European Union Law Textbook

European Union Law Textbook

Elspeth Deards LLB, Solicitor

Senior Lecturer in Law, Nottingham Law School

Sylvia Hargreaves BA, LLM, PhD, Solicitor

Principal Lecturer in Law, Nottingham Law School

OXFORD
UNIVERSITY PRESS

OXFORD

UNIVERSITY PRESS

Great Clarendon Street, Oxford OX2 6DP

Oxford University Press is a department of the University of Oxford.
It furthers the University's objective of excellence in research, scholarship,
and education by publishing worldwide in

Oxford New York

Auckland Bangkok Buenos Aires Cape Town Chennai
Dar es Salaam Delhi Hong Kong Istanbul Karachi Kolkata
Kuala Lumpur Madrid Melbourne Mexico City Mumbai Nairobi
São Paulo Shanghai Taipei Tokyo Toronto

Oxford is a registered trade mark of Oxford University Press
in the UK and in certain other countries

Published in the United States
by Oxford University Press Inc., New York

ISBN 0-19-870071-7

Typeset by SNP Best-set Typesetter Ltd., Hong Kong
Printed in Great Britain
on acid-free paper by
Antony Rowe Limited, Chippenham, Wiltshire

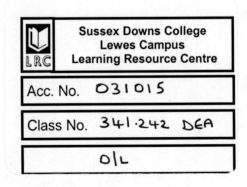

■ PREFACE

EU law is a subject which students have traditionally found difficult. Although many students will have come across EU law at work, or will have an interest in the politics, economics or history of the EU, many others find it a particularly inaccessible subject. This books aims to, and in previous editions has succeeded in, demystifying the key areas of EU law for undergraduate and graduate students approaching the subject for the first time.

We start with the background to EU law – the history of the EU, which is fundamental to an understanding of the content and function of EU law, and the institutional structure and the sources of law which it produce. We then examine the EU's legal system, explaining and analysing the way in which EU law can be utilised in actions before the domestic courts, and the actions which may be brought against the EU for illegal conduct. The remainder of the book is devoted to the major areas of substantive law – freedom of movement, competition law and equal treatment. In all these areas we explain the basic concepts, with full cross references to the Cases and Materials on the Companion Web Site. Students are able to test and consolidate their understanding in considering the questions and undertaking the exercises that appear throughout the book. There is also the opportunity to tackle more extended sample questions in each chapter, both problems and essays, to which guide answers are provided.

We have found in the past that students consider this to be a more user-friendly text for EU law than many of its competitors, but we also ensure that its coverage is sufficient for standard EU courses.

Elspeth Deards and Sylvia Hargreaves
Nottingham Law School

◼ OUTLINE TABLE OF CONTENTS

■ CONTENTS

■ SOURCE ACKNOWLEDGEMENTS

Grateful acknowledgement is made to all the authors and publishers of copyright material which appears on the companion web site to this book, and in particular to the following for permission to reprint material from the sources indicated:

Blackwell Publishing: extract from N MacCormick: *Beyond the Sovereign State* (Blackwell, 1993).

Council of Europe: extracts from *European Court Reports* (ECR), copyright © Council of Europe.

Hart Publishing: extract from W van Gerven: 'Taking article 215 EC Treaty Seriously' from J Beatson and T Tridimas (eds): *New Directions in European Public Law* (Hart Publishing, 1998)

Hodder & Stoughton: extract from J Kellett: *European Business* (Hodder & Stoughton, 1995).

Lexis Nexis UK: extracts from *All England Law Reports* (All ER).

Sweet & Maxwell: extracts from *Common Market Law Reports* (CMLR) and from *European Law Review*: A Barav: 'Some Aspects of the Preliminary Rulings Procedure in EEC Law', 2 *ELRev* 3 (1977); A Durdan: 'Restitution or Damages: National Court or European Court', 1 *ELRev* 43 (1976); Nanette A E M Neuwahl: 'Article 173 Paragraph 4 EC: Past Present and Possible Future', (1996) 21 *ELRev* 17; and J Steiner: 'Direct Effects to Francovich: Shifting Means of Enforcement of Community Law', 18 *ELRev* 3 (1993).

Every effort has been made to trace and contact copyright holders prior to going to press but this has not been possible for all material listed. Although we are continuing to seek the necessary permissions up to publication, if notified, the publisher will undertake to rectify any errors or omissions at the earliest opportunity.

■ TABLE OF CASES

■ TABLE OF STATUTES

■ HOW TO USE THIS BOOK

This book will give students of EU Law a good, clear, and accurate introduction to the subject. Our aim has been to make the material as accessible as possible for those students coming to the subject for the first time. To this end we have included a number of features throughout the text to allow for interactive use of the book by students, in testing their knowledge and checking their understanding.

Special features of the book include:

Cases and Materials

The cases and materials referred to in the textbook can be found on the book's accompanying web site (www.oup.com/uk/booksites/law/eu). Wherever the case is cited on the web site, the following symbol appears in the margin of the textbook. This allows the student access to extended extracts directly relevant to the discussion in the textbook.

Chapter Objectives

Each chapter opens with a set of objectives to help students identify the areas they should understand by the end of the chapter.

Question Boxes ?

Questions are included throughout the text to encourage students to engage critically with the issues discussed. They also provide a useful means for students to test their knowledge after reading the chapter or during the revision process.

Exercises

Exercises are included throughout the text for students to test their understanding of the issues raised by key cases, and to encourage deeper reading and analysis of cases. The cases referred to in the exercises are included on the book's accompanying web site .

Chapter Summaries

Each chapter ends with a summary of the main issues discussed in the chapter. This is not intended as a substitute for reading the chapter, but rather as a section to refresh the student's memory on the key issues discussed.

Assessment Exercise

Chapters end with an 'Assessment Exercise' that asks a question or sets up a scenario for the student to assess and answer using the knowledge gained through the reading of the chapter. A full specimen answer to the Assessment Exercise is given on the accompanying web site .

1 Origins of the European Community

1.1 Objectives

By the end of this chapter you should be able to:

1 Explain the basic economic principles underlying the formation and policies of the Community

2 Assess whether the economic and political aims of the founders of the Community have been achieved

3 Describe the changes which have taken place in the ambitions of the Community in social, economic and political spheres

4 Understand the development of the Community since its inception, including the effect of the treaties amending and supplementing the EC Treaty 1957 and in particular the Single European Act 1986

1.2 Introduction

The legal framework of the Community has developed specifically in order to support and further the aims of the Community organization, and therefore an awareness of the origins of the Community is essential in order to understand the nature of its laws and their impact on UK law.

The 'European Community' or 'EC' is now the correct term for what was formerly the 'European Economic Community' or 'EEC'. It is only one of the three 'European Communities' (see later), which in turn form part of the European Union or EU (see **Chapter 4**). Throughout this book the term 'the Community' will be used for the organization at all stages of its development and may, where appropriate, include the other two Communities.

The EC and EU Treaties were renumbered by the Treaty of Amsterdam (see 4.5.1) which came into force on 1 May 1999. In this Text the new Article numbers are used and where this number is different to the previous number, the previous number is given in brackets. In the corresponding *Cases and Materials* a table of equivalence of old and new Article numbers is included.

The official convention is that references to Treaty articles as they were prior to 1 May 1999 are made in the form 'Article 1 of the [EC/EU/ECSC/Euratom] Treaty'. References to Treaty Articles as they exist from that date are made in the form 'Article 1 [EC/EU/ECSC/Euratom]'.

1.3 Definitions

The following is not an exhaustive list of all treaties or of all institutions but of those which will most commonly be referred to in this Learning Text.

1.3.1 The treaties

The Treaty of Paris establishing the European Coal and Steel Community 1951	The ECSC Treaty
The EC Treaty establishing the EEC 1957 (note that 'EEC' has been amended to 'EC' and so this Treaty is sometimes referred to as the EEC Treaty (prior to 1992) or the EC Treaty (after 1992) as well as 'The EC Treaty').	The EC Treaty
The EC Treaty establishing the European Atomic Energy Community 1957	The EURATOM Treaty
The Single European Act 1986	The SEA
The Treaty on European Union 1992	The EU Treaty

1.3.2 The institutions

The Council of the European Communities (also known as the Council of Ministers)	The Council
The Commission of the European Communities	The Commission
The Parliament of the European Communities	The Parliament
The Court of Justice of the European Communities	The Court of Justice
The Common Agricultural Policy	The CAP
Economic and monetary union	EMU

In addition, you should note that all references to particular Articles are references to Articles of the EC Treaty as currently amended, unless otherwise stated.

1.4 The economic origins of the Community

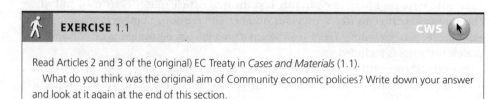

EXERCISE 1.1   CWS

Read Articles 2 and 3 of the (original) EC Treaty in *Cases and Materials* (1.1).

What do you think was the original aim of Community economic policies? Write down your answer and look at it again at the end of this section.

Article 2 set out the aims, inter alia, of balanced economic expansion, increased stability, improved living standards, and closer relations between Member States. These were to be achieved by establishing a common market and harmonizing economic policies. Article 3 set out a number of specific activities to be carried out for the purpose of achieving the aims of Article 2. Some of those which are also found in the current version of Article 3 are examined at 1.4.6.1 to 1.4.6.3 below.

The philosophy behind the economic policies of the Community was (and still is) that every individual, company and so forth, based in the Community should be free to invest, produce, work, buy, sell, or supply services wherever in the Community this can be done most efficiently and without competition being artificially distorted. This policy was to be achieved through the establishment of a common market.

? QUESTION 1.1

What do you think the term 'common market' means?

The definition of a common market will be considered shortly but for now you should be aware that it is a relatively advanced stage on the road to economic integration. At the most basic level, there is simply trade between countries.

Prior to any economic cooperation between countries, each country trades as an independent entity. It makes most sense for each country to concentrate on the goods or services which it can produce most efficiently. To take a hypothetical example, suppose that France produces wine much more efficiently than the UK, but only produces cheese slightly more efficiently.

? QUESTION 1.2

In this example, what might France and the UK gain from trading with each other?

Since France is most efficient in wine production, it should concentrate on that. Since the UK is most efficient (or least inefficient) at producing cheese, it should concentrate on that. However, the two countries can only optimize their efficiency in this way if they trade with each other in order to meet the demand for the product of which they now produce less.

? QUESTION 1.3

Can you see any potential problems for these countries in this scenario?

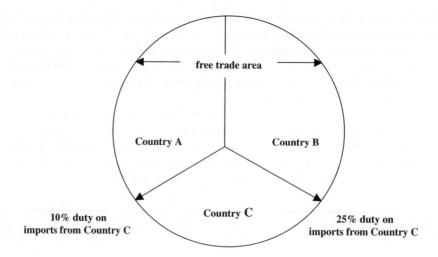

If there are no restrictions at all on trade, i.e. it is 'free trade', then there may be disadvantages. For instance, if France produces less cheese and the UK produces less wine, there will be unemployed workers in the French cheese and UK wine industries. Another problem is that few countries would wish to be totally dependent on one country of supply if the commodity involved was an essential one, such as oil or grain. A third problem is that we have been looking at two countries in isolation. In the real world, free trade does not exist between all countries because of protectionist measures by some and economic integration between others. The Community has adopted the approach of economic integration.

1.4.1 The first stage of integration is a free trade area

This is where a number of countries agree to remove all customs duties and quotas between themselves, so that when goods, capital, and so forth are moved from one country to another, there is no restriction on the amount and no border taxes on them, **but** each country keeps its own (i.e. different) duties and quotas as regards countries outside the area.

Example
Country A and Country B have joined together to create a free trade area. Country C borders on both of them, but is not part of the free trade area. Country A levies a duty of 10% on goods from countries outside the free trade area, whereas Country B levies a duty of 25% on such imports.

It will be cheaper for Country C to market goods to the whole of the free trade area (Countries A and B) through Country A. The goods will be taxed at 10% when they enter A but can then pass into B without further payment because of the free trade area.

This is good for consumers in the free trade area because the goods will be cheaper than if a 25% duty had been added, but it may affect the relative competitiveness of industry in B (which has to compete with goods from C which are cheaper than before), the trade balance (because C's exports to A will rise and to B will fall, while exports from A to B will also rise) and the customs duties received by each country.

1.4.2 **The next stage of integration is a customs union**

This consists of a free trade area **plus** an agreement by all members of the area to impose a common level of duty on goods coming into the area from non-member countries.

This common level of duty for the Community is known as the Common Customs Tariff or CCT for short.

A customs union would avoid the imbalance outlined above because the same level of duty would be charged by all the countries within the free trade area to countries outside it. In the example given above, goods from Country C would incur the same level of duty whether they enter the free trade area through A or B.

?　**QUESTION** 1.4

Jack, a chocolate manufacturer within a free trade area, can either buy cheap sugar from outside the area (on which he has to pay a 40% duty), or slightly more expensive sugar from another country within the area (on which he does not have to pay duty). Which do you think he will choose? Will this cause any problems?

The problem with a customs union from an economist's point of view is that it may encourage inefficiency. It is cheaper for Jack to buy from an inefficient producer in another country within the free trade area than from an efficient producer in a country outside the area on whose products he then has to pay import duties. Of course from the point of view of the inefficient producers, being in a customs union is not a problem at all.

Another problem is that such policies lead to international trade diversion, which may cause economic difficulties for countries outside the free trade area. This was a factor in the creation of the European Free Trade Area (EFTA), which was set up in 1960 by a number of European countries outside the Community in an attempt to counter the negative effects on trade.

1.4.3 **The next step is a common market**

This consists of a customs union **plus** an agreement by all members to remove restrictions on what are known as factors of production, e.g. labour, capital, materials, etc, between themselves. So, for example, there should be no restrictions on working in another country within a common market.

In the Community this requirement has been translated into 'freedom of movement of goods, persons, services and capital'.

The term 'common market' is an economic term used to describe an abstract model. In the context of the Community, the Single European Act 1986 has introduced a further term, the 'internal market', also known as the 'Single Market'. This has a broadly similar meaning but is a term particular to the Community, implying a common market in the precise form laid down by the Act. In the Single Market, certain restrictions on the factors of production continue to exist.

1.4.4 The final stage of the economic integration process is an economic and monetary union

This consists of a common market (including the Community's 'Single Market') **plus** unified monetary and fiscal policies. These include, inter alia, a single currency for all members, common policies on interest rates and central control by the union of each country's budget.

The process of economic and monetary union of the Community is now outlined in the Treaty on European Union (see **Chapter 4**). You should remember that this was not one of the original aims of the Community

1.4.5 The current economic status of the community

> **?** **QUESTION** 1.5
>
> Can you identify from your own knowledge which stage the Community has now reached? Give reasons for your answer.

If you have any difficulty in answering this question look back at the definition of each stage and think about your own experience. Have you ever wanted to work in another Community country or bring back expensive goods from a European holiday? What sort of restrictions, if any, have you encountered or think that you might encounter?

Despite the widespread use in the UK in the 1970s of the term 'Common Market', meaning the Community, the deadline originally envisaged by the EC Treaty for the completion of the common market (the end of 1969) passed without fulfilment. It was only the completion in the early 1990s of the Single Market which brought the Community close to achieving a full common market. In fact, as stated above, the Single Market is not a perfect market. For instance, there are still more restrictions on the right of a Briton to work in Germany than for a German to work there, and restrictions on the value of goods which that Briton might bring back into the UK with him. These are not features that one would expect to see in a genuine common market. However, the Single Market as defined by the Community has now been fulfilled.

Note also the following:

(a) The Schengen Agreements on the abolition of frontier controls were agreed by all Member States except the UK and Ireland, and have now been incorporated into the EU (see 4.5.1). The Agreements are intended to achieve the free movement of persons between these countries.

(b) A customs union between the Community and Turkey came into force on 1 January 1996 pursuant to the EEC Turkey Association Agreement (OJ L217 29.12.1964) and Protocol (OJ L293 29.12.1972).

1.4.6 Economic integration and the EC Treaty

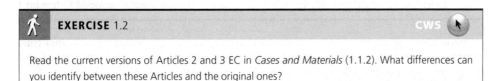

EXERCISE 1.2   CWS

Read the current versions of Articles 2 and 3 EC in *Cases and Materials* (1.1.2). What differences can you identify between these Articles and the original ones?

In addition to its original provisions, Article 2 EC now sets out the specific aim of economic and monetary union (known as EMU for short) as well as more general aims, such as equality between men and women, a high level of employment, and of social protection.

Article 3 EC now omits provisions which have been fulfilled, for instance the CCT, and adds a number of new activities for the Community, including some which go beyond purely economic matters, such as consumer protection and the establishment of a Social Fund. It also lists what the Community may do in order to achieve a common market. Three of the most important activities listed in Article 3 are as follows.

1.4.6.1 The prohibition of customs duties and quantitative restrictions between Member States

The Community has had considerable success in this area, although such duties and quotas have not been completely eliminated (see **Chapter 9**).

? **QUESTION** 1.6

'Customs duties' and 'quantitative restrictions' are important terms in understanding the economics of the Community. What do you think they mean in this context?

Customs duties are a form of tax levied on goods simply because they have crossed a border. Duties make imports more expensive than domestically produced goods and therefore less competitive.

Quantitative restrictions (more commonly referred to as quotas) are numerical limitations on imports which by their very nature restrict trade between countries.

1.4.6.2 The abolition of obstacles to the free movement of goods, persons, services and capital

Although some obstacles have been removed, others remain.

? QUESTION 1.7

Give one example of a rule or custom which you think might create such an obstacle.

Among the obstacles you might have mentioned are differences in taxation, particularly Value Added Tax (VAT), since producers will be deterred from attempting to market their goods in a country which imposes a high rate of VAT on them. Other obstacles include nationalistic public purchasing policies whereby domestic suppliers are preferred even when the foreign product is cheaper or better, and non-recognition of similar qualifications so that, for example, an accountant qualified to practise in the UK might not be permitted to practise in Belgium.

1.4.6.3 The prevention of distortion of competition

Competition policy in the Community is largely administered by the Commission and will be considered in **Chapters 11** and **12**.

? QUESTION 1.8

Imagine two chocolate manufacturers, one in Belgium and one in the UK. Can you suggest any way in which these two companies might distort the market?

If, for instance, a Belgian chocolate producer and a British chocolate producer agree not to sell their products in each other's domestic markets, then the two markets will be partitioned: the opposite of a single market. The Community competition rules outlined in Articles 81–9 (ex 85–94) are designed to prevent such distortions, although there are exceptions to these rules as we shall see later in **Chapters 11** and **12**.

1.4.7 Conclusion

This review of the Community's economic philosophy indicates first that the impetus is towards economic integration, although the original aim of a common market was more modest than the current aim of EMU, but secondly that attempts to implement this policy in practice have not met with unlimited success. However, it must be remembered that the legal framework of the Community was set up primarily to support these activities and therefore both it, and the case law of the Court of Justice, reflect these aims. In **Chapter 4** more recent economic proposals will be considered.

1.5 The political origins of the Community

Ideas of European political integration existed prior to the Second World War, but these ideas only really began to look realistic in the post-war years. Across Europe, memories were scarred by two devastating wars, successive severe winters led to a fuel crisis, there was a series of bad harvests, and foreign reserves were drained by the lack of exports. It seemed that political cooperation might be the way to a better future.

The military threat from the USSR at this time, which marked the beginning of the Cold War, was perceived as particularly acute, and in order to promote post-war stability in Europe the USA offered support in the form of the Marshall Plan (which gave aid to European countries for post-war reconstruction) and the Truman Doctrine (which pledged military support to countries resisting aggression).

? **QUESTION** 1.9

Summarize the effects of the Second World War on the awareness of the benefits of closer European cooperation.

(a) It was felt that a cooperative effort, including the pooling of resources, was needed for Europe to recover from the war and cope with the economic problems of the post-war years.

(b) The countries of Europe were too small to be economically or militarily viable independently against either the USA or the then USSR.

(c) It was felt that the likelihood of a third world war centred on Europe would be decreased by constructing close economic and political ties between European countries.

? **QUESTION** 1.10

Despite these cogent reasons, the 1940s did not see the formation of a European union. In the light of what you have read so far, can you think of a reason why the EC Treaty was not signed until 1957 rather than a decade earlier?

The problems of the immediate post-war era—depleted national reserves, decimated in-dustries and large numbers of unemployed ex-servicemen, together with a series of bad winters—meant that national reconstruction took priority over more grandiose European plans. In addition, some of the most ardent supporters of the ideal of a European union were not in a position to influence events. West Germany, which saw a European union as a way to gain re-acceptance by its neighbours had, in the immediate post-war era, little political influence and Winston Churchill, the British Prime Minister who had argued for a United States of Europe, had fallen from power. However, during the late 1940s a num-ber of organizations were set up which involved the close cooperation of European and other states. These included the Organization for European Cooperation (now the Orga-nization for Economic Cooperation and Development), the North Atlantic Treaty Orga-nization and the Council of Europe. A European Defence Community was also proposed, but failed to materialize.

1.5.1 The Treaty of Paris establishing the European Coal and Steel Community (ECSC)

A number of countries, particularly France, recognized that if West Germany's coal and steel industries were tied to that of other countries, that country would be seriously ham-pered in any war effort. In addition it was recognized that cooperation in this area could be economically advantageous.

As a result, in 1951 the Benelux countries together with France, Italy and Germany signed the ECSC Treaty, removing trade restrictions between them on coal and steel and creating a supranational authority (i.e. with powers over the Member States) to oversee the expansion of production.

In the preamble to the ECSC Treaty the signatories declared it to be only the first step towards a federal Europe, but all the members recognized the importance of establishing solidarity in fact before progressing to grander ideals. The ECSC had the same Member States as the European Community and EURATOM and shared their institutions from 1967.

The ECSC Treaty expired in July 2002.

1.5.2 The creation of the European Economic Community (now the European Community)

The six members of the ECSC, particularly the Benelux countries which were already closely linked economically by the Benelux Union, became increasingly anxious to ex-tend their fledgling alliance to other economic and political areas. In 1957, on the basis of the Spaak Report on the feasibility of European integration, the EC Treaty establishing the EEC was signed.

QUESTION 1.11

Summarize in not more than one hundred words the economic and political events which led to the creation of the Community in 1957. Check your answer against the foregoing text to make sure that you have included the most important points.

The economic and political objectives of the Community (both as originally stated and subsequently amended) have already been referred to. The preamble to the EC Treaty contains a useful, if rather general, summary of these objectives.

EXERCISE 1.3   CWS

Read the preamble to the EC Treaty in *Cases and Materials* (1.2) and consider whether you think that these aims are desirable or achievable.

1.5.3 The EC Treaty establishing the European Atomic Energy Community (EURATOM)

In 1957 the six Community countries signed this treaty, formally agreeing to cooperate in the development of the peaceful use of atomic energy. EURATOM has the same Member States as the European Community and the ECSC and has shared their institutions since 1967.

1.6 The Community

The EC Treaty was concerned primarily with the creation of a common market, but the preamble (*Cases and Materials* (1.1.2)) also makes reference to political ideals (see above).

1.6.1 The early years of the Community

The economic boom of the late 1950s and early 1960s made the Community's task easier. Many quotas and duties were removed and a common external tariff put in place. Steps were taken towards establishing the free movement of workers and protecting their social security interests, regulating competition and establishing a common agricultural policy.

Initially, all Community decisions were taken by consensus. However, during the 1960s provisions gradually came into effect requiring certain decisions to be taken by a qualified majority vote. Qualified majority voting requires a specific number of votes (rather than a simple majority) to be cast in favour of a measure in order for it to be passed. The number of votes given to a country is determined by the relative size of its population, thus giving greater power but, crucially, no veto to the larger countries such as Italy and France. Qualified majority decisions were to include, from 1966, those concerning agricultural prices, the area which absorbed most of the Community's expenditure and an area of key importance to France. The French president, Charles de Gaulle, believed that it was not in French interests for decisions in this area to be taken without French approval. He therefore refused to exercise France's vote in the final period of consensus voting so that no decisions could be taken. This tactic succeeded in forcing the other countries to compromise on the issue of qualified majority voting. The compromise was known as the Luxembourg Accords.

EXERCISE 1.4   CWS

Refer to the extract from the Luxembourg Accords in *Cases and Materials* (1.3.1). What solution did the Member States adopt to the problem of qualified majority voting?

The Luxembourg Accords stated that where the Treaty provided for qualified majority voting **and** the vitally important interests of one or more Member States were involved, the Community must try to find a unanimous solution. In practice the Accords meant that all decisions had to be unanimous. Either all Member States agreed with a decision in the first place or those which did not claimed that their vital interests were affected and refused to vote in favour until a solution was reached which they could accept. The decision would then be unanimous. Qualified majority voting was effectively sidelined and only once were the Accords ignored prior to the introduction of the Single European Act (see below). This was in 1982 when the UK opposed the adoption of certain agricultural prices as part of its campaign to limit Community expenditure. Despite this opposition, the measure was passed using qualified majority voting.

The Single European Act 1986, the Treaty on European Union 1992 (EU Treaty) and the Treaty of Amsterdam have extended the areas to which qualified majority voting applies and made it less practical for the Luxembourg Accords to operate. In addition, with the continued expansion of Community membership, it would become increasingly difficult to make decisions unless qualified majority voting is strictly applied.

However, it is interesting to note that the Treaty of Amsterdam has inserted into the EC Treaty and the EU Treaty a formula similar to the Luxembourg Accords applicable in the procedures for establishing closer cooperation. The details of closer cooperation will be discussed further at 4.7.3 but, effectively, where some but not all Member States wish to establish closer cooperation they may do so, subject to certain conditions. However, if a Member State opposes this cooperation for 'important and stated reasons of national policy' the Council may not authorize it but must instead refer the matter to the Council meeting as Heads of Government or State, which may only authorize the cooperation by unanimous agreement. This effectively applies the Luxembourg Accords to closer cooperation, since a Member State which declares that it has important reasons for opposing closer cooperation may force a decision to be taken unanimously, enabling it to block the decision.

1.6.2 **A period of stagnation for the Community**

From the mid-1960s there was a falling away of interest in the Community which lasted until well into the 1980s. The boom of the early 1960s had not been sustained and Community membership no longer appeared to guarantee economic success. In the 1970s the Member States became even less interested in the Community, as they concentrated on their own economic ills in the wake of the Organization of Petroleum Exporting Countries (OPEC) crisis of 1973, when oil prices rocketed and a world-wide slump set in.

The Merger Treaty (1965) merged the institutions of the three Communities (the ECSC, the Community, and EURATOM), but the 1969 deadline for the completion of the common market came and went, scarcely noticed and certainly unfulfilled.

The Budgetary Treaties of 1970 and 1975 introduced a special procedure for drafting and approving the Community budget which gave the Parliament greater powers (although these were still woefully inadequate by the standards of many members of the Parliament and of the public who saw the Community as alarmingly undemocratic). The 'own resources' concept was also introduced, that is to say, in addition to money contributed by the Member States, the Community had its own resources coming from the levies under the Common Agricultural Policy, the CCT and other Community inspired taxes. A Court of Auditors was appointed as a financial watchdog over Community spending.

The most important activities in this period were the development of the Community's legal system and the expansion of its membership (see 1.6.3).

 EXERCISE 1.5

Make a note of the names of the cases listed below, which will be discussed in more detail in the chapters indicated. When you reach each of these cases in later chapters, think about the impact that they had on the development of Community law and contrast this with the lack of development of other aspects of the Community at that time.

Important legal developments included the following Court of Justice decisions.

(a) Once Community measures had been taken in a particular area, Member States could no longer act independently in that area, since this would prevent the uniform application of Community law; *Commission v Council (ERTA)* (Case 22/70) [1971] ECR 263. (See **Chapter 4**.)

(b) In certain circumstances an individual could rely on Community Directives in national courts; *Van Duyn* v *Home Office* (Case 41/74) [1974] ECR 1337. (See **Chapter 5**.)

(c) Since Community law was supreme, national legislation which conflicted with it should be disapplied; *Amministrazione delle Finanze dello Stato* v *Simmenthal SpA (Simmenthal II)* (Case 106/77) [1978] ECR 629. (See **Chapter 3**.)

(d) Legislation enacted by the Council without consulting the Parliament where required was invalid; *Roquette Frères* v *Council* (Case 138/79) [1978] ECR 3333. (See **Chapter 7**.)

1.6.3 Enlargement

? **QUESTION** 1.12

From your own knowledge, can you identify the current Member States of the Community?

The original six members of the Community were Belgium, The Netherlands, Luxembourg, Italy, France, and Germany. In 1973 the UK, Denmark, and Ireland joined them, followed by Greece in 1981 and Spain and Portugal in 1986. The Twelve became the Fifteen on 1 January 1995 when Austria, Finland, and Sweden joined the Community.

The Community is conducting negotiations for accession with a number of other countries.

1.6.4 The Re-Launch of the Community

In 1984 the Draft EU Treaty, which was designed to create a federal Europe with a more powerful Parliament, was adopted by the Parliament. Although the Draft was not accepted by the Council, the Dooge Committee was set up to look into possible reforms of the EC Treaty.

The French Presidency under François Mitterrand managed to resolve the long-running dispute over the UK's contribution to the budget and pressurized the UK into accepting the work of the committee by making references to a future scenario involving a two-tier Europe, with the UK firmly in the second tier. The UK had already fallen behind its more integrationist neighbours once before, when it had refused to join the Community in the 1950s. It was not an experience which the UK, even under Margaret Thatcher, wished to repeat.

At the same time, a new President of the Commission was appointed, Jacques Delors. It was he who oversaw the White Paper on European Union which became the Single European Act (see **Chapter 4**). Ironically, given the view of the then UK government under Margaret Thatcher on European union, it was a British Commissioner, Lord Cockfield, who actually masterminded the White Paper.

? **QUESTION** 1.13

Briefly describe and explain the events leading to the introduction of the Single European Act. Check your answer against the foregoing text to make sure that you have included the most important points.

1.7 **Later developments**

In 1988 the European Regional Development Fund and the European Social Fund were restructured to channel more Community funds away from the Common Agricultural Policy (CAP) and towards regional development, as part of the Community's commitment to the harmonization of development throughout the Community, and to counter fears that the Single Market would exacerbate regional inequalities.

In 1989 all of the Member States, except the UK, adopted the Community Charter of Fundamental Social Rights of Workers. This was in addition to provisions in the EC Treaty on health and safety at work, and the prohibition of discrimination at work on grounds of sex. The Charter stated the basic rights of, amongst others, freedom of movement, the right to fair remuneration and the right to adequate social protection, but was not binding and conferred no new powers. It was simply a statement of recommended standards of worker welfare which were to be a goal for its signatories. It was the basis for the Social Protocol of the EU Treaty, the so-called 'Social Chapter', which extended the ambit and powers of Community social policy (see **Chapter 14**) and into which the UK eventually opted. These provisions have now been incorporated into the EC Treaty (Articles 136–45 EC (ex 117–22) (see 4.1.4).

In 1992, the EU Treaty was concluded. This marked another major step forward for the Community and will be considered in detail in **Chapter 4**. The Treaty of Amsterdam 1997 came into force in 1999 and will also be considered in **Chapter 4**. Most recently, the Treaty of Nice 2001 has been agreed. This has not yet been ratified by the Member States and is not yet due to come into force. The likely effect of its provisions are discussed in appropriate areas of this book, particularly at **Chapter 4**.

  CONCLUSIONS

The Community has come a long way since 1957. A rather imperfect common market is in place and full economic and monetary integration is envisaged. The Member States have achieved much in terms of political cooperation. However, the possibility that the countries of eastern Europe may be brought into the Community as a means of extending stability across the Continent is likely to conflict with the establishment of economic and monetary union. How the tension between 'deepening' the level of integration and 'widening' the number of countries to be integrated will be resolved remains to be seen.

CHAPTER 1: ASSESSMENT EXERCISE CWS

(*a*) Explain the underlying philosophy or philosophies behind the formation of the Community.

(*b*) How has this changed?

See *Cases and Materials* (1.5) for a specimen answer.

2 The institutions of the Community and the EU

2.1 Objectives

By the end of this chapter you should be able to:

1 Describe the composition and functions of the institutions of the Community and the EU

2 Analyse the relative importance and power of these institutions, including the extent of the so-called 'democratic deficit'

3 Explain the role of the Court of Justice within the framework of the Community

2.2 Introduction

When politicians and others talk of 'Brussels' what do they actually mean? Are they referring to the democratically elected Parliament, representatives of the Member State governments meeting in Council, or the full-time and independent Commissioners? The aim of this chapter is to give you an overview of the composition and functions of these and the other main institutions of the Community. While this is not a difficult topic, it is important that you are familiar with the roles of the institutions in order to understand the balance of power within the Community and to be able to 'flesh out' the legislative framework outlined in **Chapter 3**. The most important institutions are the five referred to in Article 7 (ex 4) EC (the Parliament, the Council, the Commission, the Court of Justice (to which the Court of First Instance is attached) and the Court of Auditors), but in order to gain a true picture of the Community's organization we will be considering a number of the other institutions.

Note that the Treaty of Nice has made a number of significant changes to the institutions (see further below and *Cases and Materials* (2.1)).

2.3 The 'Big Five' Institutions

 EXERCISE 2.1

From your own knowledge, try to fill in as much information as you can about the five main institutions in the following table.

	Which people make up this institution?	What kind of work do they do?
The Commission		
The Council		
The Parliament		
The Court of Justice		
The Court of Auditors		

Exercise 15 is also related to this chart.

2.3.1 The Commission

This body is based in Brussels but has an outpost in Luxembourg. It consists of twenty Commissioners, at least one from each Member State and two from the larger Member States. The convention in the UK is that one Commissioner is proposed by the Labour Party and one is proposed by the Conservatives. They are appointed for five-yearly periods by the common accord of the Member States and must be approved by the Parliament.

The Treaty of Nice (see **Chapter 4**) provides that from 2005 there be only one Commissioner per Member State, up to a maximum of twenty-seven. A system of rotation, to be decided unanimously by the Council, will then be used.

 EXERCISE 2.2   CWS

Read Article 213 (ex 157) in *Cases and Materials* (2.2.1). What qualities must Commissioners possess? In what way might the method of their appointment undermine these qualities?

Commissioners are expected to possess general competence and to be independent. They are not national representatives and should not take instructions from their Member State (or indeed anyone else). You might, however, have noted that since they ultimately owe their appointment and re-appointment to the exercise of national discretion and to Parliamentary approval, these factors may influence the exercise of their powers.

Commissioners meet weekly and take decisions by a simple majority vote (Article 219 (ex 163) EC). They have specific duties according to the policy portfolio which is allocated to them by the President of the Commission (a Commissioner nominated by the Council and approved by the Parliament). Examples of the portfolios include administrative reform (Neil Kinnock) and external relations (Chris Patten). Each Commissioner has a personal staff of civil servants, known as a 'cabinet' and they are also assisted by the Directorates General (DGs), twenty-four departments of civil servants, which each cover a policy area, for example agriculture, or the internal market and financial services. Unfortunately for the efficiency of this system, DGs do not correspond exactly with the policy portfolios of the Commissioners, so that a DG may have to report to a number of Commissioners or a Commissioner may have to direct several DGs.

The Treaty of Nice (see **Chapter 4**) provides that the powers of the President be set out in more detail and that if the President, supported by the Commission collectively, requests a Commissioner to resign, that Commissioner must do so.

The power of the Commission to delegate is severely limited, for example, decisions under Article 226 (ex 169) EC must be the subject of collective deliberation (see 2.3.1.1) and it cannot keep pace with its increasing volume of work. This causes delays in the enactment of legislation and also in the implementation of Community competition **policy**, for which the Commission is responsible (see **Chapters 11–13**). For instance, companies may have to wait years for a Commission ruling on whether a proposed business agreement is illegal under Community competition law.

 EXERCISE 2.3   CWS

Read Article 211 (ex 155) EC in *Cases and Materials* (2.2.1). Describe and explain the role(s) of the Commission as set out in the Article.

The Commission has three principal roles as outlined below: guardianship of the EC Treaty, formulation of policy and execution of policy. In addition to these functions, the Commission also has a representative function. The Commission President may speak on behalf of the Community, often with the head of government or state of the Member State which holds the Presidency of the Community, and it is the Commission which negotiates international agreements on behalf of the Community. It is also responsible for the establishment of Community diplomatic missions abroad and the accreditation of those sent to the Community.

2.3.1.1 **Guardianship of the EC Treaty**

The Commission's chief weapon in enforcing the EC Treaty is Article 226 (ex 169) EC.

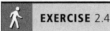 **EXERCISE** 2.4 CWS

Read Article 226 (ex 169) EC in *Cases and Materials* (2.2.1.1). How does the Article empower the Commission to safeguard the EC Treaty?

Article 226 (ex 169) EC empowers the Commission to bring enforcement proceedings before the Court of Justice against a Member State which it considers to have failed to fulfil its Treaty obligations. The Commission must first allow the Member State to state its case, and will then give its opinion. If the Member State does not comply with the opinion, the Commission may bring proceedings in the Court of Justice. Decisions by the Commission under Article 226 EC Treaty must be made collectively by the Commission (C-191/5 *Commission* v *Germany* [1998] ECR I- 5449).

As you work through the later chapters of *Cases and Materials*, you will find frequent references to Article 226 (ex 169) EC proceedings.

In addition to Article 226 (ex 169) EC, the Commission and the Member States share powers of enforcement under Article 227 (ex 170) EC.

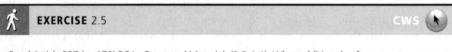 **EXERCISE** 2.5 CWS

Read Article 227 (ex 170) EC in *Cases and Materials* (2.2.1.1). What additional enforcement powers are provided by Article 170?

Under Article 227 (ex 170) EC, if a Member State considers that another Member State has failed to fulfil its Treaty obligations, it must notify the Commission, which will allow the other Member State to state its case and then give its opinion. The Commission or the complainant Member State may then bring proceedings in the Court of Justice.

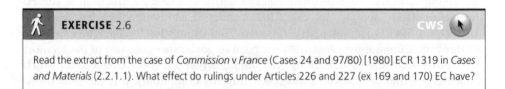 **EXERCISE** 2.6 CWS

Read the extract from the case of *Commission* v *France* (Cases 24 and 97/80) [1980] ECR 1319 in *Cases and Materials* (2.2.1.1). What effect do rulings under Articles 226 and 227 (ex 169 and 170) EC have?

The Court of Justice had ruled that French restrictions on imports of lamb and mutton from the UK were contrary to Community law. Despite this, the restrictions were continued by France on the ground that their sudden withdrawal could lead to economic damage and possibly problems of public order. The Court of Justice ruled that a judgment that a Member State had failed in its obligations amounted to a prohibition on applying the inconsistent national measures and the imposition of a duty to take all necessary action. The restrictions should therefore have been lifted with effect from the date specified in the earlier judgment.

Under Article 228 (ex 171) EC the Court of Justice, on the application of the Commission, may fine a Member State which is guilty of a continued failure to comply with a judgment against it given by the Court of Justice.

Additionally, under Articles 230 and 232 (ex 173 and 175) EC (see **Chapter 7**) any Member State or institution (including the Commission) may refer an act or omission which is contrary to Community law to the Court of Justice for annulment; and the Commission has enforcement powers in relation to the EC Treaty and secondary legislation relating to competition policy (see **Chapter 13**).

2.3.1.2 Formulation of policy

There are three ways in which the Commission can formulate policy:

(a) **A proposal for action**

This can relate to any area of Community competence and may take the form of draft legislation for the Council to adopt or more general proposals for consideration by the Council, for example the White Paper 'Completing the Internal Market'.

(b) **The draft budget**

The Commission is responsible for drafting the annual Community budget.

(c) **Policy decisions**

The Commission may take policy decisions where the EC Treaty so provides.

EXERCISE 2.7   CWS

Read the case of *Germany and Others* v *Commission* (Cases 281/85 etc.) [1987] ECR 3202 in *Cases and Materials* (2.2.1.2) in which the Court of Justice set out one of the powers of the Commission where the EC Treaty gives it a task to carry out. What was this power?

Article 137 (ex 118) EC gives the Commission the task of promoting close cooperation between Member States in social matters. In *Germany* v *Commission*, a number of Member States challenged certain Decisions taken by the Commission pursuant to this Article. The Court of Justice ruled that where the Treaty gave the Commission a specific task, it must be interpreted as giving the Commission all powers necessary to carry out the task, including the power to adopt binding legislation, such as Decisions.

2.3.1.3 Execution and administration of policy

The Commission's role here is generally an indirect one. For example, under powers delegated by the Council, it enacts rules and checks that the Member States are observing them. The use of these delegated powers is supervised by a committee of officials from the Member States, chaired by a representative of the Commission. This practice is known as 'comitology'.

? QUESTION 2.1

Can you see how the practice of comitology might undermine the powers of the Commission?

The use of supervising committees made up of representatives of the Member States gives the Member States an indirect, but pervasive influence over the work of the Commission in addition to the direct influence which they already have over the work of the Council.

The Commission also manages Community finances and enforces Community competition policy. It is responsible for the collection and expenditure of finance, including the administration of the European Social Fund, the European Regional Development Fund and the Cohesion Fund. Its enforcement powers in relation to Articles 81 and 82 (ex 85 and 86) EC include the power to declare an anti-competitive agreement invalid and the power to impose fines (**Chapter 13**).

2.3.2 The Council of the European Union (formerly known as the Council of Ministers)

This is based in Brussels, but has an outpost in Luxembourg. Unlike the Commission, it does not have a fixed membership. The 'basic' Council consists of the Foreign Ministers of the Member States, who discuss not only foreign affairs but issues of general concern. However, when a more specialised area is under discussion, the Council will consist of ministers from that policy area, for example the ministers for agriculture or for trade.

? QUESTION 2.2

Compare the composition of the Council with that of the Commission. Which do you think will represent the interests of the individual Member States more strongly?

Not only must Commissioners be independent of their Member States but their weekly meetings allow for the development of a certain solidarity along Community lines. In contrast, the fluidity of the Council means that its individual members meet rarely and develop little Community solidarity. Since they are not constrained by any formal requirement of independence, the Council is where national interests are represented more strongly. As a result, the Council is not as cohesive and forceful as the other institutions. It might be said that it is not, in effect, as 'European' as the others.

Some Council decisions must be unanimous, but most are taken by a simple majority (eight out of the fifteen votes) or a qualified majority ('QMV') (see **Chapter 1** and Article 205 (ex 148)—*Cases and Materials* (2.2.2)). QMV requires at least sixty-two out of the available eighty-seven votes must be cast in favour. The largest countries, such as the UK, have only ten votes apiece, and so even these States would need to have at least two allies in order to block a measure.

The Treaty of Nice (see **Chapter 4**) provides the extension of the use of QMV and, from 2005, the reweighting of votes and the requirement that if challenged, a decision must be carried by votes representing at least 62% of the population of the EU.

The tasks of the Council include taking decisions, coordinating the economic policies of the Member States and delegating the necessary implementing powers to the Commission. The Council may also request the Commission to undertake studies and submit proposals for legislation.

2.3.2.1 **The Presidency**

The Presidency of the Council, which is in effect the Presidency of the Community, is held by the Member States in turn for six-monthly periods. The minister from the country holding the Presidency convenes and chairs Council meetings and signs Council Acts. The government of the Member State holding the Presidency controls the Council agenda and therefore, at the start of its term, it prepares and presents a programme of action. The relevant country usually sees its Presidency as a time to make its mark upon the Community, but it may be hamstrung by the need to complete work already underway. This was the position of the British Presidency in the latter half of 1992 which inherited the final stages of the EU Treaty, and was obliged to oversee its ratification.

2.3.3 **The Parliament**

The chief provisions governing the Parliament are to be found in Articles 189 to 201 (ex 137–44) EC (*Cases and Materials* (2.2.3)).

? **QUESTION** 2.3

The Commission and the Council are based in Brussels, and the Court of Justice and Court of Auditors are based in Luxembourg. If you were an architect in charge of a project to design a new Parliament building, in which European city would you locate it?

You might have suggested that the Parliament should, like the other two legislative institutions, be based in Brussels. Alternatively you might have said that it should be located in Luxembourg alongside the courts, or even that it should be based in a third city, in order to spread the institutions evenly across the Community. What you are unlikely to have proposed is that the Parliament should be based in Strasbourg, Luxembourg, and Brussels; the current, and inefficient, state of affairs which increases the workload of the MEPs and the overall cost to the Community of the institution. It is, rather like the old air travel joke of 'breakfast in London, dinner in New York, luggage in Tokyo', with plenary (i.e. full) meetings in Strasbourg, committee meetings in Brussels and bureaucracy in Luxembourg.

The Parliament consists of 626 members (MEPs) elected five-yearly. The Treaty of Nice (see **Chapter 4**) provides that the allocation be reweighted from 2004 to accommodate new Member States without increasing the number of MEPs beyond 732. The electoral procedure is not uniform but is determined individually by the Member States. Plenary sessions are held eleven times a year and decisions are generally taken by a majority of the MEPs present.

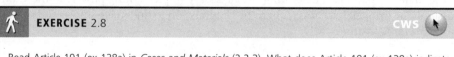

EXERCISE 2.8   CWS

Read Article 191 (ex 138a) in *Cases and Materials* (2.2.3). What does Article 191 (ex 138a) indicate about the existence of political parties at this level?

The increasing significance of political parties at the European level is reflected in the insertion into the EC Treaty (by the EU Treaty) of Article 191 (ex 138a) EC. In the early years of the Community, members of the Parliament (then known as the Assembly) were delegates from national Parliaments and were therefore unlikely to develop strong political links with members from other Member States. However, the introduction of direct and universal elections to the Parliament in 1979 loosened the ties between members of the European Parliament and their national Parliaments, and this has been reinforced by the Parliament's continuing struggle for increased powers, largely against the interests of the individual Member States. Article 191 (ex 138a) EC asserts the importance of political parties at the European level as a factor promoting integration between the Member States.

2.3.3.1 Powers

Legislative

The Parliament can make informal representations prior to the drafting of legislation, either in Parliamentary sessions, or in committee meetings (which are attended by a representative of the Commission). It may also request the Commission to submit proposals for legislation which it feels is required (Article 192 (ex 138b) EC: see *Cases and Materials* (2.2.3)).

Once legislation has been drafted, the Parliament must normally give a formal opinion on it to the Council. The procedure is that a committee scrutinizes the draft and reports to Parliament, and the Parliament passes a resolution which is presented to the Council along with the Commission's proposal.

The exact input of the Parliament into the legislative procedure is dependent upon the particular procedure which is used (see **Chapter 3**). For present purposes, the position under the most important procedures can be summarized as follows:

Legislative procedure	Parliamentary input
Consultation	The Parliament is consulted and its views may or may not be taken into account.
Co-decision	The Parliament has the right of co-decision with the Council and therefore if the Parliament rejects the measure, the Council cannot adopt it.

The Parliament has co-budgetary authority with the Council and therefore may amend or reject the Budget. The Budget must ultimately be approved by the Parliament.

Supervisory

EXERCISE 2.9   CWS

Read Articles 193–201 (ex 138c–144) EC in *Cases and Materials* (2.2.3). The supervisory powers of the Parliament are largely contained in these Articles. How many can you identify?

You should have noted that Articles 193–201 (ex 138c–144) EC give the Parliament the following supervisory powers:

(a) It can set up Committees of Inquiry to investigate alleged maladministration (Article 193 (ex 138c) EC). It did this in early 1999 in respect of allegations of fraud, maladministration, and nepotism against the Commission, and the Commission subsequently resigned.

(b) It may receive petitions from EU citizens (Article 194 (ex 138d) EC). (See also 4.8.)

(c) It may appoint an Ombudsman to investigate complaints by EU citizens (Article 195 (ex 138e)).

?   QUESTION 2.4

What advantages can you see for the Parliament in these last two powers? Write down your answer. We shall return to this issue from the point of view of the citizen in Chapter 4.

(d) It has the right to put questions to the Commission (Article 197 (ex 140) EC) at Parliamentary debates and in committee meetings.

(e) It may question the Council at Parliamentary debates (although the Council determines its own attendance at such debates (Article 197 (ex 140) EC) or in writing (Article 25 of the Council's Rules of Procedure as adopted by Council Decision 93/662/OJ 1993 L304/1).

(f) It has the right to debate the Commission's annual report (Article 200 (ex 143) EC).

(g) It can, by a two-thirds majority, require the whole Commission to resign (Article 201 (ex 144) EC).

? **QUESTION** 2.5

Can you think of any reason why the Parliament might be reluctant to require the Commission to resign? In the light of what you have learned about the appointment of the Commission, what might Member States do about any such dismissal?

This power has never been used and it is arguable that it is so Draconian—because it applies to the whole Commission only—that it never will be. It would be theoretically possible for the Member States to re-appoint the same Commissioners, which could lead to a constitutional crisis. However, similar reasons were advanced for the non-use of the power to veto the Budget, and the Parliament has in fact exercised this power twice. The Parliament has never voted to sack the Commission, but the fact that it came close to doing so in early 1999 may have been influential in the Commission's subsequent decision to resign.

Other supervisory powers of the Parliament are as follows:

(h) It must approve the incoming Commission (Article 214 (ex 158) EC).

(i) It may initiate proceedings before the Court of Justice in respect of certain acts or omissions by the other institutions (see **Chapter 7** concerning Articles 230 and 232 (ex 173 and 175) EC).

Other powers

The Parliament has a veto over a number of issues including the admission of new members to the Community and certain aspects of the work of the European Central Bank (ECB), (Article 105(6) EC)—*Cases and Materials* (2.2.3). It also has a veto in all areas where the co-decision procedure (see 3.6.2) is used.

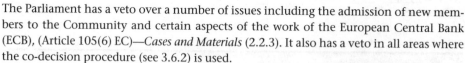

? **QUESTION** 2.6

It has been said that there is a 'democratic deficit' within the Community. In the light of what you have now read about the composition and powers of the Council, the Commission, and the Parliament, to what extent do you agree with this statement?

In **Chapter 3** it will be seen that the Community exercises sovereign powers. Within the Community it is the Council and the Commission which exercise most of these powers. The Council is not directly elected, although its ministers are usually members of their national Parliaments, and they are not collectively responsible to any representative body. The Commission is not elected at all, although its composition must be approved by the Parliament, and it similarly lacks accountability. The Parliament, which by contrast is directly and universally elected and therefore accountable to individual constituents, has relatively little legislative input. While the democratic deficit is not total, it provides a ready-made line of argument for those who oppose the grant of further powers to the Community (although it is usually these people who also oppose the extension of Parliamentary powers).

In the light of this deficit, it is not surprising that the Parliament has been keen to protect what powers it does have, and in these endeavours it has often been assisted by the Court of Justice (see **Chapter 7**).

2.3.4 **The Court of Justice**

The Court of Justice is based in Luxembourg and consists of fifteen judges, one from each Member State, who are required to be independent and to have the ability required for appointment to the highest judicial office in their country or to be a jurisconsult of recognized competence.

The judges are assisted by eight Advocates General, one of whom will be assigned to each case. They deliver a reasoned and impartial Opinion to assist the judges. The Treaty of Nice (see **Chapter 4**) provides that an Opinion will be given only in certain cases.

EXERCISE 2.10   CWS

Read the Protocol on the Statute of the Court of Justice annexed to the Treaty of Nice (*Cases and Materials* (2.2.4)) and make notes on the following:

(a) How many judges sit in the chambers which hear most cases?
(b) When will the Court sit as a Grand Chamber?
(c) When will the court sit as a full Court?
(d) When will the Advocate General be required to give an Opinion?

If you have difficulty with this Activity, look in particular at Articles 16 and 20 of the Protocol.

EXERCISE 2.11   CWS

Read the Opinion of Advocate General Gand, given in *Commission v Belgium* (Case 77/69) [1970] ECR 237 in *Cases and Materials* (2.2.4) and answer the following questions:

(a) At what point in the case is the Opinion given? (This is not necessarily the point at which it appears in this case report: see below after you have answered this Activity.)

(b) What does the Opinion consist of?

The Opinion of the Advocate General is always delivered at the conclusion of the parties' arguments and before judgment is given. (It should be noted that this order is occasionally reversed in the **report** of the case, with the Opinion being placed at the end, after the judgment.) The Opinion will contain a review of the facts, the parties' submissions and the applicable law, including previous decisions of the Court of Justice itself.

EXERCISE 2.12   CWS

Read the Grounds of Judgment in *Commission v Belgium* in *Cases and Materials* (2.2.4) and answer the following questions:

(a) Is a dissenting judgment included?

(b) Can you think of any reason why this might be so?

Now read the extract from 'How the Court of Justice Works' in *Cases and Materials* (2.2.4) for further arguments for and against the inclusion of dissenting Opinions.

Unlike the system in England and Wales, only one judgment is given by the Court of Justice and so no dissenting judgments are ever given.

2.3.4.1 Jurisdiction

The Court of Justice has often been involved in pushing forward the frontiers of Community law (see **Chapter 7**) within the confines of its jurisdiction as outlined below. It should be noted that the Court of Justice is not bound by its own previous decisions, although they are persuasive, and is therefore well able to respond to the changing needs and attitudes within the Community and the Member States.

The jurisdiction of the Court of Justice stems from Article 220 (ex 164) EC (*Cases and Materials* (2.2.4.1)) and can be categorized as follows.

Disputes about power

The Court of Justice deals with disputes between the Member States and/or the Community institutions about the balance of power between them. An action may be brought under either Article 230 (ex 173) EC or Article 232 (ex 175) EC (see **Chapter 7**) involving either a Member State or an individual alleging the wrongful exercise of power by the Community, or an institution alleging the wrongful exercise of power by another institution. An example of the latter would be the allegation by the Parliament that the Council had relied on the wrong 'legislative base' to pass a measure (see **Chapter 7**).

Disputes about the obligations of Member States
The Court of Justice deals with cases where the Commission (under Article 226 (ex 169); see *Cases and Materials* (2.2.4.1)) or a Member State (under Article 227 (ex 170); see *Cases and Materials* (2.2.4.1)) alleges that another Member State has failed to fulfil its Treaty obligations (these include obligations under secondary legislation). If an action under Article 226 (ex 169) or 227 (ex 170) is successful, Article 228 (ex 171) will apply.

EXERCISE 2.13   CWS

Read Article 228 (ex 171) in *Cases and Materials* (2.2.4.1). What are the obligations of the Member State under this Article?

Article 228 (ex 171) EC requires that the Member State comply with the judgment of the Court of Justice. If it fails to do so, a penalty payment may be imposed.

Damages
The Court of Justice has jurisdiction in cases concerning the award of non-contractual damages against the Community (Articles 235 (ex 178) and 288 (ex 215) EC; see **Chapter 8**).

Disputes about interpretation
National courts may, in certain circumstances, ask the Court for clarification of the meaning of a piece of Community legislation (under Article 234 (ex 177) EC; see **Chapter 6**).

Appellate jurisdiction
The Court of Justice has jurisdiction in appeals from the Court of First Instance (see below). These mostly involve disputes in the sphere of competition policy as to the exercise of the Commission's powers under Articles 81–9 (ex 85–94 EC) (see **Chapter 13**).

Limitations on jurisdiction
In the EU Treaty and the Treaty of Amsterdam (see **Chapter 4**) the jurisdiction of the Court of Justice in certain areas has been limited as follows.

Articles 61–9 EC (provisions establishing an area of freedom, security, and justice)

(a) It may only give preliminary rulings under Article 234 (ex 177) EC (see **Chapter 6**) on questions relating to Articles 61–9 EC (visas, asylum, immigration, and certain other matters relating to the free movement of persons) where those questions are referred by the highest courts in the Member States, rather than by any court.

(b) It has no jurisdiction at all in relation to measures under Article 62(1) EC (removing controls on persons crossing internal borders) relating to law and order or internal security.

(c) In addition, however, the Court may be required to give an interpretative ruling at the request of the Commission, the Council or a Member State.

Articles 29–42 EU (provisions on police and judicial cooperation in criminal matters)

(a) It may only give preliminary rulings under Article 234 (ex 177) EC (see **Chapter 6**) on questions relating to Articles 29–42 EU (see 4.11) where those questions are referred by courts of a Member State which has declared that it will accept such jurisdiction. A Member State may choose to limit this jurisdiction to questions referred by the highest court, rather than by all courts.

(b) It has no jurisdiction at all in respect of law and order or internal security measures taken under Articles 29–42 EU.

(c) It has no jurisdiction under Articles 230 and 232 EC (see **Chapter 7**) to review the validity of action/inaction under Articles 29–42 EU.

Articles 11–28 EU (provisions on foreign policy)

• It has no jurisdiction at all in respect of foreign policy measures taken under Article 11–28 EU (see 4.12).

2.3.4.2 Procedure

The increasing workload of the Court of Justice has resulted in longer delays, both in the hearing of direct actions, and in the giving of preliminary rulings.

? QUESTION 2.7

Given what you have learned so far about the Court of Justice and the Community legal system, what factors particular to the Court of Justice can you think of to account for these delays? Can you think of any solution(s) to the problem of delay?

EXERCISE 2.14 CWS

Read the extract from 'Judging the New Europe' in *Cases and Materials* (2.2.4.2) for some factors and suggested solutions to the problem of delay. Make a list of any factors and/or solutions that you may have missed in your answer to Question 2.7.

The Court of Justice will generally follow one of two procedures, according to whether the case has started in the Court of Justice or has been referred from a national court. (Special rules apply to appeals from the Court of First Instance to the Court of Justice and certain other categories of case.)

Procedure in direct actions (i.e. those which began in the Court of First Instance or the Court of Justice itself)

(a) written proceedings consisting of:

    (i) application;

    (ii) service of the application on the defendant;

    (iii) defence;

    (iv) reply and rejoinder (not always);

(b) preliminary enquiries by a judge (not always);

(c) oral proceedings in court or in Chambers consisting of:

    (i) report of the preliminary enquiries (where applicable);

    (ii) legal arguments by the parties;

    (iii) Opinion of the Advocate General (note that the Treaty of Nice (see **Chapter 4**) provides that an Opinion will only be essential where a new point of law is raised);

(d) judgment.

Procedure in preliminary rulings (i.e. where, in an action before a national court, that court has referred a question (or questions) to the Court of Justice)

(a) decision to refer by national court;

(b) service of the decision to refer on the parties, the Member States (accompanied by a translation into the official language of that State), the Commission and the Council;

(c) written observations by the parties, Member States and institutions (not mandatory);

(d) preliminary enquiries by a judge (not always);

(e) oral proceedings in court or in Chambers (as for direct actions (see above) but the Court may dispense with legal arguments by the parties);

(f) judgment.

？ QUESTION 2.8

Imagine that you are a lawyer based in the UK and that you have a client who is a party to proceedings before the Court of Justice in Luxembourg. What advantage does the mainly written procedure adopted by that court have for you?

The advantages of such a procedure are first, that the bulk of the work for the case may be done in your own office, with all your usual resources to hand, and secondly, that by minimizing the time spent at court in Luxembourg, the cost to your client is reduced.

2.3.5 The Court of First Instance

The Court of First Instance consists of fifteen judges, currently one from each of the Member States, who must be independent and have the ability required for appointment to judicial office in their own country. It was introduced by the SEA (see **Chapter 4**) to reduce delays in the judicial process.

? QUESTION 2.9

Given this aim, and the name of the new court, what sort of jurisdiction would you expect it to be given? Write down your answer and look at it again when you have studied this section.

The Court of First Instance has jurisdiction in the following cases:

(a) Cases brought by non-privileged applicants under Articles 230, 232, 235, and 238 (ex 173, 175, 178, and 181) EC. Articles 230 and 232 (ex 173 and 175) EC will be discussed further in **Chapter 7**. Article 235 (ex 178) EC concerns actions for compensation against the Community under Article 288 EC and will be discussed in **Chapter 8**. Article 238 (ex 181) EC concerns contracts concluded with the Community which contain an arbitration clause.

(b) Cases between the Community and its staff.

(c) Certain cases under the ECSC Treaty.

? QUESTION 2.10

Look back at your answer to Question 2.9. Is the jurisdiction of the Court of First Instance what you expected it to be?

In the UK, the court in which any particular case is first heard is described as being the court of first instance, and is often the only court to deal with that case. It might therefore be supposed that a Court of First Instance for the Community, created to lessen the workload of the Court of Justice, would deal with all cases on a preliminary basis.

However, the jurisdiction of the Court of First Instance is considerably less than that of the Court of Justice. For instance, it cannot hear cases brought under Article 234 (ex 177) EC (see **Chapter 6**) which constitute the bulk of cases before the Court of Justice. However, the Treaty of Nice (see **Chapter 4**) provides that Article 234 jurisdiction be given to the Court of First Instance in areas to be laid down in the Statute of the Court of Justice. Rulings could exceptionally be reviewed by the Court of Justice where there is a serious threat to the consistency of Community law.

Article 234 will be considered in more depth in **Chapter 6**. For the time being, note that Article 234 provides a procedure whereby national courts may, where a point of Community law is raised in a case before them, ask the Court of Justice certain questions about that Community law.

Together with the increased number of cases being received by the Court of Justice and the fact that that Court must now hear appeals from the Court of First Instance, this unlimited jurisdiction has meant that the workload of the Court of Justice has not decreased. Delays in cases being heard are now substantial in both courts.

In an attempt to reduce delays, the possibility was introduced of decisions by single judges (rather than groups of judges in chambers) in the Court of First Instance (Decision 99/291 (OJ 1999 L 114/52) amending Decision 88/591). However, this is the exception rather than the rule. The procedure before the Court of First Instance is similar to that before the Court of Justice, except that judges perform the task of Advocate Generals where a case requires an Opinion to be given.

Article 225a EC (see **Chapter 4**) provides that judicial panels be created to give first instance decisions in direct actions in areas such as staff disputes with the Community. Appeal will lie to the Court of First Instance and only then to the Court of Justice where there is a serious threat to the consistency of Community law.

2.3.6 **The Court of auditors**

This body was established in 1977 and was introduced by the EU Treaty as the 'fifth' major institution (after the Council, the Commission, the Parliament and the Court of Justice). It consists of fifteen members, one from each of the Member States, who are qualified to carry out a Community audit and whose independence is beyond doubt. Members are appointed for six-yearly terms by the Council, which is required to consult the Parliament on the appointments. Article 247 EC as amended by the Treaty of Nice (see **Chapter 4**) provides that there should be one member from each Member State.

The name 'Court' is something of a misnomer, as the function of the Court of Auditors is to examine the accounts of the Community and confirm their reliability and legality. It draws up an annual report, approved by a majority of its members, and may submit opinions or observations at any time at the request of any institution. The annual report is by no means a rubber stamp on Community finances; the Court frequently highlights inadequate documentation and control over expenditure, particularly in the Common Agricultural Policy (CAP) and recommends tighter controls.

EXERCISE 2.15   CWS

Now that you have learned about the main institutions, go back to the chart at Exercise 2.1 and try to amend it, or add further information as necessary, without looking at the text.

2.4 **The other institutions**

2.4.1 **The European Council**

The position of the European Council is set out in Article 4 (ex D) of the EU Treaty (*Cases and Materials* (2.3)). It is composed of all the heads of government or state of the Member States who meet twice a year (at the end of each Presidency) to provide the EU, which includes the Community, with its political impetus. The President of the Commission and the national foreign ministers also attend these meetings. There are also occasional interim meetings of the European Council.

2.4.2 **The economic and social committee (ECOSOC)**

This issues and policy body consists of approximately two hundred independent members (i.e. not influenced by their own Member State) appointed, in proportion to the population of each Member State, by the Council on the recommendation of the Member States. Various categories of economic and social activity are to be represented on the Committee such as employers, workers, farmers and professional associations.

ECOSOC is to be consulted by the Council and the Commission where the EC Treaty so provides or where those institutions so wish. It can also issue its own opinions on social and economic matters.

Article 258 EC (see **Chapter 4**) provides that maximum membership be set at 350 and that representatives must be elected or accountable to an elected assembly.

2.4.3 **The Committee of the Regions**

The composition and appointment of this body is similar to that of ECOSOC, except that the interests to be represented are specified as those of regional and local bodies. The UK representatives are from local authorities.

The Committee of the Regions is to be consulted by the Council and the Commission where the EC Treaty so provides or where those institutions so wish. It can also issue its own opinions where it believes that significant regional issues are affected.

Article 263 EC (see **Chapter 4**) provides that maximum membership be set at 350 and that representatives must be elected or accountable to an elected assembly.

2.4.4 **The european investment bank**

This was established by the EC Treaty to provide investment loans to assist the funding of projects to promote regional development in the Community. It receives money from the Member States but also raises its own funds on the international capital markets.

2.4.5 **The committee of permanent representatives (COREPER)**

This body consists of the ambassadors of the Member States to the Community. It carries out preparatory research and drafting for Council proposals and divides them into those on which it has already reached a unanimous decision and which can therefore be agreed by the Council without further discussion, and those which require further discussion by the Council in order to reach an agreement.

2.4.6 **The institutions of economic and monetary union (EMU)**

The following institutions were introduced by the EU Treaty solely to further the objective of economic and monetary union. They will be considered in more detail in the context of the EU Treaty (see **Chapter 4**).

(a) The European Central Bank.

(b) The European System of Central Banks.

 CONCLUSIONS

The key institutions from a legal perspective are the Commission, the Council and the Parliament, which have power (to a greater or lesser extent, depending on the legislative procedure (see **Chapter 3**)) and, of course, the Court of Justice, which has been in the forefront of promoting Community law and its enforcement in the Member States. However, despite the criticisms often levelled at the Community institutions and their powers, it should be remembered that ultimate power still lies with the Council and therefore with the Member States.

 CHAPTER 2: ASSESSMENT EXERCISE   CWS

(a) Outline the composition and functions of:
   (i) the European Council;
   (ii) the Council of the European Union.
(b) The Commission has been said to have 'a vocation to further the interests of the Community as a whole'.
   (Wyatt and Dashwood, *European Community Law*, 3rd edn.)
   In the light of its composition and powers, to what extent do you consider this proposition to be true?

See *Cases and Materials* (2.5) for a specimen answer.

3   Sovereignty and sources of law

3.1 Objectives

By the end of this chapter you should be able to:

1 Explain the impact of Community membership on the UK's sovereignty

2 Understand the concept of federalism and how it relates to the Community

3 Describe the various sources of Community law and discuss their effect and relative importance

4 Outline the main legislative processes of the Community and analyse the relative degree of power which they give to each of the institutions

3.2 Introduction

What has been the impact of the UK's accession to the Community on national sovereignty? This is a much debated topic. It is often argued by opponents of UK membership that we have entirely ceded our national sovereignty to 'Brussels'. The truth of the matter is not so simple, and in the first part of this chapter the extent to which there is now a source of law which ranks above our national laws will be examined.

In the second part of this chapter, the exact nature of these sources of law will be considered. The EC Treaty is the starting point but since 1957 a vast body of Community law has grown up which pervades virtually every aspect of UK law. It is vital for today's lawyer to be aware of these sources and to understand their potential importance as legal authorities.

3.3 Sovereignty

3.3.1 The political problem

The problem of sovereignty has both a political and a legal dimension. By way of introduction, we will consider briefly the political dimension.

QUESTION 3.1

What do you understand by the term 'national sovereignty'? Is it your opinion that this has been affected by the membership of the Community?

In the political arena, the term 'national sovereignty' is often used to mean the power of the British people, through their national government, to govern their own affairs as they see fit. There is little doubt that membership of the Community limits the power of the UK government, since decisions in certain policy areas are now taken by the Community. In theory, the position could be restored at any time by repealing the European Communities Act 1972 and leaving the Community, but it is unlikely that such extreme action will be taken in the foreseeable future.

EXERCISE 3.1   CWS

Imagine that the UK is proposing to leave the Community. Draw up a list of the advantages and disadvantages of this course of action. After you have done this, read the extract from 'European Business' by John Kellett in *Cases and Materials* (3.1.1) and see if you agree with his analysis.

The reality for the time being, therefore, is that absolute national sovereignty has been lost. The question, and this is more a matter of politics than of law, is whether this is a price worth paying for the benefits of Community membership. Lord Slynn of Hadley, in one of the Hamlyn Lecture series, *Introducing a European Legal Order*, contrasts the negative view of membership, that the Community endangers 'national sovereignty, national independence and national identity', with the positive view that the situation is not one 'of surrendering sovereignty but of pooling sovereignty in certain areas for the good of all'.

EXERCISE 3.2   CWS

Read the extract from 'Beyond the Sovereign State' in *Cases and Materials* (3.1.1) in which this topic is discussed more fully. Remember, however, that as a student of European Community law, you need to be able to separate the arguments over this question from those concerning the legal dimension of sovereignty.

3.3.2 The legal problem

The legal dimension to the question of sovereignty is more complex.

3.3.2.1 **Parliamentary sovereignty**

In the UK, the long-established doctrine of Parliamentary sovereignty means, first, that the courts may not question the validity of Parliamentary legislation (*Pickin* v *BR Board* [1994] 4 All ER 609) and, secondly, that Parliament cannot bind its successors, so a later Act of Parliament will impliedly repeal an earlier Act in so far as they are inconsistent (*Vauxhall Estates* v *Liverpool Corporation* [1932] 1 KB 733; *Ellen Street Estates* v *Minister of Health* [1934] 1 KB 590). In summary, this doctrine establishes the supremacy of Parliamentary legislation.

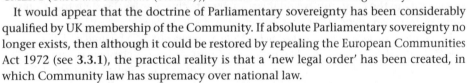

QUESTION 3.2

In what way might this doctrine conflict with giving full effect to Community law?

This doctrine is clearly in conflict with the full recognition of Community law in the UK. First, if Community law is to be fully effective, the UK courts must be able to question the validity of Acts of Parliament which conflict with, or inadequately transpose it. Secondly, if UK legislation which is inconsistent with Community law has the effect of repealing it, this would destroy any possibility of Community law applying uniformly across the Community, and in fact s. 2(4) of the European Communities Act 1972 (*Cases and Materials* (3.1.2.1)) provides that any future enactment is to take effect subject to Community law. The latter point was clearly accepted by the House of Lords in *R* v *Secretary of State for Transport ex parte Factortame Ltd (Factortame I)* (Case 213/89) [1989] 3 CMLR 1 (*Cases and Materials* (3.1.2.2)), which we shall be considering shortly.

It would appear that the doctrine of Parliamentary sovereignty has been considerably qualified by UK membership of the Community. If absolute Parliamentary sovereignty no longer exists, then although it could be restored by repealing the European Communities Act 1972 (see **3.3.1**), the practical reality is that a 'new legal order' has been created, in which Community law has supremacy over national law.

3.3.2.2 **The role of the Court of Justice**

The Court of Justice has, on a number of occasions, taken the view that the supremacy of Community law is implicit in the obligation imposed upon Member States by Article 10 (ex 5) EC.

 EXERCISE 3.3 CWS

Read Article 10 (ex 5) EC in *Cases and Materials* (3.1.2.2). How might the Article enhance the supremacy of Community law?

Article 10 (ex 5) EC provides that Member States are under a duty to take all appropriate measures to comply with their obligations under the Treaty. The national courts are therefore obliged to give effect to those Treaty obligations, even if this means disapplying national law.

All appropriate measures might include, as we shall see, repealing or refusing to apply inconsistent national law, referring all questions of interpretation of Community law to the Court of Justice or refusing to take account of the Member State's excuses for its own non-compliance with national law. The obligation to refer certain questions as to the interpretation of a piece of Community law to the Court of Justice and to follow decisions which it has made, limits, in effect, the right of UK courts to interpret the law which applies in this country.

The classic statement of the supremacy of Community law is contained in the judgment of the Court of Justice in *Costa* v *ENEL* (Case 6/64) [1964] ECR 585.

EXERCISE 3.4   CWS

Read *Costa* v *ENEL* in *Cases and Materials* (3.1.2.2). Summarize the view of the Court of Justice as outlined in *Costa* as to the position of Community law in the national legal systems.

Costa argued that the nationalization of the Italian electricity industry was contrary to Community law. ENEL and the Italian government argued that this was irrelevant, since the Italian courts were obliged to apply the later Italian law under which nationalization was legal. The Court of Justice ruled that Community law was part of the legal systems of the Member States and had to be applied by national courts. There had been a transfer of sovereignty to the Community and it was integral to this new legal system that Community law took precedence over later, inconsistent national law.

In *Amministrazione delle Finanze dello Stato* v *Simmenthal SpA (Simmenthal II)* (Case 106/77) [1978] ECR 629 (see also 1.6.2) the Court of Justice clarified its position still further. The Court of Justice had ruled, in *Simmenthal SpA* v *Italian Minister of Finance (Simmenthal I)* (Case 35/76) [1976] ECR 1871 that a fee charged on Simmenthal's imports of beef into Italy was contrary to Community law on the free movement of goods. The Italian court ordered the fee to be repaid but the Amministrazione delle Finanze appealed. Under Italian law, the constitutionality of the law imposing the fee had to be referred to the Constitutional Court. The Italian court seized of the case referred the issue to the Court of Justice.

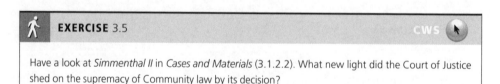

EXERCISE 3.5   CWS

Have a look at *Simmenthal II* in *Cases and Materials* (3.1.2.2). What new light did the Court of Justice shed on the supremacy of Community law by its decision?

The Court of Justice referred to the 'principle of the precedence of Community law' and stated expressly that a national court should disapply national legislation which conflicted with Community law, without waiting for it to be repealed by legislative or other means (such as a ruling by the Constitutional Court). In addition to the grounds set out in *Costa*, the Court of Justice based its ruling on the nature of Article 234 (ex 177) EC (see **Chapter 6**), under which this action was brought. Article 234 (ex 177) permits a national court to seek clarification from the Court of Justice as to the meaning or validity of Community law. The Court of Justice argued that its effect would be limited if the national court did not then apply Community law in accordance with the ruling of the Court of Justice.

 EXERCISE 3.6

Look back at paras 11–17 of the Grounds of Judgment in *Commission* v *Belgium* (Case 77/69) [1970] ECR 237 in *Cases and Materials* (2.2.4). Another instance of the loss of national sovereignty was indicated in that case. What was this?

In that case, the Belgian government had attempted to reform a timber tax which the Commission had indicated to be in contravention of Community law. However, the necessary legislation lapsed when the Belgian Parliament was dissolved and under the Belgian constitution the government was separate from, and unable to dictate to, the Parliament. The Court of Justice held that this was not a valid defence to the charge that Belgium had failed to fulfil its Treaty obligations. A Member State which had contravened Community law could not plead in its defence that its national law forced it to do so or that it had particular problems in complying.

A different problem in according supremacy to Community law arose in the *Factortame* litigation (*R* v *Secretary of State for Transport ex parte Factortame Ltd*) which involved a number of references to the Court of Justice. *Factortame II* (Case C–221/89) [1991] ECR I-3905 concerned the validity of certain provisions of the Merchant Shipping Act 1988, which the applicants claimed were in contravention of directly enforceable Community rights. *Factortame I* (Case C–213/89) concerned the possibility of interim relief being granted, in the form of a suspension of the disputed parts of the Act, a remedy which was not permitted by the UK law.

 EXERCISE 3.7

Read the extract from *Factortame I* in *Cases and Materials* (3.1.2.2). What was the decision of the Court of Justice as to the grant of interim relief and how did it justify its decision?

The Court of Justice ruled that despite the provisions of national law, the national legislation could and should be suspended pending a conclusive ruling on its validity. Rights under Community law could not be truly effective if those who sought to enforce them were prejudiced by the operation of the allegedly conflicting national legislation while the issue was being resolved. (The contested provisions of the Merchant Shipping Act were ultimately found to be contrary to Community law, and therefore invalid under s. 2(4) of the European Communities Act 1972—see *Factortame II*.)

3.3.3 Conclusion

> **?** **QUESTION** 3.3
>
> Consider your initial reaction to the question of national sovereignty (Question 3.1: see 3.3.1). What do you now consider to be the position of UK sovereignty, legal or otherwise?

The UK, and for that matter all the Member States, have surrendered, or pooled, their absolute national sovereignty. In terms of legal sovereignty, not only has the UK Parliament lost its exclusive right to legislate, but Community law will prevail over national laws. This position is subject to two provisos. First, sovereignty may be regained by withdrawing from the Community; and secondly, in those areas where the Community has no competence, such as defence, sovereignty is, for the time being, intact (although, of course, many of these areas are affected indirectly by Community law).

3.3.4 Federalism

Having noted that the sovereignty of the Member States in certain areas has been surrendered to the Community, the question of the legal status of the Community itself must be considered.

> **?** **QUESTION** 3.4
>
> In the light of what you have learned about the Community so far, would you describe it as a federation along the lines of, say, the United States of America?

In the classic federal pattern, the powers of the central or federal government and those of its Member States are exercised independently. By contrast, in the Community the lines are not always so clearly drawn and competences in some areas are shared. Other elements of a federal state are also absent. The Community has limited powers in the policy areas of defence or foreign affairs (but see 4.12) and its few powers of taxation are insufficient to fund its activities. The Parliament is excluded from decision-making in a number of key areas, such as foreign policy, a situation inconceivable in a federation such as the USA, where the federal legislature composed of representatives from the member states, is able to influence and control the activities of the federal government.

Despite these comments, it may be argued that the Community has increasingly federal tendencies. For instance, the insertion of the principle of subsidiarity into the EC Treaty (see 4.7) may lead to a clearer separation of powers between the Community and Member States, a majority of Member States are implementing a single currency, and a Briton or an Italian is now also a Community national, just as a Texan or a Californian is an American national. In addition, the Community has gradually increased its competence in all areas, including foreign policy (see 4.12).

? QUESTION 3.5

In what ways do you think that federal ideas have influenced the Community?

As discussed in **Chapter 1**, the events of the Second World War greatly influenced the move towards European integration. Amongst the myriad of ideas put forward at that time were those which envisaged a federal Europe with independent members as a counter-balance to the nation State, with its destructive capabilities. Although these were not taken up by the founders of the Community, the Preamble to the EC Treaty refers to an 'ever closer union of peoples' and it can be seen that the potential for a federal state does exist. The Community has put in place a supranational authority with sovereign power in certain policy areas, and the EU Treaty introduced a timetable of events leading to a single currency and a single economic and monetary policy. The EU Treaty also formalized, for the first time, a framework for intergovernmental cooperation between the Member States in foreign policy and defence, and in certain areas relating to justice and home affairs (see **Chapter 4**), which was built on by the Treaty of Amsterdam (see **Chapter 4**).

3.4 Attribution of powers to the Community

The issues of sovereignty and federalism discussed above are concerned with the sharing of power. The fundamental rule is that the Community may act only if the EC Treaty has given it power to do so. (The exercise of such power is subject to the principle of subsidiarity discussed in 4.7.) Articles 2 and 3 EC (see 1.46) set out the broad aims and activities of the Community and other Treaty Articles give more specific powers. For example, Article 175 (ex 130s) (*Cases and Materials* (3.2)) EC gives the Community the power to adopt measures to achieve its environmental objectives as set out in Article 174 (ex 130r) (*Cases and Materials* (3.2)). If the Treaty does not specifically give the Community the power to act, Article 308 (ex 235) EC (*Cases and Materials* (3.2)) provides a fall-back position.

EXERCISE 3.8   CWS

Look at Article 308 (ex 235) EC in *Cases and Materials* (3.2). In what circumstances may the Community take action pursuant to that Article?

Article 308 (ex 235) empowers the Community to take action where two conditions are fulfilled. First, the action must be necessary in order to achieve one of the objectives of the Community; and secondly, the EC Treaty must have failed to provide the necessary power in another Article.

Where the power in question relates to external matters, that is to say the international relations of the Community, a further rule governing the grant of power to the Community has been established (see *Commission* v *Council (ERTA)* (Case 22/70) [1971] ECR 263) (*Cases and Materials* (3.2)).

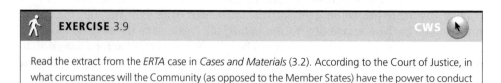

EXERCISE 3.9   CWS

Read the extract from the *ERTA* case in *Cases and Materials* (3.2). According to the Court of Justice, in what circumstances will the Community (as opposed to the Member States) have the power to conduct international negotiations?

The EC Treaty gave competence to the Community in Community-wide transport matters but did not expressly extend this to transport matters involving other countries. The Court of Justice held that, in the absence of any express provision to the contrary in the EC Treaty, the express power to act internally gave the Community the implied power to act externally and therefore to negotiate and conclude international agreements. If Member States could act independently outside the Community, this might affect the uniform policy within the Community.

This rule applies only where the Community has internal competence in all areas covered by the proposed measure. Where an international agreement relates both to areas where the Community has internal competence and areas where it does not, both the Community and the Member States may negotiate.

3.5 **Sources of Community law**

Having considered the supremacy of Community law in the national legal systems of the Member States, it is now necessary to examine the sources of law.

> **? QUESTION** 3.6
>
> In the light of what you have learned so far about the Community and its legal system, can you identify the fundamental source(s) of Community law?

3.5.1 **The treaties**

These are the fundamental sources of Community law.
  The founding Treaties are:

(a) The ECSC Treaty 1951 (due to expire in July 2002).

(b) The EEC Treaty 1957 (now the EC Treaty).

(c) The Euratom Treaty 1957.

These have been revised by:

(a) The Merger Treaty 1965.

(b) The Budgetary Treaties of 1970 and 1975.

(c) The Treaties of Accession of new Member States (i.e. one Treaty for each Member State other than the original six).

(d) The Single European Act 1986.

(e) The Treaty on European Union 1992.

(f) The Treaty of Amsterdam 1997.

(g) The Treaty of Nice 2001.

For the purposes of this chapter it is only necessary to consider the EC Treaty, as amended.
  The major amending Treaties (the Single European Act, the Treaty on European Union, the Treaty of Amsterdam and the Treaty of Nice) are discussed in **Chapter 4**.
  The EC Treaty is 'self-executing', that is to say, it becomes law in a Member State immediately upon ratification by that State, which therefore need not pass national legislation in order to implement it. The UK, in fact, chose to do so because of its approach to the status of non-national law. Unlike our European neighbours we see international law as separate from, rather than simply a superior part of, national law. In order for it to become part of our legal system it must actually be written into national law. This was achieved by s. 2(1) of the European Communities Act 1972 (*Cases and Materials* (3.3.1)).

As a result, the EC Treaty is directly applicable in the Member States. It is not, however, always directly effective. The importance of this distinction will be examined in **Chapter 5**, but for the time being it is sufficient to say that the EC Treaty is part of the law of this country in the same way as the Police and Criminal Evidence Act 1984 or the Unfair Contract Terms Act 1977, for example.

The EC Treaty consists of the following:

(a) the Preamble setting out the objectives of the Community;

(b) the body of the Treaty dealing with six broad areas (divided into Titles):

  (i) Principles of the Community

  (ii) Citizenship of the EU (see further 4.8.)

  (iii) Community policies, including policies on

- free movement of goods (see **Chapter 9**)

- free movement of persons (see **Chapter 10**)

- visas, asylum and immigration (see 4.13)

- competition (see **Chapters 11–13**)

- economic and monetary policy (see 4.10)

- employment (see 4.14)

- social policy (see 4.14 and **Chapter 14**)

- consumer protection

- the environment

  (iv) Association of overseas territories

  (v) Institutions of the Community

(c) General and final provisions

(d) Protocols on various issues, for example, the incorporation of Schengen (see 4.5.1).

3.5.2 Secondary legislation

? QUESTION 3.7

In the light of what you learned about the institutions in Chapter 2, can you identify the body/bodies responsible for making secondary legislation? Is it always the responsibility of the same body/bodies?

The Council, Commission and Parliament are responsible for law making in so far as they are granted the power to pass legislation by the Treaty. For an example of how the Treaty does this, see the Articles referred to at 3.6.1 and 3.6.2 below. Legislative acts may be adopted by the Council (e.g. under the consultation procedure (see below)), or the Commission (e.g. in competition policy) alone, or the Council and the Parliament jointly (e.g. under the co-decision procedure (see below)). Secondary legislation of the Community can be compared with statutory instruments under UK law. The Treaty or Act of Parliament confers powers and provides an outline of the law, and cannot (with some rare exceptions in the case of Acts) be challenged, whereas the secondary legislation or statutory instrument provides the detail and can be challenged in the courts. The Treaty, however, lays down a more basic framework than most Acts of Parliament, and secondary legislation is correspondingly more important in the context of Community law.

Article 249 (ex 189) EC (*Cases and Materials* (3.3.2)) defines five types of legal act which the Community may use. These are Regulations, Directives, Decisions, Recommendations and Opinions. Neither Recommendations nor Opinions have binding force but it is wise to take note of them because they are often followed by binding measures along the same lines.

 EXERCISE 3.10   CWS

Read Article 249 EC. Try to summarize the differences between Regulations, Directives and Decisions.

Regulations have the following characteristics:

(a) they are binding in their entirety, i.e. everything in the Regulation has binding force upon those to whom it applies;

(b) they are of general application, i.e. they apply to everyone in the Community (Member States, companies, individuals);

(c) they are directly applicable, i.e. implementing legislation is unnecessary for Regulations to become law in Member States.

Directives have the following characteristics:

(a) they are binding as to the result, i.e. it is only the result of the Directive which is binding, not the detail;

(b) they are only binding upon the Member State(s) to whom they are addressed;

(c) they require the Member State(s) to implement the Directive, i.e. the Member State must pass implementing legislation but the form and methods of implementation are for it to decide.

Decisions have the following characteristics:

(a) they are binding in their entirety;

(b) they bind only those to whom they are addressed (Member States, companies or individuals);

(c) there is no need for implementing legislation.

The key differences are therefore as to

(a) *What* elements of measure apply

(b) To *whom* they apply

(c) *How* they apply.

? **QUESTION** 3.8

Which of the following measures could affect you directly?

(a) A Regulation concerning public holidays.
(b) A Directive addressed to the UK concerning public holidays.
(c) A Decision addressed to your employer, concerning holiday entitlement.
(d) An Opinion concerning public holidays.

A Regulation applies directly across the whole Community and will affect you directly if the subject matter, as here, is relevant to you. A Directive will generally not have direct effect (although see **Chapter 5**), and it is the UK legislation passed to implement it that will directly affect you. The Decision will affect your employer directly, but it is the resulting action taken by the employer that affects you directly. An Opinion does not affect anyone directly.

3.5.3 **Decisions of the Court of Justice**

The rulings of the Court of Justice are authoritative on all aspects of the Treaties and other (secondary) legislation. The Court has also developed certain legal principles, some of which it has implied into the Treaties and others of which are part of the legal traditions of the Member States.

3.5.4 **General principles of Community law**

3.5.4.1 **What are they?**

Principles derived from the legal traditions of the Member States include equality, proportionality (legislation should not go beyond what is necessary to deal with the relevant problem or to achieve the desired objective) and legal certainty (it should always be possible to ascertain the law applicable to the circumstances at the time and therefore laws should not be ambiguous, nor apply retrospectively to the detriment of those who have fairly relied on them). Principles derived from both Member States and international law include respect for fundamental rights, and the Court of Justice has derived from the Treaty the principles of non-discrimination (on grounds of sex or nationality) and solidarity between Member States, which includes the duty to fulfil Treaty obligations.

3.5.4.2 **Are they useful?**

The principles can be used by all courts to interpret Community law and can be used by the Court of Justice to test the legality of Community acts and of implementing measures enacted by the Member States.

3.5.4.3 What is the basis for relying on them?

EXERCISE 3.11 CWS

Read the extracts from Articles 220 and 230 (ex 164 and 173) EC in *Cases and Materials* (2.2.4.1 and 7.1). Which words indicate that general principles of law may be relied upon?

The most important of these as authority for relying on general principles of Community law is Article 220 (ex 164) EC, which states that they should be observed in the application of the EC Treaty (the words 'the law' refer to a body of principles). Article 230 (ex 173) EC is authority for the Court of Justice to rely on 'any rule of law' when determining the validity of a Community measure (see **Chapter 7**).

3.6 Legislative procedures

In the UK, most legislation must be proposed by the government, approved by both Houses of Parliament and given Royal Assent, in order for it to become law. There are minor variations in the detail of this procedure according to the importance of the legislation and to what extent it is opposed. In some cases a different procedure is used. For example, a Private Members' Bill is proposed by a Member of Parliament, rather than the government, and certain types of delegated legislation may become law without Parliamentary approval. To a certain extent, an analogy may be drawn with Community law. The usual procedure is for a measure to be proposed by the Commission, discussed by the Parliament and adopted by the Council but there are considerable variations on this procedure and the two most important of these are set out below.

It is also necessary to note that, in some cases, a completely different procedure may be used. For example, the Parliament rather than the Commission may propose legislation concerning elections to the Parliament (Article 190 (ex 138) EC); and the Commission may enact legislation on its own in certain areas of competition policy (Article 86 (ex 90) EC) or where the Council has delegated power to it.

EXERCISE 3.12 CWS

Look back at Chapter 2 and Articles 198, 205 and 219 (ex 141, 148 and 163) EC in 2.2.3, 2.2.2 and 2.2.1 in *Cases and Materials* and make a note of the way in which each of the legislative institutions takes its decisions.

You should have noted that the Commission acts by majority (Article 219 (ex 163) EC) as does, in general, the Parliament (Article 198 (ex 141) EC). The Council also acts by majority unless a qualified majority or unanimity is expressly required (Article 205 (ex 148) EC).

3.6.1 Consultation procedure

This procedure is set out in each Article to which it applies.

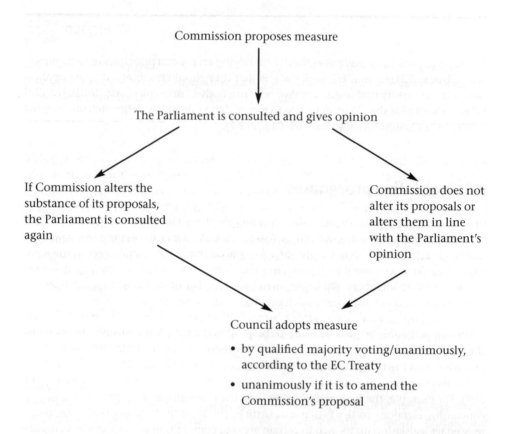

Commission proposes measure

The Parliament is consulted and gives opinion

If Commission alters the substance of its proposals, the Parliament is consulted again

Commission does not alter its proposals or alters them in line with the Parliament's opinion

Council adopts measure

- by qualified majority voting/unanimously, according to the EC Treaty
- unanimously if it is to amend the Commission's proposal

This procedure will be applied where the EC Treaty so specifies, e.g. measures involving the CAP (Article 37(2) (ex 43(2) EC), certain environmental measures (Article 175(2) (ex 130s(2) EC).

3.6.2 Co-decision procedure

This is set out in Article 251 (ex 189(b) EC).

EXERCISE 3.13   CWS

Read Article 251 (ex 189(b) EC) in *Cases and Materials* (3.4) and try to summarize the cooperation procedure in diagrammatic form. Use a separate sheet of paper.

Commission proposes measure

The Parliament is consulted for the first time

If the Parliament approves the measure or makes amendments which the Council accepts, the Council may adopt the measure by qualified majority.

Otherwise, the Council adopts a common position by qualified majority and the Commission and Council explain their positions to Parliament.

Parliament is consulted for a second time

  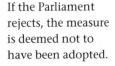

If the Parliament approves or does nothing, the measure is deemed to be adopted.

If the Parliament amends, Council may accept amendments (unanimously if the Commission opposes them) and the measure is deemed to be adopted, or reject amendments in which case the conciliation procedure is used.

If the Parliament rejects, the measure is deemed not to have been adopted.

If the Parliament insists on amendments, the measure is abandoned. If it withdraws them, Council adopts measure (by unanimity or qualified majority; see 1.6.1 and 2.3.2).

This procedure will be applied where the EC Treaty specifies that the Article 251 (ex 189b) EC procedure be used, e.g. measures concerning the internal market (Article 95 (ex 100a) EC), public health (Article 152 (ex 129) EC), vocational training (Article 150 (ex 127) EC). Note that the Treaty of Nice (see **Chapter 4**) provides that this procedure be applied to still more areas.

3.6.2.1 **Conciliation procedure**

Where the conciliation procedure is used, a Conciliation Committee, composed of equal numbers of representatives from the Council and the Parliament, has six weeks to reach agreement by a qualified majority of the Council representatives **and** a majority of the Parliamentary representatives. The agreed proposal is then adopted by both institutions. If there is no agreement the measure is deemed not to have been adopted.

 EXERCISE 3.14

Summarize as briefly as possible the procedures that will apply to the following proposed legislation:

(a) The Commission has proposed a measure reducing subsidies to llama farmers. The Parliament's opinion is that the reduction should apply only to farmers with more than ten llamas but the Commission disagrees. The Council agrees with the Parliament.

(b) The Commission has proposed a measure that would restrict admission to the professional stage of legal education (including the Legal Practice Course and the Bar Finals course) to those with fluency in at least two European languages.

Assuming that the measure proposed at (a) is part of the CAP, the consultation procedure will apply (Article 37(2) (ex 43(2) EC). The Parliament has already been consulted once and its opinion referred back to the Commission. The Council is now free to adopt the measure, but since it wishes to adopt amendments which the Commission opposes, it must adopt the measure unanimously.

Since the measure proposed at (b) relates to vocational training, the co-decision procedure applies (Article 150 (ex 127) EC). The Parliament will be consulted on the Commission's proposal, and if it approves the proposal or amends it, it will be adopted if the Council accepts any amendments. Otherwise the Council and the Commission will explain their positions to Parliament which will consider the issue again. If the Parliament then approves the measure or makes amendments which the Council can accept, the measure is adopted. If not, it goes to the Conciliation Committee. If agreement is reached the measure is adopted; if it is not, the measure is dropped.

CONCLUSIONS

Although it remains open to the UK to repeal the European Communities Act 1972 and leave the Community, this seems unlikely to happen in the near future, and in the meantime the supremacy of Community law has fundamentally qualified the doctrine of Parliamentary sovereignty. However, it is not yet true to say that our sovereignty has given way to an emerging federation. While the Community certainly has the potential to become a federation, this potential is some way from being converted into reality.

The measures which have had the greatest practical impact on our Parliamentary sovereignty have been Treaty Articles, Regulations, Directives and last, but by no means least, the decisions of the Court of Justice. In **Chapter 5** the impact of secondary legislation will be considered in detail and, throughout this Learning Text, the impact of judgments from the Court of Justice will be apparent.

 CHAPTER 3: ASSESSMENT EXERCISE **CWS**

(a) Explain the impact of Community membership on British Parliamentary sovereignty.

(b) (i) Briefly outline the main sources of Community law.

    (ii) Explain the importance of the decisions of the Court of Justice, and give three principles which it has developed.

See *Cases and Materials* (3.6) for a specimen answer.

4 The amending Treaties

4.1 Objectives

By the end of this chapter you should be able to:

1 Explain the significance of the SEA, the EU Treaty and the Treaty of Amsterdam

2 Explain the structure and underlying objectives of the EU

3 Explain the concept of subsidiarity and its importance to the powers of the Community

4 Outline the provisions relating to economic and monetary union and assess their chances of success

5 Analyse the significance of the two new 'pillars'

4.2 Introduction

Despite its rather odd name, the SEA is a European Community Treaty in the same way as the EC Treaty. However, rather than standing alone as does the EC Treaty, it consists largely of provisions amending the three Treaties (the ECSC Treaty, the EC Treaty and the EURATOM Treaty), with relatively few provisions operating outside these Treaties.

Like the SEA, the EU Treaty (sometimes known as the TEU) also consists largely of provisions amending the EC Treaty, but certain provisions remain outside. The EU Treaty represents potentially the most significant advance in the Community's development since its foundation in 1957. It created an entirely new structure, the European Union, based on the Community and with the same membership, but with a much greater sphere of competence. The Community continues to exist in the form already outlined in **Chapter 1** but is now part of the European Union, rather as Scotland continues to exist as a separate entity although it is also part of the UK. The EU shares the institutions of the Community and impetus for its action and policy comes from the European Council (see 2.4.1).

The Treaty of Amsterdam was heralded as another major amending Treaty like the EU Treaty, but has in fact achieved much less. One of its main functions should have been to make institutional reforms to prepare the Community for enlargement, but it has not succeeded in this aim. As a result, a further Treaty was required, the Treaty of Nice 2001, which achieved much more in terms of institutional reform.

This Chapter will summarize each of these four Treaties and then consider the current status of the provisions introduced by them in more detail.

4.3 The Single European Act 1986

4.3.1 Amendments to the EC Treaty to ensure completion of the single internal market by the end of 1992

The EC Treaty laid down a twelve-year period for the establishment of a common market, but by the end of 1969 it was far from complete. The Court of Justice had tried to assist by prohibiting many interferences with free movement, but it could not achieve the necessary advances alone. The Commission, under the presidency of Jacques Delors, was particularly keen to set the wheels in motion.

The SEA provided the following:

- detailed definition of the Single Market (now Article 14 (ex 7a) EC—*Cases and Materials* (4.1));

- a deadline of the end of 1992 for the completion of the Single Market;

- a specific obligation on the Community to adopt the necessary measures to achieve the Single Market;

- a new law-making power to be applied to such measures, requiring the approval of either a qualified majority of the Council and a majority of the Parliament or of the Council acting unanimously. This is known as the co-operation procedure and is discussed in greater detail in **Chapter 3**.

4.3.2 Amendments to the EC Treaty to include new areas of competence

These new areas of competence were those which the Community had in practice already taken upon itself, for example, environmental matters, research and development, and regional development. They constituted new legislative bases, that is to say, legal foundations on which the Community is empowered to base legislation. For further details of the importance of legislative bases, see **Chapter 7**.

4.3.3 Amendments to the EC Treaty to introduce the Court of First Instance

This court was introduced in order to reduce the workload of the Court of Justice and thereby ease the problem of delays in the judicial process. However, it largely failed to do this.

4.3.4 Provisions (operating outside the EC Treaty) formalizing the role of the European Council

The European Council (the Council operating at the level of heads of government or state) was originally an informal forum for discussion but was brought into the Community framework by Article 2 SEA and given a more formal role by Article 4 (ex D) EU.

4.3.5 Provisions (operating outside the EC Treaty) for European Political Cooperation

The SEA set out a number of principles to bring about closer and more systematic cooperation in the formulation and implementation of foreign policy. This was built upon both by the EU Treaty and the Treaty of Amsterdam (see **Chapter 4**)

4.4 The Treaty on European Union 1992

As mentioned at 4.2, the EU Treaty created the EU. This is closely related to the Community, but is a separate entity and must be considered in a little more detail.

4.4.1 Structure of the EU

The EU consists of the Communities (the Community, EURATOM and, originally, the ECSC), a common foreign and security policy and cooperation on justice and home affairs. It has no legal personality of its own and uses the Community's institutions and resources.

? **QUESTION** 4.1

What do you think is meant by the expression 'the three pillars of the EU'? Draw a diagram illustrating the structure of the EU.

The 'three pillars' of the EU are the central pillar of the Communities and the two side pillars of the foreign and security policy, and justice and home affairs. To make this clear, a diagram may be drawn as follows.

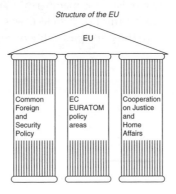

Structure of the EU

4.4.2 **Objectives of the EU**

These are set out in Article 2 (ex B) EU and were amended by the Treaty of Amsterdam.

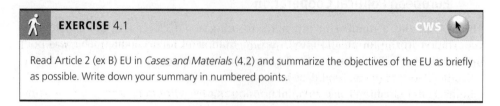

EXERCISE 4.1

CWS

Read Article 2 (ex B) EU in *Cases and Materials* (4.2) and summarize the objectives of the EU as briefly as possible. Write down your summary in numbered points.

The objectives of the EU are as follows:

(a) to promote economic and social progress, a high level of employment and balanced and sustainable development through economic and social cohesion and EMU (see 4.9 and 4.10);

(b) to assert its international identity, in particular through a common foreign and security policy (see 4.12);

(c) to strengthen individual rights by the introduction of EU citizenship (see 4.8);

(d) to maintain and develop the EU as an area of freedom, security and justice (see 4.11 and 4.13);

(e) to maintain the '*acquis communautaire*' (the existing laws and conventions of the Community).

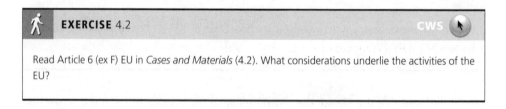

EXERCISE 4.2

CWS

Read Article 6 (ex F) EU in *Cases and Materials* (4.2). What considerations underlie the activities of the EU?

Article 6 EU states that the national identity of the Member States should be respected, indicates that democracy is a pre-requisite for membership and states that fundamental human rights must be observed by the EU. Article 6 was amended by the Treaty of Amsterdam to refer additionally to the principles of liberty and the rule of law.

4.4.3 **Key provisions of the EU Treaty**

* Change of name.

As mentioned in **Chapter 1**, the EU Treaty changed the name of the Community from the European Economic Community to the European Community.

? QUESTION 4.2

What significance, if any, do you consider that this change of name might have?

This change of name reflects the change of emphasis within the organisation, from an economic and market oriented body to one with competences in areas such as education, culture and consumer protection.

* Subsidiarity (see 4.7).
* Citizenship (see 4.8).
* Economic and social cohesion (see 4.9).
* Economic and monetary union (see 4.10).
* Cooperation of justice and home affairs (now police and judicial cooperation in criminal matters (see 4.11)).
* The common foreign and security policy (see 4.12).

4.5 **The Treaty of Amsterdam**

This Treaty was negotiated against the background of anticipated enlargement, requiring both institutional reform to ensure that a larger Community would be administratively workable and greater flexibility to ensure that those Member States which wish to do so can proceed to greater integration. The Treaty of Amsterdam was also intended to build on the achievements of the EU Treaty.

4.5.1 **Key Provisions of the Treaty of Amsterdam**

* Renumbering of the Treaties:

  As mentioned at 1.2 the Treaty of Amsterdam provides for the renumbering of the EC and EU Treaties.

The following amendments to the EC Treaty are discussed elsewhere in this Text.

* Institutional reform:
  * the reform of the co-decision procedure (see 3.6.2);

- the extension of the co-decision procedure, giving equal rights of decision making to the Parliament and the Council in most areas (see 3.6.2);
- the extension of qualified majority voting (see 1.6.1 and 2.3.2);
- amendments to subsidiarity (see 4.7).

However, the Treaty of Amsterdam failed to deal with the following institutional problems which will arise on enlargement to over twenty Member States:

- the number of Commissioners, since the present system (see 2.3.1) would mean that there would be almost thirty Commissioners, which could have adverse consequences for effective decision-making in the Commission;
- the system of the Presidency, since the present system would mean that Member States would hold the Presidency less than once every ten years, which could have adverse consequences politically and in terms of consistency.

- Introduction of new Title IV EC on visas, asylum, immigration and other policies relating to the free movement of persons (see 4.13).
- Introduction of new EC Titles on Employment and Social Policy (see 4.14).
- The renaming and amending of Cooperation on Justice and Home Affairs—now Police and Judicial Cooperation in Criminal Matters (see 4.11).
- Amendments to the Common Foreign and Security Policy (see 4.12).
- Introduction of Article 7 EU (see 4.15).
- Introduction of Closer Cooperation (see 4.16).
- Incorporation of Schengen.

The Protocol (No 2) integrating the Schengen acquis into the framework of the European Union (1997) provides that those Member States which had signed the Schengen Agreements (all Member States except the UK and Ireland) now conduct their cooperation on the abolition of internal borders under the institutional and legislative framework of the EU. Ireland and the UK may take part in such arrangements subject to the unanimous approval of the other Member States. Denmark is not involved in the incorporation into the EC Treaty and further development of the Schengen acquis but retains its existing obligations under Schengen.

? **QUESTION** 4.3

What does the term 'acquis' mean? (If you have difficulty in answering this question, look back at 4.4.2).

The term 'acquis' refers to existing laws, conventions, and decisions. In this context it refers to those existing measures passed pursuant to the Schengen agreements.

EXERCISE 4.3   CWS

Read the extract 'Introducing Schengen' from A. Duff 'The Treaty of Amsterdam: Text and Commentary' (1997) in *Cases and Materials* (4.3) for a summary of the provisions constituting the Schengen acquis.

The Protocol provides that until the Council determines the legal basis of the measures constituting the Schengen acquis, they are to be regarded as based on Title VI EU (see 4.11).

EXERCISE 4.4   CWS

Read 'Schengen: The Pros and Cons' in *Cases and Materials* (4.3) and think about whether you agree with the Schengen countries or the UK and Ireland on the elimination of restrictions on the free movement of persons.

4.6 The Treaty of Nice

4.6.1 Key Provisions of the Treaty of Nice

The following amendments to the EC Treaty are discussed elsewhere in this Text:

• Institutional reform.

Certain of these amendments—in relation to the number and allocation of MEP's, the requirements of QMV and the number of Commissioners—are contained in the Protocol on the Enlargement of the European Union which is annexed to the Treaty of Nice, rather than in the body of the Treaty itself:

  • reforms to the Commission (see 2.3.1);

  • extension and reweighting of QMV (see 2.3.2);

  • reforms to the Parliament (see 2.3.3);

  • reforms to the procedures of the Court of Justice (see 2.3.4);

  • extension of the jurisdiction of the Court of First Instance (see 2.3.5);

  • reforms to the Court of Auditors (see 2.3.6);

  • extension of co-decision (see 3.6.2);

  • alterations to the locus standi of the Parliament under Article 230 EC (see 7.3.3.1 and 7.3.3.2).

• Amendments to Police and Judicial Cooperation (see 4.11).

• Amendments to the Common Foreign and Security Policy (see 4.12).

- Amendments to Social Policy (see 4.14).
- Amendments to Article 7 EU (see 4.15).
- Enhanced Cooperation (see 4.16).

  The Treaty of Nice provides a number of amendments to the scope, conditions, and procedure for closer cooperation which it renames 'enhanced cooperation'.

4.7 Subsidiarity

Article 5 (ex 3b) EC now sets out three principles to be observed by the Community when it takes action. It must act:

- within the powers laid down in the EC Treaty;
- in accordance with subsidiarity;
- in proportion to the objective to be achieved.

The EU Treaty broadened the definition of subsidiarity, a principle first introduced by the SEA in 1986. Subsidiarity concerns the effective allocation of power between the different authorities of the Community, namely the Community institutions and the Member States. On the face of it, this seems fairly straightforward.

4.7.1 The use of subsidiarity

Subsidiarity certainly acts as a political guideline to be borne in mind by the Community institutions when deciding whether they have power to take a particular measure. Subsidiarity is already affecting political decision-making, particularly by the Commission (see, for example, the Conclusions of the Presidency at the Edinburgh European Council meeting 11–12 December 1992.

Subsidiarity can also be used by the Court of Justice as a guide in interpreting Community legislation, in particular its scope.

However, whether the Court of Justice would have to be prepared to use it as a test of the validity of legislation, so that a Community measure which deals with a matter which might be dealt with equally well (or better) by Member States would be annulled by the Court of Justice, is unclear.

? QUESTION 4.4

Why do you think that the Member States themselves might favour this possibility?

This would give Member States a second chance after their initial input in the legislative process (in Council) to restrict Community competence to those areas where the Community is better placed than individual Member States to take action. However, in order for Member States to enforce this restriction, they must be able to challenge the validity of Community measures before the Court of Justice, on the ground of failure to comply with subsidiarity. It remains to be seen whether the Court would be prepared to annul legislation on this ground.

4.7.2 **The application of subsidiarity**

Article 5 (ex 3b) EC provides that the Community may take action only where it has exclusive competence, **or** where its action would be in accordance with the principle of subsidiarity. If a proposed measure relates to an area of exclusive competence, the Community may take action without regard to subsidiarity because by definition the Member States have no power to take action in that area. It is therefore useful to understand a little more about the areas in which the Community has 'exclusive competence'.

 EXERCISE 4.5 CWS

Look back at the extract from *Commission* v *Council (ERTA)* (Case 22/70) [1971] ECR 263 in *Cases and Materials* (3.2). What rule did the Court of Justice apply in that case to determine whether the Community's competence had become exclusive?

Article 70 (ex 74) EC (*Cases and Materials* (4.4)) provides that transport matters should be dealt with by Member States within the framework of a common transport policy drawn up by the Community. In the *ERTA* case, the Court of Justice ruled that once the Community had drawn up such a policy, the Member States could no longer make rules (in this case by entering into an international transport agreement) which affected that policy. The Community, not the Member States, therefore had competence to negotiate and conclude the agreement in question. We can therefore say that once the Community has taken action, it has exclusive competence in that area and can act regardless of subsidiarity.

? **QUESTION** 4.5

Can you identify a problem with the application of subsidiarity if 'exclusive competence' is taken to refer to all areas in which the Community has already acted?

If subsidiarity is only applicable to measures concerning policy areas where the Community has not yet acted, its scope and importance will be gradually diminished as the Community continues to legislate. However, it is difficult to identify an alternative rule for identifying areas of exclusive competence. There are some areas, such as EU citizenship (see 4.8) where the Community must, logically, have exclusive competence, and it also seems clear that the Community has sole power to pass measures relating to the Single Market (under Article 14 (ex 7a), see *Cases and Materials* (4.1)). If Member States could pass their own measures in this area, markets would continue to be partitioned along national lines and it would be impossible to achieve the Single Market. The Treaty of Amsterdam introduced a Protocol (*Cases and Materials* (4.4)) dealing, inter alia, with subsidiarity.

In conclusion, although cases such as *ERTA* indicate that the Community has exclusive competence in areas where it has already acted, it remains to be seen whether this definition will be applied when considering the scope of subsidiarity, given the disadvantage of this mentioned above. The Community also has exclusive competence in specific areas such as the Single Market. Certainly, in all situations where Community competence is not exclusive, its actions will be liable to be tested, at some stage, against the requirement of subsidiarity.

4.8 **Citizenship**

The EU Treaty established for the first time the concept of EU citizenship (there was no parallel provision for the Community), which applies to all nationals of all the Member States. It is now to be found in Article 17 (ex 8) (*Cases and Materials* (4.5)).

> **?** **QUESTION** 4.6
>
> In the light of the above paragraph, can you see a way in which a Member State might exclude certain members of its population from citizenship of the EU, despite Article 17 (ex 8)?

Consider the qualification for EU citizenship. It is *nationality of a Member State*. As yet there is no Community ruling on what constitutes nationality and therefore each Member State may define it in its own way. So in one Member State, for example, the law might automatically grant nationality to all persons born there, while in another, it might not. In this hypothetical situation, two people with equal links to a Member State could find that their rights to Community citizenship, and therefore their rights under Community law, differ. Such a situation is clearly incompatible with full economic and political integration.

In addition to this criticism, while Article 17 (ex 8) EC may look impressive at first sight, the rights of the newly created EU citizen are not much greater than those previously enjoyed by the same individuals. The right of free movement conferred by Article 18 (ex 8a) EC (*Cases and Materials* (4.5)) is stated to be subject to the rest of the Treaty. In order therefore to exercise this 'new' right, the citizen must be economically active (a worker or self-employed person), or a member of the family of an economically active person, or a student or retired person who is financially independent (see **Chapter 9**). Since these categories of people had the right to free movement prior to the EU Treaty, it cannot really be said to be a new right. Note that Article 18 EC was amended by the Treaty of Nice to introduce co-decision and QMV to measures taken under this Article.

The rights granted by Article 19 (ex 8b) EC (*Cases and Materials* (4.5)) to stand and vote in local and European elections in another Member State in which the citizen is resident, are new, but it should be noted that national elections are excluded. The right to participate in such elections is governed by national law and does not arise merely by virtue of EU citizenship.

The right given by Article 20 (ex 8c) EC (*Cases and Materials* (4.5)) to diplomatic pro- tection provided by another Member State in a non-EU country where the citizen's own Member State is not represented is officially new, but reflects what formerly happened in practice. The rights given by Article 21 (ex 8d) EC (*Cases and Materials* (4.5)) to petition the Parliament or the EU Ombudsman are also technically new, although in practice it was always possible to petition the local MEP.

 EXERCISE 4.6   CWS

In Chapter 2 (Question 2.5) you were asked to think about the advantages of these rights for Parliament. Now try to assess the advantages for the citizen. If you have difficulty in doing this, refer to the extract from 'The Right to Petition the European Parliament after Maastricht' in *Cases and Materials* (4.5).

You should have concluded that for both the Parliament and the citizen, the key importance of these rights is the element of democracy. The ability to receive petitions gives the Parliament (the only directly elected Community institution) direct contact with the people of the Community. Equally, the right to present petitions to the Parliament or the Ombudsman gives citizens their most direct influence on the activities of the Parliament and through it, on those of the Community generally.

 EXERCISE 4.7   CWS

Briefly explain Articles 17–22 (ex 8–8e) EC in *Cases and Materials* (4.5) in terms of:

(a) any genuinely new rights they confer;
(b) any existing practices or rights which they merely restate or formalize.

As mentioned above, these Articles are as much a restatement of existing rights (free movement of workers) and practices (diplomatic protection) as a grant of new ones (participation in elections, petitioning the Parliament). However, Article 17 EC is of some importance because, for the first time, individual political rights were gathered together and bestowed directly on the citizens of the EU, rather than simply on the nationals of individual Member States.

4.9 Economic and social cohesion

As a result of the EU Treaty, the strengthening of economic and social cohesion is now included in the activities of the Community listed under Article 3 EC and in the Protocol on Economic and Social Cohesion annexed to the EC Treaty (see *Cases and Materials* (4.6)). The Community has decided that, in order to spread the benefits of the Single Market, it must take positive action to reduce the economic and social disparities between different regions. This is considered to be particularly important if economic and monetary union is to be achieved. A new Cohesion Fund has been set up to contribute to projects involving the international transport infrastructure or the environment. At present it is concentrating its efforts towards Greece, Ireland, Portugal and Spain.

4.10 Economic and Monetary Union (EMU)

Before examining this rather complex topic, the following description of the provisions on EMU is of interest: 'it is true that the provisions of the Treaty on this subject contain the finest examples of obscurity and unreadability . . .'. (J. C. Piris, 'After Maastricht, are the Community Institutions More Efficacious, More Democratic and More Transparent?' (1994) 19 EL Rev 449.)

4.10.1 Introduction

It is perhaps surprising to learn that the first proposals for EMU were, in fact, made in the 1970s. In 1979 the European Exchange Rate Mechanism (ERM) was set up, and the European Currency Unit (ECU) introduced in order to create monetary stability. Participation in the ERM was initially optional and several countries, such as the UK, Italy, and Spain, entered it only to be forced by monetary pressures to withdraw.

The EU Treaty attempted to get the ball of economic and monetary union rolling by providing specific objectives together with details of how and when these objectives were to be achieved.

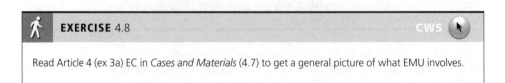

EXERCISE 4.8   CWS

Read Article 4 (ex 3a) EC in *Cases and Materials* (4.7) to get a general picture of what EMU involves.

Article 4 (ex 3a) EC now provides that the activities of the Member States and the Community are to include:

(a) An economic policy involving:

    (i) the coordination of the Member States' economic policies;

    (ii) the internal market;

    (iii) the definition of common objectives; and

    (iv) an open market economy with free competition.

(b) A monetary policy involving:

    (i) the permanent fixing of exchange rates leading to the introduction of a single currency, the ECU; and

    (ii) a single monetary and exchange rate policy.

In December 1995, the European Council decided that when the ECU became the single currency it would be known as the Euro (€).

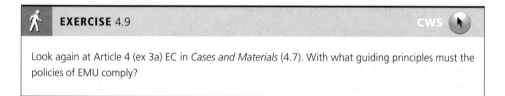

EXERCISE 4.9   **CWS**

Look again at Article 4 (ex 3a) EC in *Cases and Materials* (4.7). With what guiding principles must the policies of EMU comply?

The principles are those of stable prices, sound public finances and monetary conditions, and a sustainable balance of payments. It may be interesting to follow the future development of these policies and note the extent to which these principles are followed.

4.10.2 The timetable for EMU

The specific steps laid down to achieve EMU will be examined shortly, but it is also important to be aware of the timetable in which these steps are to be carried out. The timetable, for both economic and monetary steps consists of three stages:

(a) 1st stage   Now over.

(b) 2nd stage   Now over for Member States which fulfilled the convergence criteria (see 4.10.3). Those Member States which did not do so remain partly in the second stage, but are subject to some of the third stage provisions (with the exception of the UK, to which none of the third stage provisions will apply)

(c) 3rd stage   This commenced on 1 January 1999, but only those Member States which fulfilled the convergence criteria (see 4.10.3) for a single currency entered fully into it.

Towards the end of 1997 the Chancellor of the Exchequer, Gordon Brown stated that a positive answer must be given to each of the following questions before the UK would enter EMU.

(a) Would joining EMU improve prospects for foreign investment in the UK?

(b) Would adopting the single currency be beneficial for our financial services?

(c) Have the business cycles of the UK and the rest of Europe converged to the extent that Euro interest rates are close to those of the UK and the exchange rate at which the pound would be fixed against the Euro is satisfactory for the UK?

(d) Is there sufficient flexibility in the labour market to cope with future problems?

(e) Will joining EMU promote higher growth, stability and a lasting increase in jobs?

These are not, of course, legal questions and therefore will not be discussed further in this text.

4.10.3 The convergence criteria for entry into the third stage

These criteria are set out in Article 121 (ex 109j) EC (see *Cases and Materials* (4.7.1)):

(a) price stability (that is to say, low inflation);

(b) sustainable government finances (that is to say, an absence of an excessive budget deficit);

(c) membership of the ERM for two years without devaluation;

(d) durability of convergence and ERM membership (in the light of long-term interest rates).

4.10.4 The first two stages of EMU

During the first two stages Member States had to:

(a) prohibit restrictions on the movement of capital;

(b) enforce budget discipline by public bodies at all levels of the Community. (Community institutions and national and local governments may not borrow from central banks or the ECB, and may not enjoy privileged access to these institutions unless there are prudent financial reasons for this);

(c) to adopt programmes to achieve the convergence criteria (see 4.10.3);

(d) take steps to ensure the independence of their central banks (Article 116 (ex 109e) EC);

(e) try to avoid excessive deficits.

4.10.5 The third stage of EMU

In the third stage the following provisions apply to those Member States which entered into it:

(a) The 'excessive deficit' procedure is tightened up (Article 104(1), (9) and (11) (ex 104c) EC—see *Cases and Materials* (4.7.2)).

EXERCISE 4.10

Look at Article 104 (ex 104c) EC, paragraphs 1, 9, and 11 in *Cases and Materials* (4.7.2). How does this 'excessive deficit' procedure work?

   (i) Member States are under a duty to avoid excessive deficits, rather than simply having to try to avoid them.
   (ii) If the Member State does not respond to recommendations from the Council, which may be made public, the Council may take or intensify one of a number of measures, including the imposition of fines.
(b) The ESCB maintains price stability and support the economic policies of the Community (Article 105 EC, see *Cases and Materials* (4.7.2)). Its tasks include:
   (i) the definition and implementation of Community monetary policy;
   (ii) the conduct of foreign exchange operations;
   (iii) the management of the official foreign reserves of the Member States.

According to Article 7 of the Protocol on the Statute of the European System of Central Banks and of the European Central Bank, outside bodies such as the Community institutions or Member State governments may not seek to influence the ECB or the national banks, which in turn may not take instructions from them.

(c) The ECB (Articles 106 and 110 (ex 105a and 108a) EC):
   (i) has sole rights to authorize the issue of bank notes;
   (ii) may make Regulations or take Decisions to achieve the tasks of the ESCB set out at (b) above and may make Regulations in relation to a number of other areas;
   (iii) may make Recommendations and deliver Opinions.
(d) The Council adopted fixed conversion rates for national currencies against the euro and took other measures necessary for the rapid introduction of the euro as the single currency (Article 123 (ex 109l) EC).
(e) In early 2002, national currencies ceased to be legal tender in the twelve Member States which had joined EMU and were replaced by the euro.

4.10.6 Exceptions

The provisions for the commencement of the third stage envisaged that some Member States would not be ready to enter into it at the same time as the others. In addition, Denmark and the UK were given the possibility of opting out of the third stage even if they fulfilled the criteria.

The general exception is contained in Article 122 (ex 109, 109k) EC (see *Cases and Materials* (4.7.2)). Member States which do not fulfil the criteria for a single currency, for example those whose inflation rate is too high or whose budget deficit is too great, have a derogation, for as long as necessary, from the single currency provisions, the transfer of power from the national central bank to the ECB and the imposition of fines or other penalties under the excessive deficit procedure. All other third stage provisions will apply.

This exception was deemed necessary in order to avoid damage to any weak national economies and to the stability of the economic and monetary union itself. In addition, the UK and Denmark negotiated op-outs which they themselves could exercise, regardless of whether they fulfilled the convergence criteria.

4.10.7 Conclusion on economic and monetary union

Two questions remain unanswered in the context of EMU. The first is whether the project will succeed, and this only time will tell. The second relates to what happens to the Member States which did not join in the first wave. Is a two-tier system feasible and, if so, how will it work?

4.11 Police and judicial cooperation in criminal matters

As introduced by the TEU, Cooperation on Justice and Home Affairs covered the treatment of non-Member State nationals and aspects of law enforcement which fell outside Community competence but which had the potential to affect the operation of the Single Market.

More specifically, Article 29 (ex K.1) of the EU Treaty listed nine areas which are of 'common interest' to the Member States and over which therefore they could be required to cooperate. These included areas such as asylum policy and immigration policy, which were moved from the Treaty of Amsterdam into the EC Treaty itself (see 4.13). The remaining areas of competence in this pillar were renamed Police and Judicial Cooperation in Criminal Matters.

The aim of these provisions (contained in Title VI EU (Articles 29–41 EU) (ex K.1–K.14 EU)) is to provide citizens with a high level of safety within 'an area of freedom, justice and security'. This is to be achieved by three methods:

(a) Closer cooperation between police forces and customs authorities, involving:

    (i) operational co-operation including Europol;

    (ii) exchange of information;

    (iii) joint initiatives in training and exchanges;

    (iv) common development of detective techniques.

(b) Closer judicial cooperation in criminal matters, such as:

    (i) enforcement of judgments;

    (ii) extradition.

(c) harmonization of criminal law.

The legislative procedure is different to that applicable under the EC Treaty. A measure may be proposed by a Member State or the Commission, Parliament need only be consulted and the Council takes the final decision (unanimously or by qualified majority according to the type of measure).

The jurisdiction of the Court of Justice in this area is limited (see 2.3.4.1). It may only give preliminary rulings under Article 234 EC (ex 177) (see **Chapter 6**) on questions of interpretation and validity relating to Articles 29–42 EU where those questions are referred by courts of a Member State which has declared that it will accept such jurisdiction. A Member State may limit this jurisdiction to question referred by the highest court, rather than by all courts. The Court of Justice has no jurisdiction in respect of law and order or internal security measures taken under Articles 29–42 EU. No jurisdiction is provided in relation to Article 230 (ex 173) EC (see **Chapter 7**).

The Treaty of Nice provides limited amendments to this pillar. The European Judicial Cooperation Unit (Euro Just) is to be set up, composed of national prosecutors, magistrates or police officers of equivalent competence. Euro Just will facilitate coordination between national prosecuting authorities, support international criminal investigations, and cooperate with the European Judicial Network.

4.12 **The Common Foreign and Security Policy**

The Common Foreign and Security Policy introduced by the TEU represents an advance on the SEA's Political Cooperation and covers all areas of foreign and security policy, eventually including a common defence policy and possibly a common defence. The defence role is fulfilled by the existing Western European Union, of which ten Member States are members and five Member States are observers. This pillar was further developed by the Treaties of Amsterdam and Nice.

These provisions (contained in Title V EU (Articles 11–28) (ex J.1–J.18)) potentially cover all areas of foreign and security policy.

EXERCISE 4.11   **CWS**

Read Articles 11 and 12 (ex J. 1 and J. 2) EU (*Cases and Materials* (4.8)). Try to summarize how the common foreign and security policy is to be achieved.

This policy is to be achieved by:

(a) the definition of general principles (by the European Council (see 2.4.1));

(b) common strategies (to be implemented by the EU where Member States have important interests in common);

(c) joint actions (that is to say, operational action in specific circumstances);

(d) common positions (to which Member States must conform in their national policies);

(e) the strengthening of systematic cooperation between Member States.

The legislative procedure is different to that applicable under the EC Treaty. A measure may be proposed by a Member State or the Commission, Parliament need only be consulted and the Council takes the final decision (unanimously or by qualified majority according to the type of measure).

Article 23 EU provides that where Member States are required to act unanimously in the common foreign and security policy, a Member State may abstain without prejudice to action being taken ('constructive absention'). In effect, this means that other Member States may proceed to act. However, Article 23 further provides that abstentions may be qualified and that if more than a third of weighted votes are thus qualified, the decision may not be adopted.

Article 23 EU also provides that where Member States are required to act by qualified majority in the common foreign and security policy, and no decision having military or defence implications is involved, a vote may not be taken if a Member State declares that it opposes this 'for important and stated reasons of national policy'. The matter may then be referred to the Council acting in the composition of Heads of Government or State, which must act unanimously to authorize the action.

The Court of Justice has no jurisdiction in this area (see 2.3.4.1).

The Treaty of Nice provides limited amendments to this pillar. The role of the WEU is to be reduced and that of NATO emphasized.

4.13 New Title IV EC on visas, asylum, immigration, and other policies relating to the free movement of persons

The Treaty of Amsterdam introduced this as a new Title (Articles 61–9) within the EC Treaty, although it incorporates some former provisions EU on justice and home affairs (asylum and immigration). It is intended to contribute to the formation of the area of freedom, security and justice, along with the provisions in the EU Treaty on police and judicial cooperation in criminal matters (see 4.11) and the incorporation of Schengen (see 4.5.1).

Protocol (No 5) on the position of Denmark (1997) provides that Denmark is not taking part in measures under this Title. Protocol (No 7) on the position of the UK and Ireland (1997) provides that these countries are not taking part in measures under this Title, but that they may choose to take part in a measure. Ireland has already declared that it will do so to the extent compatible with maintaining its Common Travel Area with the UK.

It is worth noting in this connection that the UK and Ireland also have a limited opt out from Article 14 EC (ex 7a) which provides for the establishment of the internal market (Protocol (No 3) on the application of certain aspects of Article 14 of the Treaty Establishing the European Community to the United Kingdom and the Ireland (1997)). The UK is permitted to exercise border controls for limited purposes and the UK and Ireland may continue to make arrangements between themselves regarding the free movement of persons between their territories (the Common Travel Area).

The jurisdiction of the Court of Justice in this area is limited (see 2.3.4.1). It may only give preliminary rulings under Article 234 EC (ex 177) (see **Chapter 6**) on questions of interpretation and validity relating to Articles 29–42 EU (ex K.1–K.14) where those questions are referred by the highest courts in the Member States, rather than by all courts, and it has no jurisdiction in respect of law and order or internal security measures taken under these Articles. In addition, the Commission, the Council or Member States may request a ruling from the Court of Justice (see **Chapter 6**) on the interpretation of this Title or secondary legislation based on it.

4.14 New Titles VIII and XI EC on employment and social policy

The Treaty of Amsterdam has introduced a new Title on Employment (Title VIII (ex VIa)) into the EC Treaty. This provides that the EU will coordinate a strategy for employment intended, inter alia, to provide a skilled and adaptable workforce and labour markets which are responsive to economic change. The Council is to coordinate Member State employment policies and encourage cooperation between them.

The Treaty of Amsterdam also introduced a new Title on Social policy, education, vocational training, and youth (Title XI (ex VIII), incorporating the Protocol on social policy (see 1.7 and **Chapter 14**) (Articles 136–45) (ex 117–22). The Protocol was originally excluded from the Treaties because the UK refused to accept it, but it subsequently agreed to do so.

The Treaty of Nice introduces a Social Protection Committee. The Commission and each Member State will have the right to appoint two members. The Committee will monitor the social situation and social policies in Member States, exchange information, and prepare reports.

4.15 Article 7 EU

Article 7 EU, as introduced by the Treaty of Amsterdam, provides that if a Member State seriously breaches the fundamental principles set out in Article 6 EU (liberty, democracy, respect for human rights and fundamental freedoms, and the rule of law) its Treaty rights, including voting rights, may be suspended. A breach is determined unanimously by the Council on a proposal by one-third of the Member States or by the Commission, and the Parliament's assent is required. A decision on whether to suspend the rights of the Member State is broken by the Council by QMV.

Under the Treaty of Amsterdam, the first and only step which the EU could take if a Member State seriously breached the fundamental principles enshrined in Article 6 EU was the suspension of its Treaty rights, including voting rights. The Treaty of Nice permits the Council to take lesser measures designed to give the Member State an opportunity to stave off this more serious sanction. The Parliament, Commission or one-third of the Member States may make a proposal and if the Parliament assents, the Council may by a four-fifths majority determine the existence of a 'clear risk' of a serious breach of the principles in Article 6 and address recommendations to the Member State. Before doing so it must hear the Member State and may commission an independent report on the Member State concerned.

4.16 **Enhanced cooperation**

The Treaty of Amsterdam authorised 'closer cooperation' in the context of the EC Treaty generally and Title VI EU (police and judicial cooperation). This was a revolutionary concept, as it recognized the general principle that EU action could be taken by just some Members. Previously this had been limited to opt outs by particular Member States in specific areas. The Treaty of Nice 'closer cooperation' renounced 'enhanced cooperation' and made substantial amendments to it. It also extended it to the implementation of joint actions and common positions under the common foreign and security policy. Such cooperation may not apply to matters with military or defence implications.

4.16.1 **Conditions**

Article 43, 43a, and 43b EU (*Cases and Materials* (4.9.1)) provide that the general conditions for co-operation are that it must:

(a) be aimed at furthering the objectives of the Community the EU and reinforcing integration;

(b) respect the Treaties;

(c) respect the acquis communautaire;

(d) not undermine the internal market;

(e) involves an area of joint competence;

(f) not constitute a barrier to, or discrimination in, trade between Member States, or the distortion of competition;

(g) involve at least eight Member States;

(h) respect the rights of non-participating Member States;

(i) not affect the Schengen Protocol;

(j) be open to all Member States.

Article 27a EC (*Case and Materials* (4.9.2)) provides that enhanced cooperation in the area of police and judicial cooperation in criminal matters must also have as its objective enabling the EU to develop more rapidly into an area of freedom, security and justice.

Enhanced cooperation in the common foreign and security policy must also:

(a) be aimed at safeguarding the interests and values of the EU by asserting its internal identity;

(b) respect the principles and decisions of the common foreign and security policy;

(c) respect the powers of the Community;

(d) respect consistency between the EU's internal and external policies.

4.16.2 **Procedure**

Under both Treaties, with the exception of the Common Foreign and Security Policy, the Member States request the Commission to make a proposal for enhanced cooperation and the Commission must give reasons if it refuses to make a proposal. Under the EU Treaty (Article 40a EU—*Case and Materials* (4.9.2)) the Member States may then submit a proposal directly to the Council but under the EC Treaty there is nothing more they can do. The Parliament is consulted unless it is an area of the EC Treaty to which the co-decision procedure (see 3.6.2) applies, in which case, Parliament's assent is required (Articles 40a EU and 11 EC—*Case and Materials* (4.9.2)). Under the EU Treaty, the Parliament is only informed.

Under the Common Foreign and Security Policy, Member States make a request to the Council (Article 27c EU). The Commission and Parliament are informed and the former may offer its opinion. Under both Treaties the final decision is taken by the Council by qualified majority voting (Articles 40b EU and 11 EC—*Case and Materials* (4.9.2) and Article 23(2) EU).

If States wish to opt in to cooperation under the EC Treaty by qualified majority voting, it is for the Commission to approve this (Article 11a EC—*Case and Materials* (4.9.2)). Under the EU Treaty (Articles 27e and 40b EU) it is the Council which decides, but this need not simply be a positive or negative decision; a decision may be held in abeyance and reconsidered at a later date.

 CONCLUSIONS

The EU Treaty (and to a lesser extent the SEA and the Treaties of Amsterdam and Nice) has fundamentally changed the political, economic and legal assumptions underlying the Community.

In political terms, the agenda for EMU and the new policy areas relating to foreign and defence policy, and justice and home affairs, gave a radical new direction to the Community.

In economic terms, the new goal of economic and monetary union attempted to build a common market which, as we saw in **Chapter 1**, was far from complete. As a result both of this and other factors, the move to economic and monetary union has been far from smooth and scepticism still surrounds the project.

In legal terms, the EU Treaty has firmly established the principle of subsidiarity and inserted into the EC Treaty some of its most detailed provisions (those on EMU). It has also introduced new policy areas which are outside the legal framework of the Community.

The Treaty of Amsterdam built on these policy areas and began to incorporate some of them into the Community's legal framework. It also introduced for the first time a general principle of closer cooperation among some Member States. The potential significance of this principle remains to be seen.

The Treaty of Nice attempts to prepare for enlargement by reforming the institutions and procedures of the EU. Although it achieves a number of reforms, not all of these are in force as yet, and the true test of their success will come when enforcement actually takes place.

CHAPTER 4: ASSESSMENT EXERCISE   **CWS**

(a) Why was the Single European Act necessary and how does it provide for the achievement of its objectives?

(b) Summarise the most significant effects of the EU Treaty on the EC Treaty.

See *Cases and Materials* (4.11) for a specimen answer.

5 Community law in national courts

5.1 Objectives

By the end of this chapter you should be able to:

1 Understand and analyse the concept of direct effect

2 Explain the concept of indirect effect and the way in which it has been interpreted by the UK courts

3 Explain the key elements of the decisions in *Francovich*, *BT*, and *Factortame III* and apply them to any given factual situation

4 Discuss the rules which apply to the grant of remedies for breach of Community law

5 Explain generally the rights of an individual or company to rely on a provision of Community law in their national courts

5.2 Introduction

The ability of litigants to enforce Community law in national courts is an essential feature of the integrated legal system set up by the Community. Although the Court of Justice is the supreme court in that system, the lower, that is to say national, courts must also be able to apply Community law. In later chapters it will be seen that certain remedies in respect of Community law may be administered only by the Court of Justice, and of course if national law grants the same rights as Community law, it will be sufficient for the applicant to rely directly on national law. However, where national law provides lesser rights than Community law, it is vital that an applicant can enforce his Community rights in the national courts. In the case of Community law which should have been transposed into national law, such as Directives, the applicant may request the Commission to take proceedings under Article 226 (ex 169) EC against the Member State for failing to do so, but this is a relatively circuitous route and increases both delay and expense for the applicant. Where the measure is not designed to be transposed, the applicant has no alternative but to rely directly on the Community measure. It is therefore necessary to identify those rights which may be enforced in the national courts.

5.3 **Direct effect**

Although, as discussed in **Chapter 3**, Community law is part of our legal system and is therefore directly applicable in the UK, not all Community law is directly effective, that is to say, capable of judicial enforcement. In practice, the same situation arises under national law. For example, if a statute is passed enabling the government to privatize the roads, the provisions of the statute could not be enforced against the government if it in fact decided not to go ahead with the privatization.

The Court of Justice has ruled in a number of cases that in order for a Treaty Article, Regulation, or Decision to be directly effective it must be sufficiently clear and unconditional for reliance to be placed on it, and there must be no scope for the exercise of Member State discretion in implementing it. The position with regard to Directives is slightly different and will be considered separately.

5.3.1 **Treaty Articles, regulations, and decisions**

The case which first established the concept of direct effect of Community law related to Treaty Articles. In *Van Gend en Loos* v *Nederlandse Administratie der Belastingen* (Case 26/62) [1963] ECR 1, Van Gend en Loos was required by Dutch law to pay an increased customs duty on imports. It argued in the Dutch courts that this was a violation of Article 25 (ex 12) of the EC Treaty which provided *inter alia* that Member States should not increase such charges. The Dutch court asked the Court of Justice to rule on whether a litigant before a national court could rely directly on the EC Treaty, and in particular, on Article 25 (ex 12).

EXERCISE 5.1   CWS

Summarize the decision reached by the Court of Justice in *Van Gend en Loos* (see *Cases and Materials* (5.1.1)).

The Court of Justice ruled that certain Treaty obligations, such as Article 25 (ex 12) EC could be relied upon in the national courts. However, such direct effect should be restricted to Treaty Articles which were clear and unconditional.

After its ruling in *Van Gend en Loos* the Court of Justice went on in other cases to rule that Regulations and Decisions could also have direct effect.

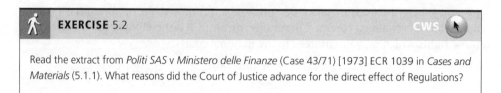

EXERCISE 5.2   CWS

Read the extract from *Politi SAS* v *Ministero delle Finanze* (Case 43/71) [1973] ECR 1039 in *Cases and Materials* (5.1.1). What reasons did the Court of Justice advance for the direct effect of Regulations?

The Court of Justice ruled that Regulations could be directly effective because, by reason of their nature and function within the Community legal system, they created individual rights which national courts must protect. The direct effect of Decisions was recognised in *Grad* v *Finanzamt Traunstein* (Case 9/70) [1970] ECR 825 (*Cases and Materials* (5.1.1)).

? **QUESTION** 5.1   CWS

Why did the Court of Justice in *Grad* (see *Cases and Materials* (5.1.1)) rule that Decisions could have direct effect?

The Court of Justice ruled that since Decisions had binding effect, they must be capable of enforcement by those who were affected by them. The Court also adduced the argument that since Article 234 (ex 177) (see **Chapter 6**) permitted national courts to refer to the Court of Justice questions concerning 'all acts' of the Community, this presupposed that those courts could in the first place apply 'all acts'. (On the facts, however, Grad lost because the date for the Decision to come into effect had not yet passed.)

The two preconditions for the direct effect of Treaty Articles, Regulations, and Decisions will now be considered in more detail.

5.3.1.1 The measure must be clear and unconditional

In practice there is some overlap between clarity and unconditionability. For example, a provision may be unclear because it is conditional on other factors, or it may be conditional because it is for the Member State to implement it in detail. However, a measure may be sufficiently clear even if its precise scope requires interpretation by the Court of Justice under the Article 234 (ex 177) EC procedure (see **Chapter 6**).

In *Van Gend en Loos*, the Court of Justice ruled that the statement in Article 25 (ex 12) EC that 'Member States shall refrain from introducing any new customs duties . . . and from increasing those which they already apply . . .' imposed a clear prohibition on such measures.

A further example is provided by *Defrenne* v *SABENA* (Case 43/75) [1976] ECR 455 (*Cases and Materials* (5.1.1)) which involved a dispute over the policy of the Belgian airline, SABENA, compulsorily to retire its female air hostesses, but not its male crew, at age 40. Ms Defrenne alleged that the loss she thereby sustained in terms of salary and pension entitlement was in breach of Article 141 (ex 119) which provides that men and women should receive equal pay for equal work. The Court of Justice held that this imposed a clear and unconditional prohibition on direct discrimination (discrimination based directly on grounds of sex) but was not sufficiently clear in respect of more indirect discrimination (discrimination purportedly based on factors other than sex, but resulting in discrimination between men and women), since it did not identify what might constitute such discrimination. The concepts of direct and indirect discrimination will be discussed in more detail in **Chapter 14**.

Similarly, Regulations and Decisions must be sufficiently clear and unconditional. As Advocate General Warner stated, in *R* v *Secretary of State for Home Affairs, ex parte Santillo* (Case 131/79) [1980] 2 CMLR 308, 'not every provision of every Regulation has direct effect, in the sense of conferring on private persons rights enforceable by them in national courts'.

In *Grad* the Court of Justice ruled that decisions must be 'unconditional and sufficiently clear and precise to be capable of creating direct effects'.

5.3.1.2 There must be no scope for the exercise of Member State discretion in implementation

In the context of Treaty Articles, Regulations and Decisions it is relatively rare for Member States to be required to pass implementing legislation (see **3.5.2**). However, where such implementation is required, as with Article 141 (ex 119) EC as originally drafted, it seems that as long as the deadline date for implementation has passed the measure can take effect directly as it did in *Defrenne* (5.3.1.1), so long as it is sufficiently clear and unconditional.

5.3.2 Directives

Directives, as we saw in **Chapter 3**, are binding as to their result, but unlike Treaty Articles, Regulations and Decisions, leave the detail of implementation to the Member States. Direct effect should therefore not be an issue since it should be possible to rely on the national, implementing measure before a national court. Unfortunately, the position is not so simple, as the implementing measure may be defective or non-existent. The Court of Justice has therefore recognized that in certain circumstances a Directive may have direct effect.

The case in which the concept of direct effect was established in relation to Directives is *Van Duyn* v *Home Office* (Case 41/74) [1974] ECR 1337. Van Duyn, a Dutch national, applied for permission to enter the UK to work for the Church of Scientology. As the UK authorities officially disapproved of this organization, permission was refused under Article 39 (ex 48) EC, which allowed Member States to derogate on public policy grounds from the right to freedom of movement for workers (see **Chapter 10**).

Van Duyn sought to enforce Directive 64/221 which stated that such derogations could be based only on the personal conduct of the applicant. She lost on the facts because the Court of Justice held that personal conduct could include membership of a particular organization.

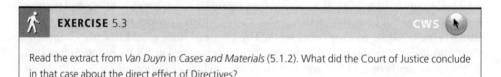

EXERCISE 5.3   CWS

Read the extract from *Van Duyn* in *Cases and Materials* (5.1.2). What did the Court of Justice conclude in that case about the direct effect of Directives?

The Court of Justice ruled that in order for Directives to have a useful effect, they must be capable of producing direct effects, subject to the nature and wording of the Directive in question.

The preconditions which Directives must satisfy in order to have direct effect will now be considered.

5.3.2.1 The directive must be sufficiently clear and unconditional

This is the same requirement as for Treaty Articles, Regulations and Decisions (see **5.3.1.1**). In *Van Duyn* (see 5.3.2) the Court of Justice ruled that the Directive at issue was sufficiently clear and unconditional to be given effect to.

5.3.2.2 The deadline for implementation must have passed

As noted at 5.3.1.2, Treaty Articles, Regulations and Decisions may only have direct effect if there is no scope for the exercise of Member State discretion in implementation. This requirement is not appropriate for Directives.

? QUESTION 5.2   CWS

Given what you have learned about the nature of Directives, why do you think that this requirement would be problematic for Directives? (If you have difficulty in answering this question, look back at 3.5.2).

The problem with Directives is that they are simply instructions to Member States to transpose particular provisions into national law, and so it is almost inevitable that some discretion is left to Member States. The Court of Justice has therefore adapted this requirement for Directives, which can have direct effect so long as the deadline for implementation has passed.

In *Pubblico Ministero* v *Ratti* (Case 148/78) [1979] ECR 1629, Ratti's company had complied with a Directive as to the information to be supplied on labels on chemicals. However, Italy had failed to implement the Directive and prosecuted Ratti under its own, stricter laws.

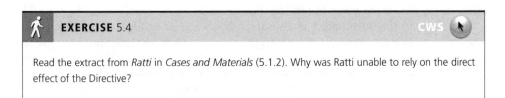

EXERCISE 5.4   CWS

Read the extract from *Ratti* in *Cases and Materials* (5.1.2). Why was Ratti unable to rely on the direct effect of the Directive?

The Court of Justice ruled that the Directive had not become directly effective because the deadline for its implementation had not passed. Until that time, it was not intended to have legal effect and Ratti could not rely on it.

This means that if a Member State wishes to take advantage of the discretion provided by a Directive, it must pass implementing legislation. If it does not, it cannot rely on an option in the Directive which it has failed to exercise. For example, in *East Riding of Yorkshire Council v Gibson* [2000] 3 CMCR 329, a swimming instructor employed by a local authority sought to rely directly on Directive 93/104 (the Working Time Directive), which provided for four weeks paid leave annually and which the UK had not implemented by the deadline. The House of Lords held that the provision on paid leave was not directly effective. However, the House of Lords stated that had the provision been directly effective, the local authority could not have relied on the provision in the Directive permitting Member States to opt for a three-week leave period, rather than four, during a transitional period. It was not open to the State, or an emanation of it, to rely upon an option which it had not exercised.

Before leaving this issue, brief mention should be made of a rather exceptional point. If it is a principle of law of the Member State in question that more favourable laws should apply retroactively, a Directive may be applied retroactively by the courts of that Member State, even where the cause of action arose before the date set for compliance with the Directive. For example, in *Criminal proceedings against Ibiyinka Awoyemi* (Case C-230/97) [1998] ECR I-6781 the Court of Justice ruled that Awoyemi could rely on the directly effective provisions of Directive 91/439 on the mutual recognition of driving licences even before the deadline for transposition of that Directive into national law had passed, if the relevant Member State recognized the principle that more favourable provisions of criminal law had retroactive effect. However, the Court stressed the fact that the Directive was directly effective, because it was clear and precise and the deadline date had passed (albeit after the cause of action arose) without the Member State having taken the measures necessary to implement it. It therefore appears that this exception will apply only where the Member State in question has a rule of law that more favourable criminal laws should apply retroactively and where the Directive in question is capable of direct effect.

5.3.3 Directives only have vertical direct effect

The term 'vertical direct effect' is used where an individual, at one level of the legal system, seeks to enforce a Community measure against the State, which occupies a different level in the system. It can be contrasted with the concept of horizontal direct effect (see below) where an individual wishes to rely on a Community measure against someone at the same level in the system, i.e. an individual. (You should note that 'individual' here refers to any private party and can include businesses.)

The law as to the direct effect of Directives draws a clear distinction between cases where the applicant seeks to enforce a Directive against a Member State, and those where enforcement is sought against a private party. In the latter situation a Directive cannot have direct effect (although a Treaty, Article, Regulation, or Decision could).

In *Marshall v Southampton and South West Area Health Authority (Teaching) (No 1)* (Case 152/84) [1986] ECR 723 (*Cases and Materials* (5.1.2)), Miss Marshall, a dietician, sought to rely on the provisions of Directive 76/207 (*Cases and Materials* (5.1.2)) which prohibited discrimination at work on grounds of sex, in opposing her enforced retirement at the age of 62 which was three years earlier than her male colleagues. The Court of Justice ruled that the Directive was directly effective against the Area Health Authority. Directives were binding only against the State (and emanations of the State), but the capacity in which the State or emanation thereof acted (here as public authority or employer) was irrelevant. Miss Marshall thus succeeded in her claim.

Subsequent cases have given further guidance on which bodies may be included in the definition of the State. The most important of these cases is *Foster* v *British Gas* (Case C-188/89) [1990] ECR 1-3313. British Gas employees were compulsorily retired at age 60 if female but at age 65 if male. Mrs Foster alleged that this was contrary to Directive 76/207 (above).

 EXERCISE 5.5 CWS

Read the extract from *Foster and others* v *British Gas plc and others* in *Cases and Materials* (5.1.2). What did the Court of Justice say about the nature of an emanation of a Member State?

The Court of Justice ruled that, as the deadline for implementation of the Directive had passed without transposing measures having been taken by the UK, the directive itself could be directly effective. It relied on *Marshall* as authority for the proposition that the State could not take advantage of its own failure to implement a Directive. Organizations which were to be treated as an emanation of the State, and against which direct effect could be pleaded were those which, like British Gas:

(a) had been made responsible by the State for providing a public service; and

(b) provided that service under the control of the State; and

(c) had special powers to provide that service, beyond those normally applicable in relations between individuals.

 EXERCISE 5.6 CWS

Read the extract from *Doughty* v *Rolls Royce plc* [1992] 1 CMLR 1045 in *Cases and Materials* (5.1.2). Rolls Royce had a policy similar to that of British Gas (above), and a female employee sought to rely on Directive 76/207. In what way did the Court of Appeal elaborate on the explanation given in *Foster*.

In this case the Court of Appeal ruled that the Directive could not be directly effective against Rolls Royce because it did not fulfil the test set out in *Foster*. It was 100% owned by the State and therefore any service it provided was under the control of the State. However, it was involved in a commercial undertaking and was therefore not responsible for any public service, and it did not exercise any special powers of the type enjoyed by British Gas.

This case makes it clear that all elements of the test in *Foster* must be proved. They are not alternatives, and therefore State control of an organization is not sufficient by itself to make that organization an emanation of the State and liable to direct effect. The fact that British Gas has now been privatized would not, of itself, prevent it from being treated as an emanation of a Member State, provided that all the elements of the *Foster* test were present (i.e. so long as it provides a public service under the control of the State and has special powers to do so).

In other cases, local authorities and the police force have been held to be emanations of the State (*Fratelli Constanzo SpA v Comune di Milano* (Case C 103/88) [1989] ECR 1-1839, see *Cases and Materials* (5.1.2); and *Johnston v Chief Constable of the RUC* (Case 222/84) [1986] ECR 1651, see *Cases and Materials* (5.1.2).

In *Mighell and others v Motor Insurers Bureau* ([1999] 1 CMLR 1251) plaintiffs in three actions, who were victims of motor accidents, sought to rely on Directive 84/5 (the Second Directive on Motor Insurance), which provided for Member States to compensate the victims of accidents caused by uninsured drivers. In the United Kingdom this role was performed by the Motor Insurers' Bureau (MIB). The judges agreed (two of them expressing the opinion *obiter*) that the MIB was not an emanation of the State and therefore the Directive could not be relied upon against it.

One further complication is that in *National Union of Teachers v Governing Body of St. Mary's Church of England (Aided) Junior School* [1997] 3 CMLR 630 the Court of Appeal suggested that there might be bodies which did not satisfy the *Foster* test but which might nonetheless constitute emanations of the State. However, no further tests have been provided by the Court of Justice, and so *Foster* remains the prime test.

 EXERCISE 5.7 CWS

Try to summarize the *Foster* test in your own works without looking at the text. If you have difficulty in doing this, re-read both this section and the extract from *Foster* in *Cases and Materials* (5.1.2).

Before leaving the topic of the direct effect of Directives, brief mention should be made of the concept of horizontal direct effect. This refers to the situation where an individual seeks to rely on a direct effect of a measure against another individual. Treaty Articles, Regulations and Decisions may have horizontal as well as vertical direct effect. However, in *Marshall*, the Court of Justice ruled out the possibility of horizontal direct effect on the grounds that the binding nature of a Directive applied only to its Member State addressee(s). It could not impose obligations on an individual and should not be relied upon against them. The Court of Justice restated this position in *Faccini Dori v Recreb Sri* (Case C-91/92) [1994] ECR I-3325, despite the Opinion of Attorney General Lenz in which he persuasively argued that Directives should have horizontal direct effect.

QUESTION 5.3

Would a woman in the same position as Miss Marshall, but employed by a private hospital, be able to rely on the equal pay Directive in the same way?

In *Marshall* the Court of Justice clearly stated that a Directive could not be relied upon against another individual. It would therefore be possible to rely on the Directive in this situation only if the private hospital could be shown to be an emanation of the Member State. In the light of *Foster* and *Doughty* it would be necessary for the hospital to be operating a public service under the control of the State and to have special powers to do so. It is unlikely that these criteria would be fulfilled (since private healthcare is not a public service) and if they were not, the woman would be unable to rely on the terms of the Directive.

5.3.4 **Recommendations and opinions**

The key case concerning the direct effect of Recommendations is *Grimaldi* v *Fonds des Maladies Professionnelles* (Case C-322/88) [1989] ECR 4407. Grimaldi suffered from a disease which was classified by a Recommendation, but not by French law, as an occupational disease. Under French law, this meant that Grimaldi was not entitled to any compensation, although he would have been so entitled had his illness been classified according to the Recommendation.

EXERCISE 5.8   CWS

Read the extract from *Grimaldi* in *Cases and Materials* (5.1.3). Why was Grimaldi unable to rely directly on the Recommendation?

The Court of Justice ruled that since Recommendations were not intended to have binding effect, it would clearly be inappropriate for them to have direct effect, and therefore Grimaldi could not rely directly on the Recommendation.

Opinions are similar to Recommendations in effect, and therefore this ruling is equally applicable to them.

We have now covered the concept of direct effect. This is one of the most important concepts in EU law, and if you have difficulty in understanding this topic, you should review the foregoing text before passing on to the next topic.

5.4 **Indirect effect**

This term refers to the use of Community law to interpret national law. Community law is then said to have an 'indirect effect' since it influences the interpretation of national law (as opposed to a direct effect where it is relied upon directly).

5.4.1 **Treaty Articles, Regulations, and Decisions**

Although Treaty Articles, Regulations, and Decisions can have indirect effect, it is a relatively unimportant concept in relation to them. This is because they will generally only fail to have direct effect if they are unclear or conditional, in which case they are unlikely to be of much assistance in interpreting national law.

5.4.2 **Recommendations and Opinions**

Indirect effect has more importance in relation to Recommendations and Opinions because they cannot have direct effect (see 5.3.4).

Although in *Grimaldi* the Court of Justice ruled out direct effect, it stated that Recommendations could have indirect effect. It argued that since Recommendations must have some legal effect, they should be taken into consideration when interpreting national implementing measures, or Community measures which the Recommendations were designed to supplement.

As with direct effect, this ruling can be taken to apply equally to Opinions.

Indirect effect is of most importance in relation to Directive and so this topic will be examine in some detail.

5.4.3 **Directives**

Since direct effect is restricted to those Directives which are sufficiently clear and unconditional, and may be relied upon only against the State, the doctrine of direct effect is of somewhat limited use. However, the possibility exists that a Directive may have indirect effect, that is to say, it may be used in a national court in interpreting the relevant national legislation, even if the Directive is too vague to be applied itself, or if the action is against another individual.

Von Colson and Kamann v *Land Nordrhein-Westfalen* (Case 14/83) [1984] ECR 1891 involved the appointment of two men as social workers. Two disappointed female applicants alleged that they had been discriminated against contrary to Directive 76/207. Under German law, the applicants were only entitled to recover their travel expenses.

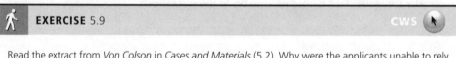

EXERCISE 5.9   CWS

Read the extract from *Von Colson* in *Cases and Materials* (5.2). Why were the applicants unable to rely directly on Directive 76/207? In what way could they rely on it?

The Court of Justice held that the provisions of the Directive as to remedies were not sufficiently precise and unconditional to be directly effective. However, national law should be interpreted in the light of its provisions, which required that an effective remedy be available. The nominal remedy available under German law (the award of expenses) was not adequate.

The case left open the question of precisely **which** national legislation should be construed in this way. The domestic legislation in *Von Colson* had been passed specifically in order to implement the Directive, but in its judgment the Court of Justice referred to 'national law **and** in particular the provisions of a national law specifically introduced in order to implement Directive 76/207' (emphasis added). This implies that legislation not specifically passed to implement a Directive could also fall to be construed in accordance with it. In particular, where the national legislation predates the Directive, such an interpretation might prove difficult, but it could be argued that if indirect effect were to be limited to implementing legislation, an unscrupulous Member State could simply fail to pass any implementing legislation and thus avoid both actions based on national implementing law and actions based on the Directive itself.

It should be noted that the duty of consistent interpretation applies only to legislation. In *White (A.P.)* v. *White and the Motor Insurers Bureau* [2001] 2 CMCR 1, the victim of a motor accident caused by an uninsured driver sought to rely on the agreement made between the Secretary of State for the Environment, Transport and the Regions and the Motor Insurers Bureau ('MIB') in implementation of Directive 84/5 (the Second Directive on Motor Insurance). The agreement provided, inter alia, for the compensation of victims who had obtained judgment against an uninsured driver, unless he 'knew or ought to have known' that the driver was uninsured. The Directive only referred to victims who 'knew'.

In determining the meaning of this phrase, the House of Lords ruled that there was no obligation to interpret the agreement in line with the Directive since it was not legislation. This is surprising given that the agreement was made with the Secretary of State, and that it was made in fulfilment of the UK's obligations under the Directive. However, the House of Lords ruled that a purposive approach to the interpretation of the agreement should be taken. Account must therefore be taken of the Directive, since the purpose of the agreement was to give effect to the provisions of the Directive. The result of this was that the House of Lords took account of the Directive in interpreting the agreement, but did so not in order to give indirect effect to the Directive, but in accordance with the usual domestic rules of statutory interpretation.

Although courts in the UK have recognized the concept of indirect effect, they have tended to rely on it somewhat sparingly. One example of its use is in *Litster* v *Forth Dry Dock and Engineering Co. Ltd* [1989] 1 All ER 1134 (*Cases and Materials* (5.2)). Litster and others were dismissed by their employer, a shipyard, one hour before it was sold to another company and new employees taken on. UK law designed to implement a Directive provided the employees with a remedy only if they had been employed immediately before such a transfer. Litster argued that 'immediately before' must be interpreted in the light of the Directive, which was clearly intended to protect all employees dismissed in the event of a transfer of employer.

QUESTION 5.4   CWS

Read the extract from *Litster and others* v *Forth Dry Dock and Engineering Co. Ltd and another* in *Cases and Materials* (5.2). What restrictions did the House of Lords impose upon the doctrine of indirect effect?

The House of Lords accepted the principle of indirect effect but restricted its scope. It took the view that the duty of construction imposed on national courts by *Von Colson* applied to legislation 'issued for the purpose of complying with directives'. On the facts, the relevant UK law had been so intended, and therefore the employees were entitled to compensation.

The Court of Justice subsequently clarified its position in *Marleasing SA* v *La Comercial Internacional de Alimentación SA* (Case C-106/89) [1990] ECR I-4135. Spanish law laid down a number of grounds on which a company could be struck off the register, including lack of cause, meaning that the company had no real function. Spain had failed to implement a company law Directive which omitted this particular ground. La Comercial sought to rely on the Directive when Marleasing attempted to have it struck off for lack of cause.

EXERCISE 5.10   CWS

Read the extract from *Marleasing* in *Cases and Materials* (5.2). What did the Court of Justice decide? Can you think of wider policy reasons why it might have decided the issue this way?

The Court of Justice confirmed that the Directive could not have horizontal direct effect against Marleasing but ruled that Spanish law, even though it predated the Directive, must be interpreted 'as far as possible' in accordance with it. This meant that lack of cause was not a ground on which a company could be struck off and therefore La Comercial could not be struck off.

It should be borne in mind that the Court of Justice has consistently attempted to promote and expand the application of Community law and to have given indirect effect a more narrow application would have gone against this policy.

However, the 'as far as possible' caveat in *Marleasing* provides a potential loophole. In the case of *Wagner Miret* v *Fondo de Garantía Salarial* (Case C-334/92) [1995] 2 CMLR 49, the Court of Justice confirmed the existence of this loophole and took a more restrictive approach to indirect effect.

Wagner Miret was a senior manager in a company which became insolvent. Directive 80/897 obliged Member States to set up a fund to recompense employees whose employers became insolvent. Although Spain had set up such a fund, it did not cover payments to higher management staff.

EXERCISE 5.11 CWS

Read the extract from *Wagner Miret* in *Cases and Materials* (5.2). What remedy did the Court of Justice rule should be provided to Wagner Miret? Why were the other potential remedies not appropriate?

The Court of Justice ruled that Directive 80/897 was not sufficiently precise to be directly effective. The relevant Spanish law clearly restricted the coverage of the existing fund and the Court of Justice accepted that the law governing the fund could not be interpreted as permitting higher management employees to claim from it. The only possible remedy for Wagner Miret was that the State should recompense him for his losses since its failure to transpose the Directive had caused his loss. (This is sometimes referred to as the *Francovich* remedy, and will be discussed shortly.)

The first case involving indirect effect to come before the UK courts after *Marleasing* was *Webb* v *EMO Air Cargo (UK) Ltd.* Ms Webb was employed to cover the maternity leave of another colleague. Prior to taking employment, Webb discovered that she was pregnant, and was dismissed as a result.

Webb's argument that her dismissal was contrary to the Sex Discrimination Act 1975 was rejected by the House of Lords (see *Cases and Materials* (5.2)). As to Webb's argument that her dismissal was contrary to Directive 76/207, which prohibited discrimination at work on grounds of sex, the House of Lords accepted that *Marleasing* required it to interpret the Sex Discrimination Act consistently with the later Directive, but 'only if it is possible to do so'. A reference was therefore made to the Court of Justice as to whether the dismissal was contrary to Directive 76/207.

The Court of Justice ruled that Webb's dismissal did indeed contravene Directive 76/207.The House of Lords was therefore left with the task of attempting to interpret the Sex Discrimination Act consistently with the requirements of the Directive.

 EXERCISE 5.12 CWS

Read the extract from *Webb* v *EMO Air Cargo (UK) Ltd (No. 2)* [1995] 4 All ER 577 in *Cases and Materials* (5.2) and answer the following questions:

(a) Did the House of Lords decide that it was possible to construe the Sex Discrimination Act in such a way as to comply with Directive 76/207?
(b) What reason(s) did the House of Lords give for this decision?

The House of Lords concluded that the Sex Discrimination Act could be interpreted consistently with the Directive.

Section 1(1)(a) of the Act prohibits the discriminatory treatment of women on the ground of their sex. Section 5(3) of the Act states that in order to show discrimination, any comparison between the treatment of women and that of men must be made on the basis of similar 'relevant circumstances'. Prior to the ruling of the Court of Justice, the House of Lords had interpreted 'relevant circumstances' in Webb's case to mean her unavailability for work. Since a male employee who was unavailable to work would have been treated in the same way, there was no discrimination.

In the light of the Court of Justice ruling that Webb's dismissal contravened Directive 76/207, the House of Lords interpreted 'relevant circumstances' to mean Webb's unavailability for work due to pregnancy. Since a male employee could not have been dismissed for this reason, the dismissal was discriminatory.

The *Webb* case clearly indicates that the House of Lords has accepted the ruling of the Court of Justice in *Marleasing* that even national legislation which pre-dates Community law must be interpreted consistently with it.

5.4.4 Relationship between indirect effect and the sovereignty of Community law

> **?** **QUESTION** 5.5
>
> How does the concept of indirect effect relate to what you learned about the sovereignty of Community law in **Chapter 3**?

First, indirect effect is a practical manifestation of the sovereignty of Community law, because an interpretation of national law which is consistent with Community law takes precedence over an interpretation which does not. Secondly, where national law clearly conflicts with Community law and cannot be interpreted consistently with it, the national court is under a duty to refuse to apply the conflicting elements of national law.

Where national law imposes a duty or prohibition on an applicant which is contrary to Community law, the applicant could benefit form it being disapplied. For example, in *Brasserie du Pêcheur SA* v *Germany* and *R* v *Secretary of State for Transport ex parte Factortame* (*'Factortame III'*) (see 5.5.2) the applicants were Spanish fishermen who were prevented from fishing in British waters by the provisions of the Merchant Shipping Act 1988. They therefore sought to have the Act disapplied so that they could legally resume fishing.

By contrast, where national law gives the applicant certain rights which are not as favourable as those granted by Community law, the applicant could be worse off if the national law is disapplied. This is because, if the Community measure in question has no direct or indirect effect, the applicant's only rights are under national law. In these circumstances, national law would not be disapplied.

We have now covered the concept of indirect effect. If you have difficulty in understanding this topic, or its application by the UK courts (and most students do!) you should review this section of the text before going on to the next topic.

5.5 Member State liability

In addition to the doctrines of direct and indirect effect, the Court of Justice has developed a third potential remedy for those individuals who have suffered as a result of breach of Community law. The Member State may, in certain circumstances, be liable in damages for its own breach of Community law. For this purpose, the 'Member State' includes not only the national government, but other public-law bodies such as territorial bodies to which certain legislative or administrative tasks have been devolved (*Haim* v *Kassenzahnärztliche Vereinigung Nordrhein* (Case C-424/97)). The Court of Justice has developed two different sets of conditions governing such liability, commonly known as the *Francovich* conditions and the *Factortame III* conditions. These will now be examined.

5.5.1 *Francovich* liability

In *Francovich and Others* v *Italian Republic* (Cases C-6/90 & C-9/90) [1991] ECR I-5357 (*Cases and Materials* (5.3.1)), Francovich was owed wages by his employer, a company which had become insolvent. Under Italian law, Francovich had no remedy but, under a Directive which Italy had failed to transpose, the State was required to set up a scheme under which employees of insolvent companies would receive at least some of their outstanding wages. The Court of Justice ruled that the Directive was not sufficiently precise to have direct effect. It could not be indirectly effective because there was no relevant Italian legislation in accordance with which it could fall to be construed.

> **? QUESTION** 5.6
>
> In the light of these problems, what reasoning did the Court of Justice adopt in order to provide a remedy to Francovich? What was this remedy?

The Court of Justice ruled that the Italian State must make good the loss suffered by Francovich. It gave two reasons for the imposition of liability on Member States. First, the full effectiveness of Community law would be impaired if individuals could not obtain redress directly from a State which was responsible for a breach of Community law that had caused them loss. Secondly, Article 10 (ex 5) EC (see *Cases and Materials* (3.1.2.2)) obliged Member States to take all measures to ensure that they fulfilled their Treaty obligations, and this included making good the consequences of a breach of these obligations.

The Court of Justice restricted Member State liability for failure to implement a Directive to situations where three conditions were fulfilled:

(a) The result prescribed by the Directive must involve the grant of rights to individuals.

(b) The content of those rights must be clear from the Directive.

(c) There must be a causal link between the breach of the State's obligation and the damage suffered by the individual.

In this case, the Directive gave employees the right to be paid their wages and it was clear from the Directive that these were to be paid in full up to a certain time. However, the Directive only applied to employees whose employer had been made subject to specified types of insolvency proceedings. Under Italian law, Francovich's employer could not be subjected to such proceedings, and so in the later case of *Francovich* v *Italian Republic* (Case C-479/93) [1993] ECR I-3843 (*Francovich II*), the Court of Justice ruled that Francovich was not covered by the protection of the Directive. Italy's failure to implement the Directive by setting up an appropriate scheme had therefore not caused Francovich loss.

From the judgment in *Francovich* (and in later cases on Member State liability—see below), it appears that the Court of Justice will only consider Member State liability where direct and indirect effect cannot provide a remedy.

? **QUESTION** 5.7 CWS

Do you agree with this approach? Should this remedy be used in preference to direct and indirect effect, or only where those doctrines are inapplicable? Read the extract from 'From direct effects to *Francovich*: shifting means of enforcement of Community law' in *Cases and Materials* (5.3.1) for a further discussion of this point.

The basic requirement for liability is that there has been a breach of Community law which has caused loss to the applicant. Beyond this, as the Court stated in *Francovich*, 'the conditions under which that liability gives rise to a right to reparation depend on the nature of the breach of Community law giving rise to the loss and damage'. In other words, further conditions may attach to liability, depending on the type of wrongful act. Where the wrongful act consists of a failure to transpose a Directive, as in *Francovich*, the applicant must show that the Directive would have conferred clear rights on him. This is part of causation.

If Member State's wrongful act consists of something other than the failure to transpose a Directive, the *Francovich* conditions will not apply. However, the *Factortame III* conditions, which are slightly different, may apply. In *Dillenkofer and others* v *Germany* (Joined Cases C-178 and 179/94 & C-188 to 190/94) [1996] 3 CMLR 469 (*Cases and Materials* (5.3.3)), a case involving the total non-transposition of a Directive, the Court of Justice applied the *Francovich* conditions but also attempted to reconcile them with the *Factortame III* conditions. This point will be discussed further at 5.5.3 after the *Factortame III* conditions have been considered.

5.5.2 *Factortame III* liability

Where the Court of Justice has found the Member State to be guilty of any breach other than a total failure to implement a Directive, it has applied the *Factortame III* conditions.

These conditions were first stated by the Court in *Brasserie du Pêcheur SA v Germany* and *R v Secretary of State for Transport ex parte Factortame ('Factortame III')* (Joined Cases C-46 and C-48/93) [1996] 1 CMLR 889, in which the Court of Justice considered together claims for damages by a French brewery against the German government and by Spanish fishermen against the UK government, in respect of national legislation which conflicted with Community law.

 EXERCISE 5.13

We have already looked at other aspects of the *Factortame* litigation (see **Chapter 3**). Try to summarize in writing the facts giving rise to the litigation and the judgments prior to this particular ruling. This will help you to understand the nature of the claim for damages. (If in doubt, see 3.3.2.2 above.)

Factortame and other Spanish fishermen claimed damages from the UK government after the Merchant Shipping Act 1988, which had made it unlawful for them to fish in UK waters, was declared by the Court of Justice to be contrary to Community law. Their action for damages was joined by the Court with that of Brasserie du Pêcheur, a French brewery. It claimed damages from the German government after the prohibition on its export from France imposed by Germany was declared by the Court of Justice to be contrary to Community law.

In *Factortame III* the Court restated the principles of State liability which it had outlined in *Francovich*. It stated that although the Treaty did not expressly provide for Member State liability in damages, such liability must be possible in order to ensure the full effectiveness of Community law and as part of the duty of Member States under Article 5 to fulfil their Treaty obligations. Indeed, the Court considered that this reasoning applied even more strongly in the present case, which involved rights upon which individuals were entitled to rely in national courts, than in *Francovich*, in which the rights infringed were not enforceable in the national courts.

As to the conditions under which Member State liability would arise, the Court reasoned that these must be similar to those laid down in Article 288 (ex 215) of the Treaty under which the Community institutions could incur liability for breach of Community law. Put simply, Article 288 (ex 215) imposes liability where there is a wrongful act, damage to the applicant and causation. In addition, if the allegedly wrongful act is a piece of legislation over which the institution has been given a wide degree of discretion (which the Court assumed to be the case in both *BT* (see below) and *Factortame III*), a further test, known as the *Schöppenstedt* test, applies. (Note that both Article 288 (ex 215) EC and the *Schöppenstedt* test will be considered in more depth in **Chapter 8** in the context of Community liability.)

In *Factortame III* the Court of Justice reformulated this test and ruled that where the Member State acts pursuant to a wide discretion, the State will be liable for its breach of Community law if:

(a) the breach infringes a rule of law intended to confer rights on individuals;

(b) the breach is sufficiently serious;

(c) there is a direct causal link between the breach of the State's obligation and the damage to the applicant.

The Court of Justice has applied the *Factortame III* test in a number of later cases, such as *R v HM Treasury ex parte British Telecommunications plc* (Case C-392/93) [1996] 2 CMLR 217 and *R v Secretary of State for the Home Department ex parte Gallagher* [1996] 2 CMLR 951 (*Cases and Materials* (5.3.2)) (which both involved a Member State's failure to implement a Directive correctly) *R v Ministry of Agriculture, Fisheries and Food ex parte Hedley Lomas* (Case C-5/94) [1996] 2 CMLR 391 (*Cases and Materials* (5.3.2)) (which concerned the refusal of a Member State to issue licences for certain goods to be exported to another Member State) and *Köbler v Austria* (Case C-224/101 [2003] 3 CMLR 28, not yet reported (which concerned a court of last instance's incorrect ruling on community law) (*Cases and Materials* (5.3.2)).

The elements of this test will now be examined.

5.5.2.1 Infringement of a rule of law intended to confer rights on individuals

The Court of Justice appears to have accepted that almost any rule of law breached is a law intended to confer rights on individuals, since in none of the cases on Member State liability so far decided has the Court found that this condition is not satisfied.

EXERCISE 5.14

Read Article 43 (ex 52) in *Cases and Materials* (5.3.2). What rights, if any, do you think that this Article confers on individuals? Read the first extract from *Factortame III* in *Cases and Materials* (5.3.2) to see if your view coincides with that of the Court of Justice.

In *Factortame III* the Court of Justice accepted that Article 43 (ex 52) EC, which provides that Member State nationals may move to another Member State as self-employed persons or in order to manage a business, confers rights on individuals which national courts must protect.

5.5.2.2 Sufficiently serious breach

The Court of Justice stated in *Factortame III* that a breach of Community law would be sufficiently serious if the Member States had 'manifestly and gravely disregarded the limits on its discretion'. In determining whether this was so, the Court set out a number of factors which could be taken into account.

EXERCISE 5.15 CWS

Read the extract at 5.3.2 in *Cases and Materials* and see how many of these factors you can list.

The factors which the Court suggested could be taken into account were:

(a) the clarity and precision of the rule breached;

(b) the extent of any discretion left to the Member State;

(c) whether the breach was intentional or involuntary;

(d) whether the error of law was excusable or inexcusable;

(e) whether the position taken by a Community institution had contributed towards the Member State's action;

(f) the adoption or retention of practices contrary to Community law

There is potential overlap between these factors. For example, an error of law might be considered excusable if the rule of law breached is extremely unclear.

 QUESTION 5.8

What other information do you think you might need in order to assess whether the error of law was excusable? (If you have difficulty in answering this question, think about the sources you might consult in order to try to understand a piece of legislation.)

Whether an error of law is excusable or inexcusable will turn largely on the clarity of that law, as mentioned above, and also on the existence of any judgments of the Court of Justice on the meaning of the particular law. For example, in *BT* (see below), the Court of Justice ruled that the UK's error of law was excusable because the law in question was unclear and there had been no previous rulings as to its meaning.

In applying these factors in *Factortame III*, the Court of Justice ruled that regard should be had, *inter alia*, to the common fisheries policy, the fact that proceedings before the Court of Justice had indicated that the Act was likely to be found invalid, the fact that the Commission had warned the UK that its actions could be contrary to Community law and the allegation by one of the claimants that the UK had delayed complying with the ruling from the Court of Justice in *Commission v UK* (Case C-246/89) [1989] ECR 3125, that parts of the Merchant Shipping Act 1988 were unlawful. These factors made the Member State's breach of the Community law all the more blatant and therefore all the more 'manifest'. In fact, the Court indicated that one of these factors—the alleged failure of the UK to comply immediately with a judgment of the Court of Justice—was so serious that, if proved, it would automatically constitute a 'sufficiently serious breach' without any need to consider the factors set out above for determining the existence of such a breach.

This approach has been taken by the Court of Justice in another case; that of *Hedley Lomas*, which involved a breach by the UK of Article 28 (ex 30) EC on the free movement of goods. The Court applied the *Factortame III* test but ruled that the Member State had no discretion as to whether to comply with Article 28 (ex 30) EC and so **any** infringement of it must be a sufficiently serious breach. The UK was therefore liable in damages to Hedley Lomas.

This judgment has been criticized as going beyond *Factortame III*. In *Factortame III* the Court of Justice referred to a breach of law—the failure to comply with a judgment by it—over which the Member State clearly had no discretion. After all, Member States cannot choose whether to comply with judgments of the Court of Justice; they are under a strict duty to do so. However, as we shall see in **Chapter 9**, Member States do effectively have a discretion over the implementation of Article 28 (ex 30) EC, because they can restrict the free movement of goods if one of the exceptions contained in Article 30 (ex 36) EC applies. In *Hedley Lomas*, the UK had argued that one of these exceptions did indeed apply. Admittedly the Court did not accept this argument, but it seems a little unjust for the Court then to rule that since the UK had been wrong about the application of Article 30 (ex 36) EC, it had had no discretion and therefore must be guilty of a sufficiently serious breach. After all, the UK could not have known that its interpretation of Article 30 (ex 36) EC would be adjudged to be incorrect until the Court of Justice gave judgment.

EXERCISE 5.16   **CWS**

Read *R v Ministry of Agriculture, Fisheries and Food ex parte Hedley Lomas* in *Cases and Materials* (5.3.2) and make a brief note of the facts. When you have studied **Chapter 9**, review these notes for a better understanding of this judgment.

A further criticism which may be levied at the whole idea of according to certain breaches the automatic status of a 'sufficiently serious breach', is that the main element of the *Factortame III* test—and the feature which distinguishes it from *Francovich*—is the very examination of **whether** there has been a sufficiently serious breach, and yet the Court appear to be prepared to omit that examination on a rather arbitrary basis.

Perhaps the best approach is to treat this possibility as a rather anomalous exception to the general application of the *Factortame III* test, and to concentrate on understanding and applying *Factortame III* and the case we are about to look at, namely *BT*.

In *R v HM Treasury ex parte British Telecommunications plc* (Case C-392/93) [1996] 2 CMLR 217, the Court of Justice held that there was no sufficiently serious breach because the interpretation of the Directive on which the flawed implementing measures were based was reasonable in the circumstances. There was no appropriate case law for the UK to consult, and the Commission had not raised the matter when the UK adopted the implementation measures. The UK did not, therefore, incur liability in damages.

The Court of Justice came to a similar conclusion in *Denkavit International BV and VITIC Amsterdam BV and Voormeer BV* v *Bundesamt für Finanzamt* (Cases 283, 291 and 292/94) [1996] ECR I-5063. In that case the German government had failed to implement correctly a Directive on the taxation of parent and subsidiary companies. The Court ruled that the Member State was not liable in damages for this breach of Community law because the rule breached was not clear and precise. Almost all Member States had adopted the same, incorrect interpretation as Germany, and there had been no case law from the Court of Justice as to how this Directive was to be interpreted.

In *R* v *Secretary of State for the Home Department ex parte Gallagher* [1996] 2 CMLR 951 (*Cases and Materials* (5.3.2)), the Court of Appeal applied the *Factortame III* test to the UK's failure, in the form of the Prevention of Terrorism (Temporary Provisions) Act 1989, to transpose correctly a Directive on the free movement of persons. It ruled that the UK's breach of Community law was not sufficiently serious because persons subject to the Act were not 'obviously worse off' as a result of that breach, and the Commission had not objected to the Act when notified of it.

In *Köbler* v *Austria* (*Cases and Materials* (5.3.2)) the Court of Justice ruled that the breach of law was insufficiently serious. Community law did not expressly state whether discrimination such as that at issue could be justified, this point had not been dealt with previously by the Court, and the answer was not obvious. In reaching an incorrect conclusion and refusing to make a reference, the national court had not committed a sufficiently serious breach of Article 39 EC and Regulation 1612/68 on the free movement of workers.

5.5.2.3 **Causation of damage**

The issue of causation is for the national court to determine on the facts (see *Francovich II* above).

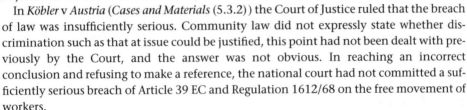

EXERCISE 5.17 CWS

Read the extract from *Gallagher* in *Cases and Materials* (5.3.2) and summarize what the Court of Appeal said about the issue of causation in that case.

In *Gallagher*, the Court of Appeal ruled that in addition to the fact that the breach of Community law was not sufficiently serious, there was no causal link between the breach and Gallagher's losses. Even if the UK had properly implemented the Directive, Gallagher could properly—and indeed would—have been excluded from the UK.

An important point to note is that in *Factortame III* the Court of Justice stated that in determining the extent of the loss or damage for which compensation would be awarded, the national court should have regard to 'whether the injured person showed reasonable diligence in order to avoid the loss or damage or limit its extent and whether, in particular, he availed himself in time of all the legal remedies available to him'. So not only must the applicant mitigate his loss, but this mitigation could include the duty to take legal action against other parties. Therefore, an applicant who has a potential claim against another defendant, by relying on the direct or indirect effect of Community law against that defendant, will be expected to pursue that claim before making a claim against the State for damages. If he does not do so, then the amount of damages payable by the State may be reduced.

5.5.3 Conclusion on Member State liability

There are now two tests for Member State liability: the *Francovich* test, applicable where a Member State has completely failed to transpose a Directive; and the *Factortame III* test, applicable in a number of other situations. While this is perhaps the simplest way to approach the issue, the Court of Justice has (as mentioned in 5.5.1) attempted to reconcile the two tests. In *Dillenkofer* the Court observed that the two sets of conditions were in fact very similar. Both required: (a) a sufficiently serious breach of (b) a rule of law which gave rights to individuals which (c) caused loss to the applicant. The key difference, according to the Court, was that instead of expressly requiring a sufficiently serious breach, the *Francovich* test required the total non-transposition of a Directive, which is, of course, simply a clear example of a sufficiently serious breach.

 EXERCISE 5.18   CWS

Read the extract from *Dillenkofer and others* v *Germany* (Joined Cases C-178 and 179/94 & C-188 to 190/94) [1996] 3 CMLR 469 in *Cases and Materials* (5.3.3) to ensure that you have understood the Court's reasoning in this respect.

Despite the Court's comments in *Dillenkofer*, it did not attempt to produce or apply a combined test on the facts, and so it seems that it will be acceptable to go on applying the *Francovich* or *Factortame III* tests separately, as applicable.

As a final point it is also worth noting that although the rules on Member State liability have been based on those applicable to Community liability, the two areas of law are quite separate. For example, in imposing liability on Community institutions (see **Chapter 8**), the Court of Justice has interpreted 'manifest' as meaning that the measure affected a limited and ascertainable group (see, e.g., *Dumortier Frères*).

? **QUESTION** 5.9

There was a very large number of applicants in *Factortame III*. In what way would you have expected this fact to have affected the Court's assessment of whether the breach was 'manifest and grave'?

You might have expected the number of applicants in *Factortame III* to have been taken as an indication that the breach was not manifest, i.e. obvious, since it affected a wide range of persons. This has been the Court's approach to the context of Community liability. However, in dealing with the liability of Member States in *Factortame III* the Court made no mention of the numbers of those potentially affected by the measure, even though there were ninety-seven applicants in that case alone.

The final point about *Factortame III* is that although the Court refused to restrict the retrospective application of its judgment for claims not already brought, it accepted that the national courts could do so. The issue of Member State liability is a complex one, not least because the jurisprudence of the Court in this area is continuing to develop. However, it is important to be able to identify the key elements of the decisions so far and apply them to any given set of facts. You may need to read this section several times in order to do this.

5.6 Remedies available

The full range of remedies available in respect of national law is applicable to Community law. However, the two most important remedies for breach of Community law are the disapplication of national law (see **Chapter 3**) and damages.

5.6.1 Disapplying national legislation

The Court of Justice clearly stated in *Amministrazione delle Finanze dello Stato* v *Simmenthal (Simmenthal II)* (see 3.3.2.2) that national courts had a responsibility to disapply national law which conflicted with Community law.

In *Factortame I* (see 3.3.2.2), the applicants sought to suspend an Act which allegedly conflicted with Community law, pending a decision by the Court of Justice. Under national law, such a remedy was not available. However, the Court of Justice ruled that in order for the Community right to be fully effective, this remedy must be granted and the Act temporarily suspended.

5.6.2 Damages

As we have seen in this chapter, damages may be awarded in any of the following circumstances for breach of Community law:

(a) Against an individual or private or public body for breach of a directly effective Treaty Article, Regulation, or Decision (see 5.3.1).

(b) Against a public body which is an 'emanation of the Member State' for breach of a directly effective Directive (see 5.3.2).

(c) Against the State for:

  (i) failure to transpose a Directive (see 5.5.1);

  (ii) certain other breaches of Community law (see 5.5.2).

In all these cases the damages will actually be awarded by the national courts and so national laws governing the award of damages will apply subject to the conditions which the Court of Justice has laid down (see below). In addition, damages may be awarded for breach of national law interpreted in the light of Community law, but this is an action under national, rather than Community, law and the principles set out do not apply. (Damages may also be awarded, in certain circumstances, against the Community institutions, but any such action must be brought in the Court of Justice rather than in the national courts—see **Chapter 8**.)

5.7 Principles governing the award of a remedy

Although, in an action in the national courts, the award of any remedy for breach of Community law is governed by national law, the Court of Justice has laid down a number of principles with which the award of this remedy must comply. These principles have been developed over time and in some cases appear to conflict.

5.7.1 Non-discrimination

The remedy must be available on conditions as favourable as those applicable to an equivalent breach of national law.

For example, if certain time limits or rights of appeal are laid down for actions based on national law, no lesser time limits or more restricted rights of appeal may be imposed for an action based on Community law.

5.7.2 The remedy must be effective

The Court of Justice has repeatedly stated that national laws must not make the obtaining of a remedy in practice 'impossible or excessively difficult'. In two areas in particular, national laws have often fallen foul of this principle: the time limits imposed, and the amount of damages awarded. Each of these will be considered in turn.

5.7.2.1 Time limits

Although the question of time limits on bringing an action is governed by national procedural rules (three years for most actions in the UK), these will not apply if they make it virtually impossible to exercise Community law rights. In *Emmott* v *Minister for Social Welfare and another* (Case C-208/90) [1991] ECR I-4269 (*Cases and Materials* (5.4)) Ireland had not implemented the necessary measures to comply with a Directive equalizing disability benefits until two years after the implementation deadline. Emmott claimed compensation in respect of underpaid benefit during this two-year period, but the Irish authorities alleged that her claim was outside the three-month time limit set by Irish law.

? **QUESTION** 5.10

Did the Court of Justice accept the argument put forward by the Irish authorities?

The Court of Justice ruled that the time limit should not start to run until the Directive had been properly transposed, and therefore that the claim could be heard.

The key to this ruling was that the time limit made it **virtually impossible** for Emmott to exercise her Community law rights since the three-month time limit expired long before the relevant Directive was implemented and therefore before Emmott could have become aware of her rights.

However, where a time limit on the bringing of another action does **not** make the exercise of Community law rights virtually impossible, that time limit will not be in conflict with Community law and will therefore be valid. In *Edilizia Industriale Siderurgica Srl (Edis) v Ministero delle Finanze* (Case C-231/96) [1999] 2 CMLR 995 the Court of Justice ruled that a time limit of three years on the commencement of actions to recover charges levied in contravention of Community law was compatible with Community law, even though at the time those charges were levied, the relevant Directive had not been properly implemented under national law. The charges had been levied between 1986 and 1992 and the Directive was correctly implemented in 1993, so it was still possible to bring an action for recovery of the charges once the Directive had been implemented (albeit not for all the charges paid).

In later cases such as *Johnson* v *Chief Adjudication Officer* (Case C-410/92) [1994] ECR I-5493 and *Steenhorst-Neerings* v *Bestuur van de Bedriffsvereniging voor Detailhandel* (Case C-338/91) [1993] ECR I-5475 the Court of Justice has made it clear that time limits which do not prevent the bringing of an action, but simply limit the arrears of benefit payable, are applicable.

5.7.2.2 **The amount of damages**

Where national law imposes an unduly severe limit on the maximum amount of damages that can be awarded, this may make the remedy ineffective to protect the applicant's Community law rights.

In *Marshall* v *Southampton and South West Area Health Authority (No. 2)* (Case C-271/91) [1993] 3 CMLR 293 (for the facts, see *Marshall (No. 1)* at 5.3.3), Marshall disputed the severe restrictions which the Sex Discrimination Act imposed on the amount of damages which could be awarded.

🚶 EXERCISE 5.19   CWS

Read the extract from *Marshall (No. 2)* in *Cases and Materials* (5.4). Did the Court of Justice uphold this limit on damages? On what grounds did it base its decision?

The Court of Justice ruled that the Act conflicted with Article 249 (ex 189) EC which provided that Member States must ensure that the objectives of Directives were fulfilled. The objective of Directive 76/207 was to achieve real equality of opportunity. This required that where such equality had not been achieved, the victim of discrimination could be reinstated or compensated in full for the loss and damage sustained. The limit on damages was therefore contrary to Community law.

It should be noted that this Directive expressly imposed a duty on Member States to take the necessary measures to enable applicants to pursue their claims. It has been argued that had such a specific duty been absent, the Court of Justice might have been less willing to override the provisions of national law.

However, there have been other cases in which the Court of Justice has made it clear that a national limit on the amount of damages is incompatible with Community law if it renders the remedy ineffective.

In a case considered earlier (at 5.4.3), *Von Colson*, two women who had attended an interview, but failed to secure the post, brought a claim for damages on the grounds of sex discrimination. The Court of Justice ruled that the compensation must be adequate in relation to the damage sustained and that a German law which limited the amount of damages to a 'purely nominal amount such as . . . the expenses incurred by them in submitting their application', did not effectively protect the applicants' rights under Community law.

In *Draehmpaehl* v *Urania Immobilienservice OHG* (Case C-180/95) [1997] 3 CMLR 1107 the Court of Justice ruled that a national law which prescribed an upper limit of three months' salary for compensation for sex discrimination in the appointment of candidates to a job was contrary to Community law. However, the Court qualified this ruling by stating that such a rule was only invalid in so far as it applied to applicants who would have obtained a post had it not been for the selection process. Where an applicant would not have obtained the position anyway, and therefore suffered little or no loss, the ceiling of three months' salary was compatible with Community law.

Similar problems occur in the context of business as well as personal losses. In *Factortame III*, the Court of Justice ruled that the total exclusion of loss of profit as a head of damages which could be awarded for breach of Community law was incompatible with Community law. It stated that in the context of commercial litigation, such a total exclusion would make genuine reparation of losses suffered practically impossible.

5.7.3 New remedies need not be created

In the case of *Rewe Handelsgesellschaft Nord Mbh and Rewe-Markt Steffen* v *Hauptzollamt* (Case 158/80) [1981] ECR 1005 (*Cases and Materials* (5.4)), the Court of Justice acknowledged that national courts need not create new remedies to ensure that Community law is fully effective if those remedies do not exist in national law. The remedy available therefore depended on the provisions of national law.

This principle may, on occasion, conflict with the principle of effectiveness. More recent case law (*Marshall No. 2, Factortame III*) appears to indicate that new remedies may be necessary in the interests of effectiveness.

5.7.4 **No further substantive conditions**

Where liability has arisen under Community law, no further substantive conditions may be imposed by national law. In the case which established this principle, *Dekker* v *Stichting VJV* (Case 177/88) [1990] ECR I-3941. Dekker's name had been put forward as the most suitable candidate for a job, but after she informed the employer that she was pregnant, she was rejected. She sought a remedy for breach of Directive 76/207.

 EXERCISE 5.20   CWS

Read the extract from *Dekker* in *Cases and Materials* (5.4). What extra substantive conditions did the employer try to impose upon the grant of a remedy for sex discrimination? Was he successful?

The employer argued that under Dutch law, Dekker had to show not merely discrimination, but unjustified discrimination. It claimed that its action was justified because its insurance would not cover the cost of her maternity leave in these circumstances. The Court of Justice held that since the Directive imposed liability purely on the basis of discrimination, regardless of any fault, national provisions requiring such fault to be proved could not be applied.

A further example of this principle is the statement in *Factortame III* that if the conditions for Member State liability are satisfied, no further requirement of proof of fault may be imposed by national law.

You should now have achieved all the learning objectives set out in 5.1. If you are still unsure about any area, don't panic. This chapter contains some complex material. However, it is a vital area of Community law for you to grasp and you should be prepared to review those elements of it which you do not understand as many times as is necessary.

CONCLUSIONS

It is essential to the supremacy and effectiveness of Community law that that law should be capable of being enforced in national courts, as a matter both of principle and of practice. In the national courts the most satisfactory course of action for a litigant is, of course, to rely directly on Community law or on any implementing legislation. Where this is not possible, he or she may seek to rely on the indirect effect of the measure; this is to say, its effect on the interpretation of national law. Where a Directive is concerned, there is a fall-back position, namely to seek damages from the Member State which has failed properly, or indeed at all, to implement it. As a result of the decision in *Factortame III*, individuals may also have a remedy in respect of national law which conflicts with Community law.

If the applicant is successful under any of these headings, the availability and nature of any remedy will be governed by national law, subject to a number of guidelines laid down by the Court of Justice. While this system has its loopholes, the effects of the Court of Justice in this area have been quite remarkable in changing the approach of the national courts.

CHAPTER 5: ASSESSMENT EXERCISE　　　　　　　　　　　CWS

Alf works for Humber plc, a company created to build and operate a railway bridge across the Humber estuary. It is authorized to do so under s. 1 of the (fictitious) Estuary Bridges Act 1990, which also gives it powers to regulate the connecting train service.

(Fictitious) Directive 999/93 requires Member States to take all measures necessary to ensure that bridge workers are provided with appropriate safety equipment, including hard hats. The deadline for implementation of the Directive has passed without UK compliance. The Estuary Bridges Act merely provides that licence holders must ensure that their employees are aware of safety hazards and advised to wear appropriate clothing.

Alf sustained a serious head injury when a cable fell on him during construction of the bridge, and as a result is unfit to work. He claims that his injury was caused by the company's failure to provide workers with hard hats. Humber plc claims that it had made Alf aware of the risks and had advised him to wear a hard hat, although the company itself was unable to provide them. It argues that the Act requires only the provision of information and advice.

(a) Advise Alf as to whether he has any cause of action against Humber plc.

(b) Would it make any difference to your answer if the company did not have the power to regulate the train service referred to above but was wholly owned by the State?

See *Cases and Materials* (5.6) for a specimen answer.

6 Preliminary references

6.1 Objectives

By the end of this chapter you should be able to:

1 Identify the types of issues which may be the subject of a preliminary reference under Article 234 (ex 177) EC

2 Explain the circumstances in which national courts are obliged to make a reference and those in which they merely have a discretion as to whether to do so

3 Analyse the different approaches taken to Article 234 (ex 177) EC by the Court of Justice and the UK courts

4 Explain the guidelines laid down in *Bulmer* v *Bollinger*

5 Explain the *CILFIT* guidelines

6 Discuss the importance of Article 234 (ex 177) EC references to the difference between questions of validity and those of interpretation

6.2 Introduction

What fundamental problem underlies the Community's legal system? It is that, although it purports to be part of the legal system of each Member State, the initiation, enactment, and interpretation of Community law are performed by entities entirely distinct and indeed distanced from those national courts which are, as we saw in **Chapter 5**, expected to apply Community law. Not only that, those national courts apply Community law independently of one another, leading potentially to different interpretations of the same piece of legislation or decision of the Court of Justice. If Community law is to be supreme it must have the same meaning and effect in all Member States, and therefore that meaning and effect must be determined by the Court of Justice.

To overcome this problem, the EC Treaty provides a procedure whereby national courts may consult the Court of Justice on particular issues of Community law. The national court will deliver judgment in the case, but is able to clarify certain issues of Community law with the Court of Justice before doing so. This is known as the preliminary reference or preliminary rulings procedure and is to be found in Article 234 (ex 177) EC (*Cases and*

Materials (6.1)). The Treaty of Nice (see **Chapter 4**) provides for the transfer of some Article 234 jurisdiction to the Court of First Instance (see 2.3.5).

This chapter will concentrate on the distinction between situations where a national court is generally **obliged** to make a reference ('mandatory references') and those in which it may make a reference but is **not obliged** to do so ('discretionary references'). As a general rule, it is the status of the court in the national legal system which determines this.

 EXERCISE 6.1

Read Article 234 (ex 177) EC in *Cases and Materials* (6.1). On what two issues may the Court of Justice give preliminary rulings?

Article 234 (ex 177) provides that a national court may, or in certain circumstances must, refer certain questions to the Court of Justice if it considers that a decision on the question is necessary to enable it to give judgment. The questions that may be referred are those as to the **interpretation** of the EC Treaty or of secondary legislation and those as to the **validity** of secondary legislation.

? **QUESTION** 6.1

In what areas has the Court of Justice's jurisdiction under Article 234 EC (ex 177) EC been limited? (If you cannot remember the answer to this question, refer back to 2.3.4.1.)

Note that jurisdiction is limited to Community law and does not extend to national law. Once the Court of Justice has interpreted Community law, it is for the national courts to apply it to the facts and, if appropriate, decide on the compatibility of national law. In *Factortame III* (see 5.5.2), the Court of Justice strayed beyond this and asserted that since it had sufficient information, it would apply its ruling on Community law to the facts. The national court accepted this application. However, it was not strictly obliged to do so. In *Arsenal Football Club plc* v *Matthew Reed* [2002] EWHC 2695 (Ch) not yet reported, the Hight Court rejected the Court's application of the law to the facts on the ground that it had exceeded its jurisdiction and had erred as to the facts.

 EXERCISE 6.2

Read the extract from the judgment in *Arsenal Football Club* in *Cases and Materials* (6.1) to see how the High Court dealt with this rather sensitive issue.

Criminal and civil legal aid are available for Article 234 (ex 177) EC references. Any existing criminal legal aid certificate will automatically cover Article 234 (ex 177) EC proceedings but an existing civil legal aid certificate will need to be amended. Where there is no certificate, a legal aid application may be made for the proceedings in the UK, which will then include the reference to the Court of Justice.

6.3 The status of the National Court

> **? QUESTION** 6.2
>
> Article 234 (ex 177) EC provides that while some national courts have a discretion as to whether to refer an issue to the Court of Justice, others have no choice. From which courts is a reference obligatory?

Article 234 (ex 177) provides that a reference is obligatory from a court 'against whose decisions there is no judicial remedy under national law'. The House of Lords is such a court. A court against whose decision there *is* such a remedy is not obliged to refer, although it has a discretion to do so.

In *Costa* v *ENEL* (Case 6/64) (see 3.3.2.2) an Italian magistrates' court made a reference to the Court of Justice under Article 234 (ex 177). The Court of Justice ruled that 'national courts against whose decisions, as in the present case, there is no judicial remedy, must refer the matter to the Court of Justice'.

Under the Italian legal system, certain categories of cases could be appealed from the magistrates' court while other categories could not. The present case fell into the latter category, that is to say, there was no possibility of an appeal.

As a result of this decision, a reference is obligatory from lower courts whose decision in a particular case is automatically final. In the English legal system this would include, for example, the Court of Appeal in probate and insolvency proceedings, since statute provides that its decisions in such actions are final (County Courts Act 1984, s. 82 and Insolvency Act 1986, s. 375(2), respectively).

> **? QUESTION** 6.3
>
> The question we now need to consider is whether a court from which an appeal is theoretically possible in a particular case should be considered to be a final court if leave to appeal is, in fact, refused.

EXERCISE 6.3 CWS

Read the extracts in *Cases and Materials* (6.2) from the following cases:

Magnavision v *General Optical Council (No. 2)* [1987] 2 CMLR 262

R v *Pharmaceutical Society of Great Britain, ex parte the Association of Pharmaceutical Importers* [1987] 3 CMLR 951

Hagen v *Fratelli D. & G. Moretti SNC and Molnar Machinery Limited* [1980] 3 CMLR 253

What is the view of the UK courts on the question posed in Question 6.3 above?

In *Magnavision* v *General Optical Council (No. 2)* counsel argued that, since the High Court had refused leave to appeal, it had turned itself into a final court and was obliged to make the reference to the Court of Justice which it had refused to make during the case. The High Court dismissed this argument. It stated that the prospect of leave being refused could not affect its decision as to whether to make the reference. The High Court also pointed out that it had declined to exercise its discretion to refer because it considered the relevant Community law to be clear. As we shall see, this is a ground on which even a final court may refuse to make a reference.

In *R* v *Pharmaceutical Society*, the Court of Appeal made a reference to the Court of Justice but remarked, *obiter dicta*, that a judicial remedy from its decisions lay in the possibility of applying for leave to appeal and that a court or tribunal below the House of Lords could be a final court only if there was no possibility of appeal (for instance the Court of Appeal in certain proceedings—see above).

In *Hagen*, the Court of Appeal commented, *obiter dicta*, that where leave to appeal to the House of Lords was 'not obtainable', the Court of Appeal itself constituted a final court. In the light of *Magnavision* and *R* v *Pharmaceutical Society* it would seem that 'not obtainable' means 'impossible' rather than 'not given in this particular case'.

It is evident from these cases that the UK courts have accepted that a court below the House of Lords will constitute a final court for the purposes of Article 234 (ex 177) EC only where, as a matter of procedure, there is no possibility of appeal. This may be perceived as unfair by parties who are in fact denied leave to appeal, but preferable to the alternative, which would be to re-open decided cases in which leave to appeal is subsequently refused.

6.4 **Discretionary references**

 EXERCISE 6.4

Try to think of as many examples as you can of English courts or tribunals from which here is generally a judicial remedy under national law.

You might have listed, among others, the Court of Appeal, the High Court, the county court, magistrates' courts and employment tribunals. The key question to be asked is whether the alleged court or tribunal exercises a judicial function. Thus, the Employment Appeal Tribunal has been held to be able to make a reference under Article 234 (ex 177) (*Jenkins* v *Kingsgate (Clothing Productions) Ltd* (Case 96/80) [1981] ECR 911) as has the Social Security Commissioner (*Drake* v *Chief Adjudication Officer* (Case 150/85) [1986] ECR 1995) and the Special Commissioners for Income Tax (*Lord Bruce of Donington* v *Aspden* (Case 208/80) [1981] ECR 2205).

Although the exercise of the discretion to refer is a matter for the court seized of a particular case, both the Court of Justice and national courts have purported to lay down guidelines as to when and how the discretion should be exercised.

6.4.1 Court of justice guidelines

The view of the Court of Justice is that the extent of the national courts' discretion is dependent on the correct interpretation of Article 234 (ex 177) EC and that it (the Court of Justice) is the only body which is competent to make authoritative pronouncements on such an interpretation.

EXERCISE 6.5   CWS

Read the extracts in *Cases and Materials* (6.3.1) from the following cases:

Rheinmühlen-Dusseldorf v *Einführ-und Vorratsstelle für Getreide und Futtermittel* (Cases 146 & 166/73) [1974] ECR 33

Irish Creamery Milk Suppliers Association v *Ireland* (Cases 36 & 71/80) [1981] ECR 735

Dzodzi v *Belgian State* (Cases C-297/88 & C-197/89) [1990] ECR I-3763

What guidelines can you discern from these cases? Make a note of your answers.

6.4.1.1 *Rheinmühlen*

In *Rheinmühlen*, the plaintiff had succeeded on appeal but the case was referred back to the lower court to reconsider. The lower court attempted to make an Article 234 (ex 177) reference and the plaintiff appealed against the making of this reference. The higher court referred to the Court of Justice the question of whether the lower court could make a reference in spite of the fact that under German law, the lower court was bound by the decision of the higher court. The Court of Justice ruled that the lower court could exercise its discretion to refer. A national court was not precluded from making a reference on a particular issue by the existence of a domestic rule of law which required that court to follow the judgment of a higher court on that issue.

In *Trent Taverns Ltd* v *Sykes* [1999] NPC 9 the Court of Appeal ruled that this principle applied equally to the domestic rule of law requiring the Court of Appeal to follow its own judgments. However, on the facts, the Court of Appeal concluded that a reference need not be made.

> **? QUESTION** 6.4
>
> Suppose that the House of Lords had ruled, as a matter of law in the case of *Smith*, that the word 'workers' in Article 39 (ex 48) EC should be interpreted as meaning 'male workers'. The case of *Brown*, which also involves a dispute as to the meaning of 'workers' in Article 39 (ex 48) EC is now before the High Court. Could the English law doctrine of precedent prevent the High Court from making a reference?

Even if the doctrine of precedent obliged the High Court to apply the previous ruling of the House of Lords on the matter, the ruling of the Court of Justice in the *Rheinmühlen* case makes it clear that the High Court could still make a reference if it so wished.

6.4.1.2 *Irish Creamery Milk Suppliers*

In *Irish Creamery Milk Suppliers*, agricultural producers argued that an Irish levy on certain agricultural products was contrary to Community law. The government wished to delay the Article 234 (ex 177) reference until the facts had been established. In its reference to the Court of Justice, the Irish court asked not only for an interpretation of the Community law involved, but also for clarification as to the timing of the reference. The Court of Justice ruled that it was for the national court to decide on the most appropriate time to make a reference. However, the Court also stated that it might therefore be more convenient to make a reference after the facts of the case and questions of national law had been determined. The Court of Justice would then have a clear legal context in which to give its ruling and so the ruling would be more likely to assist the national court.

6.4.1.3 *Dzodzi*

This case involved a rather unusual reference. The *Dzodzi* case involved a claim for Belgian residency by the Togolese widow of a Belgian national under a Belgian law which gave the spouses of Belgian nationals the same residency rights as Community nationals. The Belgian government argued that since the case turned on the meaning of Belgian law, a reference to the Court of Justice was unnecessary. The Court of Justice ruled that it was for the Belgian court to determine the relevance of Community law in these circumstances, but that if a ruling was requested, the Court of Justice had jurisdiction. Article 234 (ex 177) did not preclude jurisdiction in such circumstances, and it would destroy the system of uniform interpretation of Community law envisaged by that Article if national courts could interpret Community law themselves in purely internal cases.

6.4.2 Case law of the UK courts

A number of guidelines have been laid down by UK courts over the years. The leading cases are *R v International Stock Exchange of the UK and the Republic of Ireland Limited ex parte Else (1982) Limited and others* [1993] QB 534 and *Commissioners of Customs and Excise v Samex ApS* [1983] 1 All ER 1042 (*Cases and Materials* (6.3.2)).

In *ex parte Else* the Court of Appeal held that the issue must be 'critical' to the final decision. Since it is impossible to access this until the reference is made and a ruling given, this must require that the issue could be critical to the final decision. The national court should consider whether it could 'with complete confidence resolve the issue itself'. In deciding whether this was so, a court should take into account a number of factors.

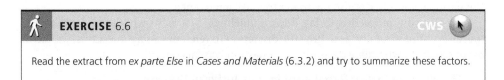

EXERCISE 6.6

Read the extract from *ex parte Else* in *Cases and Materials* (6.3.2) and try to summarize these factors.

Sir Thomas Bingham MR stated that the issues relevant to the exercise of the discretion to refer were:

(a) the differences between national and Community legislation;

(b) the difficulties in dealing with what might be an unfamiliar field;

(c) the need for a uniform interpretation throughout the Community;

(d) the advantages enjoyed by the Court of Justice in interpreting Community law.

These advantages had previously been elaborated upon in the first instance case of *Commissioners of Customs and Excise* v *Samex ApS* [1983] 1 All ER 1042. In that case, Bingham J expressed the view that the Court of Justice is much better placed than national courts to deal with matters of Community law for a number of reasons.

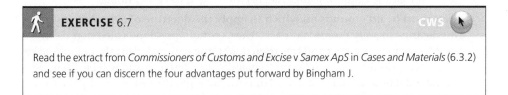

EXERCISE 6.7

Read the extract from *Commissioners of Customs and Excise* v *Samex ApS* in *Cases and Materials* (6.3.2) and see if you can discern the four advantages put forward by Bingham J.

You should have found that the following advantages are, according to Bingham J, possessed by the Court of Justice:

(a) The ability to take an overall view of the Community and its legal framework.

(b) The opportunity to receive submissions from the other institutions and Member States on the issue in question.

(c) The linguistic advantage of being able to consider all the authentic texts, which might make the meaning clearer.

(d) Familiarity with the purposive and creative approach to interpretation required by Community law, which tended to be less detailed than English law.

Another famous—but much less authoritative case—is that of *Bulmer Ltd and Another* v *Bollinger SA and Others* [1974] 2 CMLR 91, which involved an application by UK producers of 'champagne cider' for a declaration that they could use the description 'champagne'. French producers argued that this contravened Community law on the origin of wines and requested an Article 234 (ex 177) reference. The Court of Appeal upheld the refusal of the trial judge to make a reference on the basis that it was not 'necessary', and referred to *Rheinmühlen* as Court of Justice authority for the complete discretion of the national court in deciding whether to make a reference.

Lord Denning proceeded to lay down guidelines, first as to whether a decision was 'necessary' and secondly, as to how the discretion to refer 'necessary questions' should be exercised. As to whether a decision on a question was 'necessary':

(a) **The question to be referred must be conclusive of the case**
   This is in potential conflict with the assumption of the Court of Justice in cases such as *Dzodzi* that the question need only be relevant, not conclusive. In practice the best that a referring court can say is that the reference could be conclusive, but this inevitably depends upon the ruling given. In *Samex*, Bingham J. stated that the reference should be 'substantially, if not quite totally, determinative of [the] litigation'.

(b) **There must be no previous Court of Justice ruling on the question**
   At first sight, this appears to conflict with the Court of Justice's ruling in *Da Costa en Schaake NV, Jacob Meijer NV and Hoechst-Holland NV v Nederlandse Belastingadministratie* (Cases 28-30/62) [1963] ECR 31 (*Cases and Materials* (6.3.2)) (in the context of mandatory references), that the existence of a previous Court of Justice ruling on a similar question does not preclude a reference. However, Lord Denning did recognise that the Court of Justice was not bound by its decisions and that a decision could be necessary where new factors existed or where the national court felt that the Court of Justice had been wrong in its earlier ruling.

(c) **There must be no grounds on which to apply the doctrine of *acte clair***
   This doctrine literally means 'clear act'. The Court of Appeal indicated that if the point was reasonably clear and free from doubt, the national court should not make a reference. This doctrine is relevant to mandatory references and will be discussed in greater detail at 6.5.1.1 and 6.5.2. For now, note that the test set out by the Court of Justice in a case called *CILFIT* (see 6.5.1) is much more stringent than that envisaged by Lord Denning. For example, according to the Court of Justice, a national court must be sure that the law at issue is clear in all its different language versions, before concluding that it is *acte clair*. The UK courts have, in practice, developed a third definition of *acte clair*, based on whether all the judges so far seized of a particular case have agreed on the meaning and application of Community law. The *Bulmer* approach is therefore discredited.

(d) **The facts must have been established**
   Lord Denning observed that a reference might be desirable at an earlier stage, but was unlikely to be necessary until all the facts were known.

QUESTION 6.5

Assume that a decision is 'necessary' in a particular case and that the discretion to refer arises. What factors did Lord Denning say should be taken into account when considering whether to exercise this discretion?

Lord Denning indicated that the national court should particularly bear in mind the delay and expense, the danger of overloading the Court of Justice, the difficulty and importance of the point, and the wishes of the parties.

Although a delay of more than 18 months in receiving a preliminary ruling from the Court of Justice is not unusual, it is open to the referring court to request that the matter be treated as one of urgency. For example, in referring to the Court the question of whether interim relief should be granted, Lord Bridge of Harwich in the House of Lords in *R* v *Secretary of State for Transport ex parte Factortame (Factortame I)* stated:

The adjournment of further consideration of appeal which must necessarily follow is . . . a most unsatisfactory result from the appellant's point of view, and I venture to express the hope that the Court of Justice will . . . treat the reference made by your Lordships' House as one of urgency to which priority can be given.

The President of the Court decided, in accordance with the Rules of Procedure of the Court, that the case should be given priority. Judgment was given on 19 June 1990, less than a year after the reference was received by the Court of Justice.

QUESTION 6.6

Can you see a potential problem with these guidelines, so far as the Court of Justice is concerned?

The framing of these guidelines in such restrictive terms clearly encourages courts in the UK not to refer questions to the Court of Justice. This conflicts, first, with the general attitude of the Court of Justice, which has always been to take a leading role in matters of Community law, and secondly, with the specific guidelines that the Court of Justice has laid down (see 6.4.1). The *Bulmer* v *Bollinger* guidelines should therefore be treated with considerable caution.

EXERCISE 6.8   CWS

Reference has already been made in Chapter 2 to the Court of Justice. Read the first extract from '(c) Encouraging national courts to decide more questions of law without references to the ECJ' from 'The Role and Future of the ECJ', in *Cases and Materials* (6.3.2) and the extract from 'Use of the Preliminary Procedure', in *Cases and Materials* (6.3.2) and think about the advantages and disadvantages of discouraging the use of the procedure.

In *Wiener S.I. GmbH* v *Hauptzollamt Emmerich* (C-338/95 [1998] 1 CMLR 1110), Advocate General Jacobs considered the division of competence between the national courts and the Court of Justice under Article 234 EC. He argued that the Court of Justice could not cope with the workload which would result from the reference of all cases in which a point of Community law was at issue, particularly in view of the expanding volume of Community legislation. Since the Court could not rule inadmissible questions on interpretation which were properly referred, the national courts must exercise self-restraint in deciding whether to refer them. Where the Court had already established a body of principles as a result of previous references, national courts should be in a position to apply these principles to the specific facts of a case before them without making a reference. The Article 234 EC procedure should instead focus on the reference of general questions in areas of law in which there was no comprehensive body of principles. Rulings on these questions would then enable national courts to deal with more detailed questions themselves.

It should be noted that the question of when references should be made was not in fact among the questions referred by the national court in *Wiener*, and the Court of Justice subsequently answered the questions actually referred (on the interpretation of certain Regulations) without commenting on it. However, despite the fact that Court of Justice did not approve Advocate General Jacobs's comments, they have been cited by the Court of Appeal in a number of cases. In *Trinity Mirror plc* v *Commissioners of Customs and Excise* ([2001] EWCA Civ 65, [2001] 2 CMLR 33) the Court refused to make a reference. It cited *ex parte Else* as authority for the need to refer where the national court had any real doubt, but then cited Advocate General Jacobs's comments on the need for self-restraint. It concluded that there was ample guidance from the Court of Justice on the question of principle in the area of law at issue, and that it was confident in applying that principle to the facts of the case. A similar view was taken in *The Littlewoods Organisation plc and others* v *Commissioners of Custom and Excise and others* ([2001] EWCA Civ 1542, [2001] STC 1568) and *Professional Contractor's Group and others* v *Commissioners of Inland Revenue* ([2001] EWCA Civ 1945, [2002] STC 165).

Of course, an Opinion of an Advocate General is not binding on national courts, unlike the decision of the Court of Appeal in *ex parte Else*. However, the fact that the Court of Appeal is consistently citing Advocate General Jacobs's comments indicates that the national courts may now be prepared to refuse to refer where they feel that the Court of Justice has established general principles which they themselves can apply to new situations.

6.4.3 Conclusion on guidelines

The Court of Justice and the national courts have provided lower courts in the UK with a wealth of guidelines.

 EXERCISE 6.9

Try to summarize the guidelines, which UK courts should take into account when exercising the discretion to refer.

The key guidelines applicable to a court from which a reference is only discretionary may be summarized as follows:

(a) In all the circumstances of the case, is the question sufficiently relevant for an answer to it to be necessary in order for the court to give judgment in the case?

(b) Is the existence of a preliminary ruling on a similar point such as to assist the court with the issue before it?

(c) Is the measure so clear that future rulings on it by the Court of Justice or a court in another Member State would be consistent with that of the court?

In addition, the court may also consider:

(d) whether the facts have been established;

(e) the advantages possessed by the Court of Justice in interpreting Community law;

(f) the differences between domestic and Community law;

(g) the need for uniform interpretation.

R v *Ministry of Agriculture, Fisheries and Food, ex parte Portman Agrochemicals Ltd* ([1994] 3 CMLR 18) provides an instructive example. The judge referred to *ex parte Else* and concluded that he did not have 'complete confidence' that he could resolve the issue himself. However, he declined to make a reference because neither party wished the case to be referred and by the time a reference was given, the matter would have become academic as far as the parties were concerned. The issue was whether MAFF could use Portman's confidential data, but by the time a ruling was given, any right of confidentiality would have expired anyway. The interests of justice would therefore not have been served by making a reference.

6.5 Mandatory references

As stated in **6.3**, where there is no judicial remedy from a particular court, that court has no choice but to make a reference to the Court of Justice if the necessary pre-conditions are fulfilled. This may sound simple enough, but as we are about to see, mandatory references have provoked as much argument as discretionary references.

EXERCISE 6.10 CWS

To refresh your memory, refer to Article 234 (ex 177) EC in *Cases and Materials* (6.1) and write down the questions that must be referred by a court from whose decisions there is no judicial remedy.

A reference is mandatory from such a court if a question arises as to the interpretation of the EC Treaty or the validity or interpretation of the acts of the institutions. A decision on the question need not be necessary to the resolution of the case.

As with discretionary references, UK case law has not always followed Court of Justice case law, and it is therefore necessary to examine both approaches.

6.5.1 **Court of justice guidelines**

The leading case is *CILFIT and Lanificio di Gavardo SpA* v *Ministry of Health* (Case 283/81) [1982] ECR 3415, in which a number of textile firms complained that an Italian levy on wool was in contravention of Community law. The Italian government claimed that a reference was unnecessary because the meaning of the Community law in question was clear. The Court of Justice ruled that there was no obligation to refer, even from a court whose decision was final, if one of three conditions was fulfilled. (Remember that a court which thereby avoids the obligation to refer nonetheless retains the discretion to do so.)

 EXERCISE 6.11 CWS

Read the extract from *CILFIT* v *Ministry of Health* in *Cases and Materials* (6.4.1) and see if you can find the three grounds given by the Court of Justice on which a 'mandatory' reference may be avoided.

6.5.1.1 **The *CILFIT* conditions**

Under Article 234 (ex 177) EC, references from a final court would appear to be mandatory. However, the Court of Justice ruled that this was not so if one of the following three conditions was not satisfied:

The question of law is not relevant
There is no obligation to refer a question if the answer to it cannot in any way affect the outcome of the case.

The question has been decided before by the Court of Justice
In *Da Costa*, a Dutch chemical exporter alleged that certain Dutch import taxes were contrary to Community law. On a reference for a preliminary ruling under Article 234 (ex 177) the Court of Justice ruled that the existence of a prior ruling by it on the point did not preclude a reference, although it could render it unnecessary.

In *CILFIT* the Court of Justice cited *Da Costa* and reiterated that if exactly the same question has already been decided by the Court of Justice, the court is not obliged to make a reference. The discretion to refer would, of course, remain.

? QUESTION 6.7

Do you remember any particular circumstances in which a national court might wish to refer a question which has already been decided by the Court of Justice? If you have difficulty in doing this, refer back to guideline (b) from Lord Denning's judgment in *Bulmer* v *Bollinger* as stated in the answer to Exercise 6.7 above.

The correct application of Community law is clear (i.e. the acte clair *doctrine applies)*
The court must believe that there is no reasonable doubt as to the answer to the question, and that this answer would be equally clear to the Court of Justice and to the national courts of other Member States. This raises the question of whether a measure can ever be so clear that no query can be raised, and has been the most problematic of the three *CILFIT* conditions.

? QUESTION 6.8

Can you think of any problems which might arise in applying this third condition?

First, there is a difference between absolute clarity and the clarity necessary to apply the measure to the facts in question. How clear, exactly, need a measure be to obviate a compulsory reference? Secondly, a measure might clearly mean one thing to one court and another to a different court.

The Court of Justice in *CILFIT* attempted to assist with these problems by qualifying this third condition (*acte clair*) with a number of other considerations.

? QUESTION 6.9

What factors did the Court of Justice indicate should be taken into account when assessing the application of the doctrine of *acte clair*?

First, since Community legislation is drafted in different languages, each version being equally authentic, it is possible to say that the meaning of the measure is clear only if it has the same meaning in all the languages and is equally clear in all. If there is any discrepancy or lack of clarity in even one language then it is not possible to say that the application of Community law is obvious, and therefore a reference would be mandatory.

Secondly, the doctrine of *acte clair* is applicable only where legal concepts in Community law have the same meaning in all Member States. For instance, if a measure concerns 'contracts', and the concept of a 'contract' differs under French and English law, then *acte clair* cannot apply and a reference is mandatory.

Thirdly, measures must be interpreted in the context of Community law as a whole, with particular regard to the objectives and progress of Community law at the time the measure was to be applied. For instance, the interpretation of a measure concerning the Single Market might become clear when looked at in the context of the state of the Single Market at the time in question.

To summarize, the third consideration referred to above may assist a national court, but the first two considerations appear effectively to remove the possibility of relying on *acte clair*. Realistically, it is beyond the scope of a national court accurately to compare texts and legal concepts in several different languages, and it will only be those courts which are prepared to adopt a somewhat cavalier attitude to these considerations that can avoid mandatory references.

 EXERCISE 6.12

Try to list the problems which you think could be caused if courts from which there is no judicial remedy under national law make use of the grounds given in *CILFIT* in order to avoid making a reference.

Among the problems which may result are inconsistent interpretation and application of Community law across the Member States, injustice to particular applicants, and a reduction in the importance of the Court of Justice.

6.5.2 Case law of the UK courts

Strictly, the *CILFIT* conditions only apply where *acte clair* is relied on to avoid a mandatory reference, and not where it is used in the context of discretionary references. However, the term presumably has a similar meaning in both contexts and thus the CILFIT conditions are relevant where a lower court seeks to rely on *acte clair* in deciding that a reference is not necessary. It is thus useful to look at the use of *acte clair* both by the House of Lords and the lower courts. The UK courts have not adopted a uniform approach to the use of *acte clair*.

 The House of Lords has treated the doctrine of *acte clair* with varying degrees of caution. For example, in *R v Henn and Darby* [1980] 2 All ER 166 (*Cases and Materials* (6.4.2)), which was decided prior to the ruling in *CILFIT*, importers of pornographic material argued that UK restrictions on such imports were in contravention of Article 28 (ex 30) EC, which prohibited restrictions on imports, and were not saved by Article 30 (ex 36) EC, which permitted restrictions on grounds of public policy. The Court of Appeal refused to make a reference on the ground that the application of Community law was clear. The House of Lords reversed this decision and requested a preliminary ruling.

QUESTION 6.10

On what grounds did Lord Diplock consider the doctrine of *acte clair* to be inappropriate in *R v Henn and Darby*?

Lord Diplock warned that a court should not be too ready to apply *acte clair* and treat a reference as purely discretionary, simply because the meaning of the English text was clear to that court. First, the English text was only one of six of equal authority (at that time there were only nine Member States and six official languages), any one of which might be unclear or capable of a different interpretation. Secondly, the possibility of judicial disagreement over the 'clear' meaning of Community law was highlighted in this case by the contrasting views of the House of Lords, which considered that Article 28 (ex 30) EC had been breached, and the Court of Appeal, which considered that it had not.

However, in a later case involving a similar disagreement, the House of Lords abandoned its caution. In *Freight Transport Association and others* v *London Boroughs Transport Committee Ltd* [1991] 3 All ER 915, the Court of Appeal had ruled that local regulations restricting vehicle noise emissions were contrary to Community law. The House of Lords ruled that they were not and, despite this evident uncertainty, applied the *acte clair* doctrine without citing *CILFIT* or *Henn and Darby*, and declined to make a reference.

 EXERCISE 6.13 **CWS**

Read *R v Secretary of State for Transport ex parte Factortame (Factortame I)* in *Cases and Materials* (6.4.2). Were the restrictive considerations of *CILFIT* applied by the House of Lords when considering whether to make a reference in that case?

In *Factortame I*, the House of Lords considered a reference to be mandatory in the light of the ambiguous rulings made by the Court of Justice on the particular point in question and in application of the *CILFIT* guidelines.

 EXERCISE 6.14 **CWS**

Briefly summarize the case law of the UK courts on the application of *acte clair*, then read the extract from the recent case of *R v Secretary of State for the Environment ex parte RSPB* [1995] JPL 842 in *Cases and Materials* (6.4.2), in which the interpretation of the Birds Directive was at issue. Which of the possible approaches to the doctrine of *acte clair* did the House of Lords adopt in the *RSPB* case?

The UK courts have often ignored the *CILFIT* guidelines as to the use of *acte clair* and have simply declared that a measure is *acte clair* if the court in question says that the meaning is obvious (see the *Freight Transport Association* and *Magnavision* cases, and the second extract from *Magnavision* in *Cases and Materials* (6.4.2)). However, in cases such as *Henn and Darby*, *Factortame*, and *RSPB*, the courts have taken a less cavalier approach to the doctrine.

In the *RSPB* case the point at issue was whether, under the Birds Directive, the Secretary of State could properly have regard to economic considerations when deciding whether a particular area should be excluded from a Special Protection Area for Birds. The Divisional Court and the majority of the Court of Appeal had held that the Directive was *acte clair* and that the Secretary of State was indeed entitled to take into account such considerations. The dissenting judge in the Court of Appeal also considered that the Directive was *acte clair*, but argued that it was clear that the Secretary of State could **not** take economic factors into account. The House of Lords considered that these conflicting judgments made a reference obligatory.

It may be that this cautionary approach will only be used if a court is genuinely uncertain as to the meaning of the measure and that if it is certain in its own mind as to that meaning, the *CILFIT* criteria will continue to be ignored. It should also be noted that the comments of Advocate General Jacobs in *Wiener* discussed above (see 6.4.2) were expressly applied also to courts from which there is no judicial reference, a point stressed in *Trinity Mirror plc*.

6.6 Misuse of Article 234 (ex 177) EC

The Court of Justice has, on occasion, been prepared to reject a reference where it has felt that Article 234 (ex 177) EC is being misused. The three main grounds which the Court has given for such a rejection are that the referring court has failed to explain the context, that there is no genuine dispute or that the questions referred are purely hypothetical. We shall consider each of these in turn.

6.6.1 Failure to explain the factual or legal context

The commonest reason for the Court of Justice to refuse to provide a preliminary ruling is that the order from the referring court contains an inadequate explanation of the factual or legal context.

? QUESTION 6.11

Why do you think it is so important that the Court has sufficient information about the facts and the national law? Could the absence of information prejudice the role of anyone other than the Court of Justice?

As the Court pointed out in C-458/93 *Criminal Proceedings against Saddik* [1995] ECR I-511 a lack of information may mean that the Court cannot give a meaningful answer to the questions referred, or that Member States and other interested parties are not in a position to submit their observations.

In assessing whether it has sufficient information to provide answers to the questions referred, the Court of Justice may take into account the written and oral observations submitted by the parties, as well as the order from the national court (C-18/93 *Corsica Ferries* v *Corpo dei Piloti del Porto di Genova* [1994] ECR I-1783)). However, it is not obliged to do this and may simply reject the reference.

 EXERCISE 6.15

For examples of the sort of information required and the problems caused by its absence, read the extract in *Cases and Materials* (6.5.1) from C-167/94 *Criminal Proceedings against Grau Gromis and others* [1995] ECR I-1023.

Lack of factual or legal information may also mean that the questions referred are purely hypothetical (see 6.6.3).

6.6.2 **No genuine dispute**

The leading case here is *Foglia* v *Novello (No. 1)* (Case 104/79) [1980] ECR 745, where a contract between the buyer (Novello) and the seller (Foglia) provided that Novello would not be liable for any unlawfully levied taxes. The contract between Foglia and the shipper provided that Foglia was similarly not liable.

A tax was levied by France on the goods, which Foglia paid and which Novello refused to reimburse on the ground that it was contrary to Community law. Foglia and Novello brought the dispute before an Italian court, alleging that the duty was illegal, and the Italian court made a reference to the Court of Justice.

 EXERCISE 6.16

Read the extract from *Foglia* v *Novello (No. 1)* in *Cases and Materials* (6.5.2). In what way did the Court of Justice consider that Article 234 (ex 177) EC was being misused?

The Court of Justice refused to accept the reference on the ground that it had no jurisdiction because there was no real dispute between the parties. Article 234 (ex 177) EC references were designed to provide interpretations of Community law which were required for the resolution of genuine disputes. The terms of the two contracts in question had the result that the parties had the same interest in the outcome of the case (since, contractually, neither of the parties was liable to pay the tax if it was unlawful) and therefore there was no genuine dispute. The shipper had not appealed, as he was entitled to do, against the imposition of the tax, and Foglia had reimbursed the shipper contrary to the terms of their contract, which suggested that they expected the tax to be struck down. Article 234 (ex 177) EC did not confer jurisdiction on the Court of Justice in the context of a collusive action such as this, which disguised an attempt to have a foreign law struck down.

 EXERCISE 6.17 CWS

Read the extract from *Foglia v Novello (No. 2)* (Case 244/80) [1981] ECR 3045 in *Cases and Materials* (6.5.2) where the Italian court made another attempt to refer the matter to the Court of Justice. What was its argument for so doing and what was the response of the Court of Justice?

The Italian court repeated its request for a preliminary ruling on the grounds that it was for the national court to exercise its discretion as to whether to refer. The Court of Justice accepted this argument but again refused to accept the reference on the basis that it retained the right to check its jurisdiction to hear a case, and that under Article 234 (ex 177) EC the issue referred must be one on which a decision was necessary to the resolution of the case. Where there was no genuine dispute between the parties on a particular issue, it was clearly not susceptible to a reference under Article 234 (ex 177) EC.

The fact that the parties are in effect trying to challenge the laws of one Member State in the courts of another, as in *Foglia,* makes a finding that there is no genuine dispute, and hence a refusal to accept the reference, more likely. However, such a finding is not automatic, as can be seen in *Eau de Cologne* v *Provide* (Case C-150/88) [1989] ECR 3891.

Provide, an Italian company, ordered cosmetics from Eau de Cologne, a German company. The packaging complied with Community law, but not with Italian law, and therefore the goods could not be marketed in Italy. Provide refused to accept or pay for the goods and was sued by Eau de Cologne in the German courts.

 EXERCISE 6.18 CWS

Read the extract from *Eau de Cologne & Parfümerie-Fabrik v Provide Srl* (Case C-150/88) [1989] ECR 3891 in *Cases and Materials* (6.5.2). What distinction did the Court of Justice draw between the case of *Eau de Cologne* and that of *Foglia v Novello (No. 1)*?

The Court of Justice accepted the reference, despite the fact that the parties were questioning, in German courts, the compatibility of Italian law with Community law. It stated that the case involved a genuine dispute. When giving a ruling on the interpretation of Community law in order to assist a national court in determining the compatibility of national law with Community law, it made no difference that the disputed law was that of a different Member State.

The issue of whether there is a genuine dispute will also turn very much on the facts of the individual case. In C-105/94 *Celestini* v *Saar-Sektkellerie Faber* [1997] ECR I-2971 certain of the facts were similar to *Foglia* v *Novello*. A German buyer bought wine from an Italian seller, but the German authorities impounded the wine and subsequently declared it unfit for human consumption. The seller sued the buyer in the Italian courts and a reference was made to the Court of Justice. Although the buyer had not contested the actions of the German authorities, and no case had been brought in the German courts, which had sole jurisdiction to rule on the validity of those actions, the Court accepted the reference. It expressly stated that there was nothing to indicate that the parties had jointly fabricated the dispute as a device to obtain a preliminary ruling.

 EXERCISE 6.19

Read the extract from *Vinal* v *Orbat* (Case 46/80) [1981] ECR 77 in *Cases and Materials* (6.5.2). What further action is open to the Court of Justice where it appears that there is no genuine dispute?

Where it is alleged that there is no genuine dispute, the Court of Justice may request further information before it decides whether or not to accept the reference, as happened in *Vinal* v *Orbat*. An Italian importer of pure alcohol, Vinal, contracted to supply French alcohol to Orbat. The Italian authorities imposed a duty on the goods, which Orbat refused to pay. A preliminary reference was opposed by the Italian government on the grounds that there was no real dispute and that the parties simply wished to impeach the duty so as to avoid paying it. The Court of Justice requested further information, which in the event satisfied it that there was a genuine dispute and therefore valid grounds for an Article 234 (ex 177) EC reference. However, it should be noted that the Court is not obliged to request further information and it may simply reject the reference.

6.6.3 **Hypothetical questions**

This category concerns questions which the Court rejects because they are not relevant on the facts, or because the facts are so unclear that there is no evidence that they are relevant. Examples of the former include *Lourenço Dias* v *Director da Alfandega do Porto* (Case C-343/90) [1992] ECR I-4673 (*Cases and Materials* (6.5.3) and *Società Italiana Petroli SpA (IP)* v *Borsana Srl* (Case C-2/97) [1998] ECR I-8597. In *Lourenço Dias* a Portuguese van driver challenged Portuguese vehicle tax laws on the ground that they were contrary to Article 90 (ex 95) EC (see **Chapter 9**). The national court referred a number of questions on the interpretation of Community law, some of which the Court of Justice rejected as hypothetical. For example, the Court refused to answer a question about taxation of imports of second-hand vehicles since the van in question was new when imported.

In *Borsana* the Court of Justice refused to answer a question on the compatibility of certain criminal penalties laid down by national law with Community law because the dispute before the national court was a civil case.

? QUESTION 6.12

Suppose, in proceedings concerning the compatibility with Community law of a (fictitious) UK law on the transportation by air of live animals, the following questions were referred to the Court of Justice under Article 234 (ex 177):

(a) the meaning of 'air transport';

(b) the meaning of 'sea transport';

(c) the meaning of 'animals';

(d) whether 'animals' could be interpreted as including elephants.

Which of the above questions do you suspect that the Court of Justice might reject, and why? (You may find it helpful to read the extracts from *Lourenço Dias* and *Meilicke* in *Cases and Materials* (6.5.3) before attempting to answer this question.)

In this example, question (b) is clearly hypothetical since the UK law does not apply to sea transport. Question (d) would also be hypothetical if the case in which the questions were referred did not on the facts, concern elephants. Questions (a) and (c) would be accepted (unless of course, the facts revealed that there was no genuine dispute, in which case all the questions would be rejected—see 6.6.2).

An example of a case where the facts and legal context are so unclear that the questions referred are regarded as hypothetical is *Meilicke* v *ADV/ORGA AG* (Case C-83/91) [1992] ECR I-4871. In this case a German shareholder sought to rely on the Second Company Law Directive which he alleged gave him greater rights to information than German law, where the company had received payment otherwise than in cash for its shares. The Court of Justice refused to answer the questions referred on the interpretation of the Directive on the ground that they were hypothetical. It had not been established on the facts whether the payment received by Meilicke's company should be categorized as cash or not and it was therefore unclear how German law, which gave greater rights to information where payments other than cash were concerned than where payments were in cash, applied, and whether the Directive, which only applied to non-cash payments, applied at all.

6.7 Issues of validity

We have been looking so far at preliminary rulings on the interpretation of Community law, either Treaties or secondary legislation. However, Article 234 (ex 177) EC also permits preliminary references to be made concerning the validity of secondary legislation. (The validity of the Treaty may not be questioned.) Whereas a national court may often be able to interpret Community law itself, either because it is clear, or because there has been a previous Court of Justice ruling, it is less likely that it will be competent to deal with questions of validity.

EXERCISE 6.20   CWS

Read the extract from *Firma Foto-Frost* v *Hauptzollamt Lübeck-Ost* (Case 314/85) [1987] ECR 4199, in *Cases and Materials* (6.6). What is the main restriction on the power of a national court to deal with questions relating to the validity of Community law?

Frost applied to the German courts to have a Commission Decision set aside. The German court requested a preliminary ruling as to whether it could review the validity of the Decision. The Court of Justice ruled that no national court could declare a Community act invalid, although it could make a declaration of validity. Any other conclusion would destroy the uniform application of Community law.

A national court should therefore make a reference to the Court of Justice whenever there is some doubt as to the validity of a measure.

6.8 Interim measures

As has already been mentioned, it is not uncommon for up to 18 months to elapse between the making of a reference by a national court and the giving of a ruling by the Court of Justice. Given this potential delay, in certain circumstances one party may wish to request interim relief in the form of the suspension of national law. Guidelines have laid down two possibilities: the suspension of national measures implementing allegedly invalid Community law, and the suspension of national law which may, depending on the correct interpretation of Community law, be inconsistent with it.

6.8.1 National measures based on allegedly invalid Community law

In *Atlanta Fruchthandelsgesellchaft MbM and others* v *Bundesamt für Ernahrung und Forstwirtschaft* (Case C-465/93) [1996] 1 CMLR 575 the Court of Justice laid down conditions to be applied by national courts when granting interim relief, in the form of the suspension of national law implementing the disputed Community law, pending the outcome of a reference to the Court of Justice on the **validity** of that Community law. These conditions are as follows:

(a) the national court seriously doubts the validity of Community law and the issue has already been referred to the Court of Justice; and

(b) interim relief is necessary as a matter of urgency to avoid serious and irreparable damage to the applicant; and

(c) due account of the effect of any suspension on the whole regime of Community law has been taken; and

(d) due account of any decisions of the Court of Justice or the Court of First Instance on the validity of the Community law or on any similar application for interim relief has been taken.

6.8.2 Suspension of national measures which may, on the correct interpretation of Community law, be in conflict with it

An example of this is *Factortame I* (see **Chapter 3**), but although the Court of Justice ruled that such suspension must be possible, it was left for the House of Lords on receipt of this ruling to lay down guidelines. The House of Lords ruled that the applicants must demonstrate:

(a) a strong *prima facie* case that the national law was incompatible with Community law; and

(b) that the balance of convenience favoured the granting of an injunction suspending the Act.

The House of Lords concluded that a strong *prima facie* case had been shown by the Spanish fishermen that the Merchant Shipping Act was incompatible with Community law. It also concluded that the balance of convenience favoured an injunction since the damage likely to be caused (to the British fishing industry) by the injunction was outweighed by that likely to be caused (to the Spanish fishermen) by the continuance of the national law.

6.9 The effect of a ruling

A Court of Justice ruling as to the interpretation or validity of a measure provides a binding precedent for national courts. It is thus a further example of the way in which Community law (in this instance, a decision of the Court of Justice) takes precedence over national law (in this instance, the decision which the national court would otherwise have taken).

In the case of an interpretative ruling or a ruling that a measure is valid, national courts are not precluded from making further references on the point, but generally they will do so only where new evidence has come to light or where there is reason to believe that the Court of Justice may have changed its mind. In the case of a ruling of invalidity, the measure is void, that is to say, of no effect.

In general, the effect of a ruling is retrospective, but the Court of Justice may place a limitation on this.

EXERCISE 6.21 CWS

Look back at the comments already made about *Defrenne* v *SABENA* (Case 43/75) [1976] 2 ECR 455 at 5.3.1.1 and read the second extract from the case in *Cases and Materials* (6.7). What limitation did the Court of Justice impose on its ruling and what factor(s) led it to do so?

In *Defrenne,* the Court of Justice took account of the fact that several Member States had failed to comply with Article 141 (ex 119) EC by the original deadline and yet the Commission had failed to take enforcement proceedings against them. It therefore held, in the interests of legal certainty, that its ruling that Article 141 (ex 119) EC was directly effective should not be applied retrospectively except in the case of proceedings already issued.

 EXERCISE 6.22 CWS

Read the extract in *Cases and Materials* (6.8) from 'Some Aspects of the Preliminary Rulings Procedure in EEC Law' for a summary of the importance of the Article 234 (ex 177) procedure to the Community legal order.

 CONCLUSIONS

It is essential to the uniformity and effectiveness of Community law that a system exists whereby national courts, faced with a dispute as to the interpretation or validity of Community law, may ask the Court of Justice for a ruling. This system is outlined in Article 234 (ex 177) EC.

However, the system is only as good as its constituent parts, and the national courts, at least in the UK, have regularly declined to refer matters which are properly the province of the Court of Justice. While this approach has its advantages in terms of speed and cost, it does make it more likely that Community law will not be applied effectively and uniformly across the Community.

 CHAPTER 6: ASSESSMENT EXERCISE CWS

Critically discuss, with examples from case law, the obligations of national courts under Article 234 (ex 177) EC.

See *Cases and Materials* (6.10) for a specimen answer.

7 Challenging Community acts

7.1 Objectives

By the end of this chapter you should be able to:

1 Explain the ability of the Parliament to bring actions under Article 230 (ex 173) EC and relate changes in this area of law to the development of the Parliament's role generally

2 Illustrate the importance of relying on the correct legislative base

3 Analyse the concepts of direct and individual concern

4 Identify the circumstances in which a plea of illegality under Article 241 (ex 184) EC may be made

5 Identify the circumstances in which an action under Article 232 (ex 175) EC is likely to be successful

6 Explain the effect of a successful action under Article 230 (ex 173) or Article 232 (ex 175) EC

7.2 Introduction

The most usual way of challenging Community measures is to rely on Article 230 (ex 173) EC, alleging that the Community has done something which it should not have done. The Parliament has, on occasion, alleged that the Community has adopted a measure on an incorrect legal base, a flaw which could be detrimental to the Parliament since it is that base which determines the appropriate legislative procedure, and hence the degree of input of the Parliament.

Although individuals and companies are also entitled to challenge measures under this Article, their capacity to do so has been hampered by the wording of Article 230 (ex 173) EC and its interpretation by the Court of Justice, which has meant that only persons immediately concerned by the measure may challenge it. This test of 'direct and individual concern' involves a number of elements which combine to create a considerable hurdle for private applicants under Article 230 (ex 173) EC.

The partner to Article 230 (ex 173) EC is Article 232 (ex 175) EC, which may be relied on where the Community has failed to do something which it ought to have done. This is far less commonly relied on than Article 230 (ex 173) EC and there has been a particular difficulty in establishing whether it, or Article 230 (ex 173), should be used to challenge a positive refusal to act. The third possible challenge to Community EC law is the so-called plea of illegality under Article 241 (ex 184) EC.

7.3 **Article 230 (ex 173) EC**

Article 230 (ex 173) permits certain Community acts to be challenged, by certain applicants, in certain circumstances. Let us consider each element of Article 230 (ex 173) in turn.

7.3.1 **Acts which may be challenged**

7.3.1.1 **Acts of the legislative institutions**

Article 230 (ex 173) EC permits challenges to be made to acts of the:

(a) Parliament and Council;

(b) Council;

(c) Commission;

(d) European Central Bank;

(e) Parliament, in so far as those acts are intended to produce legal effects.

7.3.1.2 **Acts with binding legal effect**

In the case of *IBM Corporation* v *Commission* (Case 60/81) [1981] ECR 2639, IBM challenged both:

(a) a Commission Decision to initiate proceedings under Community competition law, and

(b) a statement of objections to its marketing practices (which the Commission alleged were contrary to Article 243 (ex 186) EC) which was provided with the notification of this decision.

? QUESTION 7.1 CWS

Read the extract from *IBM* v *Commission*, in *Cases and Materials* (7.1.1). According to the Court of Justice in that case, can acts of the institutions which do not have binding legal effect be challenged under Article 230 (ex 173) EC?

The Court of Justice ruled that neither the initiation of proceedings nor the statement of objections were, on the basis of their nature and legal effect, acts capable of challenge under Article 230 (ex 173) because they did not have binding legal effect. The act to be challenged must be a final statement of an institution's position and not merely an interim position.

QUESTION 7.2

In the light of this case, can you explain why Article 230 (ex 173) EC expressly excludes Recommendations and Opinions from the acts which may be challenged?

Recommendations and Opinions are expressly excluded from challenge under Article 230 (ex 173) for the very reason that they do not produce legal effects (see **Chapter 3**).

7.3.2 **Applicants under Article 230 (ex 173)**

Community institutions, Member States and private parties are all referred to in Article 230 (ex 173) EC, but some of them are restricted as to the acts which they may challenge.

 EXERCISE 7.1   CWS

Read Article 230 (ex 173) EC in *Cases and Materials* (7.1) and attempt to summarize the acts which may be challenged by the different types of applicant.

Not all acts may be challenged by all applicants. The position may be summarised as follows:

Applicant	Acts which may be challenged
Privileged applicants (the Council, the Commission, the Parliament and Member States).	Any act (provided that it is a final statement of an institution's position and produces legal effects; see **7.3.1.2**).
'Intermediate' category of applicants (the Court of Auditors and the ECB).	Any act (as above), subject to certain restrictions.
Non-privileged applicants (companies and individuals).	Regulations and Decisions only, subject to certain restrictions.

 QUESTION 7.3

Since Article 230 (ex 173) does not permit non-privileged applicants to challenge Regulations or Directives, in what other ways might the terms of these measures be subject to review by such applicants? Try to think of as many ways as possible. (If you have difficulty in doing this, look back at Chapters 2 and 5.)

Individuals or companies (or indeed the Member State) may rely on Regulations, national legislation transposing a Directive and in certain circumstances the Directive itself (see **Chapter** 5) before the national courts. National courts are then able to review the Community measure or the transposing legislation although only the Court of Justice may declare a Community measure invalid (see **Chapter** 6). Such national judicial protection is important to the Community legal system and has been expressly recognized as such by the Court of Justice, for example, in *ASOCARNE* v *Council* (Case T-99/94) [1995] 3 CMLR 458.

The restrictions on certain applicants will now be considered.

7.3.3 *Locus standi*

What is meant by the term '*locus standi*'? It means the standing, or legal ability, to bring an action. The *locus standi* of each type of applicant considered above is different, and we shall consider the position of each in turn.

7.3.3.1 **Privileged applicants**

As mentioned at 7.3.2, these include the Commission, the Council, the Parliament, and the Member States. They have locus standi to challenge any act.

7.3.3.2 **The intermediate category of applicants**

This consists of the Court of Auditors and the ECB. These bodies may challenge any act, but only in order to protect their prerogatives. Although the cases discussed in this section relate to the Parliament which, prior to the Treaty of Nice, was an intermediate applicant, they are still relevant to what is meant by the protection of an applicant's prerogatives.

? **QUESTION** 7.4   CWS ⬤

Read the extract from *Parliament* v *Council (Chernobyl)* (Case C-70/88) [1970] ECR I-2041 in *Cases and Materials* (7.1.2.1). What do you understand by the expression 'to protect its prerogatives', in the context of Article 230 (ex 173) EC?

According to *Chernobyl*, the Parliament's prerogatives include the right to influence the legislative process to the extent provided for in the EC Treaty. This prerogative would be infringed if the Parliament had been accorded less influence than it was entitled to, because of the use of the wrong legislative base, and therefore the wrong legislative procedure, in passing a measure.

In order for the Parliament to bring an action on this ground, it must identify the legal base which was used, and then show that this was an incorrect base for the particular legislation. The legal base will normally be a Treaty provision, but may be secondary legislation.

In the case of *Commission* v *Council (Generalised Tariff Preferences)* (Case 45/86) [1987] ECR 1493 (*Cases and Materials* (7.1.2.1), a Regulation suspended duties on certain imports from developing countries, but did not include identification of its legislative base. The Court of Justice held that the obligation under Article 253 (ex 190), to include in measures a statement of the reasons behind them, required as part of those reasons a sufficient identification of the legal base. Where the choice of legislative base was unclear or incorrect, the measure would, as here, be annulled.

One of the factors which may determine the correct choice of base is the relative degree of Parliamentary input. The Court of Justice gave guidelines on the choice of legislative base in the case of *Commission* v *Council (Titanium Dioxide)* (Case C-300/89) [1991] ECR 2867. In this case, a Directive harmonizing programmes for the reduction of titanium dioxide pollution had been based on Article 175 (ex 130s) EC, which concerned environmental measures. The Commission challenged the Directive on the ground that the correct legal base was in fact Article 95 (ex 100a) EC, which dealt with the internal market. Article 95 (ex 100a) EC specified the use of the cooperation procedure, whereas Article 175 (ex 130s) utilized the consultation procedure. As the cooperation procedure gave the Parliament a greater input into decision making, you will not be surprised to learn that the Parliament also favoured Article 95 (ex 100a) EC, rather than Article 175 (ex 130s) EC.

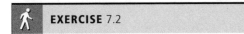 **EXERCISE** 7.2

Read the extract from *Commission* v *Council (Titanium Dioxide)* in *Cases and Materials* (7.1.2.1). What factors did the Court of Justice take into account when determining the correct legal base of a measure?

The Court of Justice stated that where two bases were appropriate, both should usually be cited. However, this was not possible here because the two bases specified the use of different legislative procedures. A joint base which effectively gave a choice of procedures would allow the consultation procedure to be used at the expense of the cooperation procedure, and thus at the expense of the Parliament's involvement in the legislative process. The Court stressed the importance of the fundamental democratic principle of Parliament's involvement in the cooperation procedure and concluded that Article 95 (ex 100a) EC was the more appropriate legislative base for the following reasons:

(a) If the burdens on businesses of measures relating to the environment were not harmonized the internal market would be distorted.

(b) Article 175 (ex 130s) EC was not the only suitable legislative base for environmental measures since Article 174 (ex 130r) EC provided that environmental protection should be a component of all Community policies. Indeed, Article 95 (ex 100a) EC specifically provided for environmental protection to be taken into account.

The Court of Justice therefore annulled the Directive on the ground that the wrong legislative base had been used.

7.3.3.3 **Non-privileged applicants**

This category covers individuals and other private parties such as companies—in other words, anyone other than an institution or a Member State.

? QUESTION 7.5 CWS

Can you remember which of the cases you have learned about so far involved a non-privileged applicant? If not, look back at the cases referred to so far in this chapter, and try to identify a case which involved such an applicant.

In *IBM Corporation* v *Commission*, IBM was a non-privileged applicant.

Article 230 (ex 173) EC restricts the *locus standi* of such applicants to actions against:

(a) a Decision addressed to the applicant; or

(b) a Decision addressed to a third party which is of direct and individual concern to the applicant; or

(c) a Decision in the form of a Regulation (i.e. a disguised Decision), which is of direct and individual concern to the applicant.

The first category is fairly straightforward, but problems have arisen in the context of the second and third categories over the meaning of 'direct and individual concern' and over which Regulations can truly be said to be disguised Decisions. We shall examine each of these problems in turn but before doing so, it should be noted that neither true Regulations nor Directives may be challenged by non-privileged applicants.

? QUESTION 7.6

Since Article 230 (ex 173) EC does not permit non-privileged applicants to challenge Directives or genuine Regulations, in what other ways might the terms of these measures be subject to review? Try to think of as many ways as possible. (If you have difficulty in doing this, look back at Chapters 2 and 5.)

As we have seen at 7.3.3.1, privileged applicants (the Member States, the Council, the Commission, and the Parliament) may challenge any acts under Article 230 (ex 173). They may therefore challenge Regulations and Directives. Member States also have the opportunity, through their representatives in the Council, to review the framing of Regulations and Directives before they are adopted. They also have a discretion when transposing Directives into national law. Individuals or companies (or indeed the Member State) may rely on regulations, national legislators transposing a Directive or, in certain circumstances, the Directive itself (see **Chapter 5**) before the national courts. National courts are then able to review the Community measure or the transposing legislation, although only the Court of Justice may declare a Community measure invalid (see **Chapter 6**). Such national judicial protection is important to the Community legal system and has been expressly recognized as such by the Court of Justice in, for example, *ASOCARNE v Council* (Case T-99/94) [1995] 3 CMLR 458.

7.4 **Direct concern**

The act complained of must have a direct effect on the applicant. What does this mean? For the effect to be direct the act of the Community must cause an effect on the applicant without any intervening act. Intervening acts may occur where a Member State has some discretion in the application of a measure.

   UNICME and Others v Council (Case 123/77) [1978] ECR 845 involved a Council Regulation which, *inter alia*, made the importing of Japanese motor cycles subject to the issue of a licence from the Italian government. Italian importers of such motor cycles, together with their trade association, UNICME, attempted to challenge the Regulation under Article 230 (ex 173) EC. As it was not a decision addressed to them, the importers had to show that they were directly and individually concerned by the Regulation.

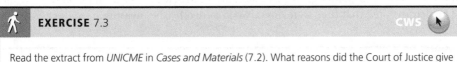

EXERCISE 7.3   CWS

Read the extract from *UNICME* in *Cases and Materials* (7.2). What reasons did the Court of Justice give in that case for holding that the importers were not directly concerned by the measure?

You should have concluded that the Court of Justice held that the importers were not directly concerned because the Italian government retained a discretion over the grant of import licences. It was not the Regulation which directly concerned the importers, but any subsequent refusal by the Italian government to issue import licences to them.

QUESTION 7.7

What alternative action did the Court of Justice suggest that the importers might be able to bring?

The Court of Justice stated that if the Italian government did indeed refuse licences to the importers, they could bring an action in the national courts. A national court could then, if necessary, refer the question of the validity of the Regulation to the Court of Justice under Article 234 (ex 177) EC.

   In *Bock v Commission* (Case 62/70) [1971] ECR 897, Bock applied for a licence to import Chinese mushrooms, but the German authorities replied that they would refuse to grant the licence as soon as they were authorized by the Commission to do so. The Commission issued a Decision allowing Germany to refuse to issue import licences for Chinese mushrooms. The Court of Justice ruled that Bock was directly concerned by the Decision.

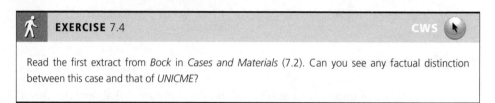

EXERCISE 7.4   CWS

Read the first extract from *Bock* in *Cases and Materials* (7.2). Can you see any factual distinction between this case and that of *UNICME*?

In *Bock*, the Court of Justice held that there was no intervening discretion, because the German authorities had already exercised their discretion when they notified Bock of their intention to refuse his application as soon as they were able. It was therefore the Decision itself which actually affected Bock. In contrast, in *UNICME* the Regulation did not directly concern *UNICME* because the Member State involved had yet to exercise its discretion at the time the Regulation was issued.

In *Piraiki-Patraiki and others* v *Commission* (Case 11/82) [1985] ECR 207 a Commission Decision authorized France to impose quotas on imports of yarn from Greece. The Greek importers sought to challenge this Decision under Article 230 (ex 173) EC, and the Court of Justice accepted that they were directly concerned by the measure.

EXERCISE 7.5   CWS

Read the first extract from *Piraiki-Patraiki* in *Cases and Materials* (7.2). Can you see any factual distinction between this case and that of *UNICME?*

The crucial distinction between this case and *UNICME* which you should have discerned is that, on the facts, the possibility of an exercise of intervening discretion by the French government could be disregarded. France already severely restricted such imports and in fact had requested a quota more strict than that given, so the chance that it would not utilize the permission to impose quotas was 'purely theoretical'.

Whereas in *Bock* the German authorities had actually stated that the Decision would be applied directly to the applicant, in *Piraiki-Patraiki* it was simply the opinion of the Court of Justice that the French authorities would apply the Decision directly to the applicants. The test would therefore seem to be whether the Member State has given a sufficiently clear indication of how it will use its discretion. In *Bock* and *Piraiki-Patraiki* the Court of Justice considered that the respective governments had given such an indication, whereas in *UNICME* it was clear that the Italian government had not.

7.5 **Individual concern**

The classic statement of the law in this area comes from the case of *Plaumann & Co.* v *Commission* (Case 25/62) [1963] ECR 95 in which the German government applied for permission to reduce the duty on imports of clementines. The Commission issued a Decision refusing permission and Plaumann, a clementine importer, challenged it. The Court of Justice held that Plaumann was not individually concerned by the Decision.

 EXERCISE 7.6

Read the extract from *Plaumann* in *Cases and Materials* (7.3). What factors led the Court of Justice to conclude that Plaumann was not individually concerned by this measure?

In order to show individual concern, an applicant must show that it was affected by the Decision by reason of certain attributes or circumstances:

(a) which differentiated it from all others; and

(b) which distinguished it as individually as if the Decision had been addressed to it.

In this instance, the Decision applied to all the clementine producers, and Plaumann could not be said to be in any way differentiated from the others.

Clearly, then, individual concern requires that the applicant be singled out in some way by the measure. This means that it will be more difficult to prove individual concern where the measure challenged is a Regulation, than where it is a Decision.

? **QUESTION** 7.8

Why do you think this is so? If you have difficulty answering this question, look back at the difference between these types of measure at 3.5.2.

This is because Regulations apply generally and are unlikely to concern potential applicants particularly, whereas Decisions apply to a specific entity or group of entities, and are therefore more likely to have a particular impact on them.

Unfortunately for all concerned, the Court of Justice has not developed a consistent approach to the question of whether an applicant is sufficiently singled out by a measure. A number of approaches have been discernable for some years. First, the 'closed class' test (see 7.5.1) often provides a starting point for establishing locus standi. Secondly, where an applicant fails to satisfy this test when strictly applied, the Court of Justice may consider whether it fulfils a more generous test based on the facts (see 7.5.2). Thirdly and fourthly, where the measure in question has been issued as a result of proceedings issued by the applicant or is an anti-dumping measure, the Court has developed a special test (see 7.5.3 and 7.5.4).

Each of these possibilities will be considered in turn. It should also be noted that a number of new approaches have been proposed, although not yet accepted by the Court of Jusitce, in relation to Regulations. These will be discussed at 7.6.2.

7.5.1 **The 'closed class' test**

One approach, often called the 'closed class' test, involves a consideration of whether it was possible to identify all the potential applicants at the time the measure allegedly affecting them was passed. In order to do this, the membership of the class must have been fixed at that time and it must have been possible to ascertain the identity of those members. Where is the burden of proof? It is on an applicant to show that it is a member of such a class (possibly the only member).

The test is a strict one, as can be seen from *Spijker Kwasten BV v Commission* (Case 231/82) [1983] ECR 259. Spijker, a Dutch importer of Chinese brushes, applied for an import licence which the Dutch authorities stated that they would refuse if the Commission authorized them to do so. The Commission Decision authorized the Dutch government, for a period of six months, to ban imports of Chinese brushes. Not only had the Dutch request for such a Decision been made in response to Spijker's imports, but Spijker was the only importer of such goods into the Netherlands at the time.

 EXERCISE 7.7 CWS

Despite these facts, the Court of Justice concluded that Spijker was not individually concerned by the measure. Read the extract from *Spijker* in *Cases and Materials* (7.3.1) and try to summarize the reasons for its decision.

The Court of Justice ruled that the class of those potentially affected was not closed (and therefore not ascertainable) at the time of the Decision because other importers might materialise during the six-month period, who would then be adversely affected by the Decision and form part of the class of potential applicants.

In *International Fruit Company and others v Commission* (Cases 41–4/70) [1971] ECR 411, Member States were required to notify the Commission, on a weekly basis, of the quantity of apples for which import licences had been requested. This enabled the Commission to determine the percentage of licences which should be granted. Only 80% of licence applications in the week in which the applicants had applied were granted, and their applications were amongst those refused. The applicants challenged the Regulation which applied the 80% limit.

EXERCISE 7.8

What do you think that the Court of Justice decided in this case? Read the extract from *International Fruit Company* in *Cases and Materials* (7.3.1) to see if you were correct.

The Court of Justice held that the Regulation must be regarded as a conglomeration of individual Decisions which individually concerned the applicant. It applied to a fixed and ascertainable class, that is to say, applicants in a particular week, and although it took account only of the total quantity of applications, the decision then had to be applied to each individual application. This necessarily involved a decision on each application.

A similar approach was taken in one of the many 'isoglucose cases', a series of cases in the late 1970s and early 1980s involving the introduction of quotas and levies, and the abolition of subsidies, on the production of isoglucose, a liquid sugar substitute. In *Roquette Frères* v *Council* (Case 138/79) [1978] ECR 3333 (*Cases and Materials* (7.3.1)), a Regulation established quotas for the production of isoglucose and listed in an annex the companies to which these quotas applied. Roquette Frères, one of the companies listed, challenged the validity of the Regulation.

? **QUESTION** 7.9

How might Roquette be considered to be individually concerned?

The Court of Justice ruled that the Regulation was of individual concern to the applicants and other producers listed in the annex because specific quotas were allotted to them by name and therefore the Regulation was susceptible to challenge under Article 230 (ex 173). Under the terms of Article 230 (ex 173), this could only have been possible if the Court of Justice had regarded the Regulation as, in substance, a Decision.

7.5.2 **A test based on the facts**

In many cases, the Court of Justice has found that the contested measure potentially applies to a group of applicants which is neither fixed nor ascertainable, but has then gone on to accept that the applicant in the case before it is nonetheless individually concerned. This involves a careful examination of the particular facts of the case, and an assessment as to whether the applicant is affected by the measure in a way that no other potential applicant is affected. There are a number of examples of this approach in the case law of the Court of Justice.

In *Toepfer Getreide-Import Gesellschaft* v *Commission* (Cases 106 & 107/63) [1965] ECR 405, a German maize importer, Toepfer, had applied for an import licence on 1 October, the only day on which the levy was 0%. The German authorities refused to issue the licence and the Commission issued a Decision on 4 October authorizing the refusal of licence applications up to and including 4 October. Toepfer challenged this Decision under Article 230 (ex 173) EC.

EXERCISE 7.9   CWS

Try to apply the 'factual' test set out above to these facts. Do you think that Toepfer was individually concerned by this Decision? Read the extract from *Toepfer* in *Cases and Materials* (7.3.2) to see if you were correct.

The Court of Justice held that Toepfer was individually concerned by the Decision. The 0% levy had been available only on 1 October, and so only those importers which had applied for a licence on that day were adversely affected by the Decision authorizing the refusal of their licences. (Applications made on 2–4 October which were refused, could be resubmitted thereafter without loss to the applicants, since the applicable levy would be the same.) The class of potential applicants was therefore fixed and ascertainable at the time the Decision was taken and the factual situation differentiated them from all others in the same way that a Decision addressed to them would have done.

In effect, Toepfer and the other 1 October applicants created a closed class within a larger class of 1–4 October applicants. This larger class was not closed at the date of the Decision because the Decision was issued on 4 October.

In *Bock* and *Piraiki-Patraiki* the classes of potential applicants (all importers of Chinese mushrooms and all importers of Greek yarn into France, respectively) were not closed. However, the Court of Justice held that the applicant importers were individually concerned.

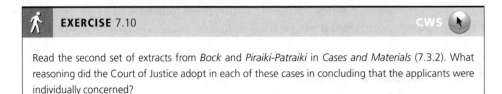

EXERCISE 7.10   CWS

Read the second set of extracts from *Bock* and *Piraiki-Patraiki* in *Cases and Materials* (7.3.2). What reasoning did the Court of Justice adopt in each of these cases in concluding that the applicants were individually concerned?

In these cases, the Court of Justice adopted a similar test to that in *Toepfer* to find that the applicants were differentiated on the facts from all other potential applicants.

In the case of *Bock* (see above), Bock did not challenge the Decision in its entirety, but only in so far as it applied to importers who had already applied for import licences. The Court of Justice considered that Bock was individually concerned by this part of the Decision because such importers constituted a fixed and ascertainable class. It therefore annulled the Decision in so far as it applied to existing licence applications.

Did you notice that the reasoning in *Piraiki-Patraiki* (see above) was similar? The Decision applied to all potential importers of Greek yarn into France, but the Court of Justice accepted that importers already bound by contractual arrangements (and who would therefore be particularly prejudiced by the Decision when it was passed) could be distinguished from importers who were not so bound. The class of such importers was therefore fixed at the date of the Decision. The Commission could scarcely argue that it was not possible to identify the members of this class, since it was required to carry out precisely that task as part of the inquiry which the Greek Act of Accession obliged it to conduct into the effects of any proposed protective measure.

The Court of Justice adopted a similar line of reasoning in *Cordonui SA* v *Council* (Case C-309/89) [1995] 2 CMLR 561 which concerned a Regulation which restricted the use of the description 'crémant' to quality sparkling wines originating in France and Luxembourg.

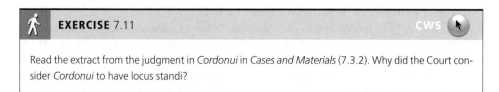

EXERCISE 7.11   CWS

Read the extract from the judgment in *Cordonui* in *Cases and Materials* (7.3.2). Why did the Court consider *Cordonui* to have locus standi?

The Court ruled that *Cordonui* was differentiated from other producers who might be affected by the Regulation because it had registered and used the word 'crémant' as part of its trademark since 1924.

In the case of *Sofrimport SARL* v *Commission* (Case C-152/88) [1990] ECR I-2477, Sofrimport had shipped apples from Chile prior to the issue of a Regulation which suspended import licences for Chilean apples. Sofrimport's subsequent application to the French authorities for an import licence was refused and it then applied for annulment of the Regulation. The Court of Justice held that the Regulation should be annulled in so far as it applied to goods in transit. When taking protectionist measures, the Commission was required, under a previous Regulation, to take into account the position of importers with goods in transit and since such importers constituted a fixed and ascertainable class, they could be said to be individually concerned. These importers therefore had locus standi to challenge the Regulation in so far as it applied to them.

The Court of First Instance reached a different decision in *Unifruit Hellas* v *Commission* (Case T-489/93) [1996] 1 CMLR 267, a case involving similar facts, but a different Regulation. The Court of First Instance ruled that although importers whose goods were in transit to the Community when the Regulation introduced a charge on those goods constituted a fixed and identifiable class of persons, that was not sufficient. The Regulation in question did not require the Commission to take into account the special position of products in transit (unlike the Regulation in *Sofrimport*) and so there was no individual concern.

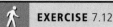 **EXERCISE** 7.12

Read the extracts from *Sofrimport* and *Unifruit Hellas* in *Cases and Materials* (7.3.2). Do you agree with the reasoning of the Court of Justice in *Unifruit Hellas*?

7.5.3 Measures issued as a result of proceedings initiated by applicant

Where the measure complained of was adopted as a result of proceedings in which the applicant was involved, the Court of Justice has been prepared to rule that the applicant is individually concerned. This is most likely to be the case where the measure concerns competition policy (see **Chapters 11–13**) or is an anti-dumping measure (designed to stop the import into the Community of goods priced below the normal price where this could cause economic harm within the Community).

For example, in *Metro-SB-Grossmärkte GmbH & Co KG v Commission* (26/76) [1977] ECR 1875 the applicant sought to challenge a Decision addressed to another company. However, the Decision had been issued in response to a complaint made by the applicant to the Commission that the other company was in breach of Community competition policy. Similarly, in *Timex Corporation v Council* [1985] ECR 849 an applicant which had initiated the complaint and given evidence in the proceedings giving rise to the anti-dumping measure was held to be individually concerned by it.

7.5.4 Anti-dumping measures

As well as those who initiate the procedure leading to the adoption of an anti-dumping measure, the Court of Justice has also recognized that producers, exporters or importers of the product at which the measure is directed may be individually concerned by it.

In *Allied Corporation v Commission* (239 &275/82) [1984] ECR 1005 the Court of Justice identified as relevant the fact that the producers and exporters had given undertakings pursuant to one of the contested Regulations, were referred to in the other contested Regulation, and their individual circumstances formed the subject matter of the two Regulations.

Where the applicant is not an exporter or a producer, but only an importer, it must prove that it is particularly singled out by the measure. For example, in *Extramet Industrie SA v Council* (C-358/89) [1991] ECR I-2501 the Court of Justice ruled that an importer was individually concerned where it was the largest importer and end user of the product, its business was dependent to a large extent upon the product and it was difficult to obtain supplies elsewhere.

7.6 **Decisions in the form of regulations**

7.6.1 **The current position**

An applicant may prove that a purported Regulation is, in fact, a Decision, in one of two ways. First, the nature and scope of the Regulation may be such that it is not legislative in character and thus not a true Regulation but a Decision. Secondly, and in the alternative, a true Regulation may be of individual concern to the applicant and thus effectively a Decision so far as it is concerned.

In earlier years, the Court on occasion applied only the first, stricter test and not the second, more generous test. For example, in *KSH NV* v *Council and Commission* (Case 101/76) [1977] ECR 797 (*Cases and Materials* (7.4.1)), an isoglucose producer challenged a Regulation which provided for the reduction, and eventual abolition, of subsidies on isoglucose production. The producer was one of only three or four such producers in the Community and because of the technology and expense involved, any potential producers would not be in a position to enter the market for at least two years. The Court of Justice ruled that the wording of this Regulation indicated that it was a measure of general application, applying objectively to a general and abstract category of persons. The fact that those persons were fixed and ascertainable at any given time was insufficient. It is possible that the Court of Justice was influenced in this case by the problem of massive isoglucose overproduction. If it had not invented this extra hurdle for applicants, it would have had to annul the Regulation, and the overproduction would have continued.

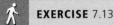 **EXERCISE** 7.13 CWS

Read the extract from the later case of *Calpak SpA and Società Emiliana Lavoraziore Frutta SpA* v *Commission* (Cases 789–790/79) [1980] ECR 1949 in *Cases and Materials* (7.4.1). Did the Court of Justice continue to consider the wording of the measure, even in the absence of such a policy factor?

In *Calpak* v *Commission*, the Court of Justice again considered the wording of the measure. A Regulation altered the calculation of subsidies to producers of processed pears, so that reference was made only to the previous year's production rather than to the average production over the previous three years. Since the reference year in question had been a bad one for Italian producers, but not for French producers (who were their sole rivals in the Community), the Italian producers complained. The Court of Justice ruled that the Regulation applied to all producers, that is to say, it applied objectively to a category of persons described in a general manner. The fact that the number and even the identity of those producers could be determined was insufficient for it to be categorized as a Decision.

However, in other cases such as *Cordonui* and *Sofrimport* (see 7.3.2), the Court applied the more generous test. More recently in *Union de Pequeños Agricultores (UPA)* v *Council*

(C-50/00 [2002] 3 CMLR 1 *Cases and Materials* (7.4.2)) the Court has referred to both tests as alternatives, either of which will be sufficient to establish that the Regulation is open to challenge if the applicant is directly and individually concerned by it.

7.6.2 **Possibilities for reform**

The difficulties for non-privileged applicants of challenging measures of general application have been considered in two recent cases. In *UPA*, a trade association representing small agricultural business in Spain brought an action under Article 230 EC for the annulment of Regulation 1638/98 which reformed the system of aid for olive oil. The Court of First Instance held the action inadmissible on the grounds that the Regulation was neither a Decision nor of individual concern to UPA. UPA appealed to the Court of Justice

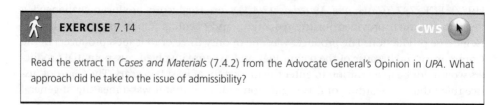

EXERCISE 7.14   CWS

Read the extract in *Cases and Materials* (7.4.2) from the Advocate General's Opinion in *UPA*. What approach did he take to the issue of admissibility?

Advocate General Jacobs argued that the caselaw on the locus standi of natural and legal persons under Article 230 EC needed to be changed in order to provide adequate judicial protection of persons affected by Community measures, and that a person should be regarded as individually concerned where 'by reason of his particular circumstances, the measure has, or is liable to have, a substantial adverse effect on his interests'. The Advocate General therefore concluded that the judgment of the Court of First Instance should be annulled.

Subsequently the Court of First Instance gave judgment in *Jégo-Quéré SA v Commission* (T-177/01 [2002] 2 CMLR).

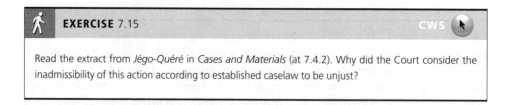

EXERCISE 7.15   CWS

Read the extract from *Jégo-Quéré* in *Cases and Materials* (at 7.4.2). Why did the Court consider the inadmissibility of this action according to established caselaw to be unjust?

The Court was concerned that if Jégo-Quéré's action was inadmissible, it would be denied any legal remedy enabling it to challenge the legality of the contested provisions. Access to the courts was an essential element of a community based on the rule of law, and was guaranteed by the establishment in the EC Treaty of a complete system of remedies and procedures enabling the Court to review the legality of acts of the institutions, and by the establishment by the Court of a right to an effective remedy. The latter had also been reaffirmed by Article 47 of the Charter of Fundamental Rights of the EU.

What other actions might have provided a remedy?

Why did the Court of First Instance not consider these to be sufficient?

There were two other routes by which an individual might obtain a declaration that a Community measure was unlawful: Article 234 EC and Article 288 EC. However, an Article 234 EC ruling was not possible in the present case because there were no acts of implementation capable of giving rise to an action in the national courts. Although Jégo-Quéré could breach the Regulation and then assert its illegality in proceedings against it, individuals could not be required to breach the law in order to gain access to justice. An Article 288 EC action could also not provide a solution because it could not result in the annulment of a Community measure which was held to be unlawful. (Actions under Article 288 EC will be discussed in depth in **Chapter 8.**)

? **QUESTION** 7.11

What new test did the Court of First Instance formulate establish whether a Regulation was of direct concern to the applicant?

The Court held that a person a person must be regarded as individually concerned by a Community measure of general application (i.e. a Regulation) if 'the measure in question affects his legal position, in a manner which is both definitive and immediate, by restricting this right or by imposing obligations on him'. It stressed that 'the number and position of other persons who are likewise affected by the measure, or who may be so, are of no relevance in that regard'. Although it was necessary for a non-privileged applicant to satisfy the conditions laid down by Article 230 EC in order to bring an action for annulment, an applicant seeking to challenge a general measure need not differentiated from all others affected by it in the same way as an addressee.

The most recent judgment on the issue is that of the Court of Justice in *UPA*, which confirmed its judgment in C-321/95 P *Greenpeace* [1998] ECR I-1651 that a non-privileged applicant could only challenge a Regulation if it was in fact a Decision, or if he was individually concerned by it so that it was a Decision in respect of him.

⚐ **EXERCISE** 7.16   CWS

Read the extract in *Cases and Materials* (7.4.2) from the judgment of the Court of Justice in *UPA*. Do you find this more or less persuasive than the judgment of the Court of First Instance in *Jégo-Quéré*?

However convincing you find the arguments of the Court of First Instance, remember that it is the judgment of the Court of Justice which is authoritative. Note that the Court of Justice accepted that applicants had rights of access to the courts and to an effective remedy, but concluded that Articles 230, 234, and 241 EC provided 'a complete system of legal remedies'. (Article 241 EC is discussed in more detail at 7.11.)

 EXERCISE 7.17 CWS

Look back at Article 230 (ex 173) EC in *Cases and Materials* (7.1) and read the extract from 'Article 173 Paragraph 4 EC: Past, Present and Possible Future' in *Cases and Materials* (7.4.2). Do you think that there should be a further hurdle, beyond those of proving direct and individual concern, for non-privileged applicants wishing to challenge a Regulation?

7.7 **Directives**

Although not mentioned in Article 230 EC as subject to challenge by non-privileged applicants, it has been held that Directives are open to challenge if an applicant is directly and individually concerned by them (see, e.g., *Salamander AG* v *Parliament* (T-172/98) [2000] ECR II-2487 and *Japan Tobacco Inc and JT International SA* v *Parliament and Council* (T-223/01) [2002] ECR II-3259).

? **QUESTION** 7.12

What problems do you think might be encountered in relation to direct concern and Directives?

Since Directives leave some discretion to Member States and cannot produce direct legal effect until their implementation deadline has passed, it will be rare for a Directive to directly concern an applicant.

7.8 **Grounds for annulment**

? **QUESTION** 7.13

Article 230 (ex 173) gives four grounds on which an application for annulment may be made. What are they?

The four grounds outlined below may be relied upon by all applicants (subject to the ful-filment of the further requirements outlined above by non-privileged applicants and those in the intermediate category). The grounds overlap and an applicant may rely on one or more in its challenge. The decision of the Court of Justice need not identify the ground on which the challenge is successful.

The four grounds are as follows.

7.8.1 Lack of competence

If an institution acts beyond its powers, that act can be annulled. An example would be an act which had no legal base in the EC Treaty or in secondary legislation, and which the Community therefore had no power to take. This ground is rarely used because of the fall-back power given by Article 308 (ex 235) (see **Chapter 3** and *Cases and Materials* (3.2)).

In *UK v Council (Working Time Directive)* (Case C-84/94) [1996] 3 CMLR 671 the UK re-quested the annulment of a Directive imposing a maximum working week of 48 hours on the ground, *inter alia*, that the Council had no competence to adopt the Directive. The UK argued that the measure did not relate to health and safety at work and therefore should not have been adopted under Article 138 (ex 118a). Instead, it should either have been proposed under Article 94 (ex 100) (as an internal market measure) or under Article 308 (ex 235) (as a measure not covered by any specific Treaty Article). In either case the Council Decision adopting the measure would have had to be unanimous and since the UK would have opposed the Directive, the Council would not have had the competence to adopt the Regulation.

The Court of Justice ruled that Article 138 (ex 118a) was the appropriate legislative base for the Directive and therefore the Council was competent to adopt it.

7.8.2 Infringement of an essential procedural requirement

Although there are a number of possibilities here, the commonest infringements are a failure to give proper reasons for an act as required by Article 253 (ex 190) EC, and use of the wrong legislative procedure, in particular involving a failure to consult the Parliament.

 EXERCISE 7.18   CWS

For a slight variation on the latter complaint, look at the second extract from *Roquette Frères* v *Council* (Case 138/79) in *Cases and Materials* (7.5). What essential procedural requirement was infringed in this case?

In *Roquette Frères* the measure challenged should have been adopted under the consulta-tion procedure. The Council asked the Parliament for its opinion but adopted the mea-sure without waiting for it to be given. The Court of Justice ruled that this amounted to an infringement of an essential procedural requirement.

7.8.3 Infringement of the EC Treaty or of any rule or law relating to its application

This ground is commonly relied upon in Article 230 (ex 173) EC actions.

 EXERCISE 7.19

Try to list as many 'rules of law' as possible. If you have difficulty in doing this, you should refer back to Chapter 3.

You might have mentioned legal certainty, non-discrimination, proportionality, fundamental human rights, or any other general principle of law.

7.8.4 **Misuse of powers**

Where an institution has been given power to act, but only for a particular purpose or purposes, then if that power is used for an illegal end or in an illegal way, this may give grounds for a challenge.

7.9 **Procedure**

The applicant has two months in which to challenge the measure in the Court of Justice. This time limit runs from the fifteenth day after publication of the measure in the Official Journal or, if the measure has not been published, from the day after receipt of notification by the applicant. If neither of these events has occurred, the time limit runs from the day on which the measure came to the applicant's knowledge.

7.10 **Effect of annulment**

If an Article 230 (ex 173) EC action is successful, the measure will be annulled, either in whole or in part. According to Article 231 (ex 174) EC, such a measure (to the extent to which it is annulled) is void, that is to say, has no legal effect. It may not be reviewed or enforced and, according to Article 233 (ex 176) EC, the defendant institution must take such steps as are necessary to comply with the judgment of the Court of Justice. The Court of Justice will determine the time from which the annulment takes effect, which may be from the date of judgment, from the future date on which the measure is replaced, or retrospectively to an earlier date.

7.11 **The plea of illegality**

Article 241 (ex 184) EC provides that in proceedings where a Regulation is at issue, an applicant may rely on the grounds for an Article 230 (ex 173) EC action (lack of competence and so forth) in order to allege that the Regulation is inapplicable in that case. This form of indirect challenge is known as the 'plea of illegality'.

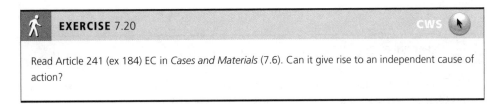

EXERCISE 7.20 CWS

Read Article 241 (ex 184) EC in *Cases and Materials* (7.6). Can it give rise to an independent cause of action?

Article 241 (ex 184) EC cannot give rise to a separate cause of action, but can be raised in the course of other proceedings. A declaration of inapplicability means that any measures adopted under the Regulation are invalid. In theory, the declaration is relevant only to the case in question but in practice, since the Court of Justice would be likely to annul the Regulation or any measures based on it if challenged correctly under Article 230 (ex 173) EC, the other institutions would be likely to replace the Regulation in question as soon as possible. The relevant time limits and rules of *locus standi* are those applicable to the underlying action, whatever that may be.

7.12 **Article 232 (ex 175) EC**

Article 232 (ex 175) EC provides that the Court of Justice may declare an institution's failure to act to be an infringement of the EC Treaty. There are a number of conditions which must be fulfilled before an action can be brought.

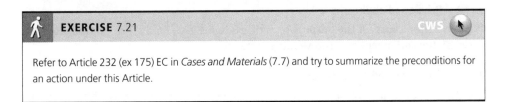

EXERCISE 7.21 CWS

Refer to Article 232 (ex 175) EC in *Cases and Materials* (7.7) and try to summarize the preconditions for an action under this Article.

You should have found two preconditions, as follows:

(a) The defaulting institution must have been called upon to act.
   It would be inequitable to sue an institution before notifying it of the complaint and calling upon it to take the action required by the complainant.

(b) The institution must have failed to define its position within two months of being called upon to act.

The institution is not obliged to take the action required by the complainant in order to avoid an Article 232 (ex 175) EC action. It is simply obliged to define its position (see 7.12.1).

7.12.1 Meaning of 'fail to act'

A failure to act on the part of the Parliament, the Council or the Commission is open to challenge.

 EXERCISE 7.22   CWS

Write down what you think 'fail to act' should mean in this context. Read the extract from *Alfons Lütticke GmbH and others* v *Commission* in *Cases and Materials* (7.7.1) to see if your view coincides with that of the Court of Justice.

In *Alfons Lütticke* v *Commission* (Case 48/65) [1966] ECR 19, the applicants alleged that a German tax on imports of dried milk was contrary to Community law. They made a formal application requiring the Commission to take infringement proceedings against Germany under Article 226 (ex 169). The Commission responded that the tax was not contrary to Community law and that therefore it would not take such proceedings. The Court of Justice ruled that proceedings for a failure to act could be brought only if the institution had failed to define its position. The Commission had defined its position by taking the decision not to initiate proceedings against Germany, and therefore it had not 'failed to act' within the meaning of Article 232 (ex 175) EC.

As a result of this interpretation of 'fail to act', actions under Article 232 (ex 175) EC are rarely successful.

7.12.2 *Locus standi*

7.12.2.1 Privileged applicants

Privileged applicants for the purpose of Article 232 (ex 175) EC are the Commission, the Council, the Parliament and the Member States.

7.12.2.2 The intermediate category

The intermediate category under Article 232 (ex 175) EC consists solely of the ECB. The ECB may bring an action, or have an action brought against it, only in respect of areas within its field of competence.

7.12.2.3 Non-privileged applicants

Such applicants are not entitled to complain about **all** failures to act but only about a failure to address **to them** an act (other than a Recommendation or an Opinion) which they were legally entitled to claim. Since a non-privileged applicant cannot be the addressee of a Regulation or a Directive, they may only challenge a failure to adopt a Decision.

In the case of *Lord Bethell* v *Commission* (Case 246/81) [1982] ECR 2277 (*Cases and Materials* (7.7.2)), the applicant had notified the Commission of alleged anti-competitive practices by European airlines, contrary to Community law, and had requested an inquiry and a Decision on the matter. The Court of Justice ruled that where a non-privileged applicant such as Lord Bethell was concerned, an action for a failure to act lay only where there had been a failure to adopt a measure which the applicant was 'legally entitled to claim' under Community law. The applicant must therefore be the potential addressee of the act.

 QUESTION 7.14

To whom do you think a Commission Decision in this case would have been addressed?

In this case, the potential addressees of any Decision on the anti-competitive behaviour of the airlines would have been the airlines themselves, and not Lord Bethell (who would also have been unlikely to have been able to prove that any such Decision would have directly and individually concerned him).

In *Gestevisión Telecinco SA* v *Commission* (Case T-95/96 [1998] 3 CMLR 1112) the Court of Justice ruled that an undertaking would be directly concerned by a decision on State aid where the national authorities clearly intended to grant the aid, and would be individually concerned where the decision would have affected them by reason of attributes or circumstances which differentiated them from all others. Where the Commission took a decision that a measure did not constitute aid, or constituted aid but was nonetheless compatible with the common market, without initiating the procedure under Article 88(2) EC (ex 93(2) on the investigation of State aids, the beneficiaries of that procedure (in particular, competing companies) could secure compliance with the procedure only by challenging the decision to grant aid before the Court of Justice. A competing company, whose interests would be affected by the grant of that aid, was therefore directly and individually concerned by the Commission's failure to act.

7.12.3 **Procedure**

 EXERCISE 7.23   CWS

Look back at Article 232 (ex 175) EC in *Cases and Materials* (7.7) and try to summarize the procedure that an applicant should follow in order to bring a claim under this Article.

The applicant must first make a formal request to the relevant institution to act. If the institution fails to define its position within two months, the applicant may apply directly to the Court of Justice within a further period of two months.

7.12.4 **Effect**

If the Court of Justice finds that a failure to act infringes the Treaty, it will order the institution concerned to take any necessary steps to remedy the omission. These steps are not necessarily those requested by the applicant.

7.13 **The relationship between Article 230 (ex 173) EC and Article 232 (ex 175) EC**

If the institution has not defined its position, Article 232 (ex 175) EC is the appropriate provision; but if the position has been defined, Article 230 (ex 173) EC should be used since the definition in itself amounts to an act which can be challenged. The two actions are often pleaded in the alternative, but a particular measure must amount either to an act, or to a failure to act, and so only one action can be correct. If the requirements of the appropriate action are not fulfilled, for example because a challenge to an act under Article 230 (ex 173) EC is made by an individual lacking direct and individual concern, it is not open to that individual to bring an action under Article 232 (ex 175) instead.

In *Eridania and others* v *Commission* (Cases 10 & 18/68) [1969] ECR 459 (*Cases and Materials* (7.8)), a Commission Decision granted aid to three Italian sugar refineries. A number of other sugar producers asked the Commission to annul this Decision, which it refused to do. The other producers then made both an Article 230 (ex 173) and an Article 232 (ex 175) application to the Court of Justice. The Court of Justice held that the Article 232 (ex 175) action could not succeed because the Commission's positive refusal to annul the Decision amounted to an act, rather than a failure to act. The Article 230 (ex 173) action could not succeed because there was no direct and individual concern. The Court of Justice stressed that Article 232 (ex 175) should not be used to circumvent the restrictions of Article 230 (ex 173). If an institution refused to annul an act, recourse against that refusal was provided by the Treaty under Article 230 (ex 173), and the refusal should not therefore be treated as a failure to act giving rise to an Article 232 (ex 175) action.

CONCLUSIONS

Although Articles 230, 232, and 241 (ex 173, 175, and 184) EC permit actions taken by the Community to be challenged, these Articles will not provide a remedy in every case. Under Article 230 (ex 173), both the intermediate category of applicants and non-privileged applicants are extremely restricted, albeit in different ways, in their opportunities to challenge Community acts.

Under Article 232 (ex 175) EC, only total inaction may be challenged, rather than positive refusals to act and non-privileged applicants must prove that the measure they are seeking would have been addressed to them. Given that Article 241 (ex 184) EC does not provide for an independent cause of action at all, it is evident that the Community is not over anxious to encourage challenges to its measures. However, it should be remembered that the Member States are equally cautious about challenges to national law and that under Community law, as we shall see in **Chapter 8**, it is possible to claim damages in respect of a Community measure which has not been successfully challenged under Articles 230, 232, or 241 (ex 173, 175, or 184) EC.

 CHAPTER 7: ASSESSMENT EXERCISE   **CWS**

The Community operates a system of production licences, administered by the Member States, in respect of soft toys, in order to avoid the development of a soft toy mountain. The Council has recently issued a Regulation, which has immediate effect, permitting Member States to prohibit the grant of production licences in respect of cuddly toy penguins.

The two Community producers of cuddly toy penguins wish to challenge the Regulation. Do they have *locus standi* to do so?

See *Cases and Materials* (7.10) for a specimen answer.

8 The liability of the Community

8.1 Objectives

By the end of this chapter you should be able to:

1 Identify the choice of law which governs the liability of the Community in contractual and non-contractual actions

2 Explain all elements of the test which must be satisfied before damages will be awarded in respect of non-contractual liability

3 Assess the factors which may lead to the reduction of damages

4 Explain and analyse the test for a wrongful act as outlined in the *Schöppenstedt* and *Second Skimmed Milk Powder* cases

5 Explain the relationship between an action under Article 288 (ex 215) EC and other actions under the EC Treaty

8.2 Introduction

If loss is suffered as a result of Community action or inaction, it may be possible to claim damages against it under Article 288 (ex 215) EC if the Community is found to have acted wrongfully. The rules regarding the liability of the Community differ according to whether the claim is contractual or non-contractual. This chapter, for reasons which will become apparent, will concentrate on the latter.

Acts which may give rise to non-contractual claims against the Community include negligence and the adoption of defective legislation. Although Community law provides other remedies, such as annulment under Article 230 (ex 173) EC (see **Chapter 7**), damages are often claimed in addition, for instance to compensate for loss incurred prior to annulment. Many of the cases already considered under other headings led to an action for damages, for example *Alfons Lütticke v Commission* and *KSH v Council and Commission* (for both cases, see **Chapter 7** and below).

This topic may seem familiar if you have already studied the topic of Member State liability (at 5.5), since the Court of Justice used Article 288 (ex 215) and Community liability as a starting point for its development of Member State liability. However, remember that Community liability in damages is a separate area of law from that of Member State liability.

 **EXERCISE** 8.1 CWS

As a reminder of the way in which Article 288 (ex 215) EC was used by the Court of Justice in cases such as *Factortame III*, read the extract from 'Taking Article 215 EC Seriously' in *Cases and Materials* (8.1).

8.3 **Contractual liability**

The first paragraph of Article 288 (ex 215) (*Cases and Materials* (8.2)) provides that Community liability for breach of contract is governed by the system of law which applies to the contract. This law is determined by reference to the rules of private international law, and will be the law chosen by the parties or, if none, the law of the country with which the contract is most closely connected. Contracts made by the Community itself normally contain a 'choice of law' clause, but since liability in this area will, in any event, be governed by national law, it is beyond the scope of this chapter to consider it further.

8.4 **Non-contractual liability**

Article 288 (ex 215) EC (*Cases and Materials* (8.3)) provides that in non-contractual cases the Community will:

(a) in accordance with the general principles common to the law of the Member States

(b) make good any damage

(c) caused by its institutions or by its servants in the performance of their duties.

In *Dubois et Fils SA* v *Council and Commission* (Case T-113/96) [1998] 1 CMLR 1335 the Court of First Instance ruled that the Treaties of the EC and the EU were not 'acts of the institutions' but agreements by the Member States. They could not, therefore, give rise to liability on the part of the Community under Article 288 (ex 215).

 EXERCISE 8.2 CWS

Read Article 235 (ex 178) EC in *Cases and Materials* (8.3). How does Article 235 (ex 178) EC relate to Article 288 (ex 215) EC?

Article 235 (ex 178) confers jurisdiction upon the Court of Justice to award damages under Article 288 (ex 215).

EXERCISE 8.3

Look back at 2.3.5 above. Does the Court of First Instance have any jurisdiction in this area?

The Court of First Instance has jurisdiction to hear actions brought under Article 288 (ex 215) EC by legal and natural persons.

Article 288 (ex 215) EC states that Community liability is to be determined in accordance with the general principles common to the law of the Member States. In the course of its judgment in *Alfons Lütticke* v *Commission* (Case 4/69) [1971] ECR 325, the Court of Justice explained the meaning of the requirement in Article 288 (ex 215) that damages be awarded in accordance with 'the general principles common to the law of the Member States'. Lütticke had first brought an unsuccessful action under Article 232 (ex 175) (Case 48/65; see **Chapter 7**). Case 4/69 involved an action under Article 288 (ex 215) to recover damages caused by the Commission's inaction.

 QUESTION 8.1   CWS

Remember that these general principles are those which are common to the laws of Member States on liability. From your knowledge of English law can you guess what might have to be proved before damages will be awarded under Article 288 (ex 215) EC? If you have difficulty with this, read the first extract from *Alfons Lütticke* v *Commission* in *Cases and Materials* (8.3.1) to confirm the three elements which make up these 'general principles'.

In this case, the Court of Justice stated that the reference to 'the general principles common to the law of the Member States' meant that the Community would be liable in damages if three elements were proved:

(a) actual damage to the applicant (personal or property damage);

(b) illegal conduct by a Community institution;

(c) a causal link between the illegal conduct and the damage.

On the facts, the Court of Justice held that the Commission's conduct had not been illegal and that therefore damages could not be awarded.

Each of these three principles will now be examined in turn.

8.5 Actual damage

It can be surprisingly difficult to prove this element of liability, as can be seen from the case of *GAEC* v *Council and Commission* (Case 253/84) [1987] ECR 123. Subsidies had been provided to German farmers pursuant to a Council Decision, and aggrieved French farmers brought an Article 288 (ex 215) action claiming damages for losses caused to them by competition from subsidized German milk, poultry, and cattle products.

 EXERCISE 8.4 CWS

Read the first extract from *GAEC* in *Cases and Materials* (8.3.1.1). What problem did the farmers encounter in proving their claim in relation to the milk and poultry?

The Court of Justice held that in respect of sales of milk and poultry, actual damage was not proved because the farmers had produced no evidence of their losses. (The result of their claim for losses in respect of cattle products will be discussed at 8.7.)

Even where the applicant is able to prove its loss, the level of damages awarded may be less than the loss sustained if the applicant has been guilty of contributory negligence or has failed to mitigate its loss.

? **QUESTION** 8.2

From your own knowledge, can you attempt to explain, or give an example of, either of these principles?

These principles are both enshrined in English law. In the law of tort it has been established that a plaintiff who has contributed through his own negligence to the tort or to the resulting damage, may be expected to bear some or all of his own loss. For example, damages awarded to a plaintiff injured in a car accident may be reduced if it is shown that he contributed to the accident by driving too fast, or contributed to the resulting damage by failing to wear a seatbelt.

In both contract and tort, English law recognizes that a plaintiff should do his best to minimize the loss that he has suffered as a result of the tort or breach of contract. If he does not do so, then in effect he has brought some of his loss upon himself and should therefore bear a proportion of it. In the example given above, damages awarded in respect of lost earnings while the plaintiff is unable to undertake his normal work may be reduced if he fails to take reasonable alternative work.

The use of both principles in Community law is similar.

8.5.1 **Contributory negligence**

In the case of *Adams v Commission* (Case 145/83) [1985] ECR 3539, Adams had supplied the Commission with confidential information concerning breaches of Community competition law by his employer, Hoffman-La Roche. In the course of proceedings, the

Commission gave papers to Hoffman-La Roche which enabled it to identify Adams as the source of the leaked information. It then failed to warn Adams that Hoffman-La Roche was planning to prosecute him, and when Adams returned to Switzerland, he was arrested and convicted of industrial espionage under Swiss law.

The Court of Justice awarded damages for Adams's loss of earnings and loss of reputation as a result of his conviction and imprisonment, which the Court of Justice attributed to the Commission's wrongful actions in allowing Adams to be identified and in failing to warn him that his identity was known. However, the damages awarded were reduced by half as a result of Adams's contributory negligence.

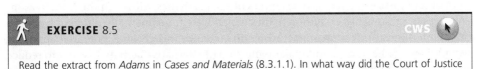

EXERCISE 8.5   CWS

Read the extract from *Adams* in *Cases and Materials* (8.3.1.1). In what way did the Court of Justice consider Adams to have been contributorily negligent? Do you agree with the Court of Justice on this?

The Court of Justice ruled that Adams had been contributorily negligent in failing to warn the Commission that he could be identified from the documents, in failing to ask that he be kept informed of progress in the case, particularly with regard to the use of the documents, and in returning to Switzerland without inquiring as to the current status of the proceedings and the use of the documentation. This decision appears to be rather harsh, both as to the existence and the level of the contributory negligence, but it is true to say that the Court of Justice has tended to be cautious in imposing liability on the Community.

8.5.2 Duty to mitigate any loss

Mulder v *Council and Commission (Mulder II)* (Cases C-104/89 & C-37/90) [1992] ECR I-3061, concerned a Council Regulation which allocated milk quotas (the amount of milk which a particular undertaking could produce without incurring a levy) to producers on the basis of the previous year's production. A number of producers, such as Mulder, had not produced any milk in the previous year as a result of a Community agreement aimed at reducing over-production. They were therefore disadvantaged by the terms of the Regulation. These producers had successfully applied for partial annulment of the measure under Article 230 (ex 173), for breach of their legitimate expectation that they would be able to resume milk production when the agreement came to an end *(Mulder* v *Minister van Landbouw en Visserij (Mulder I)* (Case 120/86) [1988] ECR 2321 and *Von Deetzen* v *Hauptzollampt Hamburg-Jonas* (Case 170/86) [1988] ECR 2355). They then claimed damages in respect of the period prior to the annulment. The Court of Justice upheld the complaint and awarded damages for loss of profit.

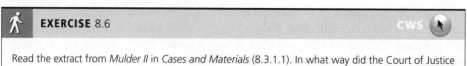

EXERCISE 8.6

Read the extract from *Mulder II* in *Cases and Materials* (8.3.1.1). In what way did the Court of Justice consider that the producers should have mitigated their loss?

The Court of Justice reduced the damages awarded by the amount of profit which the producers could reasonably have earned had they undertaken alternative activities. However, the Court of Justice failed to give examples of such activities. Although the word 'reasonably' would presumably exclude activities which were fundamentally different from the original business, such as manufacturing, no guidance was given. A potential applicant would therefore be wise to undertake some kind of alternative activity in order to reduce the actual loss, unless it is confident of proving that there is no possible alternative.

8.6 Wrongful act

In order to identify acts which may be classified as wrongful, we will examine three particular areas.

8.6.1 General legislative measures

The greatest number of applications for damages under Article 288 (ex 215) EC has been in respect of general legislative acts. As a result the Court of Justice appears to have attempted to stem the flow by applying a restrictive test as to what constitutes a 'wrongful act'. This test is commonly referred to as the *Schöppenstedt* or *Second Skimmed Milk Powder* test, after the cases in which it was respectively introduced and clarified.

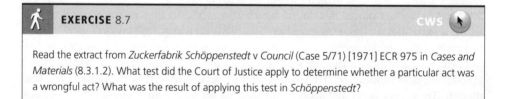

EXERCISE 8.7

Read the extract from *Zuckerfabrik Schöppenstedt* v *Council* (Case 5/71) [1971] ECR 975 in *Cases and Materials* (8.3.1.2). What test did the Court of Justice apply to determine whether a particular act was a wrongful act? What was the result of applying this test in *Schöppenstedt*?

In *Schöppenstedt*, a number of German sugar producers alleged that a Regulation imposing minimum and maximum prices for raw sugar was, in its detail, discriminatory. The Court of Justice refused to award damages on the ground that the Community could not incur liability for legislative action involving economic policy unless there had been:

(a) a sufficiently flagrant violation;

(b) of a superior rule of law;

(c) for the protection of the individual.

For this instance, the Court of Justice held that the alleged differences in the system were not discriminatory and therefore that there had not been a 'sufficiently flagrant violation' of the principle of non-discrimination.

The Court of Justice confirmed the *Schöppenstedt* test in *Bayerische HNL Vermehrungsbetriebe GmbH & Co KG and others* v *Council and Commission* (Cases 83 etc./76) [1978] ECR 1209, which is commonly referred to as the *Second Skimmed Milk Powder* case. In order to reduce Community milk stocks, a Regulation provided for the compulsory purchase of skimmed milk powder for use in animal feedstuffs. Poultry producers claimed damages against the Community for the increased price of animal feed. The Court of Justice had already accepted, in other cases, that the Regulation was void, because it discriminated between different agricultural sectors (against poultry producers for the benefit of the dairy industry) and was out of proportion to the achievement of a reduction in milk stocks.

 **QUESTION** 8.3

In the light of the *Schöppenstedt* test, do you think that the producers in the *Second Skimmed Milk Powder* case succeeded? Read the extract from the latter case in *Cases and Materials* (8.3.1.2) to see if your answer is correct.

The Court of Justice effectively repeated the *Schöppenstedt* test, substituting the words 'sufficiently serious breach' for 'sufficiently flagrant violation'. However, it refused to award damages to the producers on the grounds that it was essential for the Community to have a wide discretion in adopting economic legislation. The Community should not be hindered, in making economic policy, by the prospect of continual applications for damages.

The three elements of the *Schöppenstedt* test will now be examined in greater detail.

8.6.1.1 A sufficiently serious breach

 **QUESTION** 8.4

In the *Second Skimmed Milk Powder* case, the Court of Justice elaborated on the meaning of 'a sufficiently serious' breach. How did it do this?

The Court of Justice stated that the institution concerned must have 'manifestly and gravely disregarded the limits on the exercise of its powers'. In its application of this test to the facts, the Court of Justice indicated that both the unlawfulness of the act and the nature of its effect must be considered. In this case, the measure in question affected a wide range of traders, so that its impact on any particular undertaking was less evident; and the effect of the measure on the price of feed was relatively small in comparison to the price increases resulting from other factors. The effect of the action was therefore within the inherent economic risks of that business sector and the Community could not be said to have manifestly and gravely exceeded the limits on its powers.

Dumortier Frères SA and others v *Council and Commission* (Cases 64 & 113/76) [1979] ECR 3091 (*Cases and Materials* (8.3.1.2)) involved a Regulation under which production re-funds in respect of maize grits were abolished while those for maize starch were not. Both products were used in brewing and in baking, and were in direct competition with each other. The Court of Justice concluded that the Community had manifestly and gravely disregarded the limits on its powers by withdrawing refunds from the production of maize grits, but not from the production of maize starch, which was a competing product.

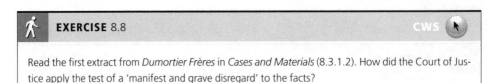

EXERCISE 8.8   CWS

Read the first extract from *Dumortier Frères* in *Cases and Materials* (8.3.1.2). How did the Court of Justice apply the test of a 'manifest and grave disregard' to the facts?

The Court of Justice ruled that the disregard of the principle of non-discrimination was manifest and grave because the damage went beyond the bounds of the inherent economic risks and the Council had ignored the advice of the Commission to re-introduce the refunds.

In *Mulder I* and *Von Deetzen* (see 8.4.1.1), the exclusion of certain producers from the milk quota system was held to be invalid. When a subsequent Regulation allocated to such producers quotas which were less generous than those given to other producers, this too was held to be invalid on the ground that it was discriminatory (*Spagl* v *Hauptzollamt Rosenheim* (Case C-189/89) [1990] ECR I-4539) and *Pastätter* v *Haupzollamt Bad Reichenhall* (Case C-217/89) [1990] ECR I-4585).

As outlined above, in *Mulder II*, the Court of Justice granted damages in respect of the original exclusion. However, it declined to do so in respect of the discriminatory quotas.

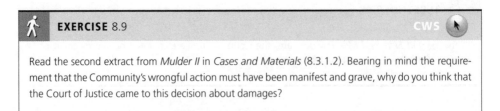

EXERCISE 8.9   CWS

Read the second extract from *Mulder II* in *Cases and Materials* (8.3.1.2). Bearing in mind the requirement that the Community's wrongful action must have been manifest and grave, why do you think that the Court of Justice came to this decision about damages?

In excluding the producers completely, the Commission had seriously breached the principles of non-discrimination and legitimate expectation but in simply granting them lower quotas than other producers, the infringement of those principles was not manifest or grave.

In *G. R. Amylum NV and Tunnel Refineries Limited* v *Council and Commission* (Cases 116 & 124/77) [1979] ECR 3497 and *Koninklijke Scholten Honig NV* v *Council and Commission* (Case 43/77) [1979] ECR 3583 (*Cases and Materials* (8.3.1.2)), a number of isoglucose producers brought actions for damages in respect of certain production levies on isoglucose which the Court of Justice, in *RSH and Tunnel Refineries* v *Commission and Council* (Joined Cases 103 & 145/77) [1978] ECR 2037 had ruled to be invalid. As outlined in 7.6.1, there were only three or four isoglucose producers in the Community, and other potential producers would not be in a position to enter the market for at least two years. The effect of the levies was clearly serious, given that one producer had been forced to close down its isoglucose business altogether.

? QUESTION 8.5 CWS

In the light of what you have read so far, what would you expect the decision of the Court of Justice to have been in this case? Read the extract from *Amylum* in *Cases and Materials* (8.3.1.2) to see if you were correct.

The Court of Justice refused to award damages, despite the factors referred to above. It stated that the Community would be liable only if its errors were so grave that its conduct could be said to be 'verging on the arbitrary' and this was not so in the present case. This appears to be an additional test, since the Community's wrongful act in this instance was both manifest and grave.

In *Roquette Frères SA* v *French Customs Administration* (Case 145/79) [1980] ECR 2917 the Court of Justice had declared invalid a Regulation which provided for compensation to be given, or levies imposed, on agricultural imports and exports, in order to compensate fully for the effect of exchange rate fluctuations. In *Roquette Frères* v *Commission* (Case 20/88) [1989] ECR 1553, Roquette Frères claimed damages for the effects of the Regulation.

? QUESTION 8.6 CWS

Read the extract from Case 20/88 *Roquette Frères* in Cases and Materials (8.3.1.2) Do you consider this to have been an appropriate case for an award of damages against the Community?

You might have concluded that if the case of the producers in *Amylum* was not considered to be sufficiently meritorious for an award of damages, then the case of these applicants would certainly not be. Indeed, despite its ruling that the Regulation was invalid, the Court of Justice refused to award damages to Roquette. It stated that the applicant's loss had been caused by the use of an incorrect basis for calculation but that this was merely a 'technical error' by the Commission, and did not amount to a manifest and grave disregard of its powers.

It can therefore be concluded that liability will exist only if the Community has obviously, and to a serious extent, disregarded the limits on its powers, as evidenced by effects on the producers which go substantially beyond the normal risks of the economic sector in question.

8.6.1.2 Of a superior rule of law

Superior rules of law have been taken to include those general principles of law discussed in **Chapters 3** and **7**.

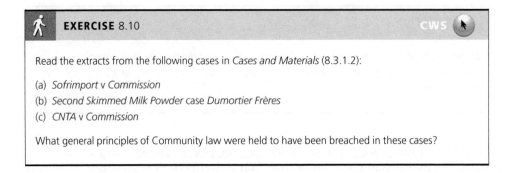

EXERCISE 8.10   CWS

Read the extracts from the following cases in *Cases and Materials* (8.3.1.2):

(a) *Sofrimport* v *Commission*
(b) *Second Skimmed Milk Powder* case *Dumortier Frères*
(c) *CNTA* v *Commission*

What general principles of Community law were held to have been breached in these cases?

In *Sofrimport* v *Commission* (see 7.3.5.2), which concerned the prohibition of import licences in respect of Chilean apples, the Court of Justice gave damages for breach of the legitimate expectation of importers that goods in transit would be protected against the sudden introduction of such a prohibition.

In the *Second Skimmed Milk Powder* case, the Court of Justice ruled that the Regulation requiring the compulsory purchase of Community stocks of skimmed milk powder was in breach (albeit not a flagrant breach) of the principle of non-discrimination and that it was 'impossible to disregard the importance of this prohibition on discrimination in the system of the Treaty'. In an Article 234 (ex 177) ruling concerning the same Regulation (*Bela-Mühle* v *Grows-Farm*, the *Skimmed Milk Powder* case (Case 114/76) [1977] ECR 1211), the Court of Justice had ruled that the measure was void not only because it was discriminatory, but also because it was out of all proportion to the end to be achieved.

In *Dumortier Frères* the Court of Justice ruled that the principle of equality 'occupies a particularly important place among the rules of Community law intended to protect the interests of the individual'.

In *CNTA* v *Commission* (Case 74/74) [1975] ECR 533 (*Cases and Materials* (8.3.1.2)), a Regulation abolished, without warning, compensation for the effect of exchange rate fluctuations on trade in colza and rape seeds. The Court of Justice awarded damages in respect of transactions which had already been entered into at the date of abolition of the compensation scheme, and for which export licences fixing the amount of compensation in advance had already been obtained. It stated that, in respect of such transactions, there was a legitimate expectation that the compensation would not be withdrawn.

EXERCISE 8.11

Read the extract in *Cases and Materials* (8.3.1.2) from 'Restitution or Damages: National Court or European Court?' concerning the meaning of 'legitimate expectation'.

In addition to these general principles, Treaty Articles will generally constitute superior rules of law, but this is not always the case. For example, in *Kind* v *EEC* (Case 106/81) [1982] ECR 2885, Kind alleged that a Community export levy on meat was in breach of Article 253 (ex 190), which required the reasons for a measure to be given. His claim for damages was rejected because a failure to state the reasons for a measure did not amount to a manifest and grave disregard of the limits on the Community's powers.

8.6.1.3 **For the protection of individuals**

Not only must the rule of law infringed be a superior one, it must also be for the protection of individuals. The case of *Kampffmeyer and others* v *Commission* (Cases 5, 7 & 13–24/66) [1967] ECR 245 involved similar facts to those of *Toepfer* (see 7.5.2). The Commission had upheld a wrongful refusal by Germany to allow the applicants to import maize at a time when large profits could be made because of the zero levy imposed by a Regulation.

 EXERCISE 8.12

Read the extract from *Kampffmeyer* in *Cases and Materials* (8.3.1.2). Did the Court of Justice consider the rule of law which had been breached (the free movement of goods) to be a rule of law for the protection of individuals?

In *Kampffmeyer*, the Regulation establishing levies on maize also provided that the Commission must investigate protective measures imposed by the Member States. The Court of Justice ruled that in failing to investigate fully, the Commission had infringed a rule of law which was for the protection of individuals. The fact that the interests protected were of a general nature (free trade, support for the relevant markets and the establishment of a single market), did not preclude their protection from being for the ultimate protection of individuals.

8.6.2 **Administrative acts**

Although the *Second Skimmed Milk Powder* test was expressed as applying only to general legislative acts of an economic nature, it may be that this reflected the fact that all Community legislation at that time was of an economic nature. Indeed, the only acts excluded from the test were administrative acts. As Community powers are extended beyond economic matters, it remains to be seen whether the test will be applied to general legislative measures other than those which involve choices of economic policy. In any event, it is clear that the test will not be applied to purely administrative measures.

? QUESTION 8.7

Where the act complained of is one to which the *Second Skimmed Milk Powder* test does not apply, such as an administrative measure, what must the applicant prove? (If you have difficulty in answering this question look back at 8.4.)

Where the act complained of is an administrative measure (and, possibly, where it is a general, but non-economic legislative measure), the applicant need prove only the general principles outlined in *Alfons Lütticke* v *Commission* (Case 4/69) [1971] ECR 325, namely damage, a wrongful act and causation. No further conditions attach to the nature of the wrongful act. In other words, it need not also amount to a sufficiently serious breach of a superior rule of law. The test is therefore more straightforward, and generally easier for an applicant to fulfil, than that applicable to general economic legislative measures.

This simpler test was applied in *Adams* (see 8.5.1), where the wrongful acts in question were not general legislative acts but the negligent acts of the Commission in revealing sensitive documents and failing to warn Adams. Adams therefore needed to prove only that the acts were wrongful, and not that they constituted a serious breach of a rule of law for the protection of individuals.

However, the Court of Justice has been as unwilling to impose liability on the Community for non-legislative acts, as it has been to impose liability for economic measures. In *Adams*, as we have seen, a wide definition of contributory negligence was applied so as to limit the liability of the Community.

An administrative issue was also considered in *Cato* v *Commission* (Case C-55/90) [1992] ECR I-2533 (*Cases and Materials* (8.3.1.2)). Cato had failed to qualify for compensation (in respect of a decommissioned fishing vessel) under a scheme which the UK had introduced pursuant to a Directive. He applied for damages under Article 288 (ex 215) on the basis that the UK scheme was in fact contrary to the Directive, and that the Commission had therefore not acted wrongfully in approving the scheme. The Court of Justice ruled that on the facts, the scheme did not contravene the Directive. The Court was therefore not obliged to address the possibility that Community approval of a **wrongful** implementing measure could in itself be wrongful, and render the Community liable in damages. However, it seems unlikely that the Court would find the Community liable in such circumstances. First, the Community has limited resources available for such supervision and secondly, the tendency of the Court of Justice is to encourage individuals to seek redress from the national authorities where Member State implementation is involved (see **Chapter 5**).

8.6.3 Acts by community servants

Article 288 (ex 215) provides that the Community must make good any damage caused, not only by its institutions, but also by its servants in the performance of their duties. Although the *Second Skimmed Milk Powder* test is inapplicable here, since individuals are not directly responsible for general legislative measures, the Court of Justice has adopted a strict approach to the causation element of the 'general principles' in order to limit the likelihood of the Community being liable. In *Sayag* v *Leduc* (Case 9/69) [1969] ECR 329, Leduc was injured in a road accident caused by a Euratom official, Sayag, who was driving his private car in performance of his official duties. Sayag alleged that any liability in damages lay with his employer, Euratom, rather than himself, under a provision of the Euratom Treaty which was equivalent to Article 288 (ex 215).

EXERCISE 8.13   CWS

Read the extract from *Sayag* in *Cases and Materials* (8.3.1.3). How did the Court of Justice interpret the words 'in the performance of his duties'?

The Court of Justice held that Euratom was not liable because the wrongful act by its servant had not been committed 'in the performance of his duties'. The Community could be liable only for acts of its servants which were a necessary extension of the tasks of its institutions. Therefore 'in the performance of his duties' in this context must be limited to occasions when the Community would be unable to fulfil its tasks unless Sayag used his private car. This test seems unduly restrictive and would fix liability on Euratom only in the event that no official car or public transport was available to Sayag to reach his destination, and that his doing so was essential to the work of the Community.

8.7 Causation

The applicant must prove that the wrongful act actually led to his loss. The Court of Justice will not simply assume causation after a wrongful act by the Community, and loss to the applicant, have been proved.

EXERCISE 8.14   CWS

Read the second extract from *GAEC* v *Council and Commission* in *Cases and Materials* (8.3.1.4). We have already seen (at 8.5 and *Cases and Materials* (8.3.1.1)) that the French farmers who brought this action failed to prove the extent of their damages in relation to milk and poultry. In relation to cattle products, they were able to prove their losses, but were still unable to recover damages. Why was this?

Although the French farmers in *GAEC* produced statistics to prove their losses in respect of beef and veal, they failed to show causation because there was evidence that French prices for these products had fallen prior to the German subsidy becoming effective.

The test is a strict one, as can be seen from *Dumortier Frères* (8.3.1.4).

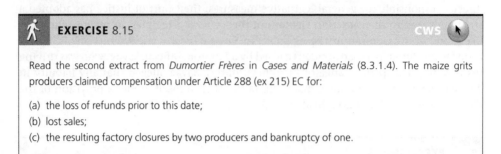

EXERCISE 8.15   CWS

Read the second extract from *Dumortier Frères* in *Cases and Materials* (8.3.1.4). The maize grits producers claimed compensation under Article 288 (ex 215) EC for:

(a) the loss of refunds prior to this date;
(b) lost sales;
(c) the resulting factory closures by two producers and bankruptcy of one.

In respect of which of these losses, if any, were damages awarded?

The Court of Justice ruled that damages should be awarded only in respect of the lost refunds. First, the reduction in sales could not be attributed to the withdrawal of the refunds, since the producers had not chosen to pass the loss of refunds on in increased prices. Secondly, even if the abolition of refunds had exacerbated the problems of certain producers, the factory closures and bankruptcy were not a sufficiently direct result of the abolition to render the Community liable. There was no obligation to make good every unfortunate consequence, however remote, of unlawful legislation.

It can be observed from this case that not only must causation be proved, but that causation must be sufficiently direct. A further illustration of this point is provided by *Kampffmeyer* v *Commission* (see 8.6.1.3), where the alleged damage had been caused by the Commission's approval of a German ban on maize importers.

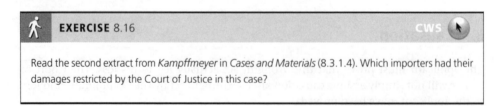

EXERCISE 8.16   CWS

Read the second extract from *Kampffmeyer* in *Cases and Materials* (8.3.1.4). Which importers had their damages restricted by the Court of Justice in this case?

Only those importers which had concluded contracts prior to the refusal of licences were awarded damages. Of these, those which had chosen to fulfil their contracts were awarded damages in respect of the higher levies which they had had to pay in order to do so. Those which had chosen to repudiate their contracts were awarded damages in respect of penalties payable for breach of contract.

> **? QUESTION 8.8**
>
> Those importers which had repudiated contracts also claimed damages for loss of expected profit. How did the Court of Justice treat this claim?

The Court of Justice ruled that the expected profit was of a purely speculative nature and therefore damages should be limited to an amount equivalent to 10% of the sums which the importers would have paid by way of levy if they had carried out the contracts.

8.8 The requirement of fault

The Court of Justice has never referred to proof of fault as a precondition for Community liability in damages. Although certain factors relevant to proving that the breach is 'sufficiently serious' may also be relevant to a finding of fault (for instance, the fact that the Commission's warning was not heeded in *Dumortier Frères*), it is not necessary to prove fault. For example, in *Biovilac* v *EEC* (Case 59/83) [1984] ECR 4057 (*Cases and Materials* (8.3.2)), Biovilac claimed damages on the ground, *inter alia*, of a lawful act which had resulted in a special sacrifice, thus giving rise to liability even in the absence of fault. The concept of special sacrifice was recognized by both French and German law, under which damages were payable where a lawful measure had adversely affected the applicant more seriously than other persons. Biovilac, a producer of piglet feedstuffs, claimed that it had been particularly harmed by the cheap sale of Community skimmed milk powder which was a competing feedstuff for piglets.

> **? QUESTION 8.9**
>
> What did the Court of Justice conclude in *Biovilac* v *EEC* about the requirement of fault?

The requirement of a 'sufficiently serious breach' is a lesser requirement than that of fault. In *Biovilac* the Court of Justice ruled that it would still be necessary to prove the existence of a 'sufficiently serious breach' even if no fault need be proved. Since the damage suffered by Biovilac was within the risks inherent in that business sector, the breach of law was not 'sufficiently serious' and the Court was not required to rule on whether fault need also be proved.

In *Dubois et Fils SA* v *Council and Commission* the Court of First Instance was required to consider whether the Community could be strictly liable for damage allegedly caused by the Single European Act or, in the alternative, liable for fault in taking particular measures to implement the SEA. As we saw at 8.4, the Court concluded that the Community could not incur liability for damage caused by Treaties, and therefore it did not have to rule on whether the Community could, in principle, be strictly liable. In addition, since the Court concluded that the measures taken by the Community to implement the SEA were not in breach of Community law, it was not required to rule on whether fault need have been proved.

8.9 The relationship between Article 288 EC and other actions

The success of an action under Article 288 (ex 215) EC is independent of any other action (for instance, under Articles 230, 234, or 241 (ex 173, 177, or 184) EC), so that the fact that there has been no other action or that such an action has been unsuccessful is irrelevant. Indeed, Article 233 (ex 176) specifically provides that where an act of an institution is annulled, the obligations imposed on that institution as a result do not affect any liability it might also incur in damages.

 In the case of *Krohn and Co. Import–Export (GmbH and Co. KG) v Commission* (Case 175/84) [1986] ECR 753 (*Cases and Materials* (8.3.3)), the Commission had authorized the German authorities to refuse to grant an import licence to Krohn for Thai manioc. Krohn brought an action for damages after it had become time barred from bringing an Article 230 (ex 173) action (see 7.3.7).

> **?** **QUESTION** 8.10 CWS
>
> In the light of the foregoing, do you think that Krohn was allowed to bring an action under Article 288 (ex 215) EC? Check your answer against the first extract in *Cases and Materials* (8.3.3).

The Court of Justice held that an action under Article 288 (ex 215) was admissible on the grounds that it was an independent action with a particular purpose. The fact that the time limit for an Article 230 (ex 173) action had passed, and that the measure had thereby become definitive, was irrelevant.

> **⚐** **EXERCISE** 8.17 CWS
>
> Read the second extract from Case 4/69 *Alfons Lütticke* in *Cases and Materials* (8.3.3). What did the Court of Justice say in that case about the relationship between Article 288 (ex 215) and other actions?

The Court of Justice stated that 'The action for damages provided for by . . . Article 288 (ex 215) was established by the Treaty as an independent form of action with a particular purpose to fulfil.'

Despite the fact that an Article 288 (ex 215) EC action is self-contained, it is common for a measure which is the subject of Article 288 (ex 215) EC proceedings to have been annulled under Article 230 (ex 173) EC or declared invalid under Article 234 (ex 177) EC. For example, the 'isoglucose cases' referred to above (see 8.6.1.1) had been preceded by an unsuccessful action under Article 230 (ex 173) EC and a successful action under Article 234 (ex 177) EC. In *Sofrimport* (see 7.3.2 and the second extract from that case in *Cases and Materials* (8.3.1.2)), the applicants successfully requested in the same action both the annulment of a Regulation and damages in respect of the losses caused to them.

8.10 **Concurrent liability**

Cases of potentially concurrent liability arise where a Community measure implemented by a Member State has adversely affected the applicant.

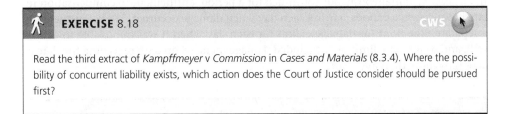

EXERCISE 8.18

CWS

Read the third extract of *Kampffmeyer* v *Commission* in *Cases and Materials* (8.3.4). Where the possibility of concurrent liability exists, which action does the Court of Justice consider should be pursued first?

In such instances, the Court of Justice has insisted that an action in the national courts, against the implementing measure itself, is pursued first. In the case of *Kampffmeyer*, the applicants challenged a refusal by the German authorities to grant import licences to them. The refusal to grant the licences had been authorised by the Commission.

The Court of Justice recognised the liability of the Community for these acts but ruled that the applicants must exhaust their rights of action against the national authorities before the Court of Justice would issue final judgment as to any Community liability in damages. In its reasoning, it stated that, 'It is necessary to avoid the applicants being insufficiently or excessively compensated for the same damage by the different assessment of two different courts applying different rules of law.'

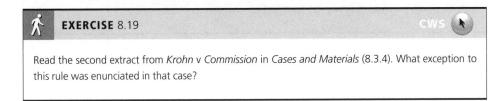

EXERCISE 8.19

CWS

Read the second extract from *Krohn* v *Commission* in *Cases and Materials* (8.3.4). What exception to this rule was enunciated in that case?

The general rule, that the national action should be pursued first, clearly applies only where the possibility of concurrent Member State liability exists. In addition, as the Court of Justice made clear in *Krohn*, it applies only where the rights of action against the national authorities will effectively compensate the applicant. Since the annulment by the German authorities of their decision to refuse Krohn an import licence would not adequately compensate it, the Court accepted that an action under Article 288 (ex 215) should not be made dependent on exhausting national remedies.

8.11 Time limits

Under Article 43 of the Statute of the Court of Justice, an applicant has five years from the event giving rise to the claim in which to bring an action. However this period does not start to run until the damage has materalized and will be suspended by any other Court of Justice proceedings.

In *Saint and Archer* v *Council and Commission* (Case T-554/93) [1997] 2 CMLR 527, a case involving similar facts to those of *Mulder I* and *II*, the Court ruled that where damage was not caused instantaneously but continued for a period, entitlement to compensation related to successive periods starting each day when damage occurred. There was therefore a separate time limit for damage claims for each day when it was impossible to deliver milk and so the time limit only excluded damage incurred on days preceding the date of action by more than five years.

 CONCLUSIONS

In order for the Community to be liable in damages, an applicant must at the very least prove that it has suffered loss and that this is due to a wrongful act by the Community. In addition, where the alleged wrongful act consists of a general legislative measure, the applicant must also prove that there has been a sufficiently serious breach of a superior rule of law for the protection of the individual. The Court of Justice has applied these tests strictly and as a result there has been no opening of the floodgates to Community liability. There are, of course, policy reasons behind Article 288 (ex 215) EC and the related jurisprudence. The Community institutions should not be hampered in their legislative activities by the threat of mass litigation and indeed the cost to the Community—and therefore ultimately to the citizens of the Member States—would be too great. Whether a correct balance has been achieved between policy decisions and providing justice for those affected by Community measures is a matter of opinion, but this question has assumed greater importance with the extension of Member State liability on principles similar to Article 288 (ex 215) EC (see also 5.5).

CHAPTER 8: ASSESSMENT EXERCISE   CWS

Critically discuss the development by the Court of Justice of the 'general principles' referred to in Article 288 (ex 215).

See *Cases and Materials* (8.5) for a specimen answer.

9 Free movement of goods

9.1 Objectives

By the end of this chapter you should be able to:

1 Explain the principle of free movement of goods and its significance within the Community internal market

2 Discuss and analyse the key Treaty provisions relating to the elimination of customs duties, charges having equivalent effect, discriminatory internal taxation, quantitative restrictions, and measures having equivalent effect

3 Discuss the nature and scope of the exceptions to the principle of free movement of goods

9.2 Introduction

Article 14 (ex 7a) EC underlines the importance of the principle of freedom of movement of goods as one of the four freedoms of the Community, defining the internal market as 'an area without internal frontiers in which the free movement of goods, persons, services and capital is ensured in accordance with the provisions of this Treaty'. This element of the internal market has as its objective the removal of all obstacles to the free circulation of goods between Member States.

Such obstacles can take a number of different forms, ranging from customs duties charged on goods as they cross internal frontiers to 'hidden barriers' to trade, which are more difficult to identify. This chapter will consider the nature of these obstacles to interstate trade, at the Treaty provisions designed to eliminate them and at the exceptions to the principle of free movement of goods.

9.3 Overview of the Community free movement provisions

9.3.1 The customs union

 EXERCISE 9.1

Turn back to Chapter 1. Write down the two essential features of a customs union.

In simple terms, a customs union consists of an agreement between countries to operate:

(a) a free trade area in which goods pass between them without restrictions, together with

(b) a system whereby a common level of duty is charged on goods coming into the free trade area from non-member countries.

In the European Community these are sometimes referred to, respectively, as the internal and external aspects of the customs union. Non-Member States are termed 'third countries'.

 EXERCISE 9.2 CWS

Read Article 23 (ex 9) EC in *Cases and Materials* (9.1.1) and write down answers to the following:

(a) What does Article 23 (ex 9) prohibit between Member States?
(b) What term is used for the common level of duty charged upon goods from third countries?

Article 23 (ex 9) sets out the Treaty definition of the Community customs union. Its internal aspect is the prohibition between Member States of 'customs duties on imports and exports and of all charges having equivalent effect'. This prohibition, which will be examined in detail in this chapter, applies to goods passing across any of the Community's internal borders.

When goods enter the Community from third countries, the Common Customs Tariff (known as the CCT) applies. The CCT, sometimes referred to as the Common External Tariff (CET), is governed by Articles 26 and 27 (ex 28 and 29) EC. These articles provide for the fixing of Common Customs Tariff duties by the Council, acting on a proposal from the Commission.

The Treaty makes no distinction between 'products' and 'goods'. When goods have passed into the Community from third countries, the necessary formalities have been complied with and the appropriate duties paid, those goods are allowed to move freely between Member States without any further restriction. Such goods, like goods which originate in the Community itself, are said to be in free circulation.

9.3.2 Application of the principle of free movement of goods

The principle of free movement of goods is one of the fundamental freedoms upon which the Community is founded. Any measure adopted by a Member State government, be it protectionist or not, which sets up a barrier to the free movement of goods will be condemned by the Court of Justice unless it falls within the scope of the exceptions provided for in the Treaty and in the case law of the Court. As will be seen later in this chapter, those exceptions are interpreted restrictively.

Although the Community comprises an internal market in which goods can circulate freely without restrictions, it is important to understand that Member States may seek to protect their own domestic products from competition from similar products crossing the Community's internal borders. A measure such as the imposition of a customs duty, which has the effect of raising the price of imported goods and making them less competitive, is protectionist if it is designed for that purpose. If a charge is imposed on imported goods for other reasons, that charge is not protectionist. A good example of a non-protectionist measure is the charge imposed on imported diamonds which was considered in *Sociaal Fonds voor de Diamantarbeiders* v *Chougol Diamond Co* (Cases 2 & 3/69) [1969] ECR 211 (*Cases and Materials* (9.1.2)). Here, as far as the Court of Justice was concerned, the distinction between protectionist and non-protectionist measures was irrelevant. The Court examined the effect of the measure on inter-state trade, not its purpose.

9.3.3 Outline of the Treaty Articles providing for the free movement of goods

Article 3(a) (*Cases and Materials* (9.1.3)) provides for the prohibition of customs duties and other kinds of charges and measures which restrict trade between Member States.

Article 14 (ex 7a) (*Cases and Materials* (9.1.3)) specifies the free movement of goods as an essential element of the internal market.

Articles 23–31 (ex 9–37), headed 'Free Movement of Goods', deal with the internal and external aspects of the customs union.

In addition, there are other provisions contained in the competition and taxation section of the Treaty (Articles 81–97 (ex 85–102) which are aimed at the elimination of measures restricting trade between Member States or threatening or distorting competition within the common market. Although the main competition rules (Articles 81 and 82 (ex 85 and 86)) are considered separately in **Chapters 11** and **12**, it should be noted that, together with the rules relating to free movement of goods, they constitute the means to achieve a unified Community internal market which functions efficiently and which allows the Community to compete effectively on a global scale.

The following Treaty Articles contain detailed rules concerning the free movement of goods:

(a) Article 25 (ex 12): the prohibition of customs duties and charges having equivalent effect to customs duties.

(b) Article 90 (ex 95): the prohibition of discriminatory taxation.

(c) Articles 28 and 29 (ex 30 and 31): the prohibition of quantitative restrictions and all measures having equivalent effect.

This chapter will consider in detail Articles 25, 90, 28, and 30 (ex 12, 95, 30, and 36).

9.4 Article 25 (ex 12): the prohibition of customs duties and charges having equivalent effect

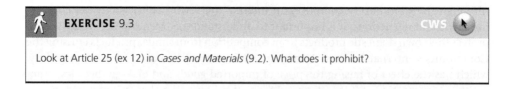

EXERCISE 9.3   CWS

Look at Article 25 (ex 12) in *Cases and Materials* (9.2). What does it prohibit?

Article 25 (ex 12) prohibits customs duties on imports and exports and charges having equivalent effect.

9.4.1 **Direct effect of Article 25 (ex 12)**

 EXERCISE 9.4

Turn back to Chapter 5 and remind yourself of the meaning of 'direct effect'. Write down the name of the case in which the Court of Justice established that Treaty Articles are capable of direct effect. Which Treaty Article did this case concern?

The Court first considered the direct effect of Treaty Articles in a case concerning Article 25 (ex 12) and the increase in a customs duty imposed by the Dutch authorities on imports of ureaformaldehyde. In *Van Gend en Loos* v *Nederlandse Administratie der Belastingen* (Case 26/62) [1963] ECR 1 (*Cases and Materials* (9.2.1)), not only did the Court establish that Treaty Articles are capable of direct effect, it also held that Article 25 (ex 12) itself is directly effective.

9.4.2 **Meaning of 'customs duties' and 'charges having equivalent effect'**

 QUESTION 9.3

How would you define a 'customs duty'? Glance back at Chapter 1 where the term is defined.

The term 'customs duty' combines two elements. First, it comprises a pecuniary charge on goods, which might be regarded as a 'tax' or a 'levy'. Secondly, that charge is imposed by reason of the fact that the goods cross a frontier.

A prohibition on customs duties alone would leave the way open for Member States to justify charges on imported goods which are not customs duties in the strict sense. Consequently, the Article 25 (ex 12) prohibition also encompasses charges of equivalent effect to customs duties. The way in which the Court of Justice has used the concept of 'charges having equivalent effect' (or, as they are commonly referred to, CEEs) to give broad scope to Article 25 (ex 12) is illustrated by the following two cases.

 EXERCISE 9.5   CWS

Consider *Commission* v *Luxembourg and Belgium (Gingerbread)* (Cases 2 & 3/62) [1962] ECR 425 in *Cases and Materials* (9.2.2) and *Sociaal Fonds voor de Diamantarbeiders* v *Chougol Diamond Co* (Cases 2 & 3/69) [1969] ECR 211 in *Cases and Materials* (9.1.2). In each case, what was the purpose of the charge imposed and how did the Court of Justice view the charge? Make a written note of your answers.

The *Gingerbread* case concerned the increase of a charge imposed by Luxembourg and Belgium on imports of gingerbread. The two governments claimed that the reason for the charge was to offset the effects on the price of domestically produced gingerbread of an internal tax on rye, one of the ingredients of gingerbread. The Court of Justice held that the purpose of Article 25 (ex 12) was to prohibit not only those measures which are clearly customs duties in the strict sense but also other measures, perhaps called by different names or with non-protectionist purposes, which nonetheless have a similar effect to customs duties. Such measures constitute CEEs. The charge on imported gingerbread resulted in the alteration of the price of the product, thereby reducing its competitiveness in the Luxembourg and Belgian markets and affecting trade between Member States. The Court of Justice reached similar conclusions in the *Sociaal Fonds* case. Here, a charge on diamonds imported into Belgium was held to be a CEE, despite the fact that the charge was not protectionist (Belgium did not produce diamonds) and was levied to provide social security benefits for Belgian diamond workers.

CEEs have been defined by the Court of Justice in similar terms in a number of cases. The definition in *Commission* v *Italy (Statistical Levy)* (Case 24/68) [1969] ECR 193 (*Cases and Materials* (9.2.2)) is typical:

any pecuniary charge, however small and whatever its designation and mode of application, which is imposed unilaterally on domestic or foreign goods by reason of the fact that they cross a frontier and which is not a customs duty in the strict sense constitutes a charge having equivalent effect . . . even if it is not imposed for the benefit of the State, is not discriminatory or protective in effect and if the product on which the charge is imposed is not in competition with any domestic product.

9.4.3 Charges for services rendered

Member States have frequently argued that charges imposed upon imported goods escape the Article 25 (ex 12) prohibition because they are levied for services rendered to the importer.

? QUESTION 9.4

What kinds of services might be relevant here?

The argument has been put forward in relation to a wide range of 'services', including, for instance, health and safety or quality control inspection services, a statistical service provided for importers and exporters and storage services.

The Court of Justice has made clear that a charge for services will fall outside the Article 25 (ex 12) prohibition only if those services are of direct benefit to the goods or traders and if the charge is proportionate to the services provided. The *Statistical Levy* case concerned a levy imposed by the Italian government on all imports and exports. The proceeds were used to compile statistics which, it was claimed, were of benefit to traders. The

Court of Justice held that any advantage gained by importers and exporters from the statistical information was so general and difficult to assess that the charge did not constitute consideration for 'a specific benefit actually conferred' and consequently comprised a CEE.

Similarly, in *Commission v Belgium (Customs Warehouses)* (Case 132/82) [1983] ECR 1649 (*Cases and Materials* (9.2.3)) concerning storage charges, it was established that when a charge is payable exclusively on imported products, it is a CEE unless it is 'the consideration for a service actually rendered to the importer'. Moreover, that charge must be 'of an amount commensurate with that service'—it must not exceed the cost of the service or the value to the trader of the service provided.

A number of cases have dealt with charges imposed in relation to health controls.

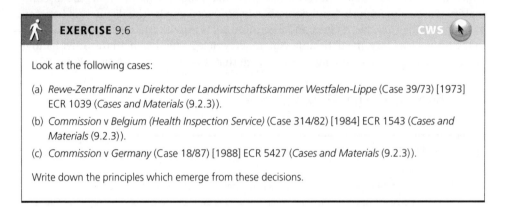

EXERCISE 9.6   CWS

Look at the following cases:

(a) *Rewe-Zentralfinanz v Direktor der Landwirtschaftskammer Westfalen-Lippe* (Case 39/73) [1973] ECR 1039 (*Cases and Materials* (9.2.3)).
(b) *Commission v Belgium (Health Inspection Service)* (Case 314/82) [1984] ECR 1543 (*Cases and Materials* (9.2.3)).
(c) *Commission v Germany* (Case 18/87) [1988] ECR 5427 (*Cases and Materials* (9.2.3)).

Write down the principles which emerge from these decisions.

In the first two judgments, the Court of Justice held that charges for inspections imposed in the 'general interest' (*Rewe*) and those which are expressly permitted under Community law (*Commission v Belgium*) do not, for those reasons alone, escape classification as CEEs.

However, charges for inspections which are mandatory under Community law are lawful, provided the charges do not exceed the cost of the inspection and the inspections themselves are obligatory and uniform for all the products concerned in the Community, are provided in the general interest of the Community and promote the free movement of goods (*Commission v Germany*). The principle that charges for inspections mandated by Community law are not CEEs was first established in *Bauhuis v Netherlands State* (Case 46/76) [1977] ECR 5. The same principle applies to charges for inspections which are mandatory under international agreements entered into by the Community (*Commission v Netherlands* (Case 89/76) [1977] ECR 1355).

9.5 Article 90 (ex 95): prohibition of discriminatory taxation

9.5.1 The scope of Article 90 (ex 95)

It has already been noted that customs duties and CEEs are charges imposed on goods by reason of the fact that they cross a frontier. Such charges are an obstacle to free movement because they increase the trader's costs. They also affect the competitive structure of the internal market by raising the price of products to the consumer. Similar effects may flow from the imposition of taxes on imported goods. The kinds of taxes referred to here are those which are levied by Member States not by reason of importation but as part of a system of internal taxation. They have been defined by the Court of Justice as charges relating to 'a general system of internal dues applied systematically and in accordance with the same criteria to domestic products and imported products alike': *Denkavit* v *France* (Case 132/78) [1979] ECR 1923 (*Cases and Materials* (9.3.1)).

Where a charge is classified as a genuine internal tax, rather than a customs duty or a CEE, Article 25 (ex 12) does not apply. Internal taxes fall within the scope of Article 90 (ex 95). This provision does not prevent Member States from setting up taxation systems which they consider suitable in relation to particular products but prohibits the discriminatory taxation of imported and domestically produced goods. The distinction between a charge having equivalent effect and a genuine tax is important. If a charge is classified in the former category, it will be unlawful under Article 25 (ex 12). If on the other hand it is a genuine tax, it will be permissible provided that it complies with Article 90 (ex 95).

9.5.2 The Article 90 (ex 95) prohibition

EXERCISE 9.7   CWS

Compare the two paragraphs of Article 90 (ex 95) in *Cases and Materials* (9.3.2). You will see that both relate to the imposition by a Member State of internal taxes on the products of other Member States. How do the provisions of the two paragraphs differ? Make a brief note of your answer.

The drafters of the Treaty were well aware that there is little point in eliminating crossfrontier charges if Member States are still able to obstruct interstate trade and reduce competition from imported products by means of discriminatory internal taxation. Under Article 90 (ex 95), internal taxation is discriminatory and therefore prohibited where:

(a) taxes imposed on imported goods exceed those levied on similar domestic products (first paragraph); or where

(b) taxes imposed on imported goods give indirect protection to other products (second paragraph).

Article 90 (ex 95) has been directly effective since 1 January 1962 (*Lütticke (Alfons) GmbH* v *Hauptzollamt Saarlouis* (Case 57/65) [1966] ECR 205 in *Cases and Materials* (9.3.2)).

9.5.3 Article 90(1) (ex 95(1)): the prohibition of discriminatory taxation of similar products

The first paragraph of Article 90 (ex 95) prohibits internal taxation of any kind on imports in excess of that imposed directly or indirectly on similar domestic products. In *Molkerei-*

Zentrale v *Hauptzollamt Paderborn* (Case 28/67) [1968] ECR 143 (*Cases and Materials* (9.3.3)) the Court of Justice indicated that the words 'directly or indirectly' must be widely construed to include taxes imposed on the domestic products at various stages of the manufacturing and marketing process.

In some cases, discrimination results not from different rates of taxation but from other connected factors, such as the rules relating to tax collection, or the basis of assessment. In *Commission* v *Ireland (Excise Payments)* (Case 55/79) [1980] ECR 481 (*Cases and Materials* (9.3.3)), national legislation imposing an equal rate of tax on imported and domestic goods was held to breach Article 90 (ex 95) because importers were required to pay immediately on importation whilst domestic producers were given more time for payment. *Outokumpu Oy* (Case C-213/96) [1998] ECR I-1777 concerned Finnish legislation which subjected domestically produced electricity to tax rates which varied according to the method of production but subjected imported electricity to a flat-rate tax. That rate was higher than the lowest tax charged on domestically produced electricity. The Court of Justice held that Article 90 (ex 95) does not preclude the rate of an internal tax on electricity from varying according to the way in which the electricity is produced, on the basis of environmental considerations. However, Article 90 (ex 95) is infringed where the taxation of the imported product and that on the similar domestic product are calculated in a different manner and on the basis of different criteria which lead, if only in certain cases, to higher taxation being imposed on the imported product.

Tax measures which openly treat domestic goods and imports differently are directly discriminatory. Because this form of discrimination is easily identifiable, Member States are generally careful to avoid it, though some cases of direct discrimination have reached the Court of Justice. A good example is to be found in *Lütticke (Alfons) GmbH* v *Hauptzollamt Saarlouis.*

A taxation system which appears neutral but has the effect of discriminating against imported products is indirectly discriminatory. *Humblot* v *Directeur des Services Fiscaux* (Case 112/84) [1985] ECR 1367 (*Cases and Materials* (9.3.3)) concerned a French two-tier system of annual car taxation which did not directly discriminate between imported and domestically produced vehicles. However, because France did not produce high powered cars falling into the higher tax category, the effect of the tax system was to place imported cars at a competitive disadvantage.

Certain cases involving allegations of indirectly discriminatory taxation seem to suggest that such discrimination is capable of objective justification, thus falling outside the scope of Article 90 (ex 95).

? **QUESTION** 9.5   CWS

How did the respective governments seek to justify the allegedly indirectly discriminatory taxation considered by the Court of Justice in *Commission* v *France* (Case 196/85) [1987] ECR 1597 in *Cases and Materials* (9.3.3) and *Chemial Farmaceutici SpA* v *DAF SpA* (Case 140/79) [1981] ECR 1 in *Cases and Materials* (9.3.3)?

The French government sought to justify the scheme of taxation of wines on the basis of its regional policy, designed to encourage production in poor growing areas. In *Chemial Farmaceutici,* the Italian government maintained that the higher taxation of synthetic alcohol constituted a 'legitimate choice of economic policy' aimed to encourage production of alcohol by fermentation rather than from ethylene, a raw material which, it was said, should be reserved for more important economic uses.

Although in both cases the Court of Justice rejected allegations that the effect of the taxation systems was to favour the domestic products over imports, the judgments suggest a willingness to allow legitimate policy objectives, which are compatible with Community aims, to preclude too strict an application of Article 90 (ex 95).

This point was further illustrated in *Commission* v *Greece* (Case C-132/88) [1990] ECR I-421/97, in which the Court of Justice considered an environmental justification for a car taxation system providing for differential rates of taxation according to power rating. Here, the Court held that such a taxation system would escape the Article 90 prohibition, notwithstanding that all cars in the highest tax band were imported, provided that no discriminatory effect disadvantaging imports could be established.

Since the first paragraph of Article 90 (ex 95) applies to 'similar' products, the issue of similarity between non-identical products which are subject to different rates of taxation has been the focus of much of the caselaw. This issue was prominent in a series of cases concerning alcoholic beverages. Here, the Commission challenged taxation regulations which, it alleged, favoured domestic alcoholic products. In these, as in other cases, Member States sought to defend their taxation systems by arguing that the products concerned were not sufficiently similar to bring the first paragraph of Article 90 (ex 95) into play.

? **QUESTION** 9.6   CWS

What factors were examined by the Court of Justice in *John Walker* v *Ministeriet for Skatter* (Case 243/84) [1986] ECR 875 when it was considering the question of product similarity? See *Cases and Materials* (9.3.3).

The Court of Justice has emphasized that the term 'similar products' should be interpreted widely to encompass similar characteristics and comparable use. In *Commission* v *France (French Taxation of Spirits)* (Case 168/78) [1980] ECR 347 the Court concluded that non-fruit spirits (whisky, gin, and vodka) were similar products to fruit spirits (brandy, armagnac, and calvados) because they 'have similar characteristics and meet the same needs from the point of view of consumers'. By contrast, in *John Walker,* following an examination of methods of production, alcohol content and consumer perception, liqueur fruit wine and whisky were held not to be similar products.

9.5.4 Article 90(2) (ex 95(2)): prohibition of taxation affording indirect protection to other products

As has been seen, the first paragraph of Article 90 (ex 95) prohibits the unequal taxation of similar products. The second paragraph of Article 90 (ex 95) prohibits internal taxation giving indirect protection to domestic products which, though they are not similar to the imported products, are nevertheless in competition with them.

The Court of Justice's approach to the distinction between the two paragraphs of Article 90 (ex 95) can be traced through the series of alcohol cases referred to above. In the earlier judgments, the Court of Justice did not distinguish between the two paragraphs at all and treated the concepts of 'similar' and 'competing' products as interchangeable.

? **QUESTION** 9.7

What do you think was the problem with this approach?

The problem with the Court of Justice's approach was that it concealed the distinction between the different effects of breaches of the two paragraphs of Article 90 (ex 95). If goods are similar, Member States are required to equalize taxation. If they are merely in competition, Member States are only required to remove the competitive effect of the tax regulation.

In one particularly difficult case (*Commission* v *United Kingdom (Excise Duties on Wine)* (Case 170/78) [1980] ECR 417, [1983] ECR 2265 in *Cases and Materials* (9.3.4)) concerning the differential taxation of wine and beer, the nature of the products led the Court of Justice to treat the two paragraphs separately. Wine and beer were clearly not similar within the terms of the first paragraph. Consequently, in order to establish a breach of Article 90 (ex 95), the Commission had the task of convincing the Court that the products were in competition with each other and that the higher tax on wine afforded indirect protection to United Kingdom beer producers, in contravention of the second paragraph.

On hearing the case for the first time, the Court of Justice declined to give a ruling and requested further information from the parties on the nature of the two products. Judgment was finally delivered three years later. After studying the Commission's detailed evidence and examining in particular the competitive relationship between beer and the cheaper varieties of wine, the Court decided that the two products were in competition. In reaching this conclusion, it considered not only current consumer preferences and purchasing habits but also possible future market developments which might place wine and beer in direct competition with each other. The Court emphasized that taxation policy must not be allowed to 'crystallize' consumer habits by taxing one product more heavily than another. Being also satisfied that the taxation system favoured the domestic product, the Court ruled that there was a breach of the second paragraph of Article 90 (ex 95).

9.6 Harmonization of taxation

The problems arising from discriminatory taxation could be solved by the harmonization of taxation between Member States. Although progress has been made in relation to the approximation of VAT, excise duty, and corporation tax regulation, Member States remain reluctant to cede power to the Community in an area which symbolizes national sovereignty.

9.7 Articles 28 and 29: the prohibition of quantitative restrictions and all measures having equivalent effect

So far barriers to trade of a pecuniary nature have been considered—customs duties, charges having equivalent effect and discriminatory taxes—which are comparatively easy to identify. There are other kinds of obstacles to the free movement of goods within the Community, often described as 'hidden' or 'non-tariff' barriers to trade, which are non-pecuniary in nature. These comprise physical and technical barriers to the free flow of goods between Member States. Articles 28 and 29 are aimed at the elimination of such barriers. This section will consider the most important of these provisions, Article 28 (ex 30).

EXERCISE 9.8   CWS

Read Articles 28 and 29 (ex 30 and 34) in *Cases and Materials* (9.4). What does Article 28 (ex 30) prohibit? Write down your answer.

Article 28 (ex 30) concerns restrictions on imports. It prohibits two kinds of barrier to trade:

(a) quantitative restrictions and

(b) all measures having equivalent effect.

The similar prohibition in Article 29 (ex 34) relates to exports.

Although Article 28 (ex 30) is addressed to Member States the Court of Justice has applied the Article widely to include measures adopted by public and semi-public bodies, such as the Royal Pharmaceutical Society (*R* v *Royal Pharmaceutical Society of Great Britain* (Cases 266 and 267/87) [1989] ECR 1295 in *Cases and Materials* (9.4)) which have powers conferred on them by national legislation. Article 28 covers not only measures applied by a Member State to the whole of its territory, but also those applying to only part of its territory. This was confirmed by the Court of Justice in *Ditlev Bluhme* (Case C-67/97 [1998] ECR 1–8033). Here it was held that a Danish prohibition on the keeping on the Danish island of Læsø of any species of bee other than the Læsø brown bee, effectively prohibiting the importation of other kinds of bee, constituted a measure having equivalent effect to a quantitative restriction.

One further key provision which should be mentioned at this point is Article 30 (ex 36). This article allows national laws to restrict the free movement of goods on certain specified grounds. The Article 30 (ex 36) grounds of derogation from Articles 28 and 29 (ex 30 and 34) will be considered later in this chapter.

9.7.1 Quantitative restrictions on imports: Article 28 (ex 30)

Quantitative restrictions are measures which limit the import (or indeed the export) of goods by reference to amount or value.

> **? QUESTION** 9.8
>
> What form do you think a quantitative restriction might take?

Quantitative restrictions can take different forms but are generally easily recognized. They have been defined by the Court of Justice as 'measures which amount to a total or partial restraint of . . . imports, exports, or goods in transit' (*Geddo* v *Ente Nazionale Risi* (Case 2/73) [1973] ECR 865). Thus, they clearly include quotas and bans. In *R* v *Henn and Darby* (Case 34/79) [1979] ECR 3795 (*Cases and Materials* (9.4.1)), a ban on the import of pornographic materials was held to amount to a quantitative restriction under Article 28 (ex 30). Quotas are limitations on imports or exports by quantity. They are sometimes concealed behind a licensing system under which certain importers are permitted to import a specified quantity of a product, determined according to value, weight or another quantitative criterion.

9.7.2 Meaning of 'measures having equivalent effect to quantitative restrictions' on imports: Directive 70/50

The notion of measures having equivalent effect to quantitative restrictions has proved both more complex and more difficult to define than that of quantitative restrictions. Some guidance on the meaning of 'measures having equivalent effect to quantitative restrictions' (referred to in the rest of this chapter as MEQRs) is provided by secondary legislation, in the form of Directive 70/50.

Although Directive 70/50 was a transitional measure and is therefore no longer formally applicable, it indicates the Commission's view of the scope of MEQRs. The Directive divides MEQRs into two groups, 'distinctly' and 'indistinctly' applicable measures. It also gives examples of the kinds of measures which constitute MEQRs.

> ## EXERCISE 9.9
>
>
>
> Consider Article 2, paragraph 1 and Article 3 of Directive 70/50 in *Cases and Materials* (9.4.2). What is the difference between the kinds of measures covered by the respective provisions as far as their *applicability to domestic and imported products* is concerned? Answer the question by completing the following:
>
> Article 2(1) covers measures other than those applicable . . .
>
> By contrast, Article 3 covers measures which are . . .

Directive 70/50 refers to a distinction which is important to an understanding of some of the case law on Article 28 (ex 30) which is considered later. The distinction is between:

(a) measures other than those applicable equally to domestic or imported products (Article 2(1)); and

(b) measures which are equally applicable to domestic and imported products (Article 3).

The two terms which are commonly used for these two categories of measures are 'distinctly applicable' (measures which do not apply equally to domestic and imported products) and 'indistinctly applicable' (measures which apply equally to domestic and imported products).

Article 2 of the Directive covers distinctly applicable measures which 'hinder imports which could otherwise take place, including measures which make importation more difficult or costly than the disposal of the domestic product' and provides an extensive non-exhaustive list of examples of such measures. For instance, Article 2(3)(b) (*Cases and Materials* (9.4.2)) refers to measures which 'lay down less favourable prices for imported products than for domestic products' and Article 2(3)(m) to measures which 'prohibit or limit publicity in respect of imported products only, or totally or partially confine publicity to domestic products only'.

Article 3 of Directive 70/50 covers indistinctly applicable measures concerning the marketing of products, in particular those which deal with 'shape, size, weight, composition, presentation, identification or putting up'. Although indistinctly applicable measures appear not to discriminate against imports because they apply equally to imported and domestic products, they frequently have discriminatory effects. For example, a Belgian requirement that all margarine for retail sale be in cube-shaped form or cube-shaped packaging did not overtly discriminate against imported margarine but was discriminatory in effect. In practice, imports of the product would become more costly since importing producers would be obliged to adapt their packaging processes in order to comply

with requirements which were not imposed upon them by their own national legislation (*Walter Rau Lebensmittelwerke* v *de Smedt PvbA* (Case 261/81) [1982] ECR 3961 in *Cases and Materials* (9.4.2)).

Article 3 of Directive 70/50 does however provide that the measures within its scope contravene Article 28 (ex 30) only 'where the restrictive effect of such measures on the free movement of goods exceeds the effects intrinsic to trade rules', that is 'where the restrictive effects on the free movement of goods are out of proportion to their purpose' or where 'the same objective can be attained by other means which are less of a hindrance to trade'. In other words, the measures are lawful provided they satisfy the principle of proportionality.

? QUESTION 9.9

Do you remember the meaning of 'proportionality'? Look back at Chapter 3 to refresh your memory. Write down the meaning of the term in one sentence.

The principle of proportionality is one of the general principles of Community law. To satisfy the proportionality principle, a measure must be suitable for the purpose of achieving the desired objective and go no further than is necessary to achieve that objective.

9.7.3 Meaning of 'measures having equivalent effect to quantitative restrictions' on imports: the *Dassonville* formula

The Court of Justice, whilst it has occasionally referred to Directive 70/50 in considering whether a particular measure constitutes an MEQR, introduced its own definition in *Procureur du Roi* v *Dassonville* (Case 8/74) [1974] ECR 837 (*Cases and Materials* (9.4.3)). This is known as the *'Dassonville* formula' and provides that:

All trading rules enacted by Member States which are capable of hindering, directly or indirectly, actually or potentially, intra-Community trade are to be considered as measures having an effect equivalent to quantitative restrictions.

The scope of the formula is wide, since it covers those measures which, although they do not actually hinder trade between Member States, are capable of doing so. Unlike Directive 70/50, the formula does not distinguish between distinctly and indistinctly applicable measures but is concerned with the restrictive effects of a measure on inter-state trade rather than its form. However, in *Dassonville*, the Court did accept that 'reasonable' restraints may not be caught by Article 28 (ex 30). The further development of what has become known as the 'rule of reason' will be considered presently.

9.7.4 Examples of distinctly applicable measures caught by Article 28 (ex 30)

The following cases provide examples of distinctly applicable measures which have been found by the Court of Justice to fall within Article 28 (ex 30).

EXERCISE 9.10   CWS

Look at the cases listed below. For each case, write down a short phrase which describes the relevant measure.

(a) *Rewe-Zentralfinanz* v *Landwirtschaftskammer Bonn* (Case 4/75) [1975] ECR 843 (*Cases and Materials* (9.4.4)).

(b) *Procureur du Roi* v *Dassonville* (Case 8/74) [1974] ECR 837 (*Cases and Materials* (9.4.3)).

(c) *Commission* v *Ireland* ('*Buy Irish*' Campaign) (Case 249/81) [1982] ECR 4005 (*Cases and Materials* (9.4.4)).

You may have written down something like this:

(a) Plant health inspections applied by the West German authorities to imported but not domestically produced apples (note that the Court of Justice held the inspections to be justified in principle on health grounds under Article 30 (ex 36), considered below).

(b) A Belgian rule requiring the production of certificates of origin for imported Scotch whisky.

(c) The introduction by the Irish government of a 'Buy Irish' campaign in order to promote Irish products to the disadvantage of imports. Similarly, the awarding of a 'quality label' by a German public body to finished products of a certain quality produced in Germany constituted an infringement of Article 28. The Court of Justice held that a label of this kind, which was designed to promote the distribution of agricultural and food products made in Germany and which indicated the German origin of the products to which it was attached, was likely to encourage consumers to buy products carrying the label in preference to imported products. Thus, even though its use was optional, the label was, at least potentially, a hindrance to the free movement of goods. (*Commission* v *Germany* (Case C-325/00) [2002] ECR 1-9977).

9.7.5 Examples of indistinctly applicable measures caught by Article 28 (ex 30)

The following cases provide examples of indistinctly applicable measures which have been found by the Court of Justice to fall within Article 28 (ex 30).

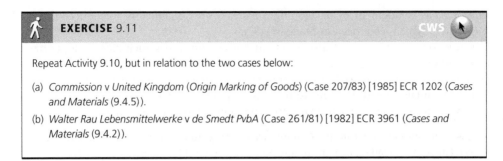

EXERCISE 9.11

Repeat Activity 9.10, but in relation to the two cases below:

(a) *Commission v United Kingdom* (*Origin Marking of Goods*) (Case 207/83) [1985] ECR 1202 (*Cases and Materials* (9.4.5)).

(b) *Walter Rau Lebensmittelwerke v de Smedt PvbA* (Case 261/81) [1982] ECR 3961 (*Cases and Materials* (9.4.2)).

You may have written down something like this:

(a) A UK requirement that certain goods offered for retail sale in the UK be marked with their country of origin.

(b) A Belgian law requiring margarine for retail sale to be in cube-shaped form or packaging.

9.7.6 Obligation of Member States to ensure free movement of goods

In *Commission v France* (Case C-265/95) [1997] ECR 1–6959, the Court of Justice held that Articles 28 (ex 30) and 10 (ex 5) require Member States to take all necessary and appropriate measures to ensure free movement of goods within their territory. Here, it was not disputed that the violent acts of individuals in France against imported agricultural products, such as the interception of lorries and destruction of loads, created obstacles to free movement. The Court found that the French government had failed to adopt adequate measures to prevent such acts. More recently, in *Schmidberger v Austria* (Case C-112/00), judgment of 12 June 2003, the Court of Justice held that the Austrian authorities' decision to permit a demonstration by environmental protesters, causing a 30-hour motorway closure, was an obstacle to free movement but was justified on the grounds of the ECHR fundamental rights to freedom of expression and assembly. However, the judgment is unclear as to whether these grounds are to be regarded as falling within the Article 30 derogations or the *Cassis* mandatory requirements, discussed below.

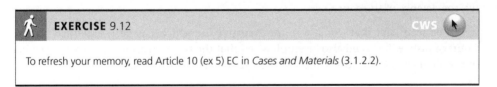

EXERCISE 9.12

To refresh your memory, read Article 10 (ex 5) EC in *Cases and Materials* (3.1.2.2).

9.7.7 *Cassis de Dijon*: the two *Cassis* principles

Rewe-Zentral AG v Bundesmonopolverwaltung für Branntwein (Case 120/78) [1979] ECR 649 (*Cases and Materials* (9.4.6)), otherwise known as *Cassis de Dijon* (because it concerned the blackcurrant liqueur 'cassis'), marks a very important stage in the development of the Court of Justice's jurisprudence on the free movement of goods. The decision builds upon the *Dassonville* judgment by developing the idea of 'reasonableness' introduced in that case and to which reference was made in 9.7.3.

Cassis concerned German legislation requiring certain spirits, including cassis, to have a minimum alcohol content of 25%. French cassis had an alcoholic strength of 15–20% and was thus effectively excluded from the German market. The applicant claimed that the German law constituted a measure having equivalent effect to a quantitative restriction and thus infringed Article 28 (ex 30). The Court of Justice stated that:

Obstacles to movement within the Community resulting from disparities between the national laws relating to the marketing of the products in question must be accepted in so far as those provisions may be recognised as being necessary in order to satisfy mandatory requirements relating in particular to the effectiveness of fiscal supervision, the protection of public health, the fairness of commercial transactions and the defence of the consumer.

This is the first *Cassis* principle, known as the 'rule of reason'. A paraphrase might help you to remember this important principle:

when the 'rule of reason' is applied, certain measures within the *Dassonville* formula will not contravene Article 28 (ex 30) if they are necessary to protect 'mandatory requirements'.

Although the *Cassis* judgment does not state this in so many words, later case law indicates that the rule of reason applies only to measures which are formally non-discriminatory, in other words to indistinctly applicable measures. Distinctly applicable measures cannot be justified by mandatory requirements, though they may be considered under one of the derogations contained in Article 30 (ex 36) (to be considered presently). In *Commission v Ireland (Restrictions on Importation of Souvenirs)* (Case 113/80) [1981] ECR 1625 (*Cases and Materials* (9.4.6)) the Court of Justice refused to apply *Cassis* principles to a measure adopted by the Irish government allegedly in the interests of fair trading and to protect consumers, which required imported souvenirs to be marked 'foreign' or with their country of origin.

You should note the guidance given by the Court as to the meaning of 'mandatory requirements':

(a) the effectiveness of fiscal supervision;

(b) the protection of public health;

(c) the fairness of commercial transactions; and

(d) the defence of the consumer.

It will be seen later that this is a non-exhaustive list which has been extended by the Court of Justice. It should also be emphasized that the rule of reason can only be applied in the absence of Community rules governing the interest concerned.

? **QUESTION** 9.10 CWS

How did the German government seek to justify its law on alcohol content in *Cassis de Dijon*? See *Cases and Materials* (9.4.6).

The German government argued that the measure was adopted in order to protect public health (low-alcohol spirits create a tolerance to alcohol and cause alcoholism) and the fairness of commercial transactions (the high rate of tax on high-alcohol drinks gave low-alcohol drinks a competitive advantage). The Court was unconvinced. Moreover, although the restriction allegedly fell within the mandatory requirements relating to public health and the fairness of commercial transactions, the German measure was not **necessary** to satisfy those requirements.

? **QUESTION** 9.11

What other means could the German government have used to achieve its stated objectives in relation to alcohol levels?

The government could have used other means which were less of a hindrance to trade, such as a requirement that products be labelled to indicate origin and alcohol content. You have no doubt recognized the use of the word 'necessary' (meaning in this context 'no more than is necessary') as a reiteration of the proportionality principle. The rule of reason requires that indistinctly applicable measures adopted to satisfy mandatory requirements be proportionate. For illustrations of the proportionality principle in this context, look at *Walter Rau Lebensmittelwerke* v *de Smedt PvbA* (Case 261/81) [1982] ECR 3961 (*Cases and Materials* (9.4.2)) and *Commission* v *Denmark (Disposable Beer Cans)* (Case 302/86) [1988] ECR 4607 (*Cases and Materials* (9.4.6)).

The *Cassis* judgment established a further principle, known as the principle of 'mutual recognition': where goods have been lawfully produced and marketed in one Member State there is no reason why they should not be introduced into another Member State. The principle operates as a presumption which, because of the importance of the principle of free movement of goods, is not easily displaced. The presumption will be displaced if it can be shown that restrictive measures are necessary to satisfy mandatory requirements. For an illustration of the application of the principle of mutual recognition, look at *Criminal proceedings against Karl Prantl* (Case 16/83) [1984] ECR 1299 (*Cases and Materials* (9.4.6)).

9.7.8 Extension of the mandatory requirements

There have been many cases in which Member States have sought to rely on the *Cassis* rule of reason. Some of these have concerned specifically the mandatory requirements set out in the *Cassis* judgment, for instance *Italian State* v *Gilli and Andres* (Case 788/79) [1980] ECR 2071 in which Italy argued that its prohibition on the sale of vinegar not produced from wine was justified on grounds of public health and the protection of the consumer. In other cases, the Court of Justice has extended the mandatory requirements beyond the four matters mentioned in *Cassis*.

> **EXERCISE** 9.13   CWS
>
> Consider the following cases and make a list of the further mandatory requirements which the Court of Justice has added to those set out in *Cassis*:
>
> (a) *Commission* v *Denmark (Disposable Beer Cans)* (Case 302/86) [1988] ECR 4607 (*Cases and Materials* (9.4.6)).
>
> (b) *Oebel* (Case 155/80) [1981] ECR 1993 (*Cases and Materials* (9.4.7)).
>
> (c) *Cinéthèque SA* v *Fédération Nationale des Cinémas Françaises* (Cases 60 & 61/84) [1985] ECR 2605 (*Cases and Materials* (9.4.7)).
>
> (d) *Torfaen Borough Council* v *B & Q plc* (Case 145/88) [1989] ECR 3851 (*Cases and Materials* (9.4.7)).

The list of mandatory requirements in *Cassis* is non-exhaustive and has been extended by the Court of Justice to include environmental protection (*Commission* v *Denmark (Disposable Beer Cans)*), legitimate interests of social and economic policy (*Oebel*), the creation of cinematographic works (*Cinéthèque*) and 'national and regional sociocultural characteristics' (*Torfaen Borough Council*).

In *Vereinigte Familiapress Zeitungsverlags- und Vertriebs GmbH* v *Heinrich Bauer Verlag* (Case C-368/95) [1997] ECR I-3689, the Court of Justice indicated that the maintenance of press diversity may constitute an 'overriding requirement' justifying a restriction on the free movement of goods. The reference from the Austrian court concerned national legislation prohibiting publishers from including prize competitions in their magazines. The Austrian government claimed that the measure was aimed to protect small publishers whose commercial survival was threatened because they could not afford to compete with large publishers offering big prizes. The Court held that, assuming that there was indeed a competitive relationship of this kind between small and large publishers, such a prohibition would not breach Article 28 (ex 30) provided that it was proportionate to the maintenance of press diversity and that that objective could not be achieved by less restrictive means.

9.7.9 Judicial developments on indistinctly applicable measures

Developments in the case law on Article 28 (ex 30) indicate growing consciousness of a distinction between:

(a) those indistinctly applicable measures which hinder, directly or indirectly, actually or potentially, trade between Member States within the meaning of *Dassonville*; and

(b) those indistinctly applicable measures which have an effect on the overall volume of trade because they are restrictive or regulatory but which are neither intended to be protectionist nor affect imports any more than they affect domestic products.

In *Criminal proceedings against Keck and Mithouard* (Cases C-267 & 268/91) [1993] ECR I-6097 (*Cases and Materials* (9.4.8)) the Court of Justice considered a measure falling into the latter category, a French law prohibiting the resale of goods at a loss. Whilst the Court recognized that the provision restricted the overall volume of sales and hence the volume of sales of products from other Member States, it declared that national measures affecting imports and restricting or prohibiting certain selling arrangements do not fall within the *Dassonville* formula 'provided that those provisions apply to all affected traders operating within the national territory and provided that they affect in the same manner, in law and in fact, the marketing of domestic products and of those from other Member States'. Where these conditions are satisfied, declared the Court, such provisions do not impede market access for imported products any more than for domestic products. Consequently such measures fall outside the scope of Article 28 (ex 30) altogether.

The Court indicated in *Keck* that its judgment was aimed at traders who invoke Article 28 (ex 30) to challenge national rules which restrict their commercial freedom. Good examples of challenges of this kind are to be found in the series of 'Sunday trading' cases (see, for instance, *Torfaen Borough Council* v *B & Q plc* (Case 145/88) [1990] 2 QB 19 in *Cases and Materials* (9.4.7)) in which traders in the UK claimed that the Sunday trading laws were incompatible with Article 28 (ex 30). Here, the Court of Justice applied the *Cassis* rule of reason and, in *Stoke-on-Trent Council* v *B & Q* (Case 169/91) [1992] ECR 1–6635 (*Cases and Materials* (9.4.8)), found that the legislation was not only justified on the basis of 'national or regional socio-cultural characteristics' (as it had done in earlier judgments) but was also proportionate.

It should be noted that the *Keck* judgment refers to restrictions relating to 'selling arrangements' (rather than rules concerning the goods themselves—packaging, content, labelling) which apply to all traders in the national territory and which affect in the same manner, in law and in fact, both imported and domestic products.

 EXERCISE 9.14   CWS

Read the extract from *Criminal proceedings against Tankstation 't Heukske vof and J.B.E Boermans* (Joined Cases C-401/92 & C-402/92) [1994] ECR I-2199 in *Cases and Materials* (9.4.8). What was the view of the Court of Justice on the application of Article 28 (ex 30) to national rules on shop closing hours? Make a written note of your answer.

The principles laid down in *Keck* have been reaffirmed by the Court of Justice in a number of cases concerning national regulation of selling arrangements. For instance, in *Tankstation 't Heukske*, it was held that Article 28 (ex 30) does not apply to national rules concerning the closure of shops which apply to all traders operating within the national territory and affect in the same manner, in law and in fact, the marketing of domestic products and of products from other Member States. The same principles have been applied to Greek rules requiring processed milk for infants to be sold only by pharmacies (*Commission* v *Greece* (Case C-391/92) [1995] ECR I-1621) and to Belgian legislation prohibiting sales yielding very low profit margins (*Groupement National des Négotiants en Pommes de Terre de Belgique (Belgapom)* v *ITM Belgium SA and Vocarex SA* (Case C-63/94) [1995] ECR I-2467).

However, it is clear that any restriction with a discriminatory effect on imports will constitute an MEQR, even where it may be characterized as a 'selling arrangement'. In *Schutzverband gegen unlauteren Wettbewerb* v *TK-Heimdienst Sass GmbH* (Case-254/98) [2000] ECR I-151, the Court considered Austrian legislation prohibiting butchers, bakers, and grocers from selling their goods on rounds from door to door unless they also carried on business selling the same type of goods from permanent establishments in the same district or an adjacent municipality. Although the legislation concerned selling arrangements applying to all traders in the national territory, traders from other Member States, in order to have the same access to the Austrian market as local traders, would be obliged to incur the additional cost of setting up a permanent establishment in the relevant locality. The legislation had the effect of impeding access to the Austrian market for imported products and was therefore incompatible with Article 28 (ex 30).

In the particular context of advertising, the Court of Justice has recognized that national rules restricting or prohibiting product advertising can be a greater impediment to market access for imported products than for domestic products.

 EXERCISE 9.15

Read the extract from *Konsumentombudsmannen (KO)* v *De Agostini (Svenska) Förlag AB* and *Konsumentombudsmannen (KO)* v *TV Shop i Sverge AB* (Cases C-34–6/95) [1997] ECR I-3843 in *Cases and Materials* (9.4.8). What was the Court's view of the potential impact of advertising restrictions on imports?

The Court took the view that a producer which is unable to promote its products in another Member State may be prevented from penetrating a new market, whereas advertising restrictions may have less impact upon the marketing of the domestic product. In these circumstances, whilst the restrictions may be classified as 'selling arrangements', the Keck exception does not apply because of their discriminatory effect. In *Agostini*, the Court of Justice left consideration of the effects of the prohibition on advertising to the national court. More recently, in *Konsumentombudsmannen* v *Gourmet International Products Aktiebolag* (Case C-405/98) [2001] ECR 1–1795, the Court of Justice considered Swedish legislation restricting the advertising of alcoholic drinks. The Court concluded that, even without a close analysis of the underlying facts, the prohibition of certain kinds of advertising of these products is liable to impede access to the market by products from other Member States more than it impedes access by domestic products.

9.7.10 Article 28 (ex 30) as a defence

It is sometimes said that Article 28 (ex 30) may be used either as a 'sword' or a 'shield'. It is used as a 'sword' by the Commission in Article 226 (ex 169) enforcement proceedings where Member States have introduced unlawful restrictions. As a 'shield', Article 28 (ex 30) is frequently raised as a defence by individuals in national courts (see for instance the

'Sunday trading' cases and *Criminal proceedings against Keck and Mithouard* (Cases C-267 & 268/91) [1993] ECR I-6097 in *Cases and Materials* (9.4.8)).

9.7.11 Article 29 (ex 34)

This section has concentrated on Article 28 (ex 30) and the prohibition relating to imports. It should be noted that similar principles apply to exports under Article 29 (ex 34). However, whereas distinctly applicable measures which discriminate against exports will generally breach Article 29 (ex 34), indistinctly applicable measures will not unless they are protectionist.

9.8 Article 30 (ex 36): derogation from Articles 28 and 29 (ex 30 and 34)

9.8.1 The Article 30 (ex 36) exceptions

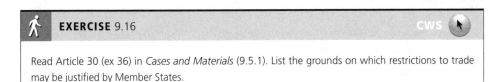

EXERCISE 9.16   CWS

Read Article 30 (ex 36) in *Cases and Materials* (9.5.1). List the grounds on which restrictions to trade may be justified by Member States.

Article 30 (ex 36) sets out a list of grounds on which Member States may justify measures which obstruct interstate trade. Measures which are justified under Article 30 (ex 36) will be lawful even though they breach Article 28 (ex 30). The provisions of Article 30 (ex 36) allow what is called 'derogation' from the principle of free movement of goods. Because this principle is fundamental to the Community system, the Article 30 (ex 36) exceptions are interpreted very strictly by the Court of Justice. The grounds of justification listed in Article 30 (ex 36) are:

(a) public morality, public policy, public security;

(b) the protection of health and life of humans, animals or plants;

(c) the protection of national treasures possessing artistic, historic or archaeological value;

(d) the protection of industrial and commercial property.

Unlike the mandatory requirements within the *Cassis* rule of reason, the list of exceptions in Article 30 (ex 36) is exhaustive (*Commission* v *Ireland* (*Restrictions on Importation of Souvenirs*) (Case 113/80) [1981] ECR 1625 in *Cases and Materials* (9.4.6)). Again, unlike the rule of reason, the Article 30 (ex 36) exceptions can apply both to distinctly and indistinctly applicable measures, though the latter would normally be considered under *Cassis*.

Article 30 (ex 36) does not give Member States complete discretion to adopt any measures which fall within the exceptions but requires such measures to be 'justified' on one of the specified grounds. To be 'justified', measures must be no more than is necessary to achieve the desired aim.

 QUESTION 9.12

What general principle of Community law do you recognize here?

You will no doubt recall that reference has been made already in this chapter to this important general principle, the principle of proportionality, which is also an essential element of the *Cassis* rule of reason.

 EXERCISE 9.17   CWS

Look again at Article 30 (ex 36) in *Cases and Materials* (9.5.1). Write down the two 'negative' conditions relating to national prohibitions or restrictions.

In addition to the proportionality requirement, Article 30 (ex 36) also lays down two other conditions which must be satisfied before restrictions can be considered lawful. Measures must not constitute 'a means of arbitrary discrimination or a disguised restriction on trade between Member States'.

Discussion now turns to the scope of the Article 30 (ex 36) grounds of justification.

9.8.2 **Public morality**

This exception to the free movement provisions has been considered by the Court of Justice in relation to restrictions on the trade in pornographic or obscene material. In *R v Henn and Darby* (Case 34/79) [1979] ECR 3795 (*Cases and Materials* (9.4.1)), the Court ruled that a ban on the import of pornographic articles into the UK breached Article 28 (ex 30) but was justified on grounds of public morality under Article 30 (ex 36). The Court stated that 'it is for each Member State to determine in accordance with its own scale of values and in the form selected by it the requirements of public morality in its own territory' and this was not affected by the fact that different rules applied in different parts of the UK. Moreover, there was no arbitrary discrimination or disguised restriction on trade despite the fact that national law did not place an absolute ban on the possession of or trade in pornographic material. Such restrictions as did exist had the clear purpose of restraining the manufacture and marketing of obscene material and from this the Court concluded that there was no 'lawful trade' in such material in the UK.

EXERCISE 9.18 CWS

Similar issues arose in *Conegate Ltd* v *Customs and Excise Commissioners* (Case 121/85) [1986] ECR 1007 (*Cases and Materials* (9.5.2)). Explain why the outcome was different in this case. Write down your answer.

In *Conegate* the Court confirmed that it is for Member States to decide upon the obscene or indecent nature of goods. However, the Court undertook a closer examination of the national rules and concluded that the restrictions placed on domestic goods—prohibition on transmission by post, restrictions on public display, licensing systems in some areas for premises from which the goods were sold—did not amount to a prohibition on manufacture and sale. Consequently, the UK could not rely on Article 30 (ex 36) to prohibit the importation of similar goods, though it was not precluded from applying the same restrictions upon imported goods once they had entered the country.

9.8.3 **Public policy**

Very few cases have raised issues of public policy and where this ground of justification has been considered by the Court of Justice, it has been very strictly interpreted. It is clear that 'public policy' cannot be used as a general justification which embraces more specific defences (such as consumer protection or economic justifications) but must be given its own independent meaning. One case in which the public policy justification was accepted by the Court is *R* v *Thompson* (Case 7/78) [1978] ECR 2247. Here, the Court of Justice recognized a state's need to protect its right to mint coinage as one of its fundamental interests and held that the right to protect coinage from destruction stems from that right. Thus a prohibition on the import and export of coins was justified on public policy grounds.

9.8.4 **Public security**

 EXERCISE 9.19 CWS

Look at *Campus Oil Ltd* v *Minister for Industry and Energy* (Case 72/83) [1983] ECR 2727 in *Cases and Materials* (9.5.3). How were the Irish national rules on the purchase of petroleum products justified?

In the *Campus Oil* case the Court of Justice found that an Irish law requiring importers to purchase a certain percentage of their requirements from a state-owned oil refinery at fixed prices was justified on public security grounds. The measure ensured that Ireland was able to maintain its own refining capacity in relation to products which were fundamental to the provision of essential services. An interruption of supplies could seriously threaten public security.

 EXERCISE 9.20

Turn back to *Campus Oil* in *Cases and Materials* (9.5.3) and mentally note the issues relating to proportionality.

9.8.5 Protection of health and life of humans, animals, or plants

---

 QUESTION 9.13

What kinds of measures do you think Member States might seek to justify on health grounds?

You may recall one specific health measure which has already been mentioned in an earlier section of this chapter, the inspection of imported (but not domestically produced) apples aimed at controlling a pest known as San Jose Scale (*Rewe-Zentralfinanz* v *Landwirtschaftskammer Bonn* (Case 4/75) [1975] ECR 843 in *Cases and Materials* (9.4.4)). Other kinds of distinctly applicable measures which Member States have sought to justify on health grounds under Article 30 (ex 36) include UK measures which effectively imposed a ban on poultry meat imports from most other Member States (*Commission* v *United Kingdom (Imports of Poultry Meat)* (Case 40/82) [1982] ECR 2793) and delays in the customs clearance of imported Italian wines at the French border caused by systematic checks on quality (*Commission* v *France (Italian Table Wines)* (Case 42/82) [1983] ECR 1013).

On occasions, indistinctly applicable measures have been considered under Article 30 (ex 36), for instance prohibitions on the use of certain additives in beer (*Commission* v *Germany (Beer Purity Laws)* (Case 178/84) [1987] ECR 1227 in *Cases and Materials* (9.5.4)) and rules prohibiting pharmacists from substituting any other product for the product specified in a doctor's prescription (*R* v *Royal Pharmaceutical Society of Great Britain* (Cases 266 & 267/87) [1989] ECR 1295 in *Cases and Materials* (9.4)).

In order to succeed under this head, Member States must show that there is a real health risk. Measures must also, of course, satisfy the proportionality requirement and must not constitute 'arbitrary discrimination or a disguised restriction on trade between Member States'.

In the *San Jose Scale* case, there was a real risk that the pest would spread to domestic apples. The Court of Justice held that the inspections were justified in principle under Article 30 (ex 36). They would not constitute arbitrary discrimination where effective measures were taken to prevent the distribution of contaminated domestic apples. By contrast, in *Commission* v *United Kingdom (Imports of Poultry Meat)*, the Court of Justice decided that the UK ban on poultry meat imports was arbitrary and a disguised restriction on trade because it was designed to protect domestic producers. Several factors pointed to this conclusion, including the haste with which the measures had been introduced, their timing (the beginning of the Christmas season) and the measures which the French had themselves introduced to prevent Newcastle disease.

Similarly, in *Commission* v *France* (*Italian Table Wines*), French quality checks on Italian imported wines were held to be arbitrary. Quality checks on French wines were much less frequent and there was no evidence supporting the need for systematic checks on the imported product.

By contrast, the Royal Pharmaceutical Society's rules prohibiting the substitution of medicines did not go beyond what was necessary to achieve the objective in view, namely to leave the entire responsibility for the treatment of a patient in the hands of the doctor. Moreover, the Court could not discount the psychosomatic factor: patients had greater confidence in the specific medicine prescribed than in a substitute, even though the latter has exactly the same therapeutic effect. (*R* v *Royal Pharmaceutical Society of Great Britain* in *Cases and Materials* (9.4).)

The public health ground has been invoked in a series of cases concerning bans on imports of foodstuffs containing additives. This is a difficult area, since medical and scientific opinion on the safety of particular substances sometimes varies. Moreover, Member States may claim that the eating or drinking habits of their own population make the addition of substances to certain products particularly harmful.

? QUESTION 9.14

In *Commission* v *Germany (Beer Purity Laws)* (Case 178/84) [1987] ECR 1227 (*Cases and Materials* (9.5.4)), the German government argued that the use of additives in beer was particularly harmful to the German population. Why?

The German beer purity laws prohibited all additives in beer. The German government pointed to the high consumption of beer in Germany and claimed that because of this, the use of additives in beer presented a greater risk to public health in Germany than in other Member States.

🚶 EXERCISE 9.21

Look again at *Commission* v *Germany (Beer Purity Laws)* (Case 178/84) [1987] ECR 1227 in *Cases and Materials* (9.5.4) and note that the Court of Justice held that the ban on the use of all additives in beer was disproportionate. The Court pointed out that German legislation permitted the use of some additives in other kinds of beverages.

The Court of Justice's approach to the prohibition of additives in foodstuffs may be summarized as follows. Where there are no Community harmonizing measures concerning particular substances, Member States remain free to adopt their own regulations, provided Community provisions on the free movement of goods are not infringed. Thus, if the additive in question is permitted in another Member State a ban in the State of importation must be shown to be proportionate, in other words necessary and effective in protecting public health. Where scientific research and the eating habits of the importing State's population indicate that there is no danger to public health and the use of the additive meets a technical or nutritional need, then a prohibition will breach Article 28 (ex 30) and will not be justified under Article 30 (ex 36).

9.8.6 Protection of national treasures possessing artistic, historic, or archaeological value

The scope of this derogation remains uncertain, for the provision has not as yet been invoked before the Court of Justice. However, in *Commission* v *Italy (Export Tax on Art Treasures, No. 1)* (Case 7/68) [1968] ECR 423, the Court indicated that quantitative restrictions (but not charges) would be justified where the object of those restrictions was to prevent art treasures from being exported from a Member State.

9.8.7 Protection of industrial and commercial property

The various kinds of industrial and commercial property rights (or 'intellectual property rights') include patents, copyright, trade marks and design rights. The use of such rights can impede the free movement of goods throughout the Community because national intellectual property law tends to partition markets along national lines. Although in principle Article 30 (ex 36) (together with Article 295 (ex 222), which precludes Community interference with national rules relating to property ownership) protects industrial property rights, these rights have been curtailed by the Court of Justice. This has been done by means of the distinction drawn between the ownership or **existence** of the rights and their **exercise**. Whilst the ownership of the right is protected, any improper exercise of it—which is anti-competitive or constitutes an obstacle to trade—will be condemned by the Court.

9.8.8 No economic justifications under Article 30 (ex 36)

Economic interests do not justify restrictions on the free movement of goods. This was made clear in *Duphar BV* v *Netherlands* (Case 238/82) [1984] ECR 523 and was later reaffirmed by the Court of Justice in *R* v *Secretary of State for Home Department ex parte Evans Medical Ltd* (Case C-324/93) [1995] ECR I-563.

 EXERCISE 9.22   CWS

Look at *Evans Medical* in *Cases and Materials* (9.5.5). Summarize the conclusions of the Court of Justice on the application of the Article 30 (ex 36) derogation to the refusal of import licences for the drug diamorphine.

The questions referred by the national court concerned the refusal of licences for the importation of the drug diamorphine from another Member State. The Court of Justice considered whether such a refusal could be justified under Article 30 (ex 36) and concluded that it cannot be justified on economic grounds—here, the Member State's desire to ensure the survival of Macfarlan, which had the exclusive right to manufacture the product in the United Kingdom. However, the derogation might apply if the maintenance of a reliable supply of drugs for essential medical purposes was necessary for the protection of the life and health of humans.

Similarly, purely economic reasons did not justify Greek legislation which, in effect, obliged petroleum marketing companies to obtain a significant part of their supplies from refineries established in Greece (*Commission* v *Greece* (Case C-398/98) [2001] ECR I-7915).

9.8.9 **Environmental justifications for distinctly applicable measures?**

It has been suggested that two decisions of the Court of Justice concerning national measures for the protection of the environment, *Commission* v *Belgium* (Case C-2/900 [1992] ECR I-4431 and *PreussenElektra AG* v *Schleswag AG* (Case C-379/98) [2001] ECR I-2099, call into question the established view that the Article 30 list of justifications is exhaustive. As previously noted, according to that established view, the Article 30 list cannot be extended in the way that the *Cassis* list of mandatory requirements, relating to indistinctly applicable measures only, has been extended.

Some commentators have argued that, in these two cases, the Court of Justice allowed environmental objectives to justify distinctly applicable measures caught by Article 28. However in *Commission* v *Belgium,* whilst the Court Justice took account of environmental protection in considering apparently unlawful national legislation concerning the disposal of waste, it held that, because of the special nature of that product, the provisions in question did not discriminate against imports.

In *PreussenElektra*, in which the Court of Justice considered German legislation requiring German electricity suppliers to purchase the electricity produced from renewable sources in their area of supply, the Court avoided discussion of the distinctions between the Article 30 justifications and the *Cassis* mandatory requirements. It held that the legislation was not incompatible with Article 28.

Notwithstanding these outcomes, neither of the two judgments is a model of clarity. It will be interesting to follow any evolution of the relevant legal principles in future decisions.

9.9 **Harmonization**

As is evident from many of the cases discussed in this chapter, the application of different product standards by different Member States, in relation for instance to health and safety requirements and consumer protection, creates a hindrance to the free movement of goods. The process of harmonization aims to eliminate these disparities by laying down Community-wide standards which are binding on all Member States. Article 94 EC provides for the adoption of Directives for this purpose, but early progress on harmonization was slow.

EXERCISE 9.23

Read Article 94 EC (*Cases and Materials* 9.6). Think of one reason why progress on the adoption of Directives under this provision was slow.

The adoption of Directives under Article 94 requires unanimous approval in the Council of Ministers. Because of this and because the initial approach to harmonization was to adopt comprehensive and detailed rules covering particular areas, consensus was difficult to achieve. However, where a measure harmonizing an area comprehensively has been put in place, a Member State has no recourse to Article 30 derogation from the free movement principles in that particular area.

A new approach to harmonization moved away from comprehensive rules and focused on a minimum level of Community regulation. A Council Resolution of 7 May 1985 states that, in relation to technical harmonization and standards, Directives are to be based upon the 'essential safety requirements (or other requirements in the general interest) with which products put on the market must conform and which should therefore enjoy free movement throughout the Community'. The detailed technical specifications needed to ensure that products meet the essential requirements are not a matter for Community legislation but for 'organizations competent in the standardization area'.

 EXERCISE 9.24

Read Article 95(1) EC (*Cases and Materials* 9.6). How does this provision further facilitate the harmonization process?

The process of harmonization was further facilitated after the insertion into the Treaty by the Single European Act 1986 of Article 95(1)EC, which provides for qualified majority voting for the adoption of measures concerning the establishment and functioning of the internal market.

 Under Article 95(4) (*Cases and Materials* 9.6), Member States wishing to apply stricter or higher standards than those comprising the essential requirements may seek approval for these from the Commission on the basis of 'major needs' referred to in Article 30 or in relation to the environment or the working environment. Similarly, after the adoption of a harmonizing measure, approval may be sought under Article 94(5) (*Cases and Materials* 9.6) for the introduction of new national provisions based on new scientific evidence relating to the protection of the environment or the working environment.

CONCLUSIONS

This chapter has underlined the importance of the free movement of goods to the Community internal market. It has been seen that obstacles to trade can take the form of customs duties, charges, taxes, quantitative restrictions and measures having equivalent effect. Member States seeking to rely on the *Cassis* rule of reason or the Article 30 (ex 36) derogation in order to justify measures breaching Article 28 (ex 30) must be able to establish not only that the measures in question are not protectionist but also that they are no more than is necessary to achieve the objective in view, in other words that they satisfy the principle of proportionality.

 CHAPTER 9: ASSESSMENT EXERCISE CWS

1   (a) Explain the distinction between distinctly applicable measures and indistinctly applicable measures. Give one example of each drawn from cases decided by the Court of Justice.

    (b) Why is this distinction important?

2   Consider the following (fictitious) measures and comment on their compatibility with Community provisions on the free movement of goods.

    (a) A recently introduced Italian tax on wine with an alcohol content exceeding 9%. Importers from other Member States are required to pay the tax at the date of importation. Domestic producers can defer payment until up to six weeks after the product has been put on the market.

    (b) A Belgian regulation requiring all imported (but not domestically produced) onions to undergo inspections. The Belgian government claims that the measure is designed to control the spread of the onion beetle, which is a very destructive pest.

    (c) German legislation requiring vegetarian cheese to be packed in triangular boxes. The government claims that the measure is aimed to protect the consumer.

    (d) English legislation which prohibits video shops and all other video retail outlets from opening between 9 p.m. and 8 a.m.

See *Cases and Materials* (9.8) for specimen answers.

10 Free movement of persons

10.1 Objectives

By the end of this chapter you should be able to:

1 Define the current scope of the right of free movement of persons throughout the Community

2 Detail the Treaty Articles and secondary legislation which give effect to the principle of freedom of movement of persons

3 Describe the rights granted to workers, the self-employed and their families by the Community free movement provisions

4 Discuss the right of Member States to derogate from the free movement provisions and, in particular, to restrict entry and residence

10.2 Introduction

The free movement of persons is identified by Article 3(1)(c) (ex 3(c)) EC (*Cases and Materials* (10.1)) as one of the four essential freedoms of the Community internal market and Article 14 (ex 7a) (*Cases and Materials* (10.1)) defines the internal market as an area without internal frontiers in which the free movement of goods, persons, services and capital is ensured. The general principle of freedom of movement is given substance by Treaty provisions and secondary legislation which confer rights of free movement and residence specifically on workers, the self-employed and their families. In purely economic terms, the purpose of granting such rights is to ensure that the economically active are able to move freely throughout the Community to locations where their skills and labour are in demand. On a broader view, the free movement provisions are concerned not only with the single market objectives of the Treaty but also with the right of the individual worker to be free from discrimination on account of nationality and to raise his or her standard of living and quality of life by working and residing in another Member State. Article 12 (ex 6) EC (*Cases and Materials* (10.1)) establishes the principle of non-discrimination on grounds of nationality 'within the scope of application of this Treaty'. This chapter examines the scope of the free movement provisions.

10.3 Freedom of movement for persons who are not economically active

The free movement rights granted to Community nationals by the Treaty and secondary legislation are limited, for the most part, to the 'economically active'.

> **? QUESTION** 10.1
>
> Which groups does this comprise?

Freedom of movement is granted to workers and to the self-employed, the latter group comprising those exercising the right of establishment and those providing services in another Member State. In addition, family members (as defined by secondary legislation) have certain rights which are derived from the rights of the workers or self-employed persons to whom they are related.

Secondary legislation has extended the right of free movement to certain groups who are not economically active:

(a) Directive 90/364: general right of free movement (subject to the conditions noted below).

(b) Directive 90/365: right of free movement for retired persons.

(c) Directive 90/366 (now replaced by Directive 93/96): right of free movement for students.

At first sight these provisions appear to widen considerably the scope of the right of freedom of movement for persons. However, in each case the extent of eligibility to free movement and residence rights is limited by the requirement that individuals have sufficient resources to avoid becoming a burden on the social assistance system of the host State and are covered by medical insurance.

10.4 Citizenship of the European Union: free movement and associated rights

Although the secondary legislation outlined above grants rights of free movement and residence to certain categories of non-workers, these rights, and the right to non-discrimination on grounds of nationality, are still to an appreciable extent tied to worker status. The concept of citizenship of the Union, introduced by the Treaty on European Union and set out in Article 17 (ex 8) EC, (*Cases and Materials* (10.2)) could signal the further extension of rights of free movement and non-discrimination beyond those who are engaged in economic activity. Indeed, in *Sala* v *Freistaat Bayern* (Case C-85/96) [1998] ECR I-2691 the Court of Justice moved closer towards such an extension of rights.

 EXERCISE 10.1 CWS

Look at the extract from *Sala* in *Cases and Materials* (10.2). How does the Court of Justice define the scope of the rights attached to the status of citizen of the Union?

The Court held that Article 8(2) (now 17(2)) EC attaches to the status of citizenship of the Union the rights and duties laid down by the Treaty. Thus, a citizen of the European Union lawfully resident in a Member State of which he or she is not a national, can rely on the non-discrimination provisions of Article 12 (ex 6) (*Cases and Materials* (10.1)) in all matters falling within the scope of application of the Treaty. The Court of Justice adopted similar reasoning in *Grzelczyk* v *Centre Public d'Aide Sociale d'Ottignes-Louvain-la-Neuve* (Case C-184/99 [2001] ECR 1–6193.

 EXERCISE 10.2 CWS

Read the extract from the *Grzelczyk* judgment (*Cases and Materials* (10.2)). Note, in paragraph 31, the Court's future vision of Union citizenship as the fundamental status of nationals of the Member States.

In *D'Hoop* v *Office national de l'emploi* (Case C-224/98) [2002] ECR 1-6191, the Court of Justice again emphasized that the status of Union citizenship forms the basis of rights to equal treatment in law, irrespective of nationality (*Cases and Materials* (10.2)).

Nevertheless, the right of every citizen of the Union to move and reside freely throughout the Community, enshrined in Article 18(1) (ex 8a(1)) EC (*Cases and Materials* (10.2)) remains subject to the limitations and conditions laid down in the Treaty and by the measures adopted to give it effect. The impact of these limitations and conditions was considered by the Court of Justice in *Baumbast* v *Secretary of State for the Home Department* (Case C-413/99) [2002] ECR 1-7091, in relation to the rights of Mr Baumbast, a German national, to reside in the UK. Mr Baumbast sought to rely directly on Article 18(1) before the UK Immigration Appeal Tribunal.

In this context, the first question raised by the Immigration Appeal Tribunal concerned the direct effect of Article 18(1).

EXERCISE 10.3

Look at paragraphs 76–9 of the *Baumbast* judgment (*Cases and Materials* (10.2)). Make a brief note summarizing the respective submissions of the UK and German Governments and Mr Baumbast on the direct effect of Article 18(1).

If necessary, look back at Chapter 5 to refresh your memory on the meaning of 'direct effect'.

The UK and German Governments took the view that the conditions and limitations contained in Article 18(1) demonstrated that the article is not intended to be a freestanding provision and thus is not directly effective. On the other hand, Mr Baumbast argued that Article 18(1) had direct effect despite those limitations and conditions.

 EXERCISE 10.4

What were the conclusions of the Court of Justice on the direct effect of Article 18(1)?

The Court of Justice held that Article 18(1) is a clear and precise provision that confers directly on every citizen of the Union the right to reside within the territory of a Member State. Although that right is subject to limitations and conditions, those limitations and conditions are subject to judicial review and thus do not prevent Article 18(1) from being directly effective.

As to the scope of the limitations and conditions referred to in Article 18(1), the Commission argued that these comprised those conditions and limitations contained in pre-existing primary and secondary legislation on free movement rights and on the categories of persons eligible for them. These rights, declared the Commission were still linked to economic activity or subject to evidence of sufficient resources.

Significantly, in its response, the Court of Justice used citizenship as the starting point. The Court pointed out that the rights of a national of a Member State to free movement and residence in another Member State are rights derived from the EC Treaty or implementing legislation. As for Treaty rights, before the entry into force of the Treaty on European Union, those rights were available only to those engaged in economic activity. However, the Treaty on European Union introduced Union citizenship into the EC Treaty and, with it, the right of every citizen to move and reside freely within the Member States. Thus, the Treaty on European Union does not make citizenship rights subject to economic activity.

In relation to the conditions and limitations resulting from secondary legislation (in Mr Baumbast's case, Directive 90/364), the Court confirmed that Member States can require nationals of the Member States and their families who wish to reside in their territory to satisfy two conditions.

EXERCISE 10.5

What are these two conditions? Look at paragraph 87 of the *Baumbast* judgment (*Cases and Materials* (10.2)).

Such persons must have medical insurance and sufficient financial resources to avoid becoming a burden on the host state. On the facts, the Court found that Mr Baumbast did indeed satisfy these requirements.

This reasoning in *Baumbast*, based on the rights arising from citizenship of the Union, represents a further weakening of the link between free movement rights and economic status.

Nevertheless, as is apparent from the *Baumbast* judgment, the conditions and limitations contained in Article 18(1) remain significant. Similar qualification is attached to the principle of free movement in Article 14 (ex 7a). That principle is ensured 'in accordance with the provisions of the Treaty'

The Court of Justice's decision in *Wijsenbeek* (Case C-378/97) [1999] ECR I-6207 is a further reminder of the conditions and limitations placed upon free movement rights. Here, the Court held that neither Article 14 (ex 7a) nor Article 18 (ex 8a) EC preclude a Member State from requiring a person, whether or not a citizen of the European Union, to establish his nationality on entry. Further, the imposition of penalties for non-compliance is not unlawful, provided that such penalties are not so disproportionate as to create an obstacle to the free movement of persons.

In addition to these developments in the case law of the Court of Justice, recent legislative developments on citizenship of the European Union allow scope for extension of the rights attached to this concept. In 2001, the Commission presented proposals for a new Directive on the right of citizens of the Union and their family members to move and reside freely within the territory of the Member States. In the introduction to its proposals, the Commission refers to the 'new legal and political environment established by citizenship of the Union' and declares that Union citizens should be able to move between Member States on similar terms as nationals moving around their own country to change their residence or employment. The contents of the proposed Directive are considered in section [10.10]. Additionally, amendments made to Article 18 by the Treaty of Nice enable the Council to adopt legislation facilitating the exercise of the free movement rights of citizens of the Union (*Cases and Materials* (10.2)).

10.5 The 'economically active': outline of the legislation

Article 3(1)(c) (ex 3(c)) EC refers to the Community aim of establishing 'an internal market characterized by the abolition, as between Member States, of obstacles to the free movement of goods, persons, services and capital'. The broad objective of freedom of movement of persons and services is given substance by a number of Treaty provisions.

Rights of free movement are granted to workers (Articles 39–42 (ex 48–51)), to those providing services (Articles 49–55 (ex 59–66)) and to those exercising rights of establishment (Articles 43–8 (ex 52–8)). These groups comprise the 'economically active', both workers and self-employed persons. These Treaty provisions have been elaborated and extended by secondary legislation. In addition, secondary legislation grants rights of free movement and other associated rights to the families of workers and of the self-employed.

10.6 The free movement of workers

10.6.1 Outline of the legislation

This part of the chapter will consider the Community free movement provisions which relate to workers and their families. Article 39 (ex 48) EC confers rights on workers.

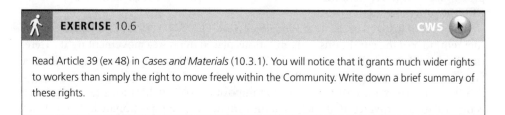

EXERCISE 10.6   CWS

Read Article 39 (ex 48) in *Cases and Materials* (10.3.1). You will notice that it grants much wider rights to workers than simply the right to move freely within the Community. Write down a brief summary of these rights.

In addition to the right of free movement, Article 39 (ex 48) provides for the abolition of discrimination based on nationality between nationals of Member States with respect to pay and conditions of employment. It also grants workers the right to accept offers of employment in other Member States, to stay there during that employment and, subject to conditions laid down by implementing legislation, to remain in that Member State after having been employed there. Article 39 (ex 48) incorporates a specific application of the general principle of non-discrimination on grounds of nationality contained in Article 12 (ex 6) EC. (The non-discrimination principle was originally contained in Article 7, which under the Treaty on European Union (the Maastricht Treaty) became Article 6—now Article 12.)

The Court of Justice has made clear that the prohibition of discrimination on grounds of nationality contained in Article 39 (ex 48) may be relied upon not only against the Member States and public authorities but also against private individuals. This has recently been confirmed in *Angonese* v *Cassa di Risparmio di Bolzano SpA* (Case C-281/98) [2000] ECR I-4139.

The Court has also held that Article 39 (ex 48) may be relied upon by an employer in order to employ workers who are nationals of another Member State. *Clean Car Autoservice GmbH* v *Landeshauptmann von Wein* (Case C-350/96) [1998] ECR I-2521 concerned Austrian legislation which provided that businesses operating in that Member State may not appoint as managers persons not resident there. This constituted indirect discrimination and an infringement of Article 39(2). (The concepts of direct and indirect discrimination are considered later at 10.6.5.4).

The main secondary legislation relating to workers is:

(a) Directive 68/360, conferring rights of entry and residence.

(b) Regulation 1612/68, governing access to employment and conditions of employment.

(c) Regulation 1251/70 on the right to remain in the territory of a Member State after having been employed there.

(d) Directive 64/221 on derogation from the free movement provisions available to Member States on grounds of public policy, public security and public health.

10.6.2 **Wholly internal situations**

The rights of free movement and associated rights conferred by the Treaty and secondary legislation do not apply in situations which are wholly internal to the Member States. This means that a national worker cannot, in his or her own Member State, claim Community rights relating to freedom of movement which are granted to nationals of other Member States working there unless he or she has already exercised Community free movement rights. This is often referred to as 'reverse discrimination'.

The potentially harsh effects of reverse discrimination in the context of free movement of persons are illustrated by *Morson and Jhanjan* v *Netherlands* (Cases 35 & 36/82) [1982] ECR 3723 (*Cases and Materials* (10.3.2)). Here, the Court of Justice held that two Surinamese women who wished to join their adult children (on whom they were dependent) in Holland had no right to do so under the Community free movement provisions. Since the children had Dutch nationality and 'had never exercised their right to free movement within the Community', this was a purely internal matter in which no link could be established with Community law. More recently, in *Land Nordrhein-Westfalen* v *Uecker* and *Jacquet* v *Land Nordrhein-Westfalen* (Joined Cases C-64 & 56/96) [1997] ECR I-3182, the Court of Justice confirmed that Community law regarding freedom of movement for workers cannot be applied to the situation of workers who have never exercised the right of freedom of movement within the Community.

However, an individual can rely on Community free movement rights against his or her own Member State in situations that are not 'purely internal'. In *R* v *Immigration Appeal Tribunal and Singh, ex parte Secretary of State for the Home Department* (Case C-370/90) ECR I-4265, the Court of Justice upheld the Community right of the Indian husband of a British woman to re-enter the UK following a period when the couple had been working in Germany. By leaving the UK to work in Germany, Mr Singh's wife had become a Community migrant worker, acquiring all the rights attached to that status. That included the right of family members to re-enter and reside in the Member State of origin.

Similarly, a Netherlands national who had been posted to the UK by his Dutch employer could rely on Article 39 (ex 48) and Regulation 1612/68 to challenge Dutch social security legislation which operated to his disadvantage as a result of his residence in another Member State. (*Terhoeve* v *Inspecteur van de Belastingdienst Particulieren/ Ondernemingen Buitenland* (Case C-18/95) [1999] ECR I-345).

More recently in *Carpenter* v *Secretary of State for the Home Department* (Case C-60/00) ECR I-6279, the Court of Justice considered the right of a Philippine national to reside in the UK with her British husband. The couple lived in the UK, where the husband's business was established.

 EXERCISE 10.7

> Look at the extracts from *Carpenter* (*Cases and Materials* (10.3.2)). On what basis did Mrs Carpenter claim that she had the right to remain in the UK under Community law? What was the Court's decision?

Unlike the British spouse in *Singh*, Mr Carpenter had not established himself in another Member State in order to engage in economic activity—in his case, the provision of services. However he had, as well as providing and receiving services in the UK where his business was established, travelled to other Member States to provide and receive services there. Mrs Carpenter claimed that she was entitled, under Community law, to remain in the UK, her right being derived from the rights of her husband to provide services and to travel within the EU under Article 49EC and Directive 73/148. (Article 49 and Directive 73/148 are considered below in section 10.8.)

The Court agreed, holding that the refusal by a Member State to grant a right of residence to a spouse of one of its nationals who provides services in other Member States is incompatible with Article 49EC. At paragraph 38, the Court referred to Regulation 1612/68 and Directive 68/360 (considered below in section 10.6.5) which recognize the importance of the protection of family life of nationals of the Member States in order to eliminate obstacles to the exercise of the fundamental freedoms guaranteed by the Treaty. It should be noted that the Court also stressed that, in the circumstances of this case, Article 49 was to be interpreted in the light of the fundamental right to respect for family life within the meaning of Article 8 of the Convention for the Protection of Human Rights and Fundamental Freedoms. Mrs Carpenter's infringement of the UK Immigration rules by staying in the UK after the expiry of her leave to remain was not sufficient to justify Mrs Carpenter's deportation.

In *D'Hoop* (*Cases and Materials* (10.2)), the Court of Justice extended the right to rely on Community law against one's own Member State, which in *Singh* and *Terhoeve* was applied to workers, to an individual who had resided in another Member State for completion of her secondary education.

The rights granted under the free movement provisions which are being considered in this section apply to workers and their families. They are available only to workers who are nationals of the Member States, though family members need not be Community nationals to be eligible. Nationality is determined according to national law. How, then, are the terms 'worker' and 'worker's family' defined?

10.6.3 **Meaning of 'worker'**

There is no Treaty definition of 'worker'. However, the Court of Justice has emphasised on many occasions that the term may not be defined by national laws but has a Community meaning (see for instance *Hoekstra (née Unger) v Bestuur der Bedrijfsvereniging voor Detail-handel en Ambachten* (Case 75/63) [1964] ECR 177 and *Levin v Staatssecretaris van Justitie* (Case 53/81) [1982] ECR 1035 in *Cases and Materials* (10.3.3)).

? **QUESTION** 10.2

Why do you think the Court of Justice has insisted that the term 'worker' be given a Community meaning?

If it were not so, and Member States were able to decide and modify the meaning of the term, the free movement rules would be frustrated because national laws would be able 'to exclude at will certain categories of persons from the benefit of the Treaty' (*Levin*).

The definition of 'worker' set out by the Court of Justice in *Lawrie-Blum v Land Baden-Württemberg* (Case 66/85) [1986] ECR 2121 (*Cases and Materials* (10.3.3)) has been referred to frequently in subsequent judgments. The Court declared that the 'essential feature of an employment relationship . . . is that for a certain period of time a person performs services for and under the direction of another person in return for which he receives remuneration'.

? **QUESTION** 10.3

Can you think of any particular circumstances in which an individual's status as a worker might be open to doubt?

The kinds of circumstances which you might have thought of are illustrated by the cases listed in the next exercise.

EXERCISE 10.8   CWS

Consider these cases:

(a) *Hoekstra (née Unger) v Bestuur der Bedrijfsvereniging voor Detailhandel en Ambachten* (Case 75/63) [1964] ECR 177 (*Cases and Materials* (10.3.3)).

(b) *Levin v Staatssecretaris van Justitie* (Case 53/81) [1982] ECR 1035 (*Cases and Materials* (10.3.3)).

continued

(c) *Kempf* v *Staatssecretaris van Justitie* (Case 139/85) [1986] ECR 1741 (*Cases and Materials* (10.3.3)).

(d) *Steymann* v *Staatssecretaris van Justitie* (Case 196/87) [1988] ECR 6159 (*Cases and Materials* (10.3.3)).

(e) *Bettray* v *Staatssecretaris van Justitie* (Case 344/87) [1989] ECR 1621 (*Cases and Materials* (10.3.3)).

Summarize in a few words each applicant's employment circumstances. Was he or she held to be a 'worker' under Community law? Write down your answers.

The concept of 'worker' included:

(a) A person who, having left her job, was not currently in employment but was capable of taking another job (*Hoekstra*).

(b) A part-time worker whose income from employment did not provide sufficient means of support and fell below the nationally recognized minimum subsistence level, where the work was 'effective and genuine' and not on such a small scale as to be 'purely marginal and ancillary' (*Levin*). In *Levin*, the Court of Justice did not consider the position of a worker whose below-subsistence income is supplemented by state benefit rather than from private funds. This issue arose in *Kempf*. Note also that in *Levin* the Court of Justice indicated that, provided the work is 'effective and genuine', a person's motives in seeking employment in another Member State are irrelevant.

(c) A part-time worker whose income was below the minimum means of subsistence in the host State and who needed to supplement that income by drawing supplementary state benefit (*Kempf*).

(d) A member of a religious community who performed general household duties and was engaged in commercial activity on behalf of the community. Although he did not receive formal wages but only his 'keep' and pocket money, the work constituted an 'economic activity' (*Steymann*).

However in the *Bettray* case, a person who was taking part in a drug-rehabilitation programme aimed to reintegrate people into the workforce and which involved work carried out under supervision and for remuneration was held not to be a worker. Here, since the objective was the rehabilitation of the individual, the work could not be regarded as an 'effective and genuine economic activity'.

10.6.4 Meaning of 'families'

The rights of family members are derived rights, in that they depend upon the worker's status as a worker and do not exist as independent rights. Such rights are however available irrespective of the nationality of the family member, though of course the worker himself or herself must be a national of a Member State.

EXERCISE 10.9   CWS

Article 10(1) of Regulation 1612/68 in *Cases and Materials* (10.3.4) defines 'workers' families'. Look at this article and list the persons who come within its scope.

The term 'workers' families' covers the worker's spouse and descendants who are under the age of 21 or are dependants and ascendants of the worker or the worker's spouse who are dependent. The status of dependant in this context results from a factual situation in which the worker is actually providing support for the family member and the Court of Justice is not concerned to determine the reasons for a family member's dependence on the worker (*Centre Public d'Aide Sociale de Courcelles* v *Lebon* (Case 316/85) [1987] ECR 2811 in *Cases and Materials* (10.3.4)).

In addition, Article 10(2) requires Member States to facilitate the admission to their territory of any other member of a worker's family who is dependent upon the worker or living under the same roof in the worker's state of origin.

10.6.4.1 **Cohabitees**

The meaning of 'spouse' is restricted to persons who are married to workers. Consequently, a cohabitee cannot claim rights as a spouse.

QUESTION 10.4   CWS

Why did Ms Reed succeed in claiming the right to reside in Holland when she was not herself a worker and was not married to her English partner (who was a worker) with whom she lived (*Netherlands State* v *Reed* (Case 59/85) [1985] ECR 1283, in *Cases and Materials* (10.3.4.1))?

Ms Reed could not claim rights as a spouse. That term, said the Court, referred to marital relationships only. However, because Dutch nationals were entitled to have living with them in Holland their (non-national) non-marital partners in stable relationships, to deny the same rights to nationals of other Member States working in Holland would amount to discrimination against those Community workers, contrary to Article 12 (ex 6, formerly 7) and 39 (ex 48) EC.

10.6.4.2 **The effect of divorce and separation**

Although the Court of Justice has not as yet given a definitive ruling as to the rights of a former spouse after divorce, it is clear that the free movement and associated rights of a worker's spouse are unaffected by separation. In *Diatta* v *Land Berlin* (Case 267/83) [1985] ECR 567 (*Cases and Materials* (10.3.4.2)) the Court of Justice held that a Senegalese national who, like her French husband, was living and working in Berlin, had the right to reside in Germany despite the fact that the couple were separated and that divorce proceedings had been initiated.

The later case of *Singh* (*R v Immigration Appeal Tribunal and Singh ex parte Secretary of State for Home Department* (Case 370/90) [1992] 3 CMLR 358) concerned the rights of re-entry and residence of an Indian national married to an English woman on the couple's return to the UK from Germany, where they had both been working. Some time after their return, the couple had divorced. The Court of Justice decided that by working in Germany the wife had exercised her Community rights of free movement. Consequently, Singh could claim rights as the spouse of a Community worker. Unfortunately, the Court chose not to comment upon the effects of the divorce on Mr Singh's rights, since the question referred by the English High Court related to the period prior to the decree absolute.

10.6.5 **The rights of workers and their families**

This section will consider the secondary legislation which gives substance to and elaborates upon the basic Treaty right of free movement for workers and which confers rights upon family members (as defined in Regulation 1612/68). This comprises Directive 68/360, Regulation 1612/68 and Regulation 1251/70. The right of Member States under Article 39 (3) (ex 48(3)) EC and Directive 64/221 to restrict entry and residence will also be examined.

10.6.5.1 **Directive 68/360: rights of entry and residence**

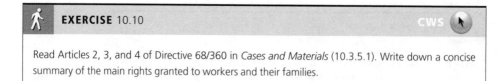

> **EXERCISE** 10.10   CWS
>
> Read Articles 2, 3, and 4 of Directive 68/360 in *Cases and Materials* (10.3.5.1). Write down a concise summary of the main rights granted to workers and their families.

You may have written down something like this, possibly with the addition of other details, for instance on the issuing of passports by the home State:

Directive 68/360 confers rights of entry and residence upon workers and their families. The main provisions grant the right:

(a) to leave their home State so that the worker can work in another Member State (Article 2);

(b) to enter the territory of another Member State on production of a valid identity card or passport (Article 3(1)). Entry visas may only be required for members of the family who are not nationals of a Member State and, where that is the case, Member States must accord to such persons every facility for obtaining the necessary visas (Article 3(2));

(c) to obtain a residence permit on the production of the document of entry and (for the worker) a certificate of employment and (for family members) a document issued by the authorities of their State of origin or the State whence they came proving their relationship with the worker and, if they are dependent on the worker, a document issued by the same authority testifying that they are so dependent or that they live under the worker's roof in that State (Article 4(3)).

The Court of Justice has established that the right of entry conferred by Community law includes the right to enter in search of work (*Procureur du Roi* v *Royer* (Case 48/75) [1976] ECR 497 in *Cases and Materials* (10.3.5.1)). However, an individual who claims to be looking for work is not entitled to remain indefinitely. Thus, the UK could lawfully deport a Community migrant who had not found employment after six months (*R* v *Immigration Appeal Tribunal, ex parte Antonissen* (Case C-292/89) [1991] ECR I-745 in *Cases and Materials* (10.3.5.1)). In *Antonissen*, no time limit was laid down but the Court indicated that a person would be entitled to remain beyond a period of six months if able to show that he or she was making genuine efforts to find work and that there was a real chance of being employed. Thus, a provision of national law automatically requiring a national of another Member State to leave the country at the expiry of a stipulated period infringes Community law (*Commission* v *Belgium* (Case C-344/95) [1997] ECR I-1035).

10.6.5.2 **Directive 68/360: residence permits**

Article 6 of Directive 68/360 contains detailed rules concerning residence permits. These must be valid for a period of at least five years from the date of issue and be automatically renewable. When a residence permit is renewed for the first time, the period of residence may be restricted (but not to less than twelve months) if the worker has been involuntarily unemployed in the host State for more than twelve consecutive months.

? QUESTION 10.5   **CWS**

Article 7(1) of the Directive (*Cases and Materials* (10.3.5.1)) provides that a valid residence permit may not be withdrawn from a worker solely because he is temporarily incapacitated by illness or accident or because he is 'involuntarily unemployed'. What might be inferred from the reference only to 'involuntary' unemployment?

Directive 68/360 makes no reference to 'voluntary' unemployment. It could be inferred from Article 7(1) that if a person leaves employment voluntarily, Member States have the right to withdraw that person's residence permit. However, if one considers the case of a worker who leaves a job which he or she dislikes and who then immediately begins to look for other work, this inference is difficult to reconcile with the Court of Justice's ruling in *Antonissen* that Article 39 (ex 48) protects the right to enter another Member State to search for work, albeit for a limited period. Nonetheless, the **issue** of a residence permit is conditional upon employment (Article 4(3)(b)).

Where employment in the host State is temporary (between three and twelve months) a temporary permit must be issued; this may be limited to the expected period of employment. There is no requirement to issue residence permits to seasonal workers and workers employed for less than three months, whose right to reside must be recognized by the host State without the issue of a permit.

Because a Community migrant worker's right to reside in the Member State where he or she is employed stems directly from the Treaty itself and from secondary legislation, a host State may not refuse entry to or deport a worker or members of the worker's family simply because they do not possess residence permits or have failed to comply with administrative requirements (*Royer* in *Cases and Materials* (10.3.5.1)).

Administrative formalities might in themselves infringe the free movement provisions if they are unduly restrictive. An Italian requirement that immigrant workers report to the police within three days of arrival in Italy was considered in two cases, *Criminal proceedings against Lynne Watson and Alessandro Belmann* (Case 118/75) [1976] ECR 1185 and *Messner* (Case C-265/88) [1989] ECR 4209 in *Cases and Materials* (10.3.5.2). *Watson and Belmann* confirmed the right of Member States to keep track of population movements within their territory and, in particular, to lay down a period of time within which foreign nationals must report their arrival. However, that period must not be unreasonable. In *Messner*, the Court of Justice held that the three-day period laid down by the Italian legislation was unreasonably short. Where administrative requirements are compatible with the free movement provisions, a Member State is entitled to sanction failure to comply, provided the sanctions are proportionate (*Watson and Belmann*).

? **QUESTION** 10.6 CWS

In *R* v *Pieck* (Case 157/79) [1980] ECR 2171 (*Cases and Materials* (10.3.5.2)) what views did the Court of Justice express on deportation, fines and imprisonment as penalties for non-compliance with formalities by Community migrant workers?

The Court viewed deportation in these circumstances as incompatible with Community law, since it negates the very right conferred and guaranteed by the Treaty. National authorities are not entitled to impose penalties which are so disproportionate to the gravity of the infringement that they become obstacles to the free movement of persons. Whilst fines might be proportionate, imprisonment is not.

Criminal Proceedings against Sofia Skanavi and Constantin Chryssanthakopoulos (Case C-193/94) [1996] ECR I-929 also concerned the imposition of criminal penalties for failure to meet an administrative requirement. Mrs Skanavi, a Greek national, had taken up residence in Germany pursuant to her right of establishment under Article 43 (ex 52). She had failed to exchange her Greek driving licence for a German licence (as she was required to do under Community provisions) and was charged with driving without a licence, a criminal offence carrying a penalty of up to one year's imprisonment or a fine. The Court of Justice held that the issue of a driving licence by the host state in exchange for the home state licence does not constitute the basis of the right to drive in the host state but only evidence of that right. Thus, the obligation to exchange a licence is an administrative requirement. To treat a person who has failed to exchange a licence as a person driving without a licence, thereby triggering criminal penalties, would be disproportionate to the gravity of the infringement. It would constitute a lasting restriction on free movement, since a criminal conviction may have serious consequences in relation to employment or self-employed activity.

10.6.5.3 Regulation 1612/68

Regulation 1612/68 gives substance to the provisions of Article 39 (ex 48) EC in three important areas. Part 1 of the Regulation, entitled 'Employment and Workers' Families' is divided into three sections:

(a) Title I, covering eligibility for employment.

(b) Title II, providing for equality of treatment in employment.

(c) Title III, dealing with families' rights.

10.6.5.4 Regulation 1612/68: eligibility for employment (Articles 1–6)

> **⚐ EXERCISE** 10.11 CWS ➤
>
> Read Articles 1–6 of Regulation 1612/68 in *Cases and Materials* (10.3.4). On a separate piece of paper write down a summary in your own words of the non-discrimination provisions in Articles 1, 3(1), 3(2), 5, and 6(1).

Your summary might look something like this:

(a) Article 1 provides that any national of a Member State has the right to take up and pursue employment activity in another Member State with the same priority as and under the same conditions applying to nationals of that Member State.

(b) Article 3(1) prohibits discrimination against non-nationals by means, for instance, of limits placed upon applications or offers of employment.

(c) Article 3(2) prohibits, in particular, special recruitment procedures for non-nationals, restrictions on advertising which are discriminatory and any other impediments to the recruitment of non-resident workers.

(d) Article 5 provides that non-nationals seeking employment must be offered the same assistance as a Member State's own nationals.

(e) Article 6(1) prohibits the use of discriminatory medical, vocational or other criteria in the engagement and recruitment of non-nationals. The provision permits vocational tests where an employer expressly requests such a test when making the offer of employment.

Commission v France (French Merchant Seamen) (Case 167/73) [1974] ECR 359 concerned Article 4 of Regulation 1612/68 which prohibits national measures restricting the employment of nationals of other Member States by number or percentage. The offending French provision was Article 3(2) of the *Code du Travail Maritime* of 1926. Ministerial orders issued pursuant to this Article imposed an overall ratio of three French to one non-French crew members on ships of the merchant fleet. By refusing to amend Article 3(2), France was found to be in breach of her Community obligations. More recently, the Court of Justice has held that rules laid down by sporting associations limiting the number of professional footballers who are nationals of other Member States which football clubs can field in official matches infringe the free movement provisions of the Treaty (*Union Royale Belge des Sociétés de Football Association ASBL* v *Bosman* (Case 415/93) [1995] ECR I-4921).

Article 3(1) does, however, permit the imposition of indirectly discriminatory conditions of eligibility for employment relating to linguistic knowledge, provided that such knowledge is required 'by reason of the nature of the post to be filled'. (The concept of 'indirect discrimination' is considered below.) This issue arose in *Groener* v *Minister for Education* (Case 379/87) [1989] ECR 3967 (*Cases and Materials* (10.3.5.3)) which concerned the refusal to appoint Mrs Groener as a full-time art lecturer. Here, the requirement that lecturers in Irish vocational schools be competent in the Irish language, although it had the effect of discriminating against non-nationals, was held to be compatible with Regulation 1612/68. This is a somewhat surprising decision, since the teaching of art in these schools was conducted in English.

? QUESTION 10.7

Why, then, did the Court of Justice consider that it was not unreasonable to require teachers to have some knowledge of the national language?

The Irish government had for some years been promoting the use of the Irish language, which was recognized by the Irish Constitution as the first official language. The Court considered that education was important in the implementation of this policy. In view of the privileged relationship of teachers with their pupils, in a role which was not confined to the classroom but extended to participation in the general life of the school, the language requirement was not disproportionate to the government's policy objective.

However, in *Angonese* v *Cassa di Risparmio di Bolzano SpA* (Case C-281/98) [2000] ECR I-4139, [2000] 2 CMLR 1120, the Court of Justice held that rules making access to employment conditional on proof of linguistic knowledge through possession of one particular language qualification issued only in one particular province of a Member State infringe Article 39 (ex 48) unless they can be justified by factors unrelated to nationality and are proportionate to their objective. *Angonese* concerned a requirement of this kind imposed by an Italian bank, the Cassa di Risparmio. Although the applicant, Mr Angonese, did not possess the language certificate required by the bank, he could provide other evidence of his linguistic ability.

QUESTION 10.8

What do you think is the difference between direct and indirect discrimination?

Measures which openly differentiate between nationals and non-nationals are directly discriminatory. Measures which appear on their face to treat nationals and non-nationals alike but in practice have a discriminatory effect are indirectly discriminatory.

In *Bosman*, the Court of Justice considered, in the context of Artcicle 39 (ex 48), rules applying to both nationals and non-nationals alike. The questions referred by the national court concerned not only the limitations placed by sporting associations on the fielding of non-national players, referred to above, but also a transfer system under which a club to which a footballer transferred was required to pay a transfer fee to his current club. The system was not directly discriminatory, for it made no distinction between national and non-national players. Moreover, it applied both to footballers transferring within a Member State and to those transferring to clubs in other Member States. Nevertheless, the Court held that the transfer fees infringed Article 39 (ex 48) because they had a direct effect on players' 'access to the employment market in other Member States'. Later, in *Graf* v *Filzmoser Maschinenbau GmbH* (Case C-190/98) [2000] ECR 1-493, the Court again emphasised that rules applying without distinction to national and non-national workers are nonetheless capable of constituting an obstacle to freedom of movement where they 'affect access of workers to the labour market', although here the provisions in question were not liable to hinder freedom of movement and did not infringe Article 39 (ex 48).

EXERCISE 10.12

Look back at 10.6.1 to find a further example of indirect discrimination in relation to access to employment in *Clean Car Autoservice GmbH*.

10.6.5.5 Regulation 1612/68: employment and equality of treatment (Articles 7–9)

Article 7(1) of Regulation 1612/68 provides that migrant workers may not be treated differently from national workers by reason of their nationality with respect to conditions of employment such as pay, dismissal, reinstatement, and re-engagement. This is a reiteration of the non-discrimination provision in Article 39(2) (ex 48(2)) EC. Such discrimination will be struck down by the Court of Justice whether it is direct or indirect.

Marsman v *Rosskamp* (Case 44/72) [1972] ECR 1243 (*Cases and Materials* (10.3.5.4)) concerned German legislation which openly differentiated between national and non-national workers by according a degree of employment protection in the event of incapacitating injury at work to all national workers irrespective of their State of residence but only to those non-national workers who were resident in Germany. This directly discriminatory measure was found to be an infringement of the principle of equality in employment.

A good illustration of indirect discrimination in relation to conditions of employment is provided by *Sotgiu v Deutsche Bundespost* (Case 152/73) [1974] ECR 153 (*Cases and Materials* (10.3.5.4)). The German Federal Post Office had increased the separation allowances paid to post office employees in Germany who lived away from home. Those who were living in Germany at the time of their recruitment were paid at a higher rate than those who had been living abroad at that time. Whilst this arrangement did not discriminate directly against non-nationals because theoretically it treated nationals and non-nationals equally, in practice it was likely to operate to the disadvantage of non-nationals. The Court of Justice ruled that this arrangement was capable of amounting to inequality of treatment contrary to Article 39 (ex 48) EC and Article 7 of Regulation 1612/68. The Court did, however, leave open the possibility that the discrimination might be objectively justified because the higher allowance was of a temporary nature and had certain conditions attached to it. More recently, the Court of Justice confirmed that a measure is indirectly discriminatory if it is liable to disadvantage a substantially higher proportion of migrant workers. It is not necessary to find that the measure has that effect in practice (*O'Flynn v Adjudication Officer* (Case C-237/94) [1996] ECR I-2617).

Article 7(2) guarantees non-national workers the same social and tax advantages as national workers. This provision has been interpreted widely by the Court of Justice.

 QUESTION 10.9   CWS

What was the 'social advantage' at issue in *Cristini* v *SNCF* (Case 32/75) [1975] ECR 1085? See *Cases and Materials* (10.3.5.4).

In *Cristini*, the Société Nationale des Chemins de Fer Français (SNCF) (French Railways) argued that the special fare reduction card issued to large families did not constitute a 'social advantage' under Article 7(2) because that Article applied only to advantages attaching to worker status. The Court disagreed, holding that the Article included within its scope all social and tax advantages, whether or not they are attached to the contract of employment. Moreover, since the card was available to the families of deceased French workers, it would be contrary to the purpose and spirit of the Treaty to deny the same benefit to the families of deceased workers of other Member States.

Following *Cristini*, the Court of Justice stated in *Ministère Public* v *Even* (Case 207/78) [1979] ECR 2019 that social advantages falling within Article 7(2) were 'those which, whether or not linked to a contract of employment, are generally granted to workers primarily because of their objective status as workers or by virtue of the mere fact of their residence on the national territory and the extension of which to workers who are nationals of other Member States therefore seems suitable to facilitate their mobility within the Community'.

In subsequent cases, 'social and tax advantages' have been held to include a disability allowance claimed by an Italian worker in France for his adult son (*Inzirillo* v *Caisse d'Allocations Familiales de l'Arondissement de Lyon* (Case 63/76) [1976] ECR 2057), a discretionary childbirth loan (*Reina* v *Landeskreditbank Baden-Württemberg* (Case 65/81) [1982] ECR 33), a guaranteed income paid to old people in Belgium claimed by an Italian widow living there with her retired son (*Castelli* v *ONPTS* (Case 261/83) [1984] ECR 3199) and the Belgian 'minimex' (minimum income allowance) claimed by an unemployed worker (*Hoeckx* v *Centre Public d'Aide Sociale de Kalmthout* (Case 249/83) [1985] ECR 973) and by members of the family of an unemployed worker (*Scrivner* v *Centre Public d'Aide Sociale de Chastre* (Case 122/84) [1985] ECR 1027). In *Lebon*, the Court of Justice held that the right to equal social and tax advantages does not extend to persons who enter another Member State in search of work (*Centre Public d'Aide Sociale de Courcelles* v *Lebon* (Case 316/85) [1987] ECR 2811 in *Cases and Materials* (10.3.4)). The later *Sala* judgment suggests that the Court of Justice may be moving towards the recognition of broader rights for jobseekers. Here, in the context of Article 39 (ex 48) and Article 7(2) of Regulation 1612/68, the Court declared that a person who is genuinely seeking work must be classified as a worker. However, it is unclear whether this classification might be applied to a national of a Member State who enters another Member State as a jobseeker as well as to a non-national Community worker whose employment in another Member State has ended and who is consequently seeking further employment in that Member State. (*Sala* v *Freistaat Bayern* (Case C-85/96) [1998] ECR I-2691.)

 EXERCISE 10.13 CWS

Look at Articles 7(3), 8 and 9 of Regulation 1612/68 in *Cases and Materials* (10.3.4). Write down three short phrases summarizing the rights granted by these provisions.

Equality of treatment accorded to workers under Regulation 1612/68 also includes:

(a) Equal access to training in vocational schools and retraining centres (Article 7(3)).

(b) Equal trade union rights (Article 8).

(c) Equal treatment in matters of housing and house ownership (Article 9).

The right of equal access to education is discussed in 10.9 below.

10.6.5.6 Regulation 1612/68: workers' families (Articles 10–12)

Articles 10–12 of Regulation 1612/68 grant certain rights to workers' families. Remember that these are not independent rights but depend upon the worker's status as a worker.

 EXERCISE 10.14

Look again at Article 10 of Regulation 1612/68 to remind yourself of the persons who come within the scope of the term 'workers' families'.

These persons, comprising the worker's spouse and their descendants under the age of 21 or dependant and dependant relatives in the ascending line of the worker and spouse, have the right, irrespective of their nationality:

(a) to install themselves with the worker (Article 10(1));

(b) to take up employment in the host State (Article 11);

Article 11 was invoked in *Gül v Regierungspräsident Düsseldorf* (Case 131/85) [1986] ECR 1573 (*Cases and Materials* (10.3.5.5)).

Under Article 10(3), the worker is required to provide housing for the family so that they may exercise their right to install themselves with the worker and take up employment in the host State. Such housing must be of the kind which is considered normal for national workers in the same region. However, Member States cannot insist that this condition continues to be satisfied once the worker and family are installed (*Commission v*

Germany (Case 249/86) [1989] ECR 1263 in *Cases and Materials* (10.3.5.5)).

Article 12 of Regulation 1612/68 provides that a worker's children residing in the host State have the same right to general education, apprenticeship and vocational training courses as nationals of that State. This provision has been interpreted liberally to include not only equal access to educational courses but also equal eligibility for 'any general measures intended to facilitate educational attendance', including grants (*Casagrande v Lan-*

deshauptstadt München (Case 9/74) [1974] ECR 773 in *Cases and Materials* (10.3.5.5)). (See section (10.9) on access to education.)

10.6.5.7 Regulation 1251/70: the right to remain in the territory of a Member State after having been employed there

Regulation 1251/70 entitles Community migrant workers and their families (as defined in Regulation 1612/68), in certain circumstances, to continue to reside in the host State after the worker's employment there has come to an end. The following have the right to remain:

(a) a worker who has reached the statutory age for entitlement to old-age pension, has worked in the host State for at least the last twelve months and has resided there continuously for more than three years (Article 2(1)(a));

(b) a worker who has resided continuously in the host State for more than two years and has ceased work because of permanent incapacity. No residence requirement is imposed where that incapacity results from an industrial accident or occupational disease entitling the worker to a state pension (Article 2(1)(b));

(c) a frontier worker, under certain circumstances (Article 2(1)(c));

(d) members of a worker's family, if the worker is entitled to remain. Family members have the right to remain permanently, even after the worker's death (Article 3(1)). Under certain circumstances, they are entitled to remain even if the worker dies before having acquired himself or herself an entitlement to remain (Article 3(2)).

10.6.5.8 Article 39(4) (ex 48(4)): exclusion of employment in the public service

Article 39(4) (ex 48(4)) EC allows Member States to deny or restrict access to employment in the public service on grounds of a worker's nationality. Potentially, this provision gives wide scope for discrimination, particularly in those Member States where the term 'public service' covers a broad spectrum of activities. However, the meaning of 'public service' is to be determined not by the Member States but by the Court, which has defined the term restrictively.

It is clear that Article 39(4) (ex 48(4)) applies only to admission to the public service. Once a national of another Member State has been appointed to a public service post, any discrimination on grounds of nationality with regard to remuneration or other conditions of employment will infringe the free movement provisions. This was emphasised in *Sotgiu* v *Deutsche Bundespost* (Case 152/73) [1974] ECR 153 (*Cases and Materials* (10.3.5.4)).

 QUESTION 10.10   CWS

In *Commission* v *Belgium (Public Employees)* (Case 149/79) [1980] ECR 3881 (*Cases and Materials* (10.3.5.6)), what posts did the Belgian government claim were in the public service?

Under Belgian law, only persons in possession of Belgian nationality were permitted to take up posts with local authorities and public undertakings. These positions included trainee drivers, loaders, platelayers, shunters, and signallers on Belgian railways, unskilled workers on local railways and nurses, night-watchmen, plumbers, carpenters, electricians, garden hands, architects, and supervisors employed by the Municipalities of Brussels and Auderghem. On challenge by the Commission in *Commission* v *Belgium*, the Belgian government argued that the regulation of entry to public office should remain a matter for Member States and that the concept of 'public service' did not have a Community meaning. The Court of Justice disagreed, insisting upon the uniform interpretation and application of Article 39(4) (ex 48(4)) throughout the Community and defining 'public service' posts as those involving 'the exercise of power conferred by public law' where there was a 'responsibility for safeguarding the general interests of the State'.

Subsequent judgments have excluded from the scope of 'public service' trainee school teachers (*Lawrie-Blum* v *Land Baden-Württemberg* (Case 66/85) [1986] ECR 2121 in *Cases and Materials* (10.3.3)), university foreign language assistants (*Allué and Coonan* v *Universita degli studi di Venezia* (Case 33/88) [1989] ECR 1591), secondary school teachers (*Bleis* v *Ministère de l'Education Nationale* (Case C-4/91) [1991] ECR I-5627) and primary school teachers (*Commission* v *Luxembourg* (Case C-473/93) [1996] ECR I-3207). These and other decisions indicate that the Article 39(4) (ex 48(4)) exception applies only to posts requiring a particular allegiance to the State. These might include, for instance, high-ranking positions in the police force, armed forces, civil service and the judiciary but does not include civil servants in general (*Lawrie-Blum*).

10.6.5.9 Restrictions on entry and residence

As has been seen, Article 39(4) (ex 48(4)) EC contains a derogation from the principle of free movement of persons within the Community. Limitations are also placed upon the rights of entry and residence of migrant workers and their families by Article 39(3) (ex 48(3)). This Article allows Member States to deny these rights on grounds of 'public policy, public security or public health'.

10.6.6 The right of Member States to restrict entry and residence

Article 39(3) (ex 48(3)) EC allows Member States to restrict entry and residence in certain circumstances. This Article is fleshed out by Directive 64/221. Because of the fundamental importance of the principle of freedom of movement of persons within the Community internal market, the Court of Justice interprets the limitations very restrictively.

10.6.6.1 The scope of Article 39(3) (ex 48(3))

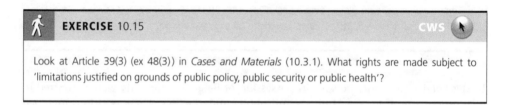

EXERCISE 10.15   CWS

Look at Article 39(3) (ex 48(3)) in *Cases and Materials* (10.3.1). What rights are made subject to 'limitations justified on grounds of public policy, public security or public health'?

The grounds of limitation apply to those rights set out in Article 39(3) (ex 48(3)) concerning entry to and residence in the territory of another Member State. They are not applicable to conditions of employment.

Whilst Article 39(3) clearly allows a Member State to exclude or deport a non-national Community worker from its territory on grounds of public policy, public security or public health, the Treaty provision is less clear as to whether the limitations include the right to impose partial restrictions on free movement within a Member State. This issue was first considered by the Court of Justice in *Rutili* v *Ministre de l'Intérieur* (Case 36/75) [1975] ECR 1219.

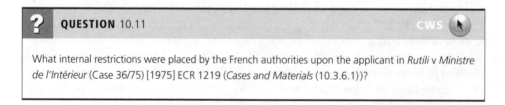

QUESTION 10.11   CWS

What internal restrictions were placed by the French authorities upon the applicant in *Rutili* v *Ministre de l'Intérieur* (Case 36/75) [1975] ECR 1219 (*Cases and Materials* (10.3.6.1))?

The applicant, an Italian national well known for his trade union activities and political activism, had been prohibited by the Ministry of the Interior from residing in certain French *départements*. The Court of Justice held that prohibitions on residence under Article 39(3) (ex 48(3)) may be imposed only in respect of the whole of the national territory. Prohibitions on residence limited to certain areas amounted to inequality of treatment between nationals and non-nationals which, if within the field of application of the Treaty, breached the non-discrimination provision contained in Article 12 (ex 6, formerly 7).

EXERCISE 10.16 CWS

Look again at paragraph 50 the *Rutili* judgment (*Cases & Materials* (10.3.6.1)). The dictum it contains must now be read in the light of the judgment of the Court of Justice in *Ministre de l'Intérieur* v *Olazabal* (Case C-100/01), [2002] ECR I-10981 (*Cases & Materials* (10.3.6.1)).

 EXERCISE 10.17 CWS

Read the extracts from the *Olazabal* judgment (*Cases & Materials* (10.3.6.1)) and note how the Court of Justice places the above dictum 'in its context'.

In *Olazabal*, the Court of Justice distinguished the circumstances of Mr Rutili and Mr Olazabal. In *Rutili*, the Court pointed out, the national court had doubts as to whether the exercise of trade union rights justified measures aimed to maintain public order. By contrast, in *Olazabal* the national court accepted not only that public policy reasons justified partial restrictions being placed on Mr Olazabal but that, if partial restrictions could not be imposed, public policy reasons would justify his exclusion from the whole of the national territory.

The Court next referred to earlier judgments in which it had held that the Community free movement provisions permit Member States to impose limitations on nationals of other Member States which they cannot apply to their own nationals, namely to exclude them from their territory. The Court reasoned that, where nationals of other Member States are liable to deportation or prohibition of residence, they may also be subject to less severe measures imposing partial limitations, even though the Member State concerned cannot apply such measures to its own nationals. Such measures are compatible with the free movement provisions provided they are based on the non-national's individual conduct and are proportionate.

10.6.6.2 The scope of Directive 64/221

The Article 39(3) (ex 48(3)) grounds of limitation are clarified and elaborated in Directive 64/221, which applies, *inter alia*, to workers of one Member State who travel to or reside in another in order to work there and to members of their families (Article 1). Articles 1–4 of the Directive deal with the scope of the public policy, public security and public health grounds. Articles 5–10 contain important procedural safeguards.

 EXERCISE 10.18 CWS

Read Article 2(1) of Directive 64/221 in *Cases and Materials* (10.3.6.2). List the measures to which it relates.

Article 2(1) of Directive 64/221 makes a clear statement of the measures to which the Directive relates, namely those measures concerning:

(a) entry into their territory;

(b) issue or renewal of residence permits;

(c) expulsion from their territory.

taken by Member States on grounds of public policy, public security or public health. Article 2(2) provides that 'such grounds shall not be invoked to service economic ends'.

'Measures' falling within the scope of Article 2(1) were defined in *R* v *Bouchereau* (Case 30/77) [1977] ECR 1999 (*Cases and Materials* (10.3.6.2)) as 'any action which affects the right of persons coming within the field of application of Article 48 to enter and reside freely in the Member States under the same conditions as the nationals of the host State'.

10.6.6.3 **Directive 64/221: provisions clarifying the scope of the grounds of limitation**

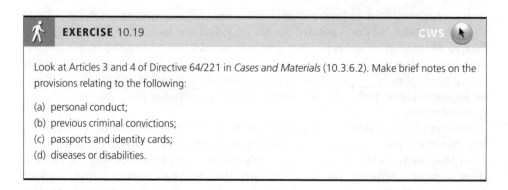

EXERCISE 10.19   CWS

Look at Articles 3 and 4 of Directive 64/221 in *Cases and Materials* (10.3.6.2). Make brief notes on the provisions relating to the following:

(a) personal conduct;

(b) previous criminal convictions;

(c) passports and identity cards;

(d) diseases or disabilities.

Articles 3 and 4 of Directive 64/221 mark out certain boundaries to the public policy, public security and public health grounds of limitation:

(a) Measures taken on grounds of public policy and public security must be based exclusively on the personal conduct of the individual whose rights of entry and residence are being challenged (Article 3(1)).

(b) Previous criminal convictions are not in themselves sufficient grounds for taking such measures (Article 3(2)).

(c) The expiry of a passport or identity card used to enter a Member State or to obtain a residence permit does not justify expulsion from that State (Article 3(3)). The State which issued those documents shall not refuse re-entry to its territory because the documents have expired or the nationality of the holder is in dispute (Article 3(4)).

(d) Only those diseases and disabilities listed in the Annex to the Directive justify the refusal of entry to a Member State or the refusal of a first residence permit (Article 4(1)). Diseases or disabilities occurring after the issue of a first residence permit do not justify expulsion or the refusal to renew a residence permit (Article 4(2)).

10.6.6.4 **Limitation on grounds of public policy**

You will recall that measures taken on grounds of public policy must be 'based exclusively on the personal conduct of the individual concerned' (Article 3(1) of Directive 64/221). Discussion now turns to the general scope of the public policy ground.

This was considered in a very well known case, *Van Duyn v Home Office* (Case 41/74) [1974] ECR 1337 (*Cases and Materials* (10.3.6.3)). Yvonne van Duyn, a Dutch national, arrived at Gatwick airport and told immigration officials that she intended to work as a secretary for the Church of Scientology at East Grinstead. She was refused entry. Although the Church of Scientology was not an illegal organization in the UK and there were no restrictions on nationals who wished to join the Church or to take up employment with it, the UK government regarded Scientology as socially harmful. It sought to justify its refusal to allow entry to Ms van Duyn on grounds of public policy. Ms van Duyn challenged the government's action in the High Court, relying on her rights under Article 39 (ex 48) EC and Article 3(1) of Directive 64/221. In response to the first two questions put to it on a reference from that court, the Court of Justice held both Article 39 (ex 48) EC and Article 3(1) of Directive 64/221 to be directly effective (see **Chapter 5**).

 EXERCISE 10.20   CWS

The third question concerned the interpretation of Article 39 (ex 48) EC and of Article 3 of Directive 64/221. Look at the Court's response in *Cases and Materials* (10.3.6.3) and write down on a separate piece of paper a summary of the main points arising from it.

Your summary might look something like this:

(a) The concept of public policy is to be interpreted strictly. Although its scope cannot be determined unilaterally by each Member State without control by Community institutions, Member States are allowed an area of discretion within the limits imposed by the Treaty.

(b) Present association with an organisation, which reflects participation in its activities and identification with its aims, is a voluntary act and therefore constitutes 'personal conduct' justifying refusal of entry to a Member State. In general, past association would not justify such action.

(c) Where a Member State has taken administrative measures to counteract the activities of an organisation, that State may rely on the public policy ground even though it has not made those activities unlawful. It may place restrictions on a national of another Member State who wishes to take up a particular employment even though no similar restrictions are placed on its own nationals.

In later cases, the scope of 'public policy' has been more narrowly defined. In *Rutili v Ministre de l'Intérieur* (Case 36/75) [1975] ECR 1219 (*Cases and Materials* (10.3.6.1)), the Court of Justice held that restrictions cannot be placed on the right of a national of a Member State to enter the territory of another Member State and remain there unless his or her presence or conduct presents 'a genuine and sufficiently serious threat to public policy'. Moreover, restrictive measures must be 'necessary' for the protection of society's interests (do you recognize the proportionality principle here?). The Court went further in *R* v *Bouchereau* (Case 30/77) [1977] ECR 1999 (*Cases and Materials* (10.3.6.2)) and declared that the threat must be such as to affect 'one of the fundamental interests of society'. Nevertheless, it was recognised that the circumstances justifying recourse to the public policy ground may vary from time to time and from one State to another and that therefore Member States must be left an area of discretion in this matter. However, the scope of that discretion does not extend to the adoption of measures which are of a general preventative nature (look at *Bonsignore* v *Oberstadtdirektor of the City of Cologne* (Case 67/74) [1975] ECR 297 (*Cases and Materials* (10.3.6.3)) for an example of a measure of a general preventative nature).

In *Van Duyn*, the Court of Justice approved the UK's refusal to admit a national of another Member State who was a member of an organisation to which its own nationals were at liberty to belong. *Adoui and Cornuaille* v *Belgian State* (Joined Cases 115 and 116/81) [1982] ECR 1665 (*Cases and Materials* (10.3.6.3)) established that a Member State may only restrict admission to individuals in respect of conduct which, if it were engaged in by that State's own nationals, would give rise to 'repressive measures or other genuine and effective measures intended to combat such conduct'.

10.6.6.5 Personal conduct

As already noted, Article 3(1) of Directive 64/221 provides that measures taken on grounds of public policy or public security must be based exclusively on the personal conduct of the individual concerned. In *Van Duyn*, the Court of Justice held that present association with an organization, reflecting participation in its activities and identification with its aims, constitutes personal conduct. However, a general preventative measure adopted by a Member State, because it is not based on an individual's personal conduct, cannot be justified on public policy grounds (see *Bonsignore, Cases and Materials* (10.3.6.3)). In *Criminal Proceedings against Donatella Calfa* (Case C-348/96) ECR I-11 (*Cases and Materials* (10.3.6.4)), the Court of Justice held that the public policy exception could not be relied on to justify an automatic expulsion for life imposed by Greek provisions on non-nationals convicted of certain criminal offences. Such measures, because they were imposed automatically, took no account of the personal conduct of the offender.

10.6.6.6 Previous criminal convictions

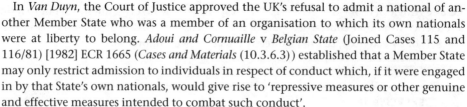

? QUESTION 10.12

Do you recall what Article 3(2) of Directive 64/221 provides on previous criminal convictions?

This article provides that previous criminal convictions shall not in themselves constitute grounds for measures taken on public policy or public security grounds. If previous criminal convictions are not **in themselves** grounds, can they be taken into account at all? This question was addressed in *R v Bouchereau* (Case 30/77) [1977] ECR 1999. Bouchereau was a French national working in England who had been convicted on two occasions of unlawful possession of drugs. The magistrates' court which heard the second of these cases proposed to recommend his deportation.

 EXERCISE 10.21 CWS

Look at the *Bouchereau* case in *Cases and Materials* (10.3.6.2). The Court of Justice held that previous criminal convictions may be taken into account in certain circumstances. Copy out the words used by the Court to describe those circumstances.

Previous criminal convictions can only be taken into account when 'the circumstances which gave rise to that conviction are evidence of personal conduct constituting a *present threat to the requirements of public policy*'. This will be the case where the individual concerned shows *'a propensity to act in the same way in the future'* (emphases added). Note, however, that the Court did not rule out the possibility that past conduct alone may be a sufficiently serious threat to the requirements of public policy.

The issue of previous criminal convictions arose again more recently in *Criminal proceedings against Donatella Calfa* (Case C-348/96) [1999] ECR I-11.

 EXERCISE 10.22 CWS

Read the extracts from *Calfa* (Cases & Materials (10.3.6.4)). Summarize, in a few sentences, the reasoning of the Court of Justice in relation to the public policy ground, previous criminal convictions and personal conduct.

The Court of Justice reiterated that the public policy exception, like all derogations from a fundamental Treaty principle, must be interpreted strictly. The Court pointed out that Article 3 of Directive 64/221 states that measures taken on grounds of public policy must be based exclusively on the personal conduct of the individual concerned. Further, previous criminal convictions cannot, in themselves, constitute grounds for taking such measures. Such a conviction can only be taken into account in so far as the circumstances giving rise to that conviction are evidence of personal conduct constituting a present threat to the requirements of public policy. The national legislation at issue imposed automatic expulsion for life without taking into account the personal conduct of the offender or of the danger posed by him for the requirements of public policy. Consequently, the public policy exception cannot be relied on to justify a restriction such as that imposed by the Greek legislation.

10.6.6.7 Limitation on grounds of public security

The public policy and public security grounds may be regarded as interrelated and overlapping. Consequently, the latter will not be considered separately.

10.6.6.8 Directive 64/221: diseases and disabilities

Directive 64/221 stipulates that only those diseases and disabilities listed in the Annex to the Directive can justify restrictions on entry and residence (Article 4(1)) and that diseases and disabilities occurring after a first residence permit has been issued shall not justify expulsion or the refusal to renew a residence permit (Article 4(2)).

EXERCISE 10.23   CWS

Turn to the Annex to Directive 64/221 in *Cases and Materials* (10.3.6.2). Make a mental note of the following:

(a) The Annex is divided into sections A and B.

(b) Section A, headed *Diseases which might endanger public health* specifies certain diseases (tuberculosis, syphilis) and includes others by reference to national provisions and to a World Health Organization Regulation.

(c) Section B, headed *Diseases and disabilities which might threaten public policy or public security* lists drug addiction and various kinds of mental illness.

10.6.6.9 Directive 64/221: procedural rights

The second part of Directive 64/221 (Articles 5–9) grants important procedural rights to individuals who are denied the rights of entry and residence granted by the Treaty and secondary legislation. These are as follows:

(a) Article 5: the right to remain in the host State pending a decision either to grant or refuse a residence permit. That decision must be taken as soon as possible and in any event not later than six months from the date of application for the permit.

(b) Article 6: the right to be informed of the grounds on which the decision has been taken, unless matters of state security are involved.

(c) Article 7: the right to official notification of refusal of a residence permit or of the decision to expel. Save in an emergency, the period allowed for leaving the host State, which must be stated in the notification, must be not less than fifteen days (where no residence permit has yet been granted) or one month (in all other cases).

(d) Article 8: the right to the same legal remedies as are available to nationals of the host State in respect of acts of the administration.

(e) In addition, Article 9 requires Member States to have in place a system for appeal to a competent authority independent of the body which adopted the measure denying or restricting the individual's rights.

10.6.7 Social security provision

If Community migrant workers were at risk of losing out on social security provision by moving to another Member State, this would act as a serious barrier to free movement. Article 42 (ex 51) EC aims to address this problem. Under this Article, Community social security measures may be adopted which provide for the aggregation of qualifying periods relating to benefit and secure the payment of benefit to persons resident in the territories of the Member States. There are a number of secondary provisions developing Community law in this area.

10.7 Provisions of the Treaty of Amsterdam: the establishment of an area of freedom, security, and justice

Building upon the framework of co-operation previously established in the Schengen Agreements between some of the Member States (see **Chapter 1**), the Treaty of Amsterdam inserted a new Title IV into the EC Treaty, headed 'Visas, asylum, immigration, and other policies related to the free movement of persons' (Articles 61–9). These provisions seek to establish progressively an area of freedom, security and justice. They provide for the adoption by the Council of measures to ensure the free movement of persons in accordance with Article 14 (ex 7a), together with measures concerning controls on the European Union's external borders, asylum and immigration and other measures to prevent and combat crime.

In particular, these include measures ensuring the absence of any controls on persons, be they citizens of the Union or not, when crossing internal borders and measures establishing standards and procedures to be followed by Member States in carrying out checks on persons at external borders. The Title also provides for the adoption of other measures concerning, *inter alia* judicial cooperation in civil matters with cross-border implications and certain aspects of immigration policy. Under the Amsterdam provisions, most of the measures referred to in the new Title IV required unanimity in the Council. The Treaty of Nice 2001 extends the use of qualified majority voting into some of the Title IV areas.

Protocols annexed to the EC Treaty secure the exclusion of the United Kingdom, Ireland, and Denmark from Title IV. These Member States are not bound by its provisions, nor do they take part in adopting the measures envisaged by the Title. Both the United Kingdom and Ireland may continue to exercise controls on persons entering their territories and other Member States remain entitled to impose controls on persons entering from the United Kingdom and Ireland.

10.8 **Freedom of movement for the self-employed**

10.8.1 **Right of establishment and to provide services**

Community rights of free movement for the self-employed are secured by provisions granting freedom of establishment (Articles 43–48 (ex 52–58) EC) and the freedom to provide services (Articles 49–55 (ex 59–66)). The main provisions are:

(a) Article 43 (ex 52) (freedom of establishment).

(b) Articles 49 and 50 (ex 59 and 60) (freedom to provide services).

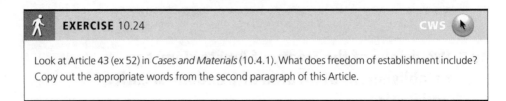

EXERCISE 10.24   CWS

Look at Article 43 (ex 52) in *Cases and Materials* (10.4.1). What does freedom of establishment include? Copy out the appropriate words from the second paragraph of this Article.

Freedom of establishment includes 'the right to take up and pursue activities as self-employed persons and to set up and manage undertakings, in particular companies or firms within the meaning of the second paragraph of Article 48 (ex 58), under the conditions laid down for its own nationals by the law of the country where such establishment is effected . . .'.

Article 48 (ex 58), paragraph 2 defines 'companies' and 'firms' as those bodies constituted under civil or commercial law, including cooperative societies, and other legal persons governed by public or private law, except those which are non-profitmaking. Where such companies or firms are formed in accordance with the law of a Member State and have their registered office, central administration or principal place of business within the Community, they are to be treated in the same way as natural persons who are nationals of Member States (Article 48 (ex 58); paragraph 1).

Article 49 (ex 59) provides for the abolition of restrictions on freedom to provide services within the Community. Article 50 (ex 60) elucidates the meaning of 'services'.

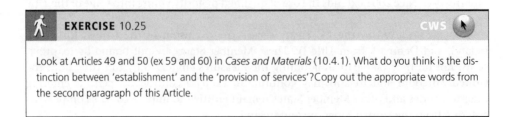

EXERCISE 10.25   CWS

Look at Articles 49 and 50 (ex 59 and 60) in *Cases and Materials* (10.4.1). What do you think is the distinction between 'establishment' and the 'provision of services'? Copy out the appropriate words from the second paragraph of this Article.

Establishment in another Member State involves setting up a business or practising a professional activity (for instance as a doctor or a lawyer) there on a permanent or semi-permanent basis. This might be done by a sole trader, a partnership or a company. By contrast, when a business is established in one Member State and simply provides services in another without being installed there, this constitutes the 'provision of services'.

This includes the situation in which the service provider does not move to another Member State in order to provide services there, as in *Alpine Investments BV* v *Minister of Finance* (Case C384/93) [1995] ECR I-1141, a case concerning 'cold calling' by telephone. With the growing use of the telephone and internet, these forms of marketing services, in which neither the service provider nor the recipient need to move physically to provide or receive the service, are becoming increasingly common.

Secondary legislation grants rights of entry and residence to the self-employed and their families. These rights are very similar to the rights granted to workers:

(a) Directive 73/148 grants rights of entry and residence.

(b) Directive 75/34 grants the right to remain in a Member State after having been self-employed there.

? QUESTION 10.13

Do you remember the two Directives which give similar rights to workers?

Directives 73/148 and Directive 75/34 correspond, respectively, to Directives 68/360 and Regulation 1251/70. However, Regulation 1612/68 has no equivalent applying to the self-employed, hence the importance of Article 12 (ex 6) EC in this area.

? QUESTION 10.14   CWS

Do you remember what general principle is contained in Article 12 (ex 6)? If not, look again at this article in *Cases and Materials* (10.1).

Article 12 (ex 6, formerly Article 7) prohibits discrimination on grounds of nationality 'within the scope of application of this Treaty'.

Member States have the right to restrict the entry and residence of self-employed persons on certain grounds.

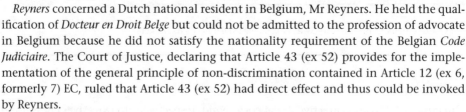

? **QUESTION** 10.15

What do you think those grounds might be?

As in the case of workers, the right of free movement of self-employed persons is subject to limitations justified on grounds of public policy, public security or public health. Articles 46 (ex 56) (in respect of those exercising the right of establishment) and 55 (ex 66) (those providing services) of the Treaty impose limitations which are substantiated in Directive 64/221. Article 45 (ex 55) of the Treaty constitutes the equivalent of Article 39(4) (ex 48(4)) (exception for employment in the public service).

10.8.2 Direct effect of Articles 43 and 49 (ex 52 and 59)

Articles 43 and 49 (ex 52 and 59) represent specific applications of the principle of non-discrimination on grounds of nationality. Their direct effect was established in *Reyners* v *Belgium* (Case 2/74) [1974] ECR 631 (Article 43 (ex 52)) and *Van Binsbergen* v *Bestuur van de Bedrijfsvereniging voor de Metaalnijverheid* (Case 33/74) [1974] ECR 1299 (Articles 49 and 50 (ex 59 and 60)). See *Cases and Materials* (10.4.2) for both cases.

Reyners concerned a Dutch national resident in Belgium, Mr Reyners. He held the qualification of *Docteur en Droit Belge* but could not be admitted to the profession of advocate in Belgium because he did not satisfy the nationality requirement of the Belgian *Code Judiciaire*. The Court of Justice, declaring that Article 43 (ex 52) provides for the implementation of the general principle of non-discrimination contained in Article 12 (ex 6, formerly 7) EC, ruled that Article 43 (ex 52) had direct effect and thus could be invoked by Reyners.

In *Van Binsbergen*, in the context of the provision of services, a residence requirement imposed by Dutch law was challenged under Articles 49 and 50 (ex 59 and 60) EC. A Dutch national who was qualified as an advocate in Holland and was providing legal services to a client there was informed, when he moved from Holland to Belgium, that he could no longer represent his client because under Dutch law only lawyers established in Holland had rights of audience before certain tribunals. The Court of Justice held that Articles 49 and 50 (ex 59 and 60), which prohibit discrimination against a provider of services, were directly effective and could therefore be invoked by an individual who was the victim of discrimination either on grounds of nationality or State of residence.

Articles 44, 47 and 52 (ex 54, 57 and 63) EC provide for the issue of Directives concerning rights of free movement for the self-employed. In *Reyners* and *Van Binsbergen*, the respective governments argued that the relevant Treaty Articles (43, 49, and 50 (ex 52, 59, and 60)) were not directly effective, because the rights they granted were conditional upon the issue of Directives. As has been noted, the Court of Justice rejected this contention, holding that in so far as non-discrimination on grounds of nationality and residence were concerned, Articles 43, 49, and 50 (ex 52, 59, and 60) granted directly effective rights. Consequently, Directives issued under Articles 44, 47, and 52 (ex 54, 57, and 63) were intended not to establish the right of free movement but simply to facilitate it.

10.8.3 **Recognition of qualifications**

Later cases raised the question as to whether Article 43 (ex 52) or Articles 49 and 50 (ex 59 and 60) could be invoked directly by individuals who were refused permission to practise a trade or profession in another Member State because they did not satisfy national rules relating to professional qualifications and educational requirements. Because such rules may not be easily satisfied by a non-national, they can constitute a very serious obstacle to the free movement of self-employed persons within the Community. These difficulties stem from Articles 43 and 50 (ex 52 and 60) EC which provide that the right of establishment and to provide services is to be exercised under the same conditions laid down by national law for nationals of the host State.

Thieffry v *Conseil de l'Ordre des Avocats à la Cour de Paris* (Case 71/76) [1977] ECR 765 (*Cases and Materials* (10.4.3)) and *Patrick* v *Ministre des Affaires Culturelles* (Case 11/77) [1977] ECR 1199 concerned the refusal by the competent national authorities to allow the applicants, who were non-French Community nationals and whose qualifications were officially recognized in France, to train for the French bar (*Thieffry*) and practise architecture in France (*Patrick*) because they did not possess French qualifications. This was found to be discriminatory and a breach of Article 43 (ex 52) and Article 12 (ex 6, formerly 7) EC. The fact that no Directives relating to these particular professions had been passed at that time did not affect the applicants' rights because Article 43 (ex 52) was directly effective.

 EXERCISE 10.26   CWS

Read paragraphs 18 and 19 of the *Thieffry* judgment (*Cases and Materials* (10.4.3)). What was the view of the Court of Justice on the restriction of access to a profession to those individuals holding national qualifications?

The Court of Justice held that it is an unjustified restriction on the freedom of establishment to refuse admission to a profession to an individual who has a qualification that has been recognized as equivalent to a national qualification in the state of establishment and who has satisfied any relevant conditions relating to professional training.

Moreover, where qualifications are not already recognized as equivalent in the host State, the national authorities must compare an individual's education and training with national requirements and must recognize a non-national's qualifications if they are equivalent. If they are not equivalent, the authorities are entitled to require the person concerned to show that he or she has acquired the knowledge and experience which are lacking. The authorities are obliged to take these into account. This applies where there is no Community harmonizing regulation of the professional qualification in question, as in *Vlassopoulou* v *Ministerium für Justiz* (Case 340/89) [1991] ECR I-2357 (*Cases and Materials* (10.4.3)), a case concerning the profession of lawyer which, at the time of the judgment, was not covered by harmonising regulation. It also applies in a situation which fails outside the scope of an existing Directive on mutual recognition (*Hocsman* v

Ministre de l'Emploi et de la Solidarité (Case C-238/98) [2000] ECR I-6623; *Conseil Nationale de l'Ordre des Architectes Dreessen* (Case C-31/00) [2002] 2 CMLR 62).

It is to the process of harmonization and of mutual recognition of diplomas that discussion now turns.

10.8.4 Mutual recognition of qualifications

The original approach to harmonization within the Community for the achievement of the mutual recognition of qualifications consisted in the production of Directives relating to individual trades and professions. Accordingly, Directives were passed covering the qualification, amongst others, of doctors, nurses, dentists, veterinary surgeons and self-employed persons in a wide range of industries. However, progress was very slow.

A new approach was adopted with Directive 89/48. This provides for the mutual recognition of qualifications in professions requiring a higher education diploma (now supplemented by Directive 92/51 on the mutual recognition of qualifications obtained on completion of non-degree post-secondary education and amended by Directive 2001/19). The Directive applies to a number of professions, such as the law, accountancy, surveying, and town planning, but not to those already covered by specific Directives. Under its provisions, an individual who holds a higher education diploma awarded on completion of at least three years professional education and has completed the professional training required for that profession is, in principle, entitled to pursue that profession in another Member State.

However, if the training and education fall short of that required by the host State by at least one year or the individual has not undertaken the entire period of supervised practice required by the host State, evidence of professional experience may be required. The Directive allows Member States, in certain circumstances, to require a non-national to pass an aptitude test examining knowledge appropriate to the profession or to complete an adaptation period (a period of supervised training in the host State). This applies, for instance, where there is a substantial difference between the matters covered by training in the host State and the State where training was undertaken. In relation to the practice of the law, Directive 98/5 allows lawyers qualified in one Member State to be integrated into the profession in another Member State following a period of professional practice in the host State under their home State professional title.

In March 2003 the Commission presented proposals for a Directive consolidating and simplifying the rules applying to the professions covered by the existing mutual recognition Directives. At the time of writing, these proposals were still under consultation.

10.8.5 Rules of professional conduct

Rules of professional conduct regulating such matters as professional ethics and organization can constitute real obstacles to the movement of self-employed persons because non-nationals may find it difficult or costly to comply with them. Nevertheless, with respect to non-nationals who exercise their right of establishment in other Member States, conditions relating to the exercise of particular professions may be imposed, provided that those conditions apply equally and without discrimination to nationals and non-nationals. This is the corollary of the non-national's right to equality of treatment in the exercise of a trade or profession.

The Court of Justice has recognized that the problem of compliance with professional rules of conduct can be particularly acute for persons providing services. Such persons are already likely to be bound by the regulations of their State of establishment and a requirement that they also comply with the professional rules of the State where the services are provided might well be an unnecessary hindrance to free movement. However, such rules will be permissible in relation to persons providing services if they are non-discriminatory, objectively justified in the interest of the general public and proportionate to their aim (*Van Binsbergen* v *Bestuur van de Bedrijfsvereniging voor de Metaalnijverheid* (Case 33/74) [1974] ECR 1299 in *Cases and Materials* (10.4.2)). These criteria were further elaborated in *Criminal proceedings against Alfred John Webb* (Case 279/80) [1981] ECR 3305 in which the Court of Justice stated that the host Member State, when applying its own national professional rules, should examine closely any existing national regulation in the State of establishment of the supplier of the service to see whether such regulation already secures the desired aim.

In the 'Insurance Cases' (*Commission* v *Germany (Insurance Services)* (Case 205/84) [1986] ECR 3755; *Commission* v *Ireland (Co-insurance services)* (Case 206/84) [1986] ECR 3817; *Commission* v *France* (Case 220/83) [1986] ECR 3663; *Commission* v *Denmark (Insurance Services)* (Case 252/83) [1986] ECR 3713) the Court of Justice made a clear distinction between the application of national professional rules to businesses established in a Member State and to those businesses providing services there. The regulation of those providing services could not be allowed to hinder the free movement of services and must be scrutinized to see whether it was objectively justified and proportionate and whether national rules in the State of establishment already achieve the aims in view.

 EXERCISE 10.27   CWS

Read the extract from *Säger* v *Dennemeyer & Co. Ltd* (Case C-76/90) [1991] ECR I-4221 in *Cases and Materials* (10.4.4). Summarize, in a few sentences, the reasoning of the Court of Justice in relation to the proportionality of the national legislation.

In *Säger*, the Court of Justice once again distinguished between the provision of services and establishment, emphasizing that the provision of services should not be made subject to all the conditions required for establishment. The Court held that the freedom to provide services may be limited only by non-discriminatory rules which are justified in the public interest and only in so far as that interest is not already protected by rules applying to the service provider in the Member State in which he is established.

In particular, requirements limiting freedom to provide services must be proportionate to their objective. The aim of the German legislation in question was to protect the recipients of legal services by ensuring that they were advised by suitably qualified persons. This objective justified a restriction of the freedom to provide services. However, national measures would be disproportionate to that objective if they required the service providers to have professional qualifications which were unnecessary for the tasks to be carried out. Here, the tasks—warning clients when renewal fees were due and paying fees on their behalf—did not require specific professional skills.

In the cases so far noted, the Court of Justice has made a distinction between limitations on the freedom to provide services and the right of establishment. The judgment in *Gebhard v Consiglio dell'Ordine degli Avvocati e Procuratori di Milano* (Case C-55/94) [1995] ECR I-4165 incorporates an assimilation of the principles to be applied in each context. Disciplinary proceedings had been opened in Milan against Gebhard, a lawyer qualified in Germany, who was accused of contravening Italian legislation by practising in Italy under the title *avvocato*. The Court of Justice confirmed that a Community national exercising the right of establishment in another Member State must comply with the conditions laid down for the pursuit of that activity, such as conditions relating to the use of a professional title. However, measures constituting a limitation on a fundamental freedom guaranteed by the Treaty must be applied in a non-discriminatory manner, must be justified in the general interest and must be suitable for and proportionate to attaining their objective.

In some areas of professional activity, Directives have been adopted providing for the harmonization and recognition of rules of conduct. A good example is Directive 77/249, governing the provision of services by lawyers in Member States in which they are not established. Article 4(1) of the Directive grants to non-national lawyers the right to practise (but not the right of establishment) subject to the conditions laid down for nationals but modifies these for non-national practitioners by dispensing with residence and registration requirements for 'the representation of a client in legal proceedings'. On the other hand, Article 5 allows Member States to require lawyers 'to work in conjunction with a lawyer who practises before the judicial authority in question and who would, where necessary, be answerable to that authority . . .' and Article 1(1) allows the exclusion of non-national lawyers from certain activities involving the preparation of formal documents.

Where a Directive has been adopted providing for harmonization or mutual recognition of particular professional rules of conduct, only those national rules which are compatible with its provisions will be permissible. It is for Member States to decide whether national rules are covered by the relevant Directive.

10.8.6 **Other kinds of restriction on the freedom to provide services**

We have so far considered restrictions on the freedom to provide services arising from educational requirements and rules of professional conduct. Other kinds of measures may limit this freedom.

 EXERCISE 10.28 **CWS**

Look at *HM Customs and Excise v Schindler* (Case C-275/92) [1994] ECR I-1039 in *Cases and Materials* (10.4.5). What was the nature of the obstacle to the free provision of services in this case? How did the United Kingdom seek to justify the restriction? Make a note of your answer.

The Court of Justice held that national legislation which, like the United Kingdom legislation on lotteries, prohibits (with exceptions) the holding of lotteries and precludes lottery organizers from other Member States from promoting their lotteries and selling their tickets, constitutes a restriction on the freedom to provide services. The United Kingdom government argued that the legislation was aimed to protect public morality, to protect the consumer, to prevent crime and fraud and to restrict demand for gambling. The Court declared that, in view of the particular nature of lotteries, national legislation of the kind in question would be justified on grounds of social policy and the prevention of fraud, provided it is not discriminatory. The Court also reiterated the requirement for proportionality, indicating that the national legislation at issue was justified as a *'necessary* part of the protection which that Member State seeks to secure in its territory' (emphasis added). The Court of Justice considered national gambling controls once again in a reference from a Finnish court. Here, the Court held that national legislation, such as the Finnish legislation, which grants a single public body the exclusive right to operate slot machines does not contravene Treaty provisions on the freedom to provide services, since that legislation was justified by public interest objectives similar to those in *Schindler* (*Läärä, Cotswold Microsystems and Oy Transatlantic Software* v *Kihlakunnansyyttäjä (Jyväskylä), Suomen Valtio (Finnish State)* (Case C-124/97) [1999] ECR I-6067.

Criminal proceedings against Michel Guiot (Case C-272/94) [1996] ECR I-1905, concerned Belgian national social security legislation. This required an employer established in Luxembourg and providing services in Belgium to pay contributions to the Belgian social security fund in relation to its employees, even though it was already paying social security contributions in Luxembourg. Such a provision, declared the Court of Justice, was liable to restrict the free provision of services because it placed an extra financial burden on the employer. Whilst the measure might be justified if it satisfied an overriding requirement relating to the social protection of workers, that would not be the case if the contributions paid in the State of establishment gave the workers in question the same or similar protection.

10.8.7 Article 45 (ex 55): activities concerned with the exercise of official authority

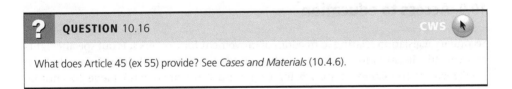

? QUESTION 10.16   CWS

What does Article 45 (ex 55) provide? See *Cases and Materials* (10.4.6).

Article 45 (ex 55) contains an exception similar to that contained in Article 39(4) (ex 48(4)) concerning employment in the public service. It provides that the right of establishment shall not apply to activities which are connected with the exercise of official authority. This derogation, which also applies to services (Article 55 (ex 66)) has, like the

Article 39(4) (ex 48(4)) derogation, been construed narrowly by the Court of Justice. Article 45 (ex 55) was invoked in *Reyners* v *Belgium* (Case 2/74) [1974] ECR 631 (*Cases and Materials* (10.4.2)) in which the Court of Justice ruled that the exception applied only to particular activities involving a direct and specific connection with the exercise of official authority and not to the whole of a profession within which only certain activities are connected with the exercise of official authority.

10.8.8 Freedom to receive services

Although the Treaty makes no express reference to the receipt of services, Directive 64/221 (concerning the public policy, public security and public health derogations) covers recipients of services (Article (1)) and Directive 73/148 requires the abolition of restrictions on the free movement of (*inter alia*) 'nationals of Member States wishing to go to another Member State as recipients of services' (Article 1(1)(b)). *Luisi and Carbone* v *Ministero del Tesoro* (Case 26/83) [1984] ECR 377 established that recipients of services include tourists, persons travelling on business or for educational purposes, and those re-

ceiving medical treatment. For an example of the freedom of a Community national to go to another Member State to receive services as a tourist, see *Calfa* (*Cases and Materials* (10.3.6.4)).

The Article 12 (ex 6, formerly 7) prohibition of discrimination was applied to the receipt of services in a case concerning a British national, Mr Cowan, who was attacked outside a Metro station during a visit to Paris (*Cowan* v *Le Trésor Public* (Case 186/87) [1989] ECR 195 in *Cases and Materials* (10.4.7)). Mr Cowan's claim that he was entitled to receive compensation for his injuries from public funds on the same basis as French nationals was upheld. The Court of Justice declared that 'the prohibition of discrimination is applicable to recipients of services within the meaning of the Treaty as regards protection against the risk of assault and the right to obtain financial compensation provided for by national law when that risk materialises'. The right of nationals of the Member States who travel to other Member States as recipients of services to be free from discrimination within the scope of the Treaty was reiterated recently by the Court of Justice in *Criminal proceedings against Bickel and Franz* (Case C-274/96) [1998] ECR 1-7637.

10.9 Access to education

Secondary legislation relating to freedom of movement for workers sets out specific rights of access to education for workers and their children. Educational rights have also been developed by the Court of Justice for Community nationals who move to another Member State in order to pursue their studies, rather than to take up employment.

10.9.1 Rights of workers

As has already been indicated Article 7(3) of Regulation 1612/68 provides that a migrant Community worker shall have, by virtue of his or her right to equality of treatment with nationals and under the same conditions applying to national workers, equal access to training in vocational schools and retraining centres. In *Lair* v *Universität Hannover* (Case 39/86) [1988] ECR 3161 (*Cases and Materials* (10.5.1)), the Court of Justice interpreted this provision quite narrowly, to include only those institutions 'which provide only instruction either alternating with or closely linked to an occupational activity, particularly during apprenticeship'. The Court further ruled, on an interpretation of Article 12 (ex 6, formerly 7) EC, that equal access to vocational training includes the payment of registration and tuition fees but not assistance given in the form of maintenance grants.

 EXERCISE 10.29 CWS

In *Lair*, the Court of Justice mitigated to some extent the harsh effects of this ruling on equal access to vocational training. Look at *Lair* in *Cases and Materials* (10.5.1) to find out how.

The Court held that workers could claim maintenance grants and similar benefits as 'social advantages' under Article 7(2) of Regulation 1612/68. However, it should be noted that the right to invoke Article 7(2) in this context is itself subject to limitations. A worker who gives up work voluntarily to undertake a course of study in the host State cannot rely on this provision unless he or she can establish continuity between the previous work and the course of study. A person who has pursued employment in the host State purely as a means to becoming a student will not be eligible for such benefits (*Lair* (Case 39/86); *Brown* v *Secretary of State for Scotland* (Case 197/86) [1988] ECR 3205). This is aimed to prevent abuse by workers who enter other Member States and take up employment there for a short time for the sole purpose of benefiting from the host State's student grant facilities.

10.9.2 **Rights of workers' children**

 EXERCISE 10.30 CWS

Look back at 10.6.5.6 and at Article 12 of Regulation 1612/68 in *Cases and Materials* (10.3.4) to remind yourself of the rights of workers' children to access to the host State's general educational, apprenticeship and vocational training courses.

? **QUESTION** 10.17

Which case established that Article 12 of the Regulation covers 'any general measures intended to facilitate educational attendance', including grants?

This liberal interpretation of Article 12 was applied in *Casagrande* v *Landeshauptstadt München* (Case 9/74) [1974] ECR 773 (*Cases and Materials* (10.3.5.5)).

In *Eternach and Moritz* v *Minister van Onderwijs en Wetenschappen* (Cases 389/87 and 390/87) [1989] ECR 723, the Court of Justice considered the position of a child of a German migrant worker who had received his primary and secondary education in the Netherlands where his father was working and who had returned to Germany with his family. Subsequently, because his Netherlands diplomas were not recognized in Germany, the child had returned alone to the Netherlands in order to complete his education. The Court of Justice held that, in circumstances such as these, a child retains his status of member of a worker's family to whom the provisions of Regulation 1612/68 apply.

More recently, in *Baumbast, R* v *Secretary of State for the Home Department* (Case C-143/99) [2002] ECR I-7091 the Court of Justice has further extended the scope of the rights under Article 12 of Regulation 1612/68. Here, the Court held that those rights are to be interpreted as entitling the parent who is the primary carer of the child, irrespective of nationality, to reside with the child, notwithstanding the fact that the parents have meanwhile divorced or that the parent from whom the rights were derived has ceased to be a migrant worker in the host state.

10.9.3 Rights of non-workers

Non-workers may have rights of access to education in a host State by virtue of Articles 12 (ex 6) (non-discrimination on grounds of nationality, formerly Article 7) (*Cases and Materials* (10.1)) and 150 (ex 127) EC (implementation of a common vocational training policy, formerly Article 128). *Gravier* v *City of Liège* (Case 293/83) [1985] ECR 593 (*Cases and Materials* (10.5.3)) concerned a claim by a French student, who was following a course at the Liège Académie Royale des Beaux-Arts, that the imposition of the 'minerval' (a fee levied on certain categories of foreign students) was discriminatory and infringed her right of free movement as a recipient of services under Article 49 (ex 59) EC. The Court of Justice chose to base its decision on former Article 12 (ex 6, formerly 7) and Article 151 (ex 128) EC, holding that access to vocational training, including the payment of fees was, as a matter covered by Community law, subject to Article 12.

⚡ EXERCISE 10.31   CWS

Look at *Gravier* v *City of Liège* (Case 293/83) [1985] ECR 593 in *Cases and Materials* (10.5.3). What was the nature of the course of study which Ms Gravier was pursuing? Find the paragraph of the judgment in which the Court of Justice defined 'vocational training'.

Ms Gravier was studying strip cartoon art. The national court asked the Court of Justice what criteria must be used in deciding whether courses in strip cartoon art constitute vocational training. The Court interpreted 'vocational training' broadly, defining the term in paragraph 30 of the judgment as any form of education or training which prepares for a qualification or provides training and skills in relation to a profession, trade, or employment, even if that training includes an element of general education.

In *Blaizot* v *University of Liège* (Case 24/86) [1988] ECR 379, the Court of Justice was even more specific, ruling that, in general, university studies can be regarded as vocational training for the purposes of the Treaty.

In both *Gravier* and *Blaizot*, the Court of Justice avoided contentious issues concerning the right to maintenance grants and scholarships from the host State in respect of vocational training. Since the Court had interpreted vocational training widely in these cases, Member States were concerned as to the implications of the decisions for the state funding of student maintenance. Such concerns were put to rest in the judgments in *Lair* (see above) and *Brown* v *Secretary of State for Scotland* (Case 197/86) [1988] ECR 3205. Further, Article 3 of Directive 93/96 on the right of residence for students (which replaced Directive 90/366 (see section 10.3)) expressly excludes any entitlement to the payment of maintenance grants by the host Member State on the part of students benefiting from the right of residence.

EXERCISE 10.32   CWS

Look again at *Grzelczyk* (*Cases and Materials* (10.2)), particularly paragraphs 38–45. Summarize in a few sentences the reasoning of the Court of Justice on the right of persons covered by Directive 93/96 to receive social security benefits.

The Court of Justice referred to the exclusion of the right to maintenance grants contained in Directive 93/96. However, the Court also pointed out that the Directive does not preclude persons covered by the Directive from receiving social security benefits. This is so, declared the Court, even though Article 1 of the Directive provides that the host State, before recognizing a right of residence, may require a student to make a declaration that he or she has sufficient resources to avoid becoming a burden on the social assistance system of the host State. A student's financial circumstances may change over time, for reasons beyond his or her control, and thus the truthfulness of the financial declaration is to be assessed at the time it is made.

10.10 Proposals for a new Directive on free movement

In May 2001 the Commission presented proposals for a new Directive on free movement. The Directive brings together the existing legislation on rights of entry and residence in a single legislative instrument. Additionally, it introduces three separate categories of residence rights, comprising the right to move and reside in another Member State for up to six months, the right of residence for more than six months and the right of permanent residence.

Under the proposals, all Union citizens and their family members, irrespective of nationality, will have the right to travel to another Member State and reside there for up to six months.

Thereafter, the right to remain is subject to conditions. For citizens of the Union who are in work, whether employed or self-employed, the only condition attached to residence rights will be that they continue to engage in economic activity. For those who are not in work, for the first four years of residence in another Member State, the conditions attached to residence rights will be that they have sufficient resources and medical insurance, so as not to become a financial burden on the host state. The rights extend to students admitted to a course of vocational training, subject to a declaration that they have sufficient resources and medical insurance, and to family members of the EU citizen.

The Directive introduces a new right of permanent residence in the host Member State for citizens of the Union and family members, irrespective of nationality, after four years of continuous legal residence there. On acquisition of permanent rights of residence, all conditions and restrictions on rights of residence are removed, though the right is lost in the event of a four-year period of continuous absence from the host state.

Rights of entry and rights of residence which have not become permanent rights are subject to restrictions on grounds of public policy, public security or public health.

Significantly, the proposed Directive is presented as a Directive 'on the right of citizens of the Union and their family members to move and reside freely within the territory of the Member States'. This reflects the shift of focus in the substance of the Directive from rights based on the economic status of the individual to rights arising from his or her status as a citizen of the Union.

 EXERCISE 10.33

Look back at section 10.4 to remind yourself of the developments in the caselaw of the Court of Justice indicating a similar change of focus in relation to free movement rights.

 CONCLUSIONS

This chapter has examined the current scope of Community law on the free movement of persons. It has been noted that, although Article 3 (ex 3) EC identifies as one of the activities of the Community the establishment of an internal market characterized (*inter alia*) by the free movement of persons, the implementation of the principle of free movement has been to a large extent confined (with some noteworthy exceptions) to the granting of rights upon workers, the self-employed and their families. The establishment of Citizenship of the Union and the provisions of the new Title IV of the EC Treaty, inserted by the Treaty of Amsterdam, signal the further extension of rights of free movement beyond those who are engaged in economic activity. These provisions also look outwards, beyond the internal market, to the external borders of the European Union. They provide the timetable for the adoption of a harmonized approach to external border control and to asylum and immigration policy. The free movement of persons is central to the organization of the internal market. This principle also has a social dimension, comprising the recognition of persons not just as economic units but as human beings. The importance of freedom of movement of persons, both in economic and social terms, is such that those provisions allowing for derogation on the part of Member States have been interpreted very narrowly by the Court of Justice.

 CHAPTER 10: ASSESSMENT EXERCISE **CWS**

(a) George, a British national, has taken up employment in Paris as a journalist with a French magazine, working 12 hours per week. He is joined by his wife Sue and daughter Anne (aged 23), also British nationals. George and his family apply for residence permits but these are refused by the French authorities. George is told that because he is a part-time worker whose earnings are insufficient to support himself and his family financially, neither he nor his family are entitled to remain in France. Advise George, Sue, and Anne.

(b) Marcel, a French national, has been offered employment in London. He is refused entry to the UK on grounds of public policy. Two years ago, Marcel was convicted by a French court of unlawful possession and supply of a controlled drug. Advise Marcel.

See *Cases and Materials* (10.7) for specimen answers.

11 Competition law: Article 81 (ex 85)

11.1 Objectives

By the end of this chapter you should be able to:

1 Outline the general aims of Community competition law and policy

2 Outline the framework of regulation contained in Article 81 (ex 85) EC

3 Explain and analyse the scope of the Article 81(1) (ex 85(1)) prohibition of agreements between undertakings, decisions of associations of undertakings and concerted practices which prevent, restrict or distort competition within the common market

4 Discuss the provisions of Article 81(3) (ex 85(3))

11.2 Introduction

The Community rules on competition are an integral part of the internal market. In particular, Articles 81 and 82 (ex 85 and 86) EC seek to eliminate obstacles to trade arising from restrictive agreements between businesses and from the behaviour of very powerful business organizations. The Commission has the power to investigate breaches and to enforce Community competition law. These powers were originally set out in Regulation 17/62. Regulation 1/2003, which enters into force on 1 May 2004 and replaces Regulation 17/62, contains similar powers. If, after an investigation, the Commission finds that a breach of the competition rules has occurred, it has the power to impose substantial fines. At the conclusion of an investigation, the Commission issues a formal decision to the parties concerned. Such decisions may be challenged in the Court of First Instance and there is a right of appeal on points of law to the Court of Justice. The role of the national courts in the enforcement of Community competition law, discussed further in **Chapter 13**, arose originally by virtue of the direct effect of Articles 81(1), 81(2) and 82 (ex 85(1), 81(2) and 86). On the entry into force of Regulation 1/2003, national competition authorities and national courts are given the power to apply Articles 81 and 82 in their entirety, including Article 81(3) (ex 85(3)) (see **Chapter 13**).

11.3 Aims of Community competition law

It is possible to identify a number of different objectives underlying Community competition law and policy.

11.3.1 **Achieving the internal market**

As has been noted in previous chapters, the creation of the European internal market is a fundamental Community goal. This is to be achieved primarily through the elimination of obstacles to the free movement of goods, persons, services and capital throughout the Member States. With respect to the free movement of goods, Community law prohibits restrictions such as bans, quotas, customs duties, and other kinds of measures which impede or prevent free movement within the common market. However, these rules are not in themselves sufficient. The single market objective can be frustrated by other barriers to free trade which arise from agreements between individuals or companies.

? **QUESTION** 11.1

Can you think of any kinds of agreement between individuals (for instance between producers or between distributors of goods) which might frustrate the internal market objective?

The kinds of agreement which threaten market integration are those which partition the common market, thereby preventing goods from moving freely throughout the Member States. Suppose, for example, that three major washing machine manufacturers operating, respectively, in the Netherlands, France, and Belgium agree that each will supply its own washing machines only to distributors located in its own national territory. The effect of such an agreement is to protect each of those manufacturers from competition from two of its potential rivals within the national market. The agreement is anti-competitive. It also partitions the market along national lines.

On a smaller scale, the distributors of the washing machines might agree that each of them will sell to customers only within a specified area, keeping out of the territory assigned to the other parties under their agreement. Again, competition between the distributors within their own territories is eliminated and the agreement constitutes an obstacle to the free movement of the products. Community competition law seeks to prevent anti-competitive practices of this kind.

11.3.2 **Efficiency**

A further aim of Community competition law and policy is the enhancement of efficiency in all aspects of production and distribution of goods and services. Efficiency is necessary not only to ensure that the European consumer has available the highest quality products and services at the lowest possible price but also to enable the Community to compete effectively on world markets.

Anti-competitive agreements can be very damaging to efficiency. Consider the market-sharing agreement between the three washing machine producers described above. Because the agreement reduces competition in the supply of washing machines in their own territories, those producers have little incentive to operate efficiently.

11.3.3 The protection of the consumer and of small and medium-sized enterprises

Community competition law is also concerned to protect individual consumers and small and medium-sized businesses from the abusive use of market power by large corporations. Such abuses may occur in monopoly-type situations, for instance where a supplier of raw materials which faces little or no competition from rival suppliers charges its customers (small and medium-sized businesses which use the raw materials in their manufacturing processes) excessive prices. This particular kind of behaviour is likely to fall within the scope of Article 82 (ex 86) EC, which prohibits the abuse of a dominant position within the common market. Article 82 (ex 86) is considered in **Chapter 12**.

A consumer or a small or medium-sized business might suffer at the hands of a group of independent suppliers of particular goods or services who reach agreement between themselves on the regulation of their trading practices. Such an agreement might, for instance, fix the prices to be charged by all the parties at an excessively high level. If there are few or no alternative sources of supply the customers, be they individual consumers or small businesses, have little choice but to pay. This is one example of a restrictive agreement falling within the scope of Article 81 (ex 85).

11.4 Outline of the Community competition rules

Article 3(g) (ex 3(g)) EC (*Cases and Materials* (11.1)) provides that the activities of the Community shall include 'a system ensuring that competition in the internal market is not distorted'. This broadly stated aim is supported by other more specific provisions including those contained in:

(a) Articles 87–9 (ex 92–4), concerning State aids;

(b) Article 81 (ex 85), prohibiting certain kinds of agreement between individuals; and

(c) Article 82 (ex 86), concerning the abuse of market power.

In addition, there is a body of secondary legislation dealing with competition matters. Regulation 17/62, concerning investigations and enforcement, will be replaced by Regulation 1/2003 when the latter enters into force on 1 May 2004. Enforcement of the competition rules is considered in **Chapter 13**.

For reasons of space, State aids must unfortunately fall outside the scope of this book. Article 82 (ex 86) is considered in **Chapter 12**. This chapter will look in detail at Article 81 (ex 85).

11.5 The framework of Article 81 (ex 85)

11.5.1 Outline of Article 81(1), (2), and (3) (ex 85)

🚶 EXERCISE 11.1   **CWS** ↖

Look at Article 81 (ex 85), see *Cases and Materials* (11.2.1). Complete the following sentences to summarize the provisions of Article 81(1), (2), and (3) (ex 85):

(a) Article 81(1) (ex 85(1)) .... certain agreements as incompatible with the common market.

(b) Article 81(2) (ex 85(2)) provides that such agreements shall be ....

(c) Article 81(3) (ex 85(3)) provides that, in certain cases, Article 81(1) (ex 85(1)) may be declared .... to agreements falling within Article 81(1) (ex 85(1)).

You have probably noticed that Article 81 (ex 85) refers to 'undertakings'. The precise meaning of this term is examined below. Broadly speaking, it means any person or entity involved in commercial activity, in other words a business or an individual engaged in business.

(a) Article 81(1) (ex 85(1)) prohibits certain agreements between undertakings. It also prohibits certain decisions of associations of undertakings and concerted practices.

(b) Under Article 81(2) (ex 85(2)), agreements falling within the Article 81(1) (ex 85(1)) prohibition are automatically void.

(c) However, under Article 81(3) (ex 85(3)), the provisions of Article 81(1) (ex 85(1)) may be declared inapplicable to an agreement if certain conditions are satisfied.

11.5.2 Article 81(1) (ex 85(1))

In addition to the general prohibition contained in the first paragraph, Article 81(1) (ex 85(1)) lists a number of examples of the types of agreement to which Article 81(1) (ex 85(1)) applies. These are contained in Article 81(1)(a)–(e) (ex 85).

11.5.3 **Article 81(2) (ex 85(2))**

Although Article 81(2) (ex 85(2)) provides that agreements falling within the Article 81(1) (ex 85(1)) prohibition shall be automatically void, the Court of Justice has held that if it is possible to remove ('sever') restrictive clauses, then those clauses alone will be held to be void and the remainder of the agreement may remain intact (*Société Technique Minière v Maschinenbau Ulm GmbH* (Case 56/65) [1966] ECR 235 in *Cases and Materials* (11.2.2)).

11.5.4 **Article 81(3) (ex 85(3))**

Article 81(3) (ex 85(3)) allows Article 81(1) (ex 85(1)) to be declared inapplicable to agreements which satisfy certain conditions. Under Regulation 17/62, the Commission **alone** had the power to apply Article 81(3) (ex 85(3)). In a White Paper issued in May 1999 (*White Paper on modernization of the rules implementing Articles 85 and 86 of the EC Treaty* (OJ 1999 C 132/1), the Commission proposed that national authorities and national courts be given the power to apply Article 81(3). This proposal has been incorporated into Regulation 1/2003 of 16 December 2002 on the implementation of the rules on competition laid down in Articles 81 and 82 EC (see **Chapter 13**). This Regulation enters into force on 1 May 2004.

Under Regulation 17/62, the Commission applied Article 81(3) either by means of individual exemptions in respect of individual agreements or through the issue of block exemptions applying to categories of agreements. On entry into force of Regulation 1/2003, the system of notification of agreements and individual exemptions is abolished.

11.6 **The Article 81(1) (ex 85(1)): prohibition**

11.6.1 **The prohibition**

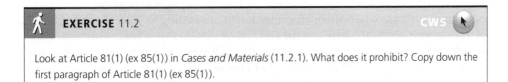

EXERCISE 11.2   CWS

Look at Article 81(1) (ex 85(1)) in *Cases and Materials* (11.2.1). What does it prohibit? Copy down the first paragraph of Article 81(1) (ex 85(1)).

In order to understand the scope of the Article 81(1) (ex 85(1)) prohibition it is necessary to look in detail at each element of the first paragraph and examine the meaning of:

(a) agreements between undertakings, decisions by associations of undertakings, and concerted practices;

(b) which may affect trade between Member States; and

(c) which have as their object or effect the prevention, restriction, or distortion of competition within the common market.

An agreement breaches Article 81(1) (ex 85(1)) only if all three elements are present.

11.6.2 Undertakings

There is no Treaty definition of 'undertaking'. The term has been interpreted widely by the Court of Justice in order to extend the application of Article 81(1) (ex 85(1)) as far as possible. 'Undertaking' has consequently been held to include both legal and natural persons engaged in commercial activity in the supply of goods or services.

? QUESTION 11.2

What do you think is meant by 'legal' persons engaged in commercial activity?

Clearly, natural persons engaged in commercial activity comprise individuals running their own businesses, perhaps as sole traders or in partnership. As for legal persons, the Court of Justice has included within the scope of Article 81(1) (ex 85(1)) various kinds of entity engaged in commercial activity, such as companies, state-owned corporations, and even sporting associations. To be classed as undertakings under Article 81(1) (ex 85(1)), such individuals or entities need not be pursuing their commercial activity with a view to profit.

11.6.3 Autonomous conduct of undertakings

Article 81 (ex 85) does not apply where the restriction of competition is not attributable to the autonomous conduct of undertakings, a point confirmed by the Court of Justice in *Commission and France* v *Ladbroke Racing Ltd* (Joined Cases C-359 & 379/95P) [1997] ECR 1-7007, [1998] 4 CMLR 27. This case concerned French legislation requiring horse racing companies authorized to operate off-course totalisator betting to place the management of those operations in the hands of the *Pari Mutuel Urbain* (PMU). Ladbroke claimed that agreements or concerted practices between the companies and between the companies and PMU granting PMU the exclusive right to manage their betting operations infringed Article 81 (ex 85). The Court of Justice reiterated that Article 81 (ex 85) only applies where undertakings engage in anti-competitive activity on their own initiative. There is no infringement where anti-competitive conduct is required by national legislation. The same principles apply in relation to Article 82 (ex 86) (see **Chapter 12**).

11.6.4 Agreements, decisions, and concerted practices

Article 81(1) (ex 85(1)) is designed to catch a wide range of agreements, including those which are made informally without writing. If that were not the case, it would be possible for undertakings to avoid the competition rules without difficulty. Accordingly, Article 81(1) (ex 85(1)) covers agreements, decisions of associations of undertakings, and concerted practices.

The term 'agreement', as might be expected, covers legally enforceable contracts. It has also been held to cover less formal agreements—the so-called 'gentleman's agreement'—and simple understandings between parties. It is not necessary to define 'agreement' precisely because the Article 81(1) (ex 85(1)) concept of 'concerted practice' has such a wide scope that it includes many forms of informal understanding between undertakings whose classification as 'agreements' might be open to doubt.

The coordination of trading activity between undertakings can arise from decisions taken collectively through a trade association. Such decisions are specifically covered by Article 81(1) (ex 85(1)) and, if all the other elements are satisfied, will constitute a breach of that article. Even non-binding recommendations—for instance to raise prices or to refuse supplies to particular categories of customers—will constitute decisions within the meaning of Article 81(1) (ex 85(1)) if members of the association normally comply with them.

? QUESTION 11.3   CWS

What recommendation was under consideration in *IAZ International Belgium NV* v *Commission* (Cases 96–102, 104, 105, 108, and 110/82) [1983] ECR 3369 (*Cases and Materials* (11.3.1))?

In *IAZ International Belgium NV*, the Court of Justice confirmed the Commission's view that a non-binding recommendation by a water suppliers' trade association that only washing machines and dishwashers carrying a conformity label issued by the Belgian association of manufacturers should be connected to the mains water supply fell within the scope of Article 81(1) (ex 85(1)).

The term 'association of undertakings' can include professional organizations. This was confirmed by the Court of Justice in *Wouters* v *Netherlands Bar* (Case C-309/99) [2002] ECR I-1577, where the Court considered a regulation of the Bar of the Netherlands prohibiting multi-disciplinary partnerships of members of the Bar and accountants. The Court declared that such a regulation expresses the intention of the delegates of the members of a profession that they should act in a particular manner in carrying on their economic activity. In adopting such a regulation, the professional organization must be regarded as an association of undertakings.

The interpretation of 'concerted practices' has given rise to many difficulties. Whilst the term is much wider in scope than 'agreements' and 'decisions of associations of undertakings', the outer limits of the concept are not easily defined. The first important case concerning concerted practices to come before the Court of Justice was *Imperial Chemical Industries Ltd* v *Commission (Dyestuffs)* (Case 48/69) [1972] ECR 619.

EXERCISE 11.3

Look at the *Dyestuffs* case in *Cases and Materials* (11.3.1). How did the Court of Justice define a concerted practice at paragraph 64? Write out the definition.

Here, ICI challenged a Commission Decision concerning certain price increases which had been introduced uniformly and almost simultaneously by a number of producers of aniline dyes, including ICI, during the 1960s. The Commission took the view that the prices had been fixed through concerted practices and fines were imposed. The Court of Justice defined a concerted practice as 'a form of coordination between undertakings which, without having reached the stage where an agreement properly so-called has been concluded, knowingly substitutes practical cooperation between them for the risks of competition'.

The producers argued that their behaviour did not amount to concerted practice but was part of the normal operation of an oligopolistic market (relatively few sellers dominating the market for a particular product). It is often argued that in oligopolistic markets where pricing policies are transparent, rival undertakings will respond naturally and without collusion to each other's market strategy. If one undertaking raises prices, the others will tend to follow with similar price increases. This is a form of 'parallel' behaviour.

 EXERCISE 11.4

Look again at the *Dyestuffs* case, in particular paragraphs 66 and 67. What view did the Court of Justice take on the significance of parallel behaviour in relation to concerted practice?

The Court ruled that whilst parallel behaviour in itself does not amount to concerted practice, it may be strong evidence of such practice. That will be the case where the conduct 'leads to conditions of competition which do not correspond to the normal conditions of the market'. This view has been criticized on the basis that it is difficult to determine with any certainty what are 'normal conditions of the market'. The *Dyestuffs* decision itself did not, however, depend upon the Court's analysis of parallel behaviour. There was sufficient evidence of communications between the companies to establish that they had knowingly cooperated with each other to eliminate the risks of competition.

 An oligopolistic market was considered once again in *Ahlström & Ors v Commission (Woodpulp)* (Cases C-89, 104, 114, 116—117, 125—129/85) [1993] ECR I-1307 (*Cases and Materials* (11.3.1)). Here, the Court of Justice accepted that parallel pricing, arising under a system of quarterly price announcements operated by a number of woodpulp producers, did not amount to concerted practice but was the result of the normal operation of an oligopolistic market. There was no evidence of communication between the parties and the parallel conduct could be satisfactorily explained by the nature of the woodpulp market.

In *Cooperatieve Vereniging 'Suiker Unie' UA v Commission* (the *Sugar Cartel* cases) (Cases 40–8, 50, 54–6, 111, 113, 114/73) [1975] ECR 1663 (*Cases and Materials* (11.3.1)), the Court of Justice rejected the contention that a concerted practice must entail the existence of a plan. There was no concerted practice, said the Court, where the undertakings concerned acted independently on the market. That did not rule out an intelligent adaptation to the current and anticipated conduct of their competitors but did preclude 'any direct or indirect contact between such operators, the object or effect whereof is either to influence the conduct . . . of an actual or potential competitor or to disclose to such a competitor the course of conduct which they themselves have decided to adopt or contemplate adopting on the market'.

Indeed, there is a presumption that operators who have exchanged such information with their competitors and are still active on the market take account of that information in the conduct of their business. In such circumstances, a concerted practice will be established without evidence of anti-competitive effects on the market. An anti-competitive object is sufficient. (Case C-199/92P *Huls AG v Commission* [1999] ECR I-4287).

11.6.5 Vertical and horizontal agreements

Article 81 (ex 85) is concerned with both vertical and horizontal agreements which restrict competition and affect trade between Member States. A vertical agreement is an agreement between undertakings which operate on different levels of the production/distribution chain.

?   QUESTION 11.4

Who do you think might be parties to a typical vertical agreement?

The most common types of vertical agreement are those which involve distribution systems, for instance an agreement between a car manufacturer and a dealer in the car retailing business. The application of Article 81 (ex 85) to vertical agreements was established in *Établissements Consten SA v Commission* (Cases 56 & 58/64) [1966] ECR 299 (*Cases and Materials* (11.3.2)) (see also *Société Technique Minière v Maschinenbau Ulm GmbH* (Case 56/65) [1966] ECR 235 in *Cases and Materials* (11.2.2)). Initiating a wide consultation exercise on vertical agreements in Community competition law in 1997, the Commission produced a Green Paper on the reform of the rules on vertical restraints (restrictions of competition in vertical agreements). Legislation was adopted in this area in 1999. (These matters are discussed further in 11.9.)

> **? QUESTION** 11.5
>
> How would you define a horizontal agreement? Who do you think might be parties to a typical horizontal agreement?

A horizontal agreement is an agreement between undertakings which operate on the same level of the production/distribution chain, for instance between a group of manufacturers or between a number of retailers. The agreement between the Dutch, French, and Belgian washing machine manufacturers described in 11.3.1 above is an example of a horizontal agreement.

For Article 81 (ex 85) to apply, undertakings must be independent of each other. Consequently, agreements between a parent company and its subsidiary or within an undertaking do not fall within its scope.

11.6.6 'Which may affect trade between Member States'

This is the second element of Article 81(1) (ex 85(1)). A restrictive agreement, decision or concerted practice does not breach Article 81(1) (ex 85(1)) unless it 'may affect trade between Member States'. If there is no such effect, an agreement falls to be considered under national law. The Court of Justice has extended Community jurisdiction in this area of competition law by adopting a very broad view of this element of Article 81 (ex 85). An effect on trade between Member States is not difficult to prove.

> **🏃 EXERCISE** 11.5 CWS
>
> Look at *Société Technique Minière* v *Maschinenbau Ulm GmbH* (Case 56/65) [1966] ECR 235 in *Cases and Materials* (11.2.2), in which the Court of Justice laid down a test to be applied in deciding whether or not an agreement has an effect on interstate trade. What is that test? Write down your answer.

The test laid down in *Société Technique Minière* is wide. Article 81(1) (ex 85(1)) applies wherever it is 'possible to foresee with a sufficient degree of probability on the basis of a set of objective factors of law or of fact that the agreement in question may have an influence, direct or indirect, actual or potential, on the pattern of trade between Member States'. *Windsurfing International* v *Commission* (Case 193/83) [1986] ECR 611 (*Cases and Materials* (11.3.3)) established that an agreement must be looked at in its entirety. It will not escape the scope of Article 81(1) (ex 85(1)) simply because individual restrictions contained in it do not affect interstate trade.

One important feature of the *Société Technique Minière* test is that it is not necessary to show that an agreement has already affected trade between Member States. A potential effect will suffice. Thus, an agreement between undertakings currently operating within one Member State may be caught by Article 81(1) (ex 85(1)). This is illustrated by *Vacuum Interrupters Ltd* (Commission Decision) OJ 1977 L 48/32, [1977] 1 CMLR D67 (*Cases and Materials* (11.3.3)), in which the Commission took the view that a joint venture agreement between two UK companies to design and manufacture switchgear in the UK was capable of affecting trade between Member States because, in the absence of an agreement between them, each company would have gone ahead with independent development of the product and would have marketed it in other Member States. Moreover, it would be more difficult for potential competitors from other Member States to enter the UK market in the product in the face of the combined economic and technical strength of the two manufacturers.

Even where it is unlikely that an undertaking would wish to extend its trading activities beyond the boundaries of a single Member State, the potential effect of restrictions will still be sufficient to bring an agreement within the scope of Article 81(1) (ex 85(1)). This situation was considered by the Court of Justice in *Pronuptia de Paris GmbH* v *Pronuptia de Paris Irmgard Schillgalis* (Case 161/84) [1986] ECR 353 (*Cases and Materials* (11.3.3)). Here, a franchise agreement restricting the franchisee's right to trade to a particular territory (a defined geographical area) was found to be capable of affecting interstate trade.

An agreement which operates within a single Member State but covers the whole territory of that State 'by its very nature has the effect of reinforcing the compartmentalization of markets on a national basis, thereby holding up the economic interpenetration which the Treaty is designed to bring about' (*Vereeniging van Cementhandelaren* v *Commission* (Case 8/72) [1972] ECR 977).

Établissements Consten SA v *Commission* (*Cases and Materials* (11.3.2)) made clear that an effect on trade between Member States means **any** effect, whether it be an increase or a decrease in trade. Moreover, the Commission and the Court will, where appropriate, look at the effect of an agreement as part of a series or a network of agreements which as a whole is capable of affecting trade between Member States (see for instance *Brasserie de Haecht SA* v *Wilkin (No. 1)* (Case 23/67) [1967] ECR 407 in *Cases and Materials* (11.3.3)).

11.6.7 **The *de minimis* principle**

Despite the wide reading of 'may affect trade between Member States', an agreement will come within the scope of Article 81(1) (ex 85(1)) only if it has an **appreciable** effect on competition or on interstate trade. If this is not the case, an agreement is described as being of minor importance or *de minimis*.

The *de minimis* principle first appeared in *Volk* v *Établissements Vervaecke Sprl* (Case 5/69) [1969] ECR 295 (*Cases and Materials* (11.3.4)), in which the Court of Justice ruled that an agreement falls outside Article 81(1) (ex 85(1)) if it has only an insignificant effect on the market. In order to determine this effect, it is necessary to look at the size of the parties to the agreement and their share of the relevant product market. However, the Court did not specify a precise market share within which the *de minimis* principle would apply.

The position has been clarified in a series of Commission Notices on agreements of minor importance. The most recent Notice, issued in 2001, sets out the Commission's view that agreements affecting trade between Member States do not appreciably restrict competition within the meaning of Article 81(1) if the parties' aggregate market share in any of the relevant markets affected by the agreement does not exceed 10% (where the parties are actual or potential competitors) or 15% (where the parties are not actual or potential competitors). In the case of parallel networks of agreements, both these thresholds are reduced to 5%.

These *de minimis* provisions do not apply to agreements containing hardcore restriction. Thus, agreements between competitors fixing sale prices, limiting production or sales or allocating markets, fall within Article 81(1), as do agreements between non-competitors which, for instance, fix minimum resale prices or restrict the territory into which the buyer may sell the relevant goods or services. Where the *de mimimis* provisions do apply the Commission will not institute proceedings and where undertakings assume in good faith that an agreement is covered by the Notice, the Commission will not impose fines.

In addition, the Notice acknowledges that agreements between small and medium-sized undertakings are rarely capable of affecting trade between Member States.

11.6.8 Object or effect

? QUESTION 11.6   CWS

Article 81(1) (ex 85(1)) refers to the anti-competitive 'object or effect' of an agreement. Is it necessary to prove both? Look at *Société Technique Minière* v *Maschinenbau Ulm GmbH* (Case 56/65) [1966] ECR 235 in *Cases and Materials* (11.2.2).

The first line of enquiry is the object of an agreement. If an agreement is clearly designed to prevent, restrict or distort competition—if for instance it contains blatant price fixing or market-sharing clauses—then there will be no need to prove an anti-competitive effect. It is only necessary to consider the effects of an agreement if it has no obvious anti-competitive purpose.

11.6.9 Prevention, restriction, or distortion of competition within the common market

This is the third element of Article 81(1) (ex 85(1)). Any agreement which may affect trade between Member States and which prevents, restricts or distorts competition within the common market will *prima facie* breach Article 81(1) (ex 85(1)).

However, this broad statement should be read with some important qualifications in mind. As has been seen, Article 81(1) (ex 85(1)) does not apply to agreements which are *de minimis* because they have no appreciable effect on competition or on interstate trade. An agreement which falls within the scope of Article 81(1) (ex 85(1)) may be exempt under Article 81(3) (ex 85(3)) if certain conditions are satisfied. In addition, the Court of Justice has, in a series of cases, held that certain kinds of agreement fall outside Article 81(1) (ex 85(1)) even though they contain restrictions and are not *de minimis*. This may apply where the restrictions are necessary to an agreement which, overall, has economic benefits.

11.6.10 Restrictive agreements which fall outside Article 81(1) (ex 85(1))

Any system of competition law which seeks to root out anti-competitive practices encounters one fundamental problem: if undertakings are to trade effectively, it is often necessary for them to impose restrictions of various kinds on each other.

Consider, for instance, the case of a UK car manufacturer which seeks to establish a market for its cars in Italy and negotiates an agreement with a Rome car dealer. The dealer is keen to buy and market the cars but will not take on the expenditure required—for showroom facilities, staff training, advertising, after sales service—unless he is protected from competition from other dealers. The manufacturer therefore agrees not to supply its cars to any other dealers in the Rome area.

> **?** **QUESTION** 11.7
>
> Would you say that this agreement is pro- or anti-competitive? Why?

This is not an easy question to answer because the agreement has both pro- and anti-competitive effects. Whilst it is anti-competitive in so far as it restricts trading between the manufacturer and other car dealers in the designated area, the agreement is also pro-competitive because it enables the penetration of the Italian car market by this manufacturer, thus enhancing competition on a broad scale. Without the restriction, the car dealer would not agree to market the product.

What approach should be adopted to agreements which, overall, are pro-competitive but which nevertheless impose restrictions? In a number of important judgments, the Court of Justice has held that restrictions on trading activity do not breach Article 81(1) (ex 85(1)) where they are necessary to protect a party who undertakes high commercial risks (*Société Technique Minière* v *Maschinenbau Ulm GmbH* (Case 56/65) [1966] ECR 235 in *Cases and Materials* (11.2.2)), where they are necessary to the performance of a particular kind of agreement (*Remia BV* v *Commission* (Case 42/84) [1985] ECR 2545 in *Cases and Materials* (11.3.6.2); *Pronuptia de Paris GmbH* v *Pronuptia de Paris Irmgard Schillgalis* (Case 161/84) [1986] ECR 353 in *Cases and Materials* (11.3.3)), or where they are necessary to ensure quality control (*Metro-SB-Grossmärkte GmbH & Co. KG* v *Commission (No. 1)* (Case 26/76) [1977] ECR 1875 in *Cases and Materials* (11.3.6.3)).

11.6.10.1 Restrictions which protect a party taking high commercial risks

>   **EXERCISE** 11.6   CWS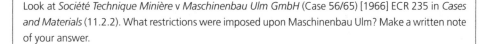
>
> Look at *Société Technique Minière* v *Maschinenbau Ulm GmbH* (Case 56/65) [1966] ECR 235 in *Cases and Materials* (11.2.2). What restrictions were imposed upon Maschinenbau Ulm? Make a written note of your answer.

The agreement under dispute between Société Technique Minière (STM) and Maschinen-bau Ulm GmbH (MU) was an exclusive supply contract relating to heavy grading machinery supplied to the distributor STM by MU. MU agreed not to supply to any other distributor within France and not to sell there itself. In entering into the agreement, STM was taking on high commercial risks, since the product was highly specialized and very expensive. The Court of Justice held that, in view of these factors, exclusivity was necessary for the penetration of a new area by MU. Consequently, the agreement fell outside Article 81(1) (ex 85(1)).

? **QUESTION** 11.8   CWS

The *STM* case is distinguishable from *Établissements Consten SA* v *Commission* (Cases 56 and 58/64) [1966] ECR 299 in *Cases and Materials* (11.3.2). How? Make a note of your answer.

The two cases are similar in that the agreements conferred exclusivity on the respective distributors. However, the *Consten* agreement contained other restrictions. Consten undertook not to re-export the goods from the designated territory and Grundig agreed to obtain similar undertakings from its distributors in other Member States. These further restrictions, amounting to what are termed 'export bans' and 'bans on parallel imports', gave absolute territorial protection to Consten on the French market. Their effectiveness was reinforced by the use of the GINT trade mark.

The partitioning of the common market resulting from export bans and bans on parallel imports was condemned by the Court of Justice. The offending clauses should be severed from the agreement. Moreover, the fact that the agreement restricted intrabrand competition (competition between products of the same brand) rather than inter-brand competition (competition between different brands) was irrelevant. This decision illustrates the importance in Community law of the single market objective and the concern that individual agreements should not be allowed to compartmentalize the common market.

11.6.10.2 Restrictions which are necessary to the performance of a particular type of agreement

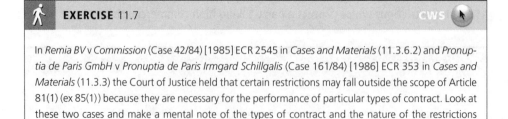

🚶 **EXERCISE** 11.7   CWS

In *Remia BV* v *Commission* (Case 42/84) [1985] ECR 2545 in *Cases and Materials* (11.3.6.2) and *Pronuptia de Paris GmbH* v *Pronuptia de Paris Irmgard Schillgalis* (Case 161/84) [1986] ECR 353 in *Cases and Materials* (11.3.3) the Court of Justice held that certain restrictions may fall outside the scope of Article 81(1) (ex 85(1)) because they are necessary for the performance of particular types of contract. Look at these two cases and make a mental note of the types of contract and the nature of the restrictions which were considered by the Court.

Remia concerned restrictive covenants, in the form of non-competition clauses, taken on the sale of two businesses. Although the Court of Justice upheld the Commission Decision that the restrictions, covering periods of five and ten years, infringed Article 81(1) (ex 85(1)) and were not eligible for exemption under Article 81(3) (ex 85(3)) because they were excessive, it held that such covenants would not breach Article 81(1) (ex 85(1)) if they were necessary to give full effect to the sale. In the absence of 'necessary' covenants, the seller would be able to compete with the buyer and gain back the business which had been sold.

In *Pronuptia*, the Court of Justice examined a distribution franchise agreement. The essence of a franchise system is that the franchisee, operating as an independent business, pays a fee for the right to use the franchisor's intellectual property rights, such as trade marks, know-how and designs. Goods or services are sold by the franchised outlets according to common standards and under a common business format imposed by the franchisor.

There were numerous restrictions in the *Pronuptia* agreement relating, for instance, to shop layout, advertising and the use of the franchisor's business methods and know-how. The Court ruled that in distribution franchise agreements, restrictions such as these, which are indispensable to protect the reputation and know-how of the franchisor and the uniform identity of the franchised outlets, do not breach Article 81(1) (ex 85(1)).

11.6.10.3 Restrictions ensuring quality: selective distribution

In order to ensure quality of sales and service, suppliers sometimes use a system of selective distribution. Under such a system, goods are retailed only through outlets chosen by the supplier on the basis of its own specific criteria, relating for instance to the suitability of the premises, the availability of after-sales service and the provision of adequately trained staff. Whilst the retailer's trading activity is restricted to some degree because of the requirement to maintain these standards, in return the retailer gains protection from competition from unsuitable outlets and the quality and brand image of the product are upheld.

In *Metro-SB-Grossmärkte GmbH & Co. KG* v *Commission (No. 1)* (Case 26/76) [1977] ECR 1875, the Court of Justice held that selective distribution systems do not breach Article 81(1) (ex 85(1)) provided that certain conditions are satisfied.

EXERCISE 11.8

What are those conditions? Look at the *Metro* case in *Cases and Materials* (11.3.6.3) and copy out the formula laid down by the Court of Justice.

The Court ruled that selective distributions systems do not breach Article 81(1) (ex 85(1)) 'provided that the re-sellers are chosen on the basis of objective criteria of a qualitative nature relating to the technical qualifications of the re-seller and his staff and the suitability of his trading premises and that such conditions are laid down uniformly for all potential re-sellers and are not applied in a discriminatory fashion'.

This statement is sometimes referred to as the *Metro* doctrine. It only applies to goods whose particular characteristics justify the restriction of the type of outlets dealing with them. These include products which are technically advanced such as computers, cars, and cameras. Such goods require, for instance, specially trained sales staff or the provision of after-sales service. Also included are products which carry a quality or luxury image— such as expensive perfumes, luxury cosmetics and high quality jewellery—which the manufacturer may seek to maintain, for instance, by requiring the retailer to provide a shop décor compatible with that image or to engage only suitably qualified staff.

However, the restrictions must be proportionate to the nature of the product. In *Ideal-Standard Agreement* (Commission Decision), OJ 1985 L20/38, [1988] 4 CMLR 627, the Commission did not accept that the sale of plumbing fittings by wholesalers required specialist staff and the provision of a specialist department. The product was not sufficiently technically sophisticated to warrant such requirements.

The reference to 'qualitative' criteria in the *Metro* doctrine rules out criteria of a 'quantitative' nature. Unfortunately, the distinction between the two is not always easily drawn. Quantitative criteria may include such matters as the holding of minimum stocks and the guarantee of a minimum turnover. In *L'Oréal NV v De Nieuwe AMCK PvbA* (Case 31/80) [1980] ECR 3775 (*Cases and Materials* (11.3.6.3)), the Court of Justice held that such requirements went beyond what was necessary to a selective distribution system and breached Article 81(1) (ex 85(1)), though it indicated that they might qualify for individual exemption under Article 81(3) (ex 85(3)).

What is clear is that, in order to escape the scope of Article 81(1) (ex 85(1)), any restrictions imposed by a supplier upon its retail outlets must be no more than is necessary to protect the quality and image of the product in question and that those restrictions must be laid down uniformly for all re-sellers and must not be applied in a discriminatory fashion.

As a result of the block exemption Regulation on categories of vertical agreements and concerted practices (OJ 1999 L336/21), which entered into force on 1 June 2000, selective distribution agreements now benefit from automatic exemption from Article 81(1), provided they fall within the scope of the Regulation (see 11.8 and 11.9).

11.6.11 Application of the rule of reason

The approach taken by the Court of Justice in the cases which have just been considered in **11.6.10** is often described as an application of the 'rule of reason'. This is a concept derived from United States competition law whereby agreements in restraint of trade are examined to see whether they are unduly restrictive of competition. This assessment entails the balancing of the pro- and anti-competitive effects of an agreement within its market context. Where an agreement is found, on balance, not to be anti-competitive, there is no breach of competition rules.

Despite the approach adopted by the Court of Justice in cases such as *STM*, *Remia*, and *Pronuptia*, the Court of First Instance has more recently emphatically denied the existence of a rule of reason under Article 81(1) (Case T-112/99 *Métropole Télévision (M6) and Others v Commission* [2001] ECR II-2459. On one view, if the rule of reason is to be applied at all within the Community context, its use should be restricted to the assessment of agreements under Article 81(3) (ex 85(3)) rather than under Article 81(1) (ex 85(1)). There is no doubt that the general scheme of Article 81 (ex 85) envisages that agreements which contain restrictions should be regarded as contravening Article 81(1) (ex 85(1)) but then scrutinized with a view to exemption under Article 81(3) (ex 85(3)).

Following the adoption of the regime set out in Regulation 17/62, the Commission alone had the power to exempt agreements under Article 81(3), the national courts being able to apply Article 81(1). The system as a whole was designed to ensure that the competition rules were applied uniformly throughout the Community. However, the Commission's heavy workload in considering agreements notified to it for individual exemption led to delays and consequent uncertainty for business. For these reasons, the system was the subject of widespread criticism. It could be streamlined, it was argued, if national courts were empowered to apply Article 81(3). This change, among others, has been adopted under the new regime of Regulation 1/2003 (see **Chapter 13**).

11.6.12 Examples of prohibited agreements: Article 81(1)(a)–(e) (ex 85(1)(a)–(e))

The words 'prevention', 'restriction', and 'distortion' used in the first paragraph of Article 81(1) (ex 85(1)) cover all forms of anti-competitive behaviour and no distinction is made between them. Article 81(1)(a)–(e) (ex 85(1)(a)–(e)) lists examples of agreements which are likely to breach Article 81(1) (ex 85(1)).

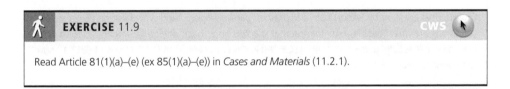

EXERCISE 11.9   CWS

Read Article 81(1)(a)–(e) (ex 85(1)(a)–(e)) in *Cases and Materials* (11.2.1).

Although many forms of anti-competitive behaviour will fall within one of the listed categories, the list is not exhaustive.

You should remember that:

(a) *de minimis* agreements fall outside the scope of Article 81(1) (ex 85(1));

(b) agreements which breach Article 81(1) (ex 85(1)) may be exempt under Article 81(3) (ex 85(3)) if they satisfy certain conditions;

(c) particular kinds of restrictive agreement and certain of the restrictions which they contain have been held by the Court of Justice not to infringe Article 81(1) (ex 85(1)) (see 11.6.10 above).

With these last two points in particular in mind, discussion now turns to some of the kinds of agreements (or restrictions) which are likely to breach Article 81(1) (ex 85(1)).

11.6.12.1 Price fixing: Article 81(1)(a) (ex 85(1)(a))

Price fixing is a classic form of anti-competitive behaviour. Horizontal price fixing agreements (for instance an agreement between independent manufacturers to fix the price of a certain product) are regarded both by the Commission and the Court as having an anti-competitive object.

Price fixing in vertical agreements (for instance between a supplier and retail outlets) infringes Article 81(1) (ex 85(1)) and exemption will apply only in exceptional cases. The Commission decided in *Hennessy/Henkell* (Commission Decision) OJ 1980 L 383/11, [1981] 1 CMLR 601 (*Cases and Materials* (11.3.7.1)) that the fixing of maximum and minimum price levels infringed Article 81(1) (ex 85(1)) and refused to grant an exemption under Article 81(3) (ex 85(3)). Here, the Commission rejected the argument that the fixing of retail prices was justified because it protected the brand image of the product. However, in *Pronuptia de Paris GmbH* v *Pronuptia de Paris Irmgard Schillgalis* (Case 161/84) [1986] ECR 353 (*Cases and Materials* (11.3.3)), the Court of Justice ruled that in a distribution franchise recommended prices would not breach Article 81(1) (ex 85(1)) provided that such recommendations were not binding on the franchisees.

11.6.12.2 Fixing other trading conditions: Article 81(1)(a) (ex 85)(1)(a)

Within this category, two trading conditions in particular have been condemned by the Commission and the Court of Justice in the strongest of terms and always breach Article 81(1) (ex 85(1)). These are the export ban and the ban on parallel imports.

EXERCISE 11.10   CWS

Explain what is meant by 'export ban' and 'ban on parallel imports' and why these particular trading conditions are incompatible with the internal market. Look back at *Établissements Consten SA* v *Commission* (Cases 56 and 58/64) [1966] ECR 299 in *Cases and Materials* (11.3.2) and 11.6.10.1 above to find the answer.

Other kinds of trading conditions to be found in distribution agreements may relate to the way in which goods or services are marketed. Commonly, such agreements set up and regulate selective distribution systems. As noted above, selective distribution agreements do not breach Article 81(1) (ex 85(1)) if they fall within the *Metro* doctrine. Certain restrictions in distribution franchise agreements will not breach Article 81(1) (ex 85(1)) if they are necessary to maintain common standards and protect the franchisor's intellectual property rights (see *Pronuptia de Paris GmbH* v *Pronuptia de Paris Irmgard Schillgalis* (Case 161/84) [1986] ECR 353 in *Cases and Materials* (11.3.3) and 11.6.10.2 above).

Selective agreements and franchise agreements falling within the scope of Article 81(1) may be covered by the block exemption on vertical agreements or, alternatively, individual agreements may be exempt if they satisfy the Article 81(3) conditions.

11.6.12.3 Other agreements likely to breach Article 81(1): Article 81(1)(b)–(e)

Article 81(1)(b) (ex 85(1)(b)) refers to agreements which control production, markets, technical developments or investments. These fall within the scope of Article 81(1) (ex 85(1)) but may be exempt under Article 81(3) (see for instance *ACEC/Berliet* (Commission Decision) JO 1968 L 201/7, [1968] CMLR D35 in *Cases and Materials* (11.3.7.3)).

Article 81(1)(c) (ex 85(1)(c)) refers to agreements to share markets or sources of supply. These fall within the Article 81(1) (ex 85(1)) prohibition but may satisfy the Article 81(3) (ex 85(3)) conditions.

 EXERCISE 11.11   CWS

Look at *Transocean Marine Paint Association* (Commission Decision) JO 1967 163/19, [1967] CMLR D9 in *Cases and Materials* (11.3.7.3). Here, an agreement providing for market sharing (but not absolute territorial protection) was granted exemption.

Article 81(1)(d) (ex 85(1)(d)) refers to agreements which apply dissimilar conditions to equivalent trading transactions with other trading parties, thereby placing them at a competitive disadvantage. Agreements to discriminate between trading parties—for instance to offer discounts to some customers but not to others in relation to identical goods or services—breach Article 81(1) (ex 85(1)) and are unlikely to be exempt.

Article 81(1)(e) (ex 85(1)(e)) refers to agreements which make the conclusion of contracts subject to acceptance by the other parties of supplementary obligations which, by their nature or according to commercial usage, have no connection with the subject of such contracts. Here, a distinction is to be made between those obligations which do have a connection and those which do not have a connection with the subject of the contract, a distinction which may not be easy to draw. The latter breach Article 81(1) (ex 85(1)) but may be exempt.

11.7 Article 81(3) (ex 85(3)): exemption

11.7.1 Exemption

Article 81(3) (ex 85(3)) provides that the prohibition in Article 81(1) may be declared inapplicable to agreements that satisfy certain conditions. Under Regulation 17/62, the Commission alone had the power to apply Article 81(3). It did so through the grant of individual exemption following the notification of an agreement by the parties.

11.7.2 Regulation 1/2003: the new regime

Notification is abolished altogether under the new enforcement regime set out in Regulation 1/2003 (see **Chapter 13**). Article 1 expressly provides that agreements caught by Article 81(1) but which satisfy the conditions of Article 81(3) will not be prohibited. They will be valid and enforceable *ab initio*, without the adoption of an exemption decision.

The following sections consider how Article 81(3) has been applied by the Commission to agreements which have been notified to it for individual exemption. Clearly, these decisions will guide national courts, national competition authorities and the Commission itself in the future application of Article 81(3).

11.7.3 The application of Article 81(3) by the Commission

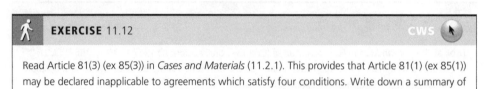

EXERCISE 11.12   CWS

Read Article 81(3) (ex 85(3)) in *Cases and Materials* (11.2.1). This provides that Article 81(1) (ex 85(1)) may be declared inapplicable to agreements which satisfy four conditions. Write down a summary of the four conditions.

You may have noticed that the first two of these conditions relate to the economic benefits of an agreement whilst the other two are negative conditions. Your summary might look something like this:

In order to be exempt under Article 81(3) (ex 85(3)) an agreement must:

(a) contribute to improving the production or distribution of goods or to promoting technical or economic progress; and

(b) allow consumers a fair share of the resulting benefit;

but must not:

(c) impose restrictions which are not indispensable to the attainment of those objectives; or

(d) afford the undertakings concerned the possibility of eliminating competition in respect of a substantial part of the products in question.

All four conditions must be satisfied.

11.7.4 Economic benefit: improving production or distribution or promoting technical or economic progress

The greater its economic benefits, the more likely it is that an agreement will be exempt. The issue is whether the restrictions in an agreement are justified by the benefits which will flow from it. Some agreements might incorporate more than one of the benefits listed in this first positive condition, others just one of them.

Improvements in production might ensue from agreements under which each party specializes in a particular area of production. For instance, under an agreement between two pharmaceutical companies, which was granted exemption by the Commission under Article 81(3) (ex 85(3)), each company agreed to give up part of its business in favour of the other, allowing one party to specialize in the production of one particular penicillin product and the other to concentrate on the production of a different penicillin product (*Bayer/Gist-Brocades* (Commission Decision) OJ 1976 L 30/13, [1976] 1 CMLR D98). Technical and economic progress can result from research and development agreements (see for instance *ACEC/Berliet* (Commission Decision) JO 1968 L 201/7, [1968] CMLR D35 in *Cases and Materials* (11.3.7.3)).

Distribution might be improved through exclusive supply or purchasing agreements. Here, the Commission has sometimes been prepared to take a surprisingly generous view of restrictions. In its Decision in *Transocean Marine Paint Association* JO 1967 163/19, [1967] CMLR D9 (*Cases and Materials* (11.3.7.3)), it granted exemption to a distribution agreement which partitioned markets on national lines (though did not give absolute territorial protection) because of its benefits in terms of improved distribution of the product.

11.7.5 Allowing consumers a fair share of the resulting benefit

The meaning of 'consumer' is not confined to the ultimate consumer of a product but includes persons (individuals or companies) at all levels of the distribution chain.

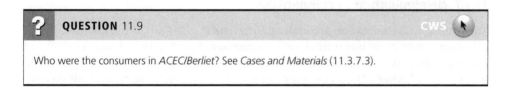

QUESTION 11.9   CWS

Who were the consumers in *ACEC/Berliet*? See *Cases and Materials* (11.3.7.3).

This Commission Decision concerned a specialisation agreement between a French bus manufacturer, Berliet, and a manufacturer of transmission systems, ACEC, for the development and marketing of a bus incorporating a new kind of electrical transmission system. Here, the consumers were held to be bus companies.

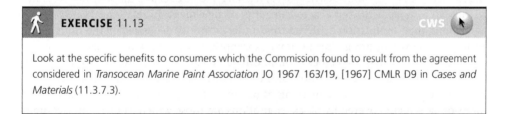

EXERCISE 11.13   CWS

Look at the specific benefits to consumers which the Commission found to result from the agreement considered in *Transocean Marine Paint Association* JO 1967 163/19, [1967] CMLR D9 in *Cases and Materials* (11.3.7.3).

In addition to specific benefits in any particular case, the Commission has recognized that any benefits resulting from an agreement, such as a better or cheaper product or service, will be passed on to the consumer only if the parties face competition from other undertakings in the same product market. Thus, an assessment must be made of the competition faced by the parties, looking carefully at the structure of the market and the size of the parties' market share.

11.7.6 No restrictions which are not indispensable

Restrictions must not go beyond what is necessary to achieve the beneficial objectives of the agreement.

? **QUESTION** 11.10

Which important general principle do you recognize here?

This is, of course, another manifestation of the principle of proportionality. Certain restrictions will rarely, if ever, be regarded as indispensable. Examples are agreements, or clauses in agreements, conferring absolute territorial protection (see, for instance, *Établissements Consten SA* v *Commission*), or fixing prices. Other kinds of restriction are to be considered in their particular context (see for instance *Transocean Marine Paint Association*).

11.7.7 **No elimination of competition**

There must be no elimination of competition in respect of the product in question. Before a decision can be made under this head, it is necessary to define the relevant product and geographical markets (in the same way that this would be done in relation to Article 82 (ex 86)—see **Chapter 12**) and, for some agreements, to take account of competition from undertakings outside the Community.

11.8 **Article 81(3) (ex 85(3)): block exemption**

Article 81(3) (ex 85(3)) allows Article 81(1) (ex 85(1)) to be declared inapplicable not only to individual agreements but also to categories of agreement. In relation to categories of agreement, the Commission achieved this, under authority delegated by the Council, by issuing block exemptions giving automatic exemption to certain kinds of agreement.

The Commission has used block exemptions as a means of reducing its own workload, which continued to increase as more and more businesses sought protection from fines by notifying any agreements which might possibly infringe Article 81(1) (ex 85(1)). The kinds of agreement covered by block exemptions are those which, though they contain restrictions, are considered overall to have beneficial effects, such as specialization agreements and technology transfer agreements (relating to patent and know-how licensing). Each block exemption is contained in a Regulation. Most of the original Regulations followed the same basic format, setting out those restrictions which were permitted, the 'white list', and those which were not permitted, the 'black list'. More recent block exemptions, including the block exemptions for specialization agreements, research and development agreements and vertical agreements, contain 'black-listed' restrictions but no 'white list' of restrictions. The Commission takes the view that the removal of the 'white-lists' will free business from the 'strait-jacket' effect of the former Regulations, under which the parties to an agreement were limited to the use of the expressly permitted restrictions.

The system of block exemptions remains unaltered by Regulation 1/2003.

11.9 Regulation 2790/99: the block exemption for vertical agreements

Regulation 2790/99, the block exemption for certain categories of vertical agreements and concerted practices, was adopted in December 1999 and came into force in June 2000. Before turning to the detail of the block exemption, it is useful to consider, generally, the nature and potential effects of vertical restraints.

11.9.1 Vertical restraints and the background to the block exemption

There is considerable debate between economists as to the harmfulness or otherwise to competition of restrictions contained in vertical agreements, or 'vertical restraints'.

 EXERCISE 11.14

What is a vertical agreement? Look back at section (11.6.5) to find the answer.

A vertical agreement is an agreement between undertakings operating at different levels of the production/distribution chain, for instance between a manufacturer and a distributor. Such an agreement may contain restrictions that could be regarded as both pro- and anti-competitive.

 EXERCISE 11.15

Consider the following circumstances:

UK Audio, a UK manufacturer of electronic sound recording equipment is seeking to establish a market for its products in Italy. Because UK Audio has no retailing expertise, the company has decided not to set up its own retailing outlets in Italy, but instead to sell through an independent retailer, which has outlets in Rome, Milan, and Naples. The retailer is prepared to undertake extensive advertising and the provision of after-sales service, without which the marketing of the products will not be successful.

What commitment do you think the retailer may well demand from UK Audio in order to ensure that its financial investment is rewarded through maximization of its sales of the products? If you need help in answering this question, look back at (11.6.10).

The retailer may be unwilling to take on the expenditure required for advertising and for the provision of after-sales service unless it is protected from competition from other retailers. It may well require UK Audio to agree not to supply its products to other retailers in the Rome, Milan, and Naples areas. Such a commitment to exclusivity is restrictive of intra-brand competition (competition within the brand, between retailers of the UK Audio's products). It is also pro-competitive, in that it may facilitate the penetration of a new market which would otherwise not have been accessible to UK Audio, thus increasing inter-brand competition (competition between different brands of sound recording equipment on the Italian market).

Before reform of Community competition law on vertical agreements, embodied in Regulation 2790/99 (see 11.9.2), the Commission had been criticized for its inflexible approach to vertical restraints, which led it to condemn them as anti-competitive and a breach of Article 81(1), without undertaking an adequate analysis of their potentially beneficial economic effects. In 1997, the Commission published the *Green Paper on Vertical Restraints in EC Competition policy*, which initiated a consultation on review of policy towards vertical restraints and proposed possible options for reform. The timing was significant, for three of the existing block exemption Regulations on distribution, covering exclusive buying and selling and franchising were due to expire.

When it published the results of the consultation on the Green Paper, the Commission recognized the need for greater flexibility in the approach to vertical agreements, based upon an effects-based economic analysis. The outcome was the adoption of a new block exemption extending to all vertical agreements.

11.9.2 **Regulation 2790/99**

This block exemption exempts from Article 81(1) (ex 85(1)) agreements or concerted practices between two or more undertakings each operating at different levels of the production or distribution chain and which relate to conditions under which the parties may purchase, sell, or resell certain goods or services. Thus it applies not only to exclusive buying and selling and franchising agreements but also to selective distribution agreements which would otherwise be prohibited by Article 81(1). The exemption applies only where the market share on the relevant market (for detailed discussion of the concept of the relevant market, see **Chapter 12**) of the supplier or buyer does not exceed 30%. The exemption does not apply to vertical agreements having certain specified objects, such as price fixing and absolute territorial protection, nor to specific obligations, such as non-competition clauses whose duration is indefinite or exceeds five years. Notably, the block exemption contains these 'black listed' restrictions but, unlike previous block exemptions, does not constrain undertakings to a 'white list' of specific permitted restrictions. This means that if a restriction in an agreement is not black-listed, it is permitted.

The following section considers the main provisions of Regulation 2790/99.

11.9.2.1 **Article 1: definitions**

Read Article 1 of Regulation 2790/99 (*Cases and Materials* (11.5)). This contains important definitions. Look at paragraphs (b) and (c). How would the following contractual obligations relating to Alpha Co, a widget manufacturer, and Omega Co, a widget distributor, be described within the terms of the Regulation:

- an obligation imposed by Alpha Co, under a contract for the supply of widgets to Omega Co, causing Omega Co not to sell widgets which compete with those supplied under the contract;
- an obligation on Omega Co to purchase from Alpha Co more than 80% of its total widget purchases from Alpha Co;
- an obligation imposed upon Alpha Co causing Alpha Co to sell widgets for resale only to Omega Co within the Community.

The first two contractual obligations restrict Omega Co's ability to sell widgets competing with Alpha Co's widgets and comprise non-compete obligations. The third obligation is an exclusive supply obligation because it causes Alpha Co to sell to only one buyer inside the Community.

11.9.2.2 **Article 2: the exemption**

Article 2 of the Regulation declares that Article 81(1) shall not apply to vertical agreements. The exemption applies to the extent that such agreements contain restrictions falling within Article 81(1).

The exemption in Article 2 is subject to the conditions contained in Article 3. Read Article 3. What conditions are set out in paragraphs 1 and 2, respectively?

Article 3 of the Regulation makes the exemption contained in Article 2 subject to a market share threshold. The exemption applies only where the supplier's market share does not exceed 30% (paragraph 1). In the case of agreements containing exclusive supply obligations, the exemption only applies where the market share of the buyer does not exceed 30% (paragraph 2).

11.9.2.3 **Article 4: hardcore, non-severable restrictions**

The benefit of the block exemption does not apply to vertical agreements which contain certain hardcore restrictions. These restrictions are set out in Article 4. They include price fixing by the supplier (restrictions on the buyer's ability to determine its sale price (paragraph (a)) and territorial restrictions (restrictions on the territory into which the buyer may sell the contract goods or services (paragraph (b)). The impact of Article 4 is that an agreement containing hardcore restrictions is, in its entirety, outside the scope of the block exemption. It is not possible to sever the offending clauses and leave the rest of the agreement within the exemption.

11.9.2.4 Article 5: severable restrictions

By contrast to Article 4, Article 5 provides that the block exemption does not apply to certain obligations contained in agreements. Although the Article 5 restrictions themselves fall outside the block exemption, they may be severed, allowing the remainder of the agreement to benefit from the block exemption.

 EXERCISE 11.18

Look at Article 5 of Regulation 2790/99. To what extent are non-compete obligations block exempted? (Remember that a 'non-compete obligation' is defined in Article 1 of the Regulation.)

The block exemption does not apply to indefinite non-compete obligations, nor to non-compete obligations of more than five years duration. However, the five-year limitation does not apply where the contract goods or services are sold by the buyer from premises and land owned or leased by the supplier, provided the non-compete obligation does not extend beyond the buyer's occupancy of the premises.

Non-compete obligations applying after the termination of the agreement are block exempted only if they are limited to one year after termination, relate to goods or services which compete with the contract goods or services, are limited to the premises from which the buyer has operated during the contract period and are indispensable to protect know-how transferred by the supplier to the buyer.

11.9.2.5 Article 6: withdrawal of the benefit of the Regulation

Under Article 6, the Commission may withdraw the benefit of the Regulation from vertical agreements which are within its scope but which, nevertheless, are incompatible with Article 81(3).

 CONCLUSIONS

One of the primary challenges for Community competition law and policy is to ensure adequate regulation of restrictive practices which threaten market integration, reduce efficiency, and prejudice the consumer—but at the same time to avoid an over-interventionist approach which strikes down all restrictions, even if they are necessary to achieve overall economic benefits. The framework of Article 81 (ex 85), specifically the provisions in Article 81(3) (ex 85(3)), allows for the assessment of the pro- and anti-competitive effects of agreements and provides scope for the necessary balance to be struck. Whether this balance is always achieved is a matter of continuing debate for businesses, economists and lawyers, alike.

CHAPTER 11: ASSESSMENT EXERCISE CWS

(a) Samcad (UK) plc (Samcad) manufactures the 'Focus', a highly technically advanced home computer, which it markets through retail outlets in the UK, France, and Denmark. Samcad has a 20% share of the total Community market for home computers. The 'Focus' is supplied only to retailers who enter into a standard form contract with Samcad requiring them to:

(i) ensure that all their sales staff are fully trained in the use of the 'Focus';

(ii) ensure that areas of their sales premises in which the 'Focus' is displayed have facilities enabling staff to give simple demonstrations of the use of the computer to customers.

Advise Samcad on the compatibility of its standard agreement with Article 81 (ex 85) EC.

(b) How would your answer to Question 1 differ if Samcad's standard agreement also required retailers to charge prices fixed by Samcad?
In view of your conclusions, advise Samcad on any action it should take.

(c) Rainco, a UK manufacturer of raincoats which has a 20% share of the relevant market, agrees to supply raincoats for resale to Pluieco, a French wholesaler of rainwear. The contract between them provides as follows:

• Rainco agrees to supply the contract goods only to Pluieco in France but is permitted to continue to supply raincoats in other Member States ('obligation 1')

• Pluieco agrees, for a period of six years from the date of the agreement, not to sell raincoats which compete with the contract goods ('obligation 2')

Does this agreement benefit from the block exemption under Regulation 2790/99?
How would your answer differ (if at all) if there were a further clause in the agreement fixing the price at which Pluieco could resell the contract goods?

See *Cases and Materials* (11.7) for specimen answers.

12 Competition law: Article 82 (ex 86)

12.1 Objectives

By the end of this chapter you should be able to:

1 Explain and analyse the prohibition of abuse of a dominant position contained in Article 82 (ex 86) EC

2 Explain and analyse the key concepts of dominance, relevant product market, relevant geographical market and abuse

12.2 Introduction

As was noted in **Chapter 11**, Article 81 (ex 85) deals primarily with the control of restrictive agreements and concerted practices between independent undertakings. The concern of Article 82 (ex 86) is the threat posed to competition within the common market by the economic power of single undertakings which enjoy a dominant position in a particular market for goods or services. Article 82 (ex 86) does not prohibit dominance. However, it does provide that any abuse of market power which is capable of affecting trade between Member States is prohibited as incompatible with the common market. Such abuses may be anti-competitive, in that they eliminate or seriously weaken existing competition in a particular market or prevent new competitors entering that market. They may also amount to exploitative behaviour, which takes unfair advantage of the consumer. Like Article 81 (ex 85), Article 82 (ex 86) pursues the broad aim of eliminating distortion of competition in the internal market which is set out in Article 3(1)(g) (ex 3(g)) (formerly Article 3(f)) EC.

12.3 The Article 82 (ex 86): prohibition

 EXERCISE 12.1   CWS

Look at the first paragraph of Article 82 (ex 86) in *Cases and Materials* (12.1). You will see that it prohibits certain behaviour by undertakings because that behaviour is incompatible with the common market. Write down the key words and phrases used to define the prohibited behaviour.

You might have written down something like this: abuse; one or more undertakings; dominant position; within the common market or a substantial part of it; affect trade between Member States.

 EXERCISE 12.2

Turn back to 11.6.2 to remind yourself of the meaning of the term 'undertaking' under Article 81 (ex 85). 'Undertaking' has the same meaning under Article 82 (ex 86).

The prohibition in Article 82 (ex 86) may be summarized as follows: it applies to the behaviour of an undertaking or undertakings when there is:

(a) a dominant position within the common market or a substantial part of it; and

(b) an abuse of that dominant position; and

(c) that abuse is capable of affecting trade between Member States.

In order to understand the scope of the prohibition in Article 82 (ex 86), it is necessary to consider each of these elements in some detail.

12.4 **Dominant position**

An undertaking is dominant when it has substantial market power. In *United Brands Co* v *Commission* (Case 27/76) [1978] ECR 207 (*Cases and Materials* (12.2)) the Court of Justice defined dominance, in paragraph 65 of the judgment, as:

a position of economic strength enjoyed by an undertaking which enables it to prevent effective competition being maintained on the relevant market by giving it the power to behave to an appreciable extent independently of its competitors, customers and ultimately of its consumers.

If an undertaking is dominant it may be able to prevent potential competitors entering the market, weaken existing competitors or drive existing competitors out of the market. A dominant undertaking may also be able to exploit its customers.

? **QUESTION** 12.1

How might a dominant undertaking drive an existing competitor out of the market or prevent a new competitor entering the market?

> **? QUESTION** 12.2
>
> How might a dominant undertaking exploit its customers?

One of the most obvious ways in which a dominant undertaking might exclude or elimi-nate competition is by temporarily lowering its prices below cost. Another is by offering discounts to customers who agree to buy all or most of their supplies from the undertak-ing. Because of its economic strength, it may be able to do this for some time. Smaller and less powerful undertakings cannot afford to compete on these terms and may go out of business. The result is a distortion of competition. The dominant undertaking may be able to exploit its customers—for instance, by charging them unjustifiably high prices or by insisting that when they buy goods from that undertaking they must also buy related services—knowing that the customers are not able, or would find it difficult, to buy elsewhere.

> **? QUESTION** 12.3
>
> What factors do you think might indicate that an undertaking is in a dominant position? Write down your answer and look at it again at the end of this section.

As indicated in *United Brands* in the passage quoted above, a dominant position is assessed in relation to a particular market. Although the illustrations in this section mainly con-cern markets for goods, the same principles also apply to services. There are three kinds of market which the Court of Justice and the Commission look at when considering domi-nant position. These are:

(a) the relevant product market;

(b) the relevant geographic market; and

(c) the relevant temporal market.

12.4.1 The relevant product market

The definition of the relevant product market (RPM) has been the subject of dispute in much of the case law on Article 82 (ex 86). This is partly because definition is often extremely difficult, involving detailed and sometimes controversial economic analysis. More importantly, the definition of the RPM may be the crucial factor in determining whether or not an undertaking is in a dominant position.

? **QUESTION** 12.4

A (fictitious) company known as Creamy plc makes a single product, luxury 'double cream' choc ices. What is the RPM in which the company is operating?

Your first reaction may be that Creamy plc's RPM is the choc ice market. Consider other possibilities. For instance, it could be argued that the RPM is the 'double cream' choc ice market or the ice cream market generally or even the general ice cream/ice lolly market. Perhaps you can think of other possible RPMs.

That raises the question as to how the RPM is determined. The Commission and the Court of Justice define the RPM in terms of product substitution or interchangeability. To decide whether goods are interchangeable and therefore in the same product market it is necessary to look, first, at consumer perception and behaviour and, secondly, at the ability of potential competitors to enter the market. In its 1997 Notice on the Definition of the Relevant Market for the Purposes of Community Competition Law, the Commission states that its starting point for definition of the RPM is demand substitutability, supply substitutability, and potential competition.

12.4.2 **Product substitution**

If products are such that customers regard them as substantially interchangeable, then they are likely to be in the same product market. To go back to the Creamy plc illustration, if customers setting out to buy choc ices are prepared to buy ice creams instead (for instance if they find that there are no choc ices available) then this is an indicator that choc ices and ice creams are substitutable and are therefore in the same product market. This is called cross-elasticity of demand or demand substitutability.

? **QUESTION** 12.5

What factors do you think are important to a consumer who is considering whether a certain product is acceptable as a substitute for another?

The consumer's willingness to accept one product as a substitute for another depends upon factors such as the characteristics of the products, the use to which the product is to be put and general similarity of price. On that basis, there is probably cross-elasticity of demand between choc ices and ice creams. Some goods, although at first sight they might appear to be in the same product market because they have similar characteristics, are not interchangeable.

Consider high quality luxury fountain pens and the kinds of fountain pens which can be bought for a few pounds. Both products are put to the same use and their basic characteristics are similar. However, a luxury fountain pen is an expensive, quality product, bought perhaps partly as a status symbol. It would be difficult to argue convincingly that these products are in the same product market.

In its 1997 Notice on the Definition of the Relevant Market, the Commission sets out a test for demand substitution based upon the consumer's response to a small but significant (between 5–10 per cent) permanent increase in the price of a product. If such an increase would cause the consumer to switch from one product to another, the two products are in the same product market. This test for product substitution, known as the SSNIP (Small but Significant Non-transitory Increase in Price) test indicates a more quantitative approach to the definition of the relevant market.

Product substitution also depends upon what is known as cross-elasticity of supply or supply substitutability. If other undertakings are able to supply similar products or are capable of switching their production to similar products, then the RPM is extended accordingly. This aspect of product substitution will be considered later when *Europemballage Corp and Continental Can Co Inc* v *Commission* (Case 6/72) [1973] ECR 215 is discussed (*Cases and Materials* (12.2.1)).

12.4.3 **Significance of the relevant product market**

> **? QUESTION** 12.6
>
> You will remember that Creamy plc manufactures only one product, luxury 'double cream' choc ices. Suppose that the company has:
>
> (a) a very large share of the Community 'double cream' choc ice market;
> (b) a large share of the Community choc ice market;
> (c) a small share of the Community general ice cream market; and
> (d) a negligible share of the Community ice cream/ice lolly market.
>
> In the course of investigations by the Commission in relation to Article 82 (ex 86), the question of the RPM is a matter of dispute between Creamy plc and the Commission. What do you think the company will claim as the RPM? Why?

Undertakings are always anxious to show that they are not dominant, so that Article 82 (ex 86) will not apply to them. Consequently, they are likely to seek to define the RPM as widely as possible. The wider the RPM, the less likely they are to be dominant in that market. Conversely, the narrower the RPM, the more likely they are to be dominant. In order to escape the scope of Article 82 (ex 86), Creamy plc will claim the widest possible market—either the general ice cream market or the ice cream/ice lolly market—as the RPM.

EXERCISE 12.3 CWS

Look at *United Brands Co* v *Commission* (Case 27/76) [1978] ECR 207 in *Cases and Materials* (12.2). Write down answers to the following questions:

(a) What did United Brands produce?
(b) What did the company claim to be the RPM?
(c) What did the Commission claim to be the RPM?
(d) What did the Court of Justice decide and why?

In *United Brands*, the Commission claimed that United Brands, a producer of bananas, acted in breach of Article 82 (ex 86) by abusing a dominant position. The first issue to be addressed was that of the RPM. The company sought to define the market broadly, as fresh fruit. The Commission claimed that the RPM was bananas. The Court of Justice agreed with the Commission. This conclusion was reached following consideration of product substitution and cross-elasticity of demand. The Court accepted the argument that bananas are unique because of their appearance, taste, softness, seedlessness, and easy handling, all characteristics which make them a particularly suitable fruit for the old, the sick and the very young (they are ideal for people without teeth!). In these important respects, no other fruits are acceptable as substitutes and there is little cross-elasticity of demand. As will be noted later, the Court of Justice went on to confirm that the company had abused its dominant position in the banana market in various ways.

 QUESTION 12.7 CWS

Look at an earlier case, *Europemballage Corp and Continental Can Co Inc* v *Commission* (Case 6/72) [1973] ECR 215 in *Cases and Materials* (12.2.1), in which the Commission Decision finding an infringement of Article 82 (ex 86) was annulled. Why did the Court of Justice consider the Commission's analysis of product substitution to be inadequate?

The Court of Justice took the view that when the Commission defined the RPM, it had failed to consider demand-side substitutability, in particular whether Continental Can's products (light metal containers for meat and fish and metal closures for glass jars) formed a separate market from the general market for light metal containers used for the packaging of fruit and vegetables, fruit juices and the like. To form a separate market, Continental Can's products must be 'individualized . . . by particular characteristics of production which make them specifically suitable for this purpose'. The Commission had also neglected to consider supply-side substitutability: how difficult would it have been for potential competitors from other sectors of the market for light metal containers to enter this market by switching their production by simple adaptation to substitutes acceptable to the consumer? Where there is high cross-elasticity of supply, an allegedly dominant firm's position is not so powerful as it might appear.

The RPM is not necessarily the market in which the ultimate consumer purchases a product. The possibility that the RPM can be an intermediate market in which there is little cross-elasticity of demand may be crucially important. This point is illustrated by the case referred to next.

 EXERCISE 12.4   CWS

List the three suggested RPMs in *Istituto Chemioterapico Italiano SpA and Commercial Solvents Corporation* v *Commission* (Cases 6 & 7/73) [1974] ECR 223 in *Cases and Materials* (12.2.2). Which was the RPM according to the Court of Justice?

As in many other Article 82 (ex 86) cases, the conclusion as to the RPM in *Istituto Chemioterapico Italiano SpA* was a crucial factor in determining whether or not Commercial Solvents Corporation (CSC) and its subsidiary Istituto Chemioterapico Italiano SpA (Istituto) had a dominant position. If the RPM was, as CSC and Istituto argued, the end product supplied to the ultimate consumer, namely anti-tuberculosis drugs (of which there were a number available), then the companies were not dominant. If the RPM was, as the Commission argued, the particular raw material (aminobutanol) supplied by CSC to Zoja for the manufacture of anti-tuberculosis drugs, there certainly was a dominant position. The third possibility was that the RPM was the range of raw materials which could be used to produce the drug; if this was the RPM, then the companies were probably not dominant. The Court of Justice did not accept that Zoja could easily adapt its manufacturing process to the use of raw materials other than aminobutanol and so the third suggested RPM was ruled out. The Court also rejected CSC's argument that the deciding factor should be consumer choice of the ultimate product, thus also ruling out drugs for treating tuberculosis as the RPM. The Court held that the RPM was CSC's raw material, aminobutanol.

Istituto Chemioterapico Italiano SpA demonstrates an aspect of Community competition policy which has already been noted in the context of Article 81 (ex 85). The Court of Justice and the Commission are particularly concerned to protect the interests of small and medium-sized businesses in the face of competition from large and powerful undertakings. In this case, that policy involved the protection of competition in the common market not only at the level of the ultimate consumer of the product but also at intermediate levels of production and distribution.

Sometimes, because of the specialist nature of the products or services which they supply, undertakings can be dominant in a very small and apparently insignificant market. This was the situation with regard to the Swedish firm Hugin, which was held to be dominant in the market for spare parts for the cash registers which it manufactured (*Hugin Kassaregister AB* v *Commission* (Case 22/78) [1979] ECR 1869 in *Cases and Materials* (12.2.2)). Similarly, General Motors had a dominant position with respect to the issuing of certificates of conformity for Opel vehicles imported into Belgium (*General Motors*

Continental NV v *Commission* (Case 26/75) [1975] ECR 1367 in *Cases and Materials* (12.2.2).

12.4.4 The relevant geographic market

Before dominance can be assessed, it is necessary also to establish the relevant geographic market and to consider whether the alleged dominant position is held 'within the common market or in a substantial part of it' (Article 82 (ex 86), see *Cases and Materials* (12.1)). Since all Community undertakings are operating within an internal market which is theoretically free from barriers to trade, the relevant geographic market will generally be taken to be the whole of the common market. Sometimes, however, there may

be factors which cause the geographic market to be defined more narrowly. In *United Brands*, see *Cases and Materials* (12.2), the Court of Justice defined the geographic market as 'an area where the objective conditions of competition applying to the product in question' are the same for all traders. Here, the relevant geographic market consisted in all the Member States except France, Italy and the UK.

> **?** **QUESTION** 12.8
>
> What do you think is meant by 'objective conditions of competition'?

One major feature of a geographic market is that within that market the cost and feasibility of transporting products is the same or similar for all traders. Thus, where goods can be easily and cheaply transported, it is economic to sell them some distance away from the point of production and consequently the whole of the Community may be the geographic market. This was the case, for instance, with respect to the nail cartridges supplied by the firm Hilti, which were very cheap to transport (*Hilti AG* v *Commission* (Case

T-30/89) [1991] ECR II-1439 in *Cases and Materials* (12.2.3)). Conversely, where the nature of the goods makes transportation expensive or difficult, the geographic market will be more narrowly defined.

A geographic market may also be characterised in other ways—as the market in which consumers are willing and able to travel to the source of supply, or in which they are prepared to look for substitute products. It may be the geographical area to which use of the goods or services is limited (remember that the RPM can be a market for goods or services). The latter point is illustrated by the 'TV listings' cases. Here, the geographic market for listings relating to BBC and ITV television programmes was held to be the area in which the applicant companies broadcasted, namely Ireland and Northern Ireland

(*RTE* v *Commission* (Case T-69/89) [1991] ECR II-485; *BBC* v *Commission* (Case T-70/89) [1991] ECR II-535; *ITP Ltd* v *Commission* (Case T-76/89) [1991] ECR II-575 in *Cases and Materials* (12.2.3)).

In summary, the 'objective conditions of competition' relate to factors such as the cost and ease of transportation, the purchasing behaviour and preferences of consumers, and any geographical limitations on the use of the goods or services.

Having examined these factors, it is necessary to consider how large a geographic market needs to be to constitute a market 'within the common market or a substantial part of it'. In fact, a geographic market need not be very extensive to be caught by Article 82 (ex 86). A Community-wide market clearly falls within the scope of the Article (*Hilti* in *Cases and Materials* (12.2.3)), as does a market which extends to a number of Member States (*United Brands* in *Cases and Materials* (12.2)). The Court of Justice has held that a single Member State can be the relevant geographic market and constitute a substantial part of the common market (*Nederlandsche Banden-Industrie Michelin NV v Commission* (Case 322/81) [1983] ECR 3461 in *Cases and Materials* (12.2.3)). In some cases, particularly in the air and sea transport sector, the geographic market has been drawn very narrowly. For instance, in *Sealink/B and I—Holyhead: Interim Measures* (Commission Decision) [1992] 5 CMLR 255 the relevant market was held to be the port of Holyhead, which served the ferry route between Holyhead and Dublin.

12.4.5 The relevant temporal market

Conditions of competition between undertakings sometimes vary from season to season. Therefore, as well as examining the product and geographic markets, it may be necessary to consider the temporal (or seasonal) market.

 QUESTION 12.9

You will recall that the relevant product market in *United Brands* was bananas. How might seasonal factors affect this market?

It was suggested in *United Brands* that there were two seasonal markets. Evidence of fluctuating cross-elasticity of demand from season to season indicated that during the summer months, when supplies of other fruits were plentiful, the company's market power was reduced. In the winter, when substitutes were not available to the consumer, its market power was restored. Despite this evidence both the Commission and the Court of Justice identified a single temporal market. By contrast, in its decision in *Re ABG Oil* OJ 1977 L 117/1, [1977] 2 CMLR D1, the Commission defined the temporal market for oil by reference to the oil crisis precipitated by the action of the OPEC states in the early 1970s.

12.4.6 Assessing dominance

Dominance is defined broadly as the ability of an undertaking to act independently on the market, free from competitive pressure. Once the relevant market has been ascertained, it is necessary to establish whether or not an undertaking is in fact dominant in that market. This can be done by reference to a number of criteria, now considered in turn. None of these criteria, save perhaps for a very large market share, is in itself conclusive of dominance but in combination the criteria may lead to a finding of dominance. The starting point is an assessment of market share.

12.4.6.1 **Market share**

In practice, total monopoly situations (in which an undertaking is the only operator in a particular market) are comparatively rare, save where monopolies are conferred by statute (see for instance *General Motors v Commission* (Case 26/75) [1975] ECR 1367 in *Cases and Materials* (12.2.2)). In this regard, it should be noted that statutory monopolies do not, as such, escape the scope of Article 82 (ex 86).

Market share is a very important factor in the assessment of dominance. A very large market share may in itself be evidence of a dominant position (see *Hoffmann-La Roche* (Case 85/76) [1979] ECR 461 and *Hilti* (Case T-30/89) [1991] ECR II-1439 in *Cases and Materials* (12.2.5.1) and (12.2.3), respectively). In *Hilti*, the Court of Justice held that a market share of between 70% and 80% in the relevant market was 'in itself a clear indication of a dominant position'. Where a market share is smaller it may be, together with other factors, a significant indicator of dominance. Because of a combination of factors, United Brands was held to be dominant with a market share of between 40% and 45%, even though this share and the company's profits had been falling. Frequently, the structure of a market is important.

? **QUESTION** 12.10

Think about the following market structures:

(a) Blue Medal Drinks plc (Blue Medal) has a 40% share of the Community soft drinks market. Its closest rivals, Thirst Quenchers plc and Sparkling Sunshine Ltd hold, respectively, 38% and 20% shares.

(b) In the Community remould tyre market, Rubber Products Ltd (Rubber Products) is the largest supplier, having a market share of 40%. The company's three nearest competitors hold, respectively, 5%, 2%, and 1% shares.

Do these figures suggest that Blue Medal and Rubber Products are dominant in their respective markets? Write down your answer, giving reasons for your conclusions.

The two companies have exactly the same share of their respective markets. The difference between them lies in the position of their competitors. Rubber Products' rivals trail a long way behind in terms of market share. With its rivals close behind, Blue Medal appears much more vulnerable to competition; only a slight fluctuation in the Community soft drinks market is required to change around the figures and put Blue Medal's nearest competitor in the lead. Consequently, Blue Medal is much less likely than Rubber Products to act without regard to its competitors and customers and is thus less likely to be in a dominant position in its particular market.

In *United Brands*, the structure of the market was an important factor. Although the company's share of the banana market was less than 50%, that share was several times greater than that of its nearest rival. Other competitors were even further behind. The Commission has indicated that, in a very fragmented market, a market share as low as 20% might be sufficient to constitute dominance.

12.4.6.2 Duration of market position

An important consideration in the assessment of dominance is the length of time that an undertaking has been in a position of market power. In *Hoffmann-La Roche & Co. AG* v *Commission* (Case 85/76) [1979] ECR 461 (*Cases and Materials* (12.2.5.1)), which concerned a drugs company which held very large shares (of between 75% and 87%) of various vitamin markets, the Court of Justice indicated that market power held 'for some time' pointed to a position of dominance on a market. If a large market share is held only for a short time before a powerful competitor enters the market, this would indicate that there was no domination of that market.

12.4.6.3 Financial and technological resources

 QUESTION 12.11

In what ways do you think extensive financial resources might assist an undertaking to establish or sustain a dominant position?

You may have thought of a number of ways in which an undertaking might use extensive financial resources. It could, for example, indulge in persistent price-cutting, perhaps selling below cost or, as United Brands had done, use its wealth to reduce cross-elasticity of demand by advertising its products heavily. The greater its financial resources, the greater an undertaking's ability to develop its technological know-how, to invest in product development and to provide technical services to its customers. All these strategies can be means to weaken existing competition, to drive competitors out of the market and to deter potential new entrants to the market.

12.4.6.4 Vertical integration

The extent of vertical integration is demonstrated by the degree of control which an undertaking exerts in the production and marketing chain, either 'upstream'—for instance in the market for raw materials—or 'downstream'—in the distribution network. The greater the vertical integration, the more likely there is to be dominance.

 EXERCISE 12.5   CWS

Look at *United Brands* in *Cases and Materials* (12.2). Write down the features of the company's production and marketing network which demonstrated, first, its 'up-stream' integration and, secondly, its 'downstream' integration.

United Brands' operations were described by the Court of Justice as 'vertically integrated to a high degree'. 'Upstream' the company owned large plantations in Central and South

America and so had virtual total control over banana supplies for the purposes of its own customers' requirements. As far as 'downstream' integration was concerned, the company controlled loading operations and had its own transportation systems, including railways and a banana fleet for carriage by sea. It also had control over banana ripeners, distributors and wholesalers through an extensive network of agents. Similarly, in *Hoffmann-La Roche & Co. AG* v *Commission*, the Court of Justice recognized that the company's highly efficient sales network was a factor indicating a dominant position.

12.4.6.5 Conduct

In *United Brands* the Court of Justice agreed with the Commission's view that the behaviour of an allegedly dominant undertaking can provide evidence of dominance. So, for example, the fact that an undertaking has cut its prices below cost can in itself indicate that it is in a dominant position. The view that abusive behaviour (a concept which we shall examine in detail presently) can indicate dominance has been criticized, since the scheme of Article 82 (ex 86) requires a finding of dominant position followed by an analysis of conduct which could amount to an abuse of that dominant position. To hold that abusive behaviour indicates dominance is to indulge in a circular argument. Nevertheless, the Commission continues to take conduct into account when assessing dominance.

12.4.6.6 Barriers to entry

? QUESTION 12.12

What kinds of factors do you think might operate as barriers which prevent or deter potential competitors from entering a particular market?

The fact that an undertaking is able to erect barriers which prevent potential competitors from entering its market may be an indication of substantial power. When thinking about barriers to entry, you may have called to mind some of the factors which have already been mentioned, such as extensive financial and technological resources, the entrenchment of market power over a long period of time and vertical integration, all of which can deter others from entry into the market because the costs of setting up a competing business would be so great.

In addition to these barriers, others could be mentioned, in particular those which arise from legal rights of various kinds. For instance, if an undertaking owns intellectual property rights such as copyright, patents and trade marks, competitors may be discouraged from entering the market through fear of infringing those legal rights. (See for instance the 'TV listings' cases referred to in 12.4.4 (copyright) (*Cases and Materials* (12.2.3)) and *Hilti* (patents) (*Cases and Materials* (12.2.3)).

EXERCISE 12.6

At Question 12.3 you should have written down the factors which you thought might indicate that an undertaking is in a dominant position. Have a look at what you wrote and see how many of the main points you identified.

In summary, in deciding whether an undertaking is dominant the Commission and the Court of Justice first identify the relevant product, geographic and temporal markets. They then assess dominance in the relevant market by reference to factors such as market share, duration of a position of market power, financial and technological resources, vertical integration, and any other barriers to entry.

12.5 Abuse of a dominant position

An undertaking does not infringe Article 82 (ex 86) merely by being in a dominant position. For a breach of Article 82 (ex 86) to occur, there must be an abuse of that dominant position.

 EXERCISE 12.7   CWS

Look at the second paragraph of Article 82 (ex 86) in *Cases and Materials* (12.1), which lists some examples of abuse. Now look at Article 81(1) (ex 85(1)) in *Cases and Materials* (11.2.1). You will notice that the Article 82 (ex 86) examples of abusive behaviour are very similar to the examples of concerted behaviour which are likely to breach Article 81 (ex 85). Such behaviour, whether by undertakings acting alone or in agreement with other undertakings, distorts competition within the common market.

Often, abuses under Article 82 (ex 86) are classified into two categories, exploitative abuses and anti-competitive abuses. Exploitative abuses are those which impose unfair conditions on consumers. Anti-competitive abuses are those which prevent or weaken competition from other undertakings in the market. Many kinds of abusive behaviour can be described as both exploitative and anti-competitive. The list of abuses in Article 82 (ex 86), like the similar list in Article 81 (ex 85), is not exhaustive but simply gives examples of abusive behaviour. Discussion now turns to some particular kinds of abuse which have been considered by the Commission and the Court of Justice.

12.5.1 Unfair prices

The imposition of unfair or excessively high prices is one of the most obvious ways in which a dominant undertaking might abuse its position and exploit its customers. However, the concept of an 'unfair' or 'excessive' price is not without difficulty.

> **? QUESTION** 12.13
>
> How would you define an 'excessive' price?

The task of defining an excessive price is not easy. In charging unfair or excessive prices the dominant undertaking relies on the fact that the consumer needs or wants the product and is prepared to pay a price which is in excess of that which would be charged in a more competitive market. One way of determining an excessive price, suggested by the Court of Justice in *United Brands* (*Cases and Materials* (12.2)), is to compare the selling price and the cost of production, in other words to calculate the size of the profit margin. Since the Commission had not analysed United Brands' production costs, the Court refused to uphold the Commission's charge of unfair pricing. In the same case, the Court defined an excessive price as one which 'has no reasonable relation to the economic value of the product supplied'. Of course, this begs the question as to how the economic value of a product is assessed. However careful and detailed the economic analysis employed in any particular case, it appears that conclusions as to unfair or excessive pricing are likely to be controversial.

When a dominant undertaking's profits reach a certain level there is a strong incentive to other firms to enter the market and to compete by undercutting any unfair or excessive prices. Thus, market forces provide some protection for the consumer. However, such forces will not operate where there are significant barriers to entry.

> **? QUESTION** 12.14   CWS
>
> What was the barrier to entry in *General Motors* v *Commission* (Case 26/75) [1975] ECR 1367? See *Cases and Materials* (12.2.2).

The Commission claimed that General Motors had charged excessive prices for the certificates of conformity required for the import of second-hand Opel cars into Belgium. The company had an exclusive right under Belgian law to provide inspection services and to issue the certificates in respect of these cars. Its statutory monopoly in this market created a complete barrier to entry. Here, the Court of Justice characterized as an abuse the imposition of a price which is 'excessive in relation to the economic value of the service provided'. However although General Motors held a dominant position, its conduct did not, on the facts, constitute an abuse. Look at paragraphs 21 and 22 of the judgment to find out why.

In a similar case, *British Leyland plc* v *Commission* (Case 226/84) [1986] ECR 3263, the Court of Justice upheld a Commission Decision finding an abuse of a dominant position by British Leyland. The Court held that the prices charged by the company for type approval certificates for imports of British Leyland cars from the continent of Europe was disproportionate to the service provided. Here, it was clear that the purpose of the excessive pricing was to reduce competition in sales of British Leyland cars on the home market by discouraging imports into the UK.

12.5.2 **Price discrimination**

This is one aspect of the wider abuse of discriminatory treatment. Price discrimination includes such practices as target discounting and loyalty rebating, both of which will be considered presently. In its simplest and most blatant form, discriminatory pricing consists in charging different prices to different customers for the same product. In *United Brands*, the Court of Justice held that the company had abused its dominant position by charging, at the port of entry of its products into the Community, different prices to customers from different Member States.

EXERCISE 12.8   CWS

Look again at the examples of abuse listed in Article 82 (ex 86) in *Cases and Materials* (12.1). Write down the example of abuse under which United Brand's discriminatory pricing policy might be classified.

The Court of Justice held that the company's pricing policy amounted to the application of 'dissimilar conditions to equivalent transactions with other trading parties, thereby placing them at a competitive disadvantage'. This policy was based purely on what the market would bear.

Sometimes, a difference in pricing may be justified by objective factors concerning the varying costs involved in supplying goods or services. For instance, the different costs of transportation of goods supplied to different locations, uneven labour costs across the market, or different marketing conditions in different regions may result in significant discrepancies in the cost of supply to different customers. Where differences in prices charged by a dominant undertaking are directly related to factors such as these, there is no abuse. This behaviour amounts to lawful price differentiation and not abusive price discrimination.

12.5.3 **Discounts**

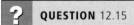

QUESTION 12.15

What kinds of discounts might a trader offer to customers?

As was noted earlier, discounts can be a form of discriminatory pricing. They may also be anti-competitive because they create a barrier to market entry. Consequently, if offered by a dominant undertaking, discounts may constitute an abuse under Article 82 (ex 86). The kinds of discounts which you may have thought of are those offered to customers who buy a certain minimum quantity of goods ('quantity' discounts), who agree to purchase all or most of their requirements from the supplier ('loyalty' or 'fidelity' discounts), or who reach a specified sales target ('target' discounts). Quantity discounts are not abusive provided they apply to all purchasers (and are therefore not discriminatory) and are linked directly to the volume of goods supplied, on the basis that bulk deliveries reduce the supplier's unit costs. Other kinds of discount are caught by Article 82 (ex 86).

? QUESTION 12.16

A (fictitious) manufacturer of a range of soap powders, Exploitem plc (Exploitem), offers fidelity discounts to retail outlets which undertake to purchase all their supplies of soap powder from the company. A clause in the agreement provides that if it transpires that other manufacturers are offering similar products at lower prices, the retailers can require Exploitem to reduce its prices accordingly. If Exploitem fails to do this, the retailers may purchase elsewhere.

Write down your opinion on the following points:

(a) Is the total arrangement exploitative? Why/why not?
(b) Is the total arrangement anti-competitive? Why/why not?

↟ EXERCISE 12.9   CWS

Now turn to *Hoffmann-La Roche & Co. AG* v *Commission* (Case 85/76) [1979] ECR 461 in *Cases and Materials* (12.2.5.1). Do your conclusions in Question 12.16 accord with those of the Court of Justice in the latter case?

The 'English' clauses in the Roche agreement allowed customers to purchase vitamins at the lowest market price, whether from Roche or from its competitors. To that extent, the agreement was not exploitative. However, the whole arrangement did limit customers' commercial freedom to a significant degree because the fidelity discounts induced them to buy their requirements of vitamins from Roche. The agreement also permitted the company to acquire information about its rivals' pricing policies, thereby enabling it to react quickly by reducing its own prices and to undermine competition. For these reasons, the Court of Justice upheld the Commission's view that the company's practices were abusive.

The Court of Justice also found the target discounting practised by Michelin to be an abuse (*Nederlandsche Banden-Industrie Michelin NV* v *Commission* (Case 322/81) [1983] ECR

3461 (*Cases and Materials* (12.2.3)) and in *Hilti AG* v *Commission* (Case T-30/89) [1991] ECR II-1439 (*Cases and Materials* (12.2.3)), the Court of First Instance upheld the Commission's decision that Hilti had abused its dominant position in various ways by, for example, offering favourable terms to the major customers of its competitors and withholding quantity discounts from customers who also bought from competing manufacturers.

12.5.4 Predatory pricing

Predatory pricing involves the reduction of prices, sometimes below cost.

> **? QUESTION** 12.17
>
> How do you think predatory pricing and 'normal' price competition between undertakings might be distinguished?

There is no easy answer to this question, which has caused some difficulty not only to the Commission and the Court of Justice but also to economists. A certain level of price competition is clearly beneficial, for it encourages efficiency and favours the consumer. In *AKZO Chemie* v *Commission* (Case C-62/86) [1991] ECR I-3359 (*Cases and Materials* (12.3.4)) the Court of Justice and the Commission took the view that 'normal' price competition becomes predatory pricing when prices are reduced below cost or when the intention is to eliminate competitors from the market. This view was reiterated in *Compagnie Maritime Belge Transports SA, Compagnie Maritime Belge SA and Dafra-Lines A/S* v *Commission* (Cases C-395-6/96P) [2000] 4 CMLR 1076.

> **? QUESTION** 12.18
>
> How might predatory pricing by a dominant undertaking disadvantage consumers in the long term?

In the *AKZO* case the Court of Justice pointed out the advantage to a dominant undertaking of reducing its prices, even to such an extent as to result in a loss. If eventually competition is eliminated, prices can then be raised to any level, with obvious detriment to the consumer. However, the Court has emphasised that predatory pricing is to be penalised wherever there is a risk that competition will be eliminated, even without proof that a dominant undertaking has a realistic chance of recouping its losses (*Tetra Pak International SA* v *Commission* (Case C-333/94P) [1996] ECR I-5951).

12.5.5 Tie-ins

Tie-in arrangements oblige or induce the purchaser of goods or services to buy other goods or services from the same supplier. Such agreements or practices may be caught both by Article 81(1) (ex 85(1)) (see **Chapter 11**) and by Article 82 (ex 86).

? QUESTION 12.19

Sometimes the inducement is a system of price discounting or rebates, examples of which have already been considered. Do you recall the cases? If not, look back at 12.5.3.

Roche, a pharmaceutical company dominant in several vitamins markets, tied its customers to purchasing all their requirements from it by offering fidelity rebates (*Hoffmann-La Roche* v *Commission*). Hilti engaged in similar practices (*Hilti AG* v *Commission*). In both cases, this constituted an abuse. In addition, Hilti was abusing its dominant position by requiring purchasers of its patented nail cartridges also to buy nails from the company, a classic case of product tied to product. Tying-in can also involve the tying of products and services—for instance, where the purchaser of goods is required to enter into a servicing agreement in respect of those goods—or the tying of services and services.

12.5.6 Refusal to supply

The characterisation of a refusal to supply as abusive can be controversial, since it is a general principle of the contract law of many legal systems that a party should have the freedom both to enter into agreements with other parties and to refuse to deal.

? QUESTION 12.20

Apart from general contractual freedom, what factors might justify an undertaking's refusal to supply a particular customer?

An undertaking might justifiably refuse to supply a customer because of stock shortages, because there are problems with production or because the customer has not paid for goods previously supplied. You have probably thought of other justifications. A dominant undertaking may infringe Article 82 (ex 86) if it refuses to supply a customer without justification. Such conduct will be abusive if it is intended to eliminate competition.

? **QUESTION** 12.21   CWS

When it refused to supply Zoja with the raw material aminobutanol, what factors made the anti-competitive intent of Commercial Solvents so obvious? (*Istituto Chemioterapico Italiano SpA and Commercial Solvents Corporation* v *Commission* (Cases 6 & 7/73) [1974] ECR 223 in *Cases and Materials* (12.2.2)).

The anti-competitive nature of Commercial Solvent's behaviour was revealed by the fact that at the same time as it was refusing further supplies to Zoja, its own subsidiary, Istituto, was emerging as a competitor in the same market as Zoja, namely the market for the manufacture of drugs for the treatment of tuberculosis.

In *Hugin Kassaregister AB* v *Commission* (Case 22/78) [1979] ECR 1869 (*Cases and Materials* (12.2.2)), the Commission suggested that Hugin had refused to supply the UK servicing firm Liptons and other undertakings outside its own distribution network with spare parts for Hugin cash registers in order to exclude competition. Hugin maintained that its commercial policy was objectively justified. It sought to reserve maintenance and repair services to itself in order to uphold the good reputation for reliability of its cash registers. In fact, this issue was not resolved, as the Commission Decision finding an abuse was annulled by the Court of Justice because there was no effect on interstate trade.

A further example of refusal to supply is provided by *United Brands (United Brands Co* v *Commission* (Case 27/76) [1978] ECR 207 in *Cases and Materials* (12.2)). Here, however, the behaviour was retaliatory rather than anti-competitive. United Brands discontinued supplies of green bananas to Olesen, a Danish ripener and distributor, because it had taken part in an advertising campaign for one of United Brands' competitors. In condemning this as an abuse, the Court of Justice described the conduct as 'a serious interference with the independence of small and medium-sized firms in their commercial relations with the undertaking in a dominant position'.

So far we have looked at cases concerning refusals to supply to existing customers. The decisions of the Court of First Instance in the 'TV listings' cases demonstrate that refusal to supply to new customers may also constitute an abuse.

Here, the television companies' refusal to supply to Magill information on weekly schedules of certain television channels prevented the introduction of a new product, a general television guide, for which there was a potential consumer demand. That refusal was likely to have the effect of excluding all competition in the market for television guides (*RTE* v *Commission* (Case T-69/89) [1991] ECR II-485; *BBC* v *Commission* (Case T-70/89) [1991] ECR II-535; *ITP* v *Commission* (Case T-76/89) [1991] ECR II-575 (*Cases and Materials* (12.2.3)). (Decisions upheld on appeal to the Court of Justice in *RTE & ITP* v *Commission* (Joined Cases C-241 & 242/91P) [1995] ECR I-743)). On the other hand, the refusal of a media undertaking to allow a rival daily newspaper, in return for appropriate remuneration, to have access to its nationwide home-delivery scheme did not constitute an abuse under Article 82 (ex 86). In order to establish an abuse, the undertaking concerned would have to show that the refusal was incapable of objective justification and would be likely to eliminate it from the daily newspaper market and that the service was indispensable to its carrying out its business. In fact, there were no technical, legal or economic obstacles preventing the company from setting up its own nationwide home-delivery service (Case C-7/97 *Oscar Bronner GmbH & Co KG* v *Mediaprint Zeitungs- und Zeitschriftenverlag GmbH & Co KG and others* [1998] ECR 1-7791)

A refusal to supply may well involve the refusal of access to a facility, rather than refusal to supply goods or services. It is sometimes said, in relation to Article 82, that this situation falls within the 'essential facilities' doctrine. Under this doctrine, a dominant undertaking abuses its position if, as the owner or controller of a facility which is essential to the conduct of a business, it refuses access to that facility to other undertakings which cannot themselves feasibly set up a similar facility to conduct that business. Sealink, for instance, which controlled the port of Holyhead, restricted B&I's access to sailing facilities there and was found to have infringed Article 82 (ex 86) (*Sealink/B and I—Holyhead: Interim Measures* (Commission Decision) [1992] 5 CMLR 255 and see 12.4.4).

12.5.7 Import and export bans

In *Hilti AG* v *Commission* (Case T-30/89) [1991] ECR II-1439 (*Cases and Materials* (12.2.3)) it emerged that Hilti had exerted pressure upon its distributors in the Netherlands not to supply Hilti's cartridge strips to the UK market. This conduct is a good example of the kind of import/export ban imposed by a dominant undertaking which is likely to breach Article 82 (ex 86). Such practices not only restrict competition but are also incompatible with the single market.

12.5.8 Mergers

Article 82 (ex 86) was first applied to a merger in *Europemballage Corp. and Continental Can Co Inc* v *Commission* (Case 6/72) [1973] ECR 215 (*Cases and Materials* (12.2.1)), which concerned a Commission Decision finding that the proposed takeover by Continental Can of Thomassen & Drijver-Verbliva NV constituted an abuse of its dominant position. Despite Continental Can's arguments to the contrary, the Court of Justice agreed with the Commission that an undertaking need not have used its market power to bring about a merger in order for there to be an abuse. It is sufficient that the merger eliminates competition in a market which the undertaking already dominates. As has been noted earlier, the outcome of this case was the annulment of the Commission's Decision because the RPM had not been proved to the satisfaction of the Court (see 12.4.3).

Although both Article 82 (ex 86) and Article 81 (ex 85) have been used as a means of controlling mergers, their usefulness in this context has now been to a large extent overtaken by the Merger Control Regulation (see 12.8). However, mergers which do not fall within the scope of the Regulation may still breach Articles 81 and 82 (ex 85 and 86).

12.6 Effect on trade between Member States

This is the third element of Article 82 (ex 86). For a breach to be established there must be an abuse of a dominant position and that abuse must be capable of affecting trade between Member States. The term 'effect on trade between Member States' in Article 82 (ex 86) has the same meaning as in Article 81 (ex 85) (see 11.6.6 above). Such an effect is not difficult to establish. An effect on the competitive structure of the common market will suffice (as in *Istituto Chemioterapico Italiano SpA and Commercial Solvents Corporation* v *Commission* (Cases 6 and 7/73) [1974] ECR 223 in *Cases and Materials* (12.2.2)), as will evidence that abusive behaviour **might** affect trade between Member States.

Hugin Kassaregister AB v *Commission* (Case 22/78) [1979] ECR 1869 (*Cases and Materials* (12.2.2)) is one of the few cases in which an effect on interstate trade was not established. As has already been noted Hugin, a Swedish company, refused to supply spare parts for its cash registers to Liptons, a London-based company which serviced the machines. The Court of Justice endorsed the Commission's view that Hugin was dominant in the market for its own spare parts but found that Hugin's restrictive practices had no effect on inter-state trade. Liptons operated within a very limited area in and around London and there was no indication that it intended to extend its activities further. Moreover, the 'normal' pattern of movement of the spare parts was not between Member States but between Liptons in the UK and Hugin in Sweden, at that time a non-member country.

12.7 Application of Article 82 (ex 86) to collective dominance

There is no doubt that the reference in Article 82 (ex 86) to the abusive behaviour and dominance of 'one or more undertakings' includes the dominant position and conduct of undertakings within the same corporate group (see *Europemballage Corp and Continental Can Co Inc* v *Commission* (Case 6/72) [1973] ECR 215 and *Istituto Chemioterapico Italiano SpA and Commercial Solvents Corporation* v *Commission* (Cases 6 & 7/73) [1974] ECR 223 in *Cases and Materials* (12.2.1) and (12.2.2), respectively).

The question as to whether Article 82 (ex 86) applies to a number of independent undertakings which are collectively dominant in a particular market (an oligopoly) is more controversial. Concerted action by such undertakings would usually be caught by Article 81 (ex 85). Nevertheless, in *Società Italiano Vetro (SIV)* v *Commission* (Cases T-68, 75, 77, 78/89) [1992] ECR II-1403, the Court of First Instance left open the possibility that, where this is not so, abuse by oligopolies may fall within Article 82 (ex 86). In *SIV* the Court of First Instance emphasized the significance, to a finding of dominance, of 'economic links' between the undertakings concerned. Later, in *Municipality of Almelo and Others* v *Energiebedrijf Ijsselmij NV* Case C-393/92 [1994] ECR I-1477, the Court of Justice declared that for collective dominance to exist, the undertakings 'must be linked in such a way that they adopt the same conduct on the market'. In *Irish Sugar plc* v *Commission* (Case T-228/97) [1999] ECR II-2969 links of this kind gave rise to the Court of Justice's finding of joint dominance between Irish Sugar and Sugar Distributors Ltd (SDL) on the Irish Sugar Market between 1985 and 1990. These links included Irish Sugar's 51% shareholding in SDL's parent company SDH and Irish Sugar's representation on the boards of both SDH and SDL, as well as arrangements between the companies relating, for instance, to technical services, marketing, commercial strategy, and advertising and undertakings by SDL to purchase all its sugar requirements from Irish Sugar and not to compete in Irish Sugar's markets. Moreover, the Court rejected the applicant's claim that joint dominance could not exist between companies in a vertical commercial relationship (upheld on appeal in *Irish Sugar* v *Commission* (Case C-497/99P) [2001] ECR I-5333).

EXERCISE 12.10

Do you remember the meaning of 'vertical' in the context of relationships or arrangements between undertakings? Look back at 11.6.5 to refresh your memory.

Recent decisions concerning joint dominance in relation to the Merger Regulation suggest that joint dominance could arise simply by virtue of the effects of a highly concentrated market, whether or not there are economic links between undertakings of the kind existing between Irish Sugar and SDL described above. It remains to be seen whether the scope of 'joint dominance' will be extended in this way in relation to Article 82. The judgment of the Court of Justice in *Compagnie Maritime Belge Transports SA, Compagnie Maritime Belge SA and Dafra Lines A/S* v *Commission* (Cases C-395-6/96P) [2000] ECR I-1365 suggests that it may be so extended. Here the Court declared that a finding of joint dominance may 'depend on an economic assessment and, in particular, on an assessment of the structure of the market in question'.

12.8 Merger control

The original Merger Regulation 4064/89 entered into force in October 1990. This is to be replaced by a new Merger Regulation, Regulation 139/2004, which received the final approval of the Council of Ministers on 20 January 2004 and enters into force on 1 May 2004. Community merger control applies to mergers, takeovers and some joint ventures ('concentrations') which have a Community dimension. Under both the original and new regimes, concentrations falling within the Regulation are normally dealt with only by the Commission. Those outside the Regulation are dealt with nationally. This is known as 'one-stop shopping' because it restricts investigations and action to a single authority, either national or Community.

Concentrations with a Community dimension must be notified to the Commission within the timeframe specified by the Regulation. Undertakings failing to notify or supplying incorrect information are liable to be fined. Once a notification is received, the Commission is required to examine it immediately and within a specified period of time (25 working days under the new regime) to decide whether or not to instigate detailed investigations (or, as it is called, to issue proceedings). Proceedings will not be issued if the Commission considers that the concentration falls outside the scope of the Regulation or if it finds that, although the concentration has a Community dimension, it does not raise competition concerns. Proceedings must be issued in relation to concentrations which both have a Community dimension and raise competition concerns. Under the new regime, proceedings must be completed within 90 days. A merger must be blocked if it would 'significantly impede effective competition'.

The merger control regime gives the Commission powers of investigation similar to those conferred by Regulation 1/2003 in relation to alleged breaches of Articles 81 and 82 (see **Chapter 13**).

CONCLUSIONS

Article 82 (ex 86) is concerned with the abuse of economic power by single undertakings which dominate a particular market for goods or services. It aims to eliminate practices which are anti-competitive, in that they seek to exclude or to weaken competition, or are exploitative, in that they take advantage of consumers. An infringement of Article 82 (ex 86) occurs when all three elements of that Article are satisfied. There must be a dominant position in the relevant market, an abuse of that position and that abuse must be capable of affecting trade between Member States.

 CHAPTER 12: ASSESSMENT EXERCISE CWS

Happy Boy plc (Happy Boy) is a UK manufacturer of pet food. The company's share of the European Community pet food market is negligible. Happy Boy's most successful product is its dog food, 'Bing', which it has supplied for many years to wholesalers throughout the Community. The company's massive financial investment in extensive advertising and research and development has paid off. Bing has become so popular that it is now a leading brand in many Member States and Happy Boy has increased its share of the Community dog food market to 45%. The company's nearest rivals in this market hold, respectively, 6%, 4%, and 2% market shares.

Waggles (UK) Ltd (Waggles) has produced dog food for the domestic market since the early 1970s. Last year, the company announced its intention to start exporting to the continent of Europe. Waggles has just learned that Happy Boy is now offering Bing to new and existing customers at considerably reduced prices and is negotiating further discounts with individual wholesalers based upon agreed sales targets for the coming year. It has also emerged that the French wholesaler Ani-Domestique SA (AD) (an established customer of Happy Boy), which agreed to distribute Waggles' promotional literature to its own customers, has been informed by Happy Boy that, as from the end of the month, no further orders from AD for Happy Boy's products will be met.

Advise Waggles.

See *Cases and Materials* (12.7) for a specimen answer.

13 Competition law: Articles 81 and 82 (ex 85 and 86): enforcement and procedure

13.1 Objectives

By the end of this chapter you should be able to:

1 Describe the role of the Commission, the national authorities, and the national courts in the enforcement of Articles 81 and 82 (ex 85 and 86) EC

2 Discuss the procedural and other safeguards provided for the protection of the rights and interests of undertakings

13.2 Introduction

The original Community competition law enforcement regime was set out in Regulation 17/62. The Commission took the central role, being empowered to investigate alleged infringements, to grant negative clearance and exemption, to order termination of infringements and to fine undertakings acting in breach of the competition rules. At the same time, the national courts had a role to play in the enforcement of Community competition law. Articles 81(1), 81(2) and 82 (ex 85(1), 85(2) and 86) are directly effective and thus can be applied by national courts in cases before them. However, under Regulation 17/62, national courts were not empowered to apply Article 81(3). Exemption could only be granted by the Commission and only after an agreement had been notified to it.

Following wide consultation, in September 2000 the Commission published a proposal for the reform of Regulation 17/62 and, in December 2002, Regulation 1/2003 on the implementation of the rules on competition laid down in Articles 81 and 82 was adopted (*Cases and Materials* (13.1)). Regulation 1/2003 replaces Regulation 17/62 and introduces a new enforcement regime. It enters into force on 1 May 2004.

The basis of the new regime is a system under which the Commission, the national courts and the national competition authorities cooperate in the effective enforcement of the Community competition rules, enabling the Community to meet the challenges of future enlargement, whilst at the same time ensuring that Articles 81 and 82 are applied uniformly across the Community. Regulation 1/2003 empowers national courts and national competition authorities to apply Articles 81 and 82 in their entirety, including Article 81(3). The notification system is abolished. These changes to the enforcement regime will allow the Commission to concentrate its limited resources on the most serious infringements of the competition rules, in particular cartel activity.

This chapter considers the enforcement regime under Regulation 1/2003, drawing comparisons, where appropriate and useful, with the old regime under Regulation 17/62.

13.3 Abolition of the notification system

Under Regulation 17/62 a decision granting exemption or negative clearance, where applicable, was issued by the Commission following the notification of an agreement to it on the prescribed form. The Commission alone had the power to apply Article 81(3) and did so in relation to individual agreements by granting individual exemption. This meant that although the agreement under consideration fell within Article 81(1), that Article was declared inapplicable and the agreement was lawful. Individual exemption was granted for a specified period of time and frequently had conditions attached to it. Negative clearance was a declaration by the Commission that an agreement or a proposed course of action did not fall within the scope of Article 81 or 82 (ex 85, 86) at all. The notification system had one immediate advantage to the parties to an agreement. It gave immunity from fines for the period from the date of notification up to the Commission's final decision.

Notification is abolished altogether under the new enforcement regime contained in Regulation 1/2003.

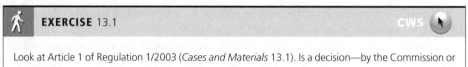

EXERCISE 13.1   CWS

Look at Article 1 of Regulation 1/2003 (*Cases and Materials* 13.1). Is a decision—by the Commission or anyone else—necessary in order that an agreement be exempt from Article 81(1)?

Article 1 expressly provides that agreements caught by Article 81(1) but which satisfy the conditions of Article 81(3) shall not be prohibited (look back at Chapter 11 to remind yourself of the Article 81(3) conditions). Such agreements are valid and enforceable *ab initio* without the adoption of an exemption decision.

QUESTION 13.1

What do you think are the advantages and disadvantages of the abolition of the notification system?

The abolition of the notification system relieves undertakings of the need to spend time and resources in dealing with notifications. However, since individual exemptions are no longer granted, undertakings must rely on their own assessment of whether their agreements amount to infringements of the competition rules. This gives rise to significant uncertainty and risk for business. If an undertaking's assessment of the compatibility of its business dealings with Article 81(1) proves to be incorrect, it will be exposed to the risk of fines or of damages claims in the national courts.

For the Commission, the abolition of the notification system allows it to focus on the investigation of complaints and on proceedings begun on is own initiative, leading to decisions punishing infringements rather than to decisions granting exemption. The Commission will therefore be able to concentrate its efforts on the most serious infringements, including the activity of cartels, and set policy in 'landmark' cases.

? QUESTION 13.2

Can you describe the features of a cartel?

In recent years, many competition regimes across the world have increased their efforts to discover and eradicate cartels. These may operate on a international level and can have a serious impact upon competition. Typically, a cartel comprises a group of undertakings in the same market that collude to fix prices, share markets or engage in other kinds of anti-competitive behaviour. Cartel members are well aware that their activity infringes competition rules and consequently act secretively, making great efforts to conceal their collusion from the competition authorities.

Regulation 1/2003 does not affect the system of block exemptions (look back at Chapter 11 to remind yourself of the nature and characteristics of a block exemption). These continue to be applicable both by the Commission and within national systems.

13.4 Powers of the Commission, the national competition authorities and the national courts

The Commission's general power to ensure the application of Articles 81 and 82 (ex 85 and 86) is derived from Article 85 (ex 89) EC (*Cases and Materials* 13.2). Article 4 of Regulation 1/2003 provides that, for the purposes of applying Article 81 and 82 of the Treaty, the Commission shall have the powers provided for by the Regulation. These powers, set out in Chapter V of the Regulation, are discussed in detail below.

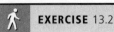 **EXERCISE** 13.2 CWS

Look at Article 5 of Regulation 1/2003 (*Cases and Materials* (13.1)). Make a list of the powers of the competition authorities of the Member States under the new regime.

The national competition authorities have the power to apply Articles 81 and 82 and, acting on their own initiative or on a complaint, may require an infringement to be brought to an end, order interim measures, accept commitments and impose fines, periodic penalty payments or any other penalty provided for in their national law. Alternatively, they may decide that there are no grounds for action in any particular case.

National courts have the power to apply Articles 81 and 82 (Article 6).

13.5 Commission decisions

Chapter III of Regulation 1/2003 confers certain decision-making powers on the Commission.

13.5.1 Requirement to bring an infringement to an end

Regulation 17/62 empowered the Commission to adopt a formal Decision requiring the undertakings concerned to terminate any infringement. This power is retained and extended by Article 7 of Regulation 1/2003. Under the new regime, the Commission may require undertakings to bring an infringement to an end and, for this purpose, impose any behavioural or structural remedy which is proportionate and necessary to end the infringement. A structural remedy may only be imposed in the absence of any effective behavioural remedy.

? **QUESTION** 13.3

Can you think of any examples of 'behavioural' and 'structural' remedies?

As you might expect, a behavioural remedy relates to the behaviour of the undertaking, for example an order to resume supplies to a customer, imposed by an undertaking found to have abused its position by refusing supplies. A structural remedy entails changes in the structure of the undertaking, for instance an order to dispose of part of its business.

13.5.2 **Interim measures**

Because of the time it can take for the Commission to investigate a complaint and to reach a decision in competition matters, it is important that undertakings which are being adversely affected by anti-competitive behaviour should be able to obtain interim relief.

The Commission had no power under Regulation 17/62 to order interim measures. However, in *Camera Care* v *Commission* (Case 792/79R) [1980] ECR 119, the Court of Justice recognized the need for the adoption of interim measures where the anti-competitive behaviour of undertakings injures the interests of Member States, causes damage to other undertakings or jeopardizes Community competition policy. Article 8 of Regulation 1/2003 contains an express power to order interim measures.

EXERCISE 13.3   CWS

Read Article 8 of Regulation 1/2003 (*Cases and Materials* 13.1) In what circumstances may interim measures be ordered by the Commission?

Acting on its own initiative, the Commission may, on the basis of a *prima facie* finding of an infringement, order interim measures in cases of urgency due to the risk of serious and irreparable damage to competition. The Decision must be for a specified period of time and may be renewed in so far as this is necessary and appropriate. In exercising this power, the Commission will doubtless draw on Decisions it adopted on the basis of the *Camera Care* judgment. The Commission Decision in *Sealink/B and I-Holyhead: Interim Measures* [1992] 5 CMLR 255 illustrates the kinds of circumstances that have given rise to an order for interim measures. Here, the Commission ordered interim measures to prevent Sealink from limiting the operations of rival ferry companies at the port of Holyhead, which Sealink controlled, through its organization of the sailing schedules. The Commission considered that the effects of the anti-competitive behaviour would have a lasting and damaging impact upon B and I's business reputation and that compensation alone would not be an adequate remedy.

13.5.3 **Commitments**

Under Article 9 of Regulation 1/2003, where the Commission intends to adopt a Decision requiring that an infringement be brought to an end, any commitments made by the undertakings concerned which meet the concerns of the Commission may, by Decision of the Commission, be made binding on the undertakings. Where this occurs, the Regulation provides that the Decision shall be for a specified period of time and shall conclude that there are no longer grounds for action by the Commission.

13.5.4 **Finding of inapplicability**

The Commission, acting on its own initiative and where the public interest of the Community so requires, may by Decision declare Articles 81 or 82 inapplicable to particular agreements or practices. This may go some way towards meeting the concerns of undertakings that, with the abolition of the notification system and of individual exemptions and negative clearance, they are now exposed to the risk of fines or to damages in national courts because, under the new regime, they must make their own assessment of whether their business dealings amount to infringements of the competition rules. However, Recital 14 of Regulation 1/2003 makes clear that Decisions on inapplicability will be adopted only in exceptional cases with a view to clarifying the law with regard to new types of agreement or to practices that are not already covered by existing Decisions.

13.6 **Cooperation**

Regulation 1/2003 sets up a system under which the Commission, national courts and national competition authorities cooperate in the effective enforcement of the Community competition rules. As the Recitals to the Regulation emphasize, such cooperation is intended to ensure the consistent application of the Community competition rules.

13.6.1 **Cooperation between the Commission and the national competition authorities**

The Commission and the national competition authorities are required by Article 11 of Regulation 1/2003 to apply the Community competition rules in close cooperation. National competition authorities must, for instance, inform the Commission in writing before or without delay after commencing the first investigative measure under Article 81 or Article 82. They must inform the Commission at least 30 days before the adoption of a final decision, providing the Commission with a summary of the case, the envisaged decision or any other documents indicating the proposed course of action. For its part the Commission is required to transmit to the national competition authorities copies of the most important documents it has collected with a view to the finding and termination of an infringement, interim measures and commitments.

Article 11 allows the Commission to take over a case itself, thus relieving the national authorities of their competence to apply the Community competition provisions in that particular case. Where a national authority is already acting on a case, the Commission is required to consult it before initiating its own proceedings. A national competition authority may suspend its proceedings or reject a complaint on the ground that another national authority is dealing with the case. Similarly, the Commission may reject a complaint on the ground that a national competition authority is dealing with the case (Article 13).

13.6.2 **Exchange of information**

For the purposes of applying Articles 81 and 82, the Commission and national competition authorities are empowered, under Article 12, to provide each other with information, including confidential information, and to use this in evidence. It should be noted here that Article 28 of Regulation 1/2003 provides that the Commission and national authorities should not disclose information exchanged between them where this is covered by the obligation of professional secrecy.

EXERCISE 13.4 CWS

Refer to Article 12 of Regulation 1/2003 (*Cases and Materials* (13.1)). What limitations are placed upon the use of information exchanged?

Article 12 places limits on the use of information exchanged between the Commission and national competition authorities. Such information may only be used in evidence in the application of Articles 81 and 82 and in relation to the subject matter for which it was originally collected. Where national competition law is applied in the same case in parallel to Community law, that information may also be used for the application of national law, provided that the outcome would be the same under both Community and national law. Further limits are placed on the use of exchanged information as evidence in cases which could result in the imposition of sanctions on natural persons.

13.6.3 **Cooperation with national courts**

Article 15 provides for the exchange of information between the Commission and national courts. National courts may ask the Commission for information or for its opinion on the application of the Community competition rules. Any national court may, of course, refer to the Court of Justice questions concerning the interpretation of Article 81 and 82 under the Article 234 EC preliminary reference procedure (look back at **Chapter 6** to remind yourself of the features of the preliminary reference procedure).

Member States are required to submit to the Commission copies of any national court judgments on the application of Article 81 and 82. Additionally, national competition authorities may, on their own initiative, submit written observations to the national courts of their Member State on the application of Articles 81 and 82 and, with the permission of the national court, may make oral observations. Equally, the Commission may, on its own initiative, make written observations to any national court and may, with permission of the court in question, make oral observation on the application of Articles 81 and 82. For this purpose, the national authorities and the Commission may request the national court to transmit to them any documents necessary for the assessment of the case.

Article 16 provides for the uniform application of Community competition law, in particular the consistency of national court decisions with Commission decisions in individual cases.

🚶 **EXERCISE** 13.5

Look back at the paragraphs relating to Article 11 of Regulation 1/2003 in section 13. 5.1. What difference do you note in this context between cooperation between the Commission and national authorities and the Commission and national courts?

Whereas the Commission is able to relieve a national competition authority of the competence to apply the Community competition provisions in any particular case by taking over the case itself, the Commission does not have a similar power in relation to a case being heard by a national court. Thus, in any particular case, national court proceedings and Commission proceedings may run in parallel or a national court may hear a case on the application of Article 81 or 82 on which a decision has already been made by the Commission.

Article 16 of Regulation 1/2003 incorporates some of the principles governing the effect of Commission Decisions on national court judgments set out by the Court of Justice in *Masterfoods Ltd* v *HB Ice Cream Ltd* (Case C-344/98) [2000] ECR I-11369. Article 16(1) states that national courts cannot take decisions that conflict with Decisions already adopted by the Commission. In *Masterfoods*, the Court of Justice further indicated that, in order to achieve this consistency, a national court should stay its proceedings pending the outcome of any appeal against the Commission Decision in the Court of First Instance or Court of Justice.

Article 16(1) also provides that national courts must avoid giving decisions which would conflict with a decision contemplated by the Commission in proceedings that it has initiated. They should therefore assess whether it is necessary to stay proceedings pending the Commission Decision.

In relation to the application of Articles 81 and 82 by national courts, important issues arise concerning the outcome of any finding of infringement, including the remedies available to a successful applicant. In accordance with Article 81(2), national courts can declare a prohibited agreement to be void, though offending clauses may be severed, leaving the rest of the agreement to stand. The general principles of equivalence and effectiveness applying to remedies for breaches of Community law indicate that damages and injunctions should be available in national courts to victims of infringements of the competition rules. More specifically, the Court of Justice has made clear that an individual who has been caused loss as a result of a prohibited agreement must, in principle, be able to claim damages in respect of that loss. (*Crehan* v *Courage* (Case C-453/99) [2001] ECR I-6297).

13.7 The Commission's powers of investigation

The Commission is authorised to instigate investigations into suspected breaches of Articles 81 and 82. The Commission's powers of investigation were originally contained in Regulation 17/62. These powers are retained and extended by Regulation 1/2003 and are set out in Chapter V. The Commission has the power to investigate sectors of the economy, to request information from undertakings and associations of undertakings, to take statements and to conduct inspections of business and other premises.

13.7.1 Investigations into sectors of the economy

The Commission's power to conduct investigations into sectors of the economy is contained in Article 17. In the course of its investigations, the Commission may request information from undertakings and carry out any necessary inspections of business premises. In relation to these kinds of investigations, the Commission may report on its findings but has no power to impose remedies.

13.7.2 Requests for information

Under Article 18, the Commission may, either by simple request or by Decision, require undertakings and associations of undertakings to supply all information necessary to its investigations. In addition to these provisions, which were originally contained in Regulation 17/62, Regulation 1/2003 also incorporates a new provision allowing such information to be provided by lawyers acting on behalf of the client undertaking. The Commission is required to forward a copy of the simple request or the Decision to the relevant national competition authority.

In a simple request, the Commission must state the legal basis and the purpose of the request, specify what information is required, fix a time limit by which the information is to be supplied and set out the penalties that will be imposed for providing incorrect or misleading information.

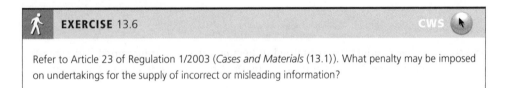

EXERCISE 13.6   CWS

Refer to Article 23 of Regulation 1/2003 (*Cases and Materials* (13.1)). What penalty may be imposed on undertakings for the supply of incorrect or misleading information?

Undertakings are under no obligation to supply information in response to a simple request, but if they do so they should bear in mind the penalties imposed for supplying incorrect or misleading information. Article 23(1) provides for fines of up to 1% of the undertaking's total turnover in the preceding business year in these circumstances.

Undertakings are, however, under an obligation to provide information when this is requested by Decision of the Commission. Like the simple request, the Decision must state the legal basis and the purpose of the request, specify what information is required and fix the time limit within which it is to be provided. It must also indicate the penalties imposed, under Article 23, for supplying incorrect or misleading information or not supplying information at all within the prescribed time limit. Again, the maximum penalty is 1% of the total turnover of the undertaking in the preceding business year.

The Commission may also request information from the governments and competition authorities of the Member States.

13.7.3 **Power to take statements**

Article 19 provides a new power. The Commission may, with their consent, interview any legal or natural person in order to gather information relating to its inquiries. The relevant national competition authorities must be informed of the interview and their officials have a right to be present and assist in the conduct of the interview. Interestingly, no penalties may be imposed for the provision of incorrect or misleading information during an interview.

13.7.4 **The commission's powers of inspection**

The Commission may conduct all necessary inspections of undertakings and associations of undertakings. Such inspections may be voluntary (conducted with the agreement of the undertaking concerned) or mandatory (often referred to as 'dawn raids'). The power to undertake mandatory inspections, in particular, is important in circumstances where undertakings have sought to conceal their anti-competitive behaviour, for instance in operating a cartel in breach of Article 81 or in abusing a dominant position in the market in breach of Article 82.

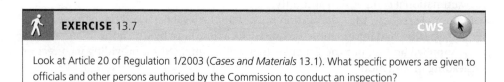

EXERCISE 13.7   CWS

Look at Article 20 of Regulation 1/2003 (*Cases and Materials* 13.1). What specific powers are given to officials and other persons authorised by the Commission to conduct an inspection?

The specific powers originally contained in Regulation 17/62 are retained and extended under the new regime. Persons authorized by the Commission to conduct an inspection are empowered to

- enter any premises, land and means of transport of undertakings;
- examine books and other records relating to the business;
- take photocopies of or extracts from books or records;
- seal any business premises or books or records;
- ask for explanations on facts or documents and record the answers.

One of the new provisions included in Regulation 1/2003 empowers persons authorized to conduct an inspection to examine books and records 'irrespective of the medium on which they are stored'. This clearly includes information stored electronically.

Officials carrying out a voluntary inspection are required to produce a written authorisation specifying the subject matter and the purpose of the inspection and the penalties for supplying incorrect or misleading information. In advance of the inspection, the Commission must notify the national competition authority in whose territory the inspection is to take place.

A mandatory inspection may only be carried out following the adoption of a Decision by the Commission requiring an undertaking to submit to the inspection. In addition to the matters specified above in relation to written authorizations, that Decision must indicate the date on which the inspection is to commence, the penalties for refusing to allow the inspection to take place and the right to judicial review of the Decision.

 QUESTION 13.4

What is the Commission required to do before it adopts a Decision ordering a mandatory inspection?

Before issuing the decision the Commission is required, under Article 20(4), to consult with the national competition authority in whose territory the inspection is to be carried out.

The Commission may undertake a mandatory inspection without having first attempted a voluntary inspection. In particular, it will carry out a mandatory inspection where the element of surprise is an important feature of its inquiry.

EXERCISE 13.8   CWS

Look at *National Panasonic (UK) Ltd* v *Commission* (Case 136/79) [1980] ECR 2033 in *Cases and Materials* (13.3.1). Is an undertaking which is to be the subject of a mandatory inspection entitled to be given prior warning of a 'raid' by the Commission?

National Panasonic sought annulment of a Commission Decision authorizing a mandatory inspection (under the powers conferred by Regulation 17/62) relating to alleged infringements of Article 81 (1) (ex 85(1)). The Commission had arrived at the company's premises without warning and had insisted that the search begin before Panasonic's lawyers could be summoned. In dismissing the company's application for annulment, the Court of Justice held that the Commission had no duty to give advance notification of such an inspection.

The Commission has the power to impose fines (Article 23) or daily penalties (Article 24) on an undertaking that refuses to allow entry to Commission officials authorised to carry out a mandatory inspection. However, the Commission has no power of forcible entry. Where an undertaking refuses to submit to an inspection, the Member State concerned is required to give the necessary assistance to Commission officials to conduct their inspection. This may entail, for instance, the issue of a search warrant and the assistance of the police.

Look at *Hoechst AG* v *Commission* (Cases 46/87 & 227/88) [1989] ECR 2859 in *Cases and Materials* (13.3.1). On what grounds did Hoechst consider that the contested Decision was unlawful? How does the judgment strike a balance between the rights of undertakings to procedural safeguards and the powers of the Commission in investigating alleged breaches of the Community competition rules? Make a note of your answer.

Commission officials sought entry to Hoechst's business premises pursuant to Article 14(3) of Regulation 17 but were refused entry. Hoechst argued that the Commission Decision ordering the investigation permitted Commission officials to carry out a search of the premises and, because no search warrant had been obtained in advance, was incompatible with fundamental rights. The Court of Justice ruled that the Commission did not exceed its powers under Article 14(3) in requiring Hoechst to permit Commission officials to enter the premises and in requiring the company to produce documents relevant to the investigation for inspection and copying.

However, the Court pointed out that in circumstances such as these there are procedural safeguards protecting an undertaking's interests. The Commission is required to specify the subject matter and the purpose of the investigation. This allows undertakings to determine the scope of their duty to cooperate. Moreover, where a mandatory investigation is opposed, an undertaking's rights must be protected by the procedural guarantees laid down by national law.

Nevertheless, the requirement for procedural safeguards, such as the production of a search warrant, does not release an undertaking from liability to fines where it refuses, while the necessary procedures are being put in place, to submit to a mandatory inspection. Measures adopted by the institutions of the Community, such as a Commission Decision ordering an investigation under Article 14(3), are fully effective so long as they have not been declared invalid by the Court. Consequently, a refusal to submit to such an investigation is an infringement of Community obligations giving rise to liability to fines.

Article 21 of Regulation 1/2003 extends the Commission's powers of inspection to the inspection of premises other than business premises, including the homes of officers and staff of an undertaking. The Commission may only carry out such inspections, however, where it has a reasonable suspicion that books or records which may be relevant to prove a serious violation of the competition rules are being kept there. A Decision ordering an inspection of other premises cannot be executed without prior authorization from a court.

13.7.5 Fines and penalties

Articles 23 and 24 empower the Commission to impose substantial fines and periodic penalty payments on undertakings found to be in breach of the competition rules. Fines of up to 10% of total turnover in the preceding business year may be levied, under Article

23, for infringements of Article 81 and 82 and, under Article 24, the Commission may impose daily penalties of up to 5% of average daily turnover in the preceding business year for continuing infringements. Fines can be heavy, since turnover figures are based upon a undertaking's world-wide turnover. For instance, in 1998, the car manufacturer Volkswagen was fined a record 102 million ecus (later reduced to 90 million ecus on appeal to the Court of First Instance) for infringements of Article 81.

? **QUESTION** 13.5

Under Article 23(3), what factors are to be taken into account when the level of a fine is fixed?

This Article refers to the gravity and duration of the infringement. Other factors which may be taken into account in determining the level of fines are to be found in the copious case law on this matter and in Commission Guidelines on the setting of fines, issued in 1997 (OJ 1998 C9/3). One important criterion which has been prominent in Commission Decisions is the nature of the infringement. Obvious and blatant breaches, such as the division of markets or price fixing, will attract heavy fines. Many other factors may be relevant, such as the economic strength of the parties to an agreement or of dominant undertakings and their share of the product market, the extent of the profits derived from the offending behaviour, any previous infringements by the undertakings concerned and whether their behaviour was inadvertent or deliberate.

In 1996 the Commission published its Notice on the Non-imposition or Reduction of Fines in Cartel Cases, thereby formalizing its policy of granting leniency to 'whistle-blower' cartel members. The later 2002 Notice on Immunity from Fines or Reduction in Fines in Cartel Cases, which replaced the 1996 notice, allows full immunity from fines to be granted to cartel members who come forward with information enabling the Commission to carry out a 'dawn raid' or to establish an infringement of Article 81 by the cartel. Reductions in fines are available to cartel members who pass on information that provides 'significant added value' to evidence of an infringement already in the possession of the Commission.

13.8 Hearings

Article 27 of Regulation 1/2003 concerns the right to be heard. Before the Commission adopts a Decision that is unfavourable to an undertaking—finding an infringement, ordering interim measures or imposing fines or penalties—that undertaking must be given the opportunity of a hearing on any matters to which the Commission has taken objection. The rights of defence of the parties must be fully respected. They have a right of access to the Commission's file, though that right of access does not extend to any confidential information or internal documents of the Commission or of the national competition authorities. The Commission must base any Decision only on objections upon which the parties concerned have been able to comment. If the Commission considers it necessary, it may hear other persons. Where they show a 'show a sufficient interest', those persons must be heard.

Before Regulation 1/2003 enters into force on 1 May 2004, the Commission is to adopt a Regulation laying down rules for the conduct of proceedings and a Notice setting out the rights of third parties.

13.9 The Commission's duty of confidentiality

Inevitably, some of the documents acquired by the Commission and the national competition authorities during the course of their investigations will be highly sensitive because they contain business secrets. They might relate, for instance, to future business plans or to valuable know-how which an undertaking would not wish to come to the knowledge or attention of its competitors. Article 27 of Regulation 1/2003, as noted above, allows parties access to the file for the purposes of their defence. However, that right is subject to the legitimate interest of undertakings in the protection of their business secrets. Similarly Article 30, which requires the Commission to publish Decisions finding and ordering termination of infringements and imposing fines and penalties, requires the Commission, in publishing these Decisions, to have regard to the legitimate interests of undertakings in the protection of their business secrets.

 EXERCISE 13.10 CWS

Look at the extracts from *AKZO Chemie BV* v *Commission* (Case 53/85) [1986] ECR 1965 (*Cases and Materials* 13.4). What course of action must be taken if there is disagreement between the Commission and an undertaking as to whether a document contains business secrets?

In *AKZO*, the Court of Justice held that business secrets should never be divulged to third party complainants. However, what constitutes a business secret may be controversial in any particular case. If there is disagreement between an undertaking and the Commission on documents which allegedly contain business secrets, the Commission must adopt a Decision setting out its view. Such a Decision is subject to challenge by the undertaking concerned before the Court of First Instance.

Article 287 (ex 214) EC (*Cases and Materials* 13.4) requires members of the institutions of the Community and Community officials not to disclose information covered by the obligation of professional secrecy. Article 28 (1) of Regulation 1/2003 requires that information collected during the course of the Commission's investigations must be used only for the purpose for which it was acquired. Article 28(2) provides that the Commission and national competition authorities shall not disclose information covered by the obligation of professional secrecy.

The duty of non-disclosure contained in Article 287 (ex 214) of the Treaty formed the basis of the damages claim brought in Article 288 (ex 215) proceedings in *Adams* v *Commission* (Case 145/83) [1985] ECR 3539.

 QUESTION 13.6

Do you recall the nature of Article 288 (ex 215) proceedings? If necessary, look back at Chapter 8.

EXERCISE 13.11   CWS

In *Adams* v *Commission*, the Court of Justice ruled that the Commission was bound by a duty of confidentiality to Mr Stanley Adams. Look at the case in *Cases and Materials* (13.4) and make a mental note of the circumstances which gave rise to that duty.

13.10 **Privilege**

As has been noted, the Commission has a general duty not to disclose to other undertakings documents containing business secrets, though undertakings are not entitled to withhold such documents from the Commission.

In *Australian Mining & Smelting Europe Ltd* v *Commission* (Case 155/79) [1982] ECR 1575 (*Cases and Materials* (13.5)), the Court of Justice was asked whether undertakings are entitled to withhold documents from the Commission on the ground that those documents comprise communications between lawyer and client made in connection with the case under consideration. In national legal systems, such documents are typically covered by legal professional privilege and are thus confidential.

 QUESTION 13.7

In the *AM & S* case the Court of Justice ruled that limited protection is available to lawyer–client communications in relation to the Commission's investigations. What conditions were attached to legal professional privilege in this context?

The Court held that privilege extends only to those documents which are created specifically in connection with the client's defence and which are either prepared after the initiation of proceedings by the Commission or are closely linked with the subject matter of the proceedings. Only those communications between an undertaking and an independent lawyer based in the Community are privileged. Communications with an in-house lawyer or a lawyer based outside the Community are not.

13.11 Self-incrimination

An undertaking is required, under Article 18 of Regulation 1/2003, to supply the Commission with all documents in its possession which are necessary to the investigation, even if those documents might establish an infringement of the competition rules. However, an undertaking is not obliged to admit to infringements and is entitled to refuse to answer questions if its responses would be self-incriminating (*Orkem* v *Commission* (Case 374/87) [1989] ECR 3283 in *Cases and Materials* (13.6)), but not otherwise (*Mannesmann-Röhrenwerke AG* v *Commission* (Case T-112/98) [2001] ECR II-729).

13.12 Judicial Review

Commission Decisions under the competition rules are subject to judicial review. Since 1989, review of competition matters has been undertaken by the Court of First Instance rather than the Court of Justice. Appeal on points of law lies to the Court of Justice.

 QUESTION 13.8

Under which Treaty Articles do you think proceedings for judicial review may be brought?

Proceedings may be brought by undertakings before the Court of First Instance in one of two circumstances. The majority of actions are those in which the complainant seeks annulment of a Commission Decision addressed to it in relation to infringements of the competition rules (Article 230 (ex 173) proceedings). Alternatively, a complainant may contest the Commission's failure to act or to take adequate action in response to its complaint with respect to the behaviour of other parties (Article 232 (ex 175) proceedings).

 QUESTION 13.9

Do you remember the features of Article 230 and 232 (ex 173 and 175) proceedings? If not, look back at Chapter 7.

Annulment of Commission Decisions on competition matters under Article 230 (ex 173) is uncommon, though not unknown. A complainant undertaking is more likely to secure the reduction of fines rather than annulment. The Court of First Instance has unlimited jurisdiction in reviewing a Decision to impose a fine or periodic penalty.

The Commission is under a duty to consider complaints of infringements of Articles 81 and 82 (ex 85 and 86) brought by persons claiming a legitimate interest. An action for failure to act under Article 232 (ex 175) may be brought against the Commission if it fails to fulfil this duty. However, the Commission is not obliged to pursue a complaint to a formal Decision. In *Automec (No 2)*, the Court of First Instance made clear that the Commission cannot be compelled to conduct an investigation, though it is required to evaluate carefully the legal and factual aspects of the matter notified to it by the applicant and to give proper reasons for closing the file (*Automec Srl* v *Commission (No 2)* (Case T-24/90) [1992] ECR II-2223).

 CONCLUSIONS

Under the old regime of Regulation 17/62, the Commission had the central role in the enforcement of the Community competition rules. With the adoption of Regulation 1/2003 and the introduction of a system based upon close cooperation between the Commission, national competition authorities and national courts and upon direct application by them all of Articles 81 and 82, the focus of enforcement of Community competition law has shifted significantly. The abolition of the Commission's exclusive role in the application of Article 81(3) is one of the prominent features of this changed focus. However, the Commission retains the extensive powers of investigation that were originally conferred on it by Regulation 17/62 and these are, in some respects, extended even further under the new regime. This will enable the Commission more effectively to concentrate its resources on the investigation of more serious infringements of Community competition law.

 CHAPTER 13: ASSESSMENT EXERCISE CWS

Outline the powers of the Commission in the enforcement of Articles 81 and 82 (ex 85 and 68). How are the rights and interests of undertakings protected?

See *Cases and Materials* (13.8) for specimen answer.

14 Sex discrimination law

14.1 Objectives

By the end of this chapter you should be able to:

1 Define and discuss the scope of Community law relating to equal pay and equal treatment for men and women in employment

2 Explain the significance of the Court of Justice's broad interpretation of 'pay'

3 Analyse the Community concepts of indirect discrimination and objective justification in relation to equal pay and equal treatment

4 Discuss the exceptions to the equal treatment principle

14.2 Introduction

The first Community provision relating to sex discrimination established the principle of equal pay for equal work for men and women and was included in the 1957 Treaty, in Article 141 (ex 119) (*Cases and Materials* (14.1)). It is frequently said that this principle was incorporated into the original Treaty not for reasons of social justice but because of economic considerations. France in particular, which already had equal pay legislation, feared that if there were no Community regulation in this area its own industry would be placed at a competitive disadvantage, since Member States which had not espoused the equal pay principle would be at liberty to take advantage of cheap female labour.

This early economic rationale was overtaken by a broader view which identified the objectives of Community sex discrimination law as both economic and social. In *Defrenne* v *SABENA* (Case 43/75) [1976] ECR 455 (*Cases and Materials* (14.1)) the Court of Justice referred to Article 141 (ex 119) as 'part of the social objectives of the Community, which is not merely an economic union, but is at the same time intended, by common action, to ensure social progress and seek the constant improvement of the working and living conditions of their peoples . . .'. From the relatively narrow starting point of the equal pay principle set out in Article 141 (ex 119), there has developed a substantial body of Community sex discrimination law which incorporates the much broader principle of equal treatment. Indeed, following Amsterdam Treaty amendments, Article 141 (ex 119) now expressly provides for the adoption of Community measures ensuring the application of the principles of equal opportunities and equal treatment of men and women in employment. Further Amsterdam amendments to the EC Treaty incorporated into Articles 2 and 3 (ex 2 and 3) more general policy statements on the elimination of inequality and the promotion of equality between men and women in relation to all the Community's activities. However, despite these wide statements of policy, Community sex discrimination law remains focused upon equality between men and women in employment and the primary provision is Article 141 (ex 119).

14.3 Article 13 EC

Following Treaty of Amsterdam amendments to the EC Treaty, Article 13 (ex 6a) empowers the Council to take action not only in relation to sex discrimination, but also in relation to discrimination based on racial or ethnic origin, religion or belief, disability, age or sexual orientation. Acting under these powers, in 2000 the Council adopted Directives 2000/43 and 2000/78 respectively implementing the principle of equal treatment between persons irrespective of racial or ethnic origin and establishing a general framework for equal treatment in employment.

EXERCISE 14.1   CWS

Read Article 13 in *Cases and Materials* (14.2).

14.4 Outline of the legislation on sex discrimination

This chapter will consider the following Community legislation on sex discrimination:

(a) Article 141 (ex 119) EC (establishes the general principle of equal pay for equal work or work of equal value for men and women);

(b) the Equal Pay Directive 75/117 (elaborates upon the principle of equal pay for equal work and work of equal value);

(c) the Equal Treatment Directive 76/207 (now amended by Directive 2002/73) (puts into effect the principle of equal treatment for men and women in employment);

Reference will also be made to:

(d) the Social Security Directive 79/7 (implements the principle of equal treatment for men and women in matters of social security).

(e) Directive 86/378, amended by Directive 96/97 (provides for equal treatment in occupational social security schemes);

(f) Directive 86/613 (extends the principle of equal treatment to self-employment);

(g) the Pregnancy and Maternity Directive 92/85 (has as its objective the protection of pregnant, new and nursing mothers in employment).

14.5 Article 141 (ex 119): Equal pay

14.5.1 Article 141 (ex 119)

Article 141 (ex 119) sets out the principle that men and women should receive equal pay for equal work or work of equal value.

>  **EXERCISE** 14.2   CWS
>
> Look at Article 141 (ex 119) in *Cases and Materials* (14.1). Copy out the definition of 'pay' contained in the second paragraph.

In the second paragraph of Article 141 (ex 119), 'pay' is defined as 'the ordinary basic or minimum wage or salary and any other consideration, whether in cash or in kind, which the worker receives, directly or indirectly, in respect of his employment from his employer'. Under paragraph 3, the principle of equal pay without discrimination based on sex means that the calculation of pay for the 'same work' is based upon the same units of measurement for piece work or the same time rates.

14.5.2 Direct effect of Article 141 (ex 119)

In *Defrenne* v *SA Belge de Navigation Aérienne* (*SABENA*) (*No 2*) (Case 43/75) [1976] ECR 455 (*Cases and Materials* (14.1)) the Court of Justice held Article 141 (ex 119) to be directly effective, thus opening the way for individual claims based on sex discrimination with respect to pay. This was an important development, since Member States had been initially very slow to implement the principle of equal pay. However, because of the potential financial consequences of the ruling for the Member States, the Court declared that only those individuals who had already made claims could rely upon Article 141 (ex 119) in respect of periods prior to the date of the judgment. In other words, the ruling on direct effect was prospective only.

The horizontal direct effect of Article 141 was once again confirmed much more recently in *Lawrence and Others* v *Regent Office Care, Commercial Catering Group and Mitie Services Ltd* (Case C-320/00) [2002] ECR I-7325. Here, however, the applicants were unsuccessful in their equal pay claim under Article 141 because the claim concerned differences of pay between men and women employed by different employers. It was undisputed that the work was of equal value. Further, the Court of Justice declared that nothing in the wording of Article 141 suggests that this provision is limited to situations in which men and women work for the same employer. However, Article 141 did not apply because the differences in pay could not be attributed to a single source and there was therefore no body which could be held responsible for the inequality or take action to restore equality.

14.5.3 The meaning of 'pay'

As already noted, the scope of the term 'pay' in Article 141 (ex 119) is wide, encompassing not only salary or wages but also any other consideration received by the worker from the employer in respect of the employment, directly or indirectly, in cash or in kind. The Court of Justice has adopted a broad definition of 'pay' and, in doing so, has pushed back the boundaries of the protection available to the individual employee under Article 141 (ex 119).

 EXERCISE 14.3 CWS

Look at the cases listed below. Make a list of the payments or benefits examined by the Court of Justice and found to fall within the scope of 'pay'.

(a) *Worringham* v *Lloyds Bank Ltd* (Case 69/80) [1981] ECR 767 (*Cases and Materials* (14.3.1)).

(b) *Garland* v *British Rail Engineering Ltd* (Case 12/81) [1982] ECR 359 (*Cases and Materials* (14.3.1)).

(c) *Bilka-Kaufhaus GmbH* v *Weber von Hartz* (Case 170/84) [1986] ECR 1607 (*Cases and Materials* (14.3.1)).

(d) *Rinner-Kühn* v *FWW Spezial-Gebäudereinigung GmbH & Co. KG* (Case 171/88) [1989] ECR 2743 (*Cases and Materials* (14.3.1)).

(e) *Barber* v *Guardian Royal Exchange Assurance Group* (Case C-262/88) [1990] ECR I-1889 (*Cases and Materials* (14.3.1)).

(f) *Kowalska* v *Freie und Hansestadt Hamburg* (Case C-33/89) [1990] ECR I-2591 (*Cases and Materials* (14.3.1)).

(g) *Vroege* v *NCIV Instituut voor Volkshuisvesting BV and Stichting Pensioenfonds NCIV* (Case C-57/93) [1994] ECR I-4541 (*Cases and Materials* (14.3.1)).

These cases illustrate the wide meaning given to the concept of 'pay' by the Court of Justice. The Court found that 'pay' included:

(a) *Worringham*: Contributions paid by an employer directly into an occupational pension scheme.

The payments were made to male, but not female, employees under the age of 25. If an employee left the employment before becoming entitled to a pension, the sums paid into the scheme were reimbursed to the employee. Moreover, the employee's gross salary figure (used for calculating the level of other benefits linked to salary) included the amount of the pensions contributions.

(b) *Garland*: Special travel facilities extended to former employees for their families on the employees' retirement.

Here, the Court of Justice considered for the first time the status of benefits in kind. In this case, the benefits were denied to female retired employees of the company. The Court held that the special travel facilities constituted pay even though the employer had no contractual obligation to grant them and they were received after retirement.

(c) *Bilka*: Benefits under an occupational pension scheme financed by the employer.

This case, which is considered in more detail below, is important with regard both to pensions as pay and to the concept of indirect discrimination.

(d) *Rinner-Kühn*: Sick pay.

The Court of Justice held that statutory sick pay constituted pay. National legislation which allowed employers to exclude part-time workers (who were predominantly female) from entitlement to sick pay was indirectly discriminatory and thus incompatible with Article 141 (ex 119) unless it was objectively justified (see 14.7.2).

(e) *Barber*: Contracted-out occupational pensions and redundancy benefits.

The *Barber* decision had far-reaching consequences for the organization of occupational pension schemes. This case is considered below in the broader context of pay, social security provision, and Article 141 (ex 119).

(f) *Kowalska*: A severance grant.

Even though the severance grant was made on termination of employment, it fell within the scope of Article 141 (ex 119) as pay because the worker was entitled to it by reason of her employment.

In *Vroege*, the Court of Justice further developed its ruling in *Bilka*:

(g) *Vroege*: Article 141 (ex 119) covers not only entitlement to benefits paid under an occupational pension scheme but also the right to be a member of such a scheme.

More recently, the Court of Justice has included in the definition of 'pay' the award of compensation for unfair dismissal (Case C-167/97 *R* v *Secretary of State, ex parte Seymour-Smith* [1999] ECR 1-623).

14.5.4 **Pensions as pay**

In the first *Defrenne* case (*Defrenne* v *Belgium (No. 1)* (Case 80/70) [1971] ECR 445 in *Cases and Materials* (14.3.2)), the Court of Justice considered a pension scheme set up under Belgian legislation for civil aviation air crews. The scheme excluded air hostesses. Ms Defrenne, an air hostess employed by the airline SABENA, claimed that the difference in treatment between men and women contravened Article 141 (ex 119) because the benefit of the pension constituted pay. The Court disagreed. The contributions made by the employer to the scheme were in the nature of social security benefits and, although such benefits were not in principle excluded from the concept of pay, they were excluded from the scope of Article 141 (ex 119) in this case. This was because the pension scheme was directly governed by legislation without any element of agreement between employee and employer and was obligatorily applicable to workers in general. The characterization of the pension scheme as a social security scheme was not affected by the fact that the employer made contributions. Those contributions did not amount to direct or indirect payments to the worker, since workers received their pension not by virtue of the employer's contribution but because they satisfied the relevant legal requirements. Consequently, Ms Defrenne's claim failed.

Since *Defrenne (No. 1)*, the Court of Justice has extended the scope of Article 141 (ex 119) in relation to pensions. Two cases in particular—*Bilka-Kaufhaus GmbH* v *Weber von Hartz* (Case 170/84) [1986] ECR 1607 and *Barber* v *Guardian Royal Exchange Assurance Group* (Case C-262/88) [1990] ECR I-1889—should be noted.

Bilka-Kaufhaus GmbH v *Weber von Hartz* (Case 170/84) [1986] ECR 1607 concerned an occupational pension scheme which supplemented state pension provision.

QUESTION 14.1　　　　　　　　　　　　　　　　　　　　　CWS

Look at *Bilka* (Case 170/84) [1986] ECR 1607 in *Cases and Materials* (14.3.1). What view did the Court of Justice take on the nature of the company's pension scheme?

Although the scheme in *Bilka* was set up in accordance with statutory provisions, it was based on an agreement between the company and its employees and was funded entirely by the employer. The Court of Justice held that since the scheme was not directly governed by statute but was contractual in nature, being part of the contracts of employment between the firm and its employees, benefits paid to employees under the scheme constituted pay and thus fell within Article 141 (ex 119).

Barber concerned an occupational pension scheme which partially replaced state pension provision—a 'contracted-out' pension scheme.

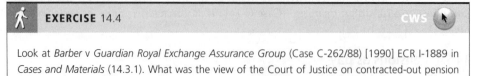

EXERCISE 14.4　　　　　　　　　　　　　　　　　　　　　CWS

Look at *Barber* v *Guardian Royal Exchange Assurance Group* (Case C-262/88) [1990] ECR I-1889 in *Cases and Materials* (14.3.1). What was the view of the Court of Justice on contracted-out pension schemes?

In *Barber*, the Court of Justice examined the characteristics of contracted-out pension schemes of the kind which had been set up by Guardian and identified their characteristics as follows: they result either from an agreement between workers and the employer or from a unilateral decision taken by the employer; they are financed solely by the employer or by both the employer and workers, with no contribution from the state; and they apply only to workers in a particular undertaking and not to general categories of workers. The Court pointed out that such schemes may provide greater benefits than those available under the statutory scheme which they replace and may consequently have a similar function to supplementary schemes like the one in *Bilka*. The Court held that retirement pensions paid under contracted-out schemes having these features constitute pay, even though such schemes partially substitute statutory pension provision and are established in conformity with national legislation. Moreover, since Article 141 (ex 119) applies to consideration received indirectly from the employer, these findings are not affected by the fact that a fund is administered by trustees (confirmed in *Coloroll Pension Trustees Ltd* v *James Richard Russell* (Case C-200/91) [1994] ECR I-4389 in *Cases and Materials* (14.3.2)).

Under the pension scheme considered in *Barber*, employees who were made redundant were entitled to receive an immediate pension provided they had reached the age of 50 (for women) or 55 (for men). Mr Barber was made redundant at 52 and, in accordance with the rules of the scheme, payment of his pension was deferred until normal pensionable age. Having established that payments under the scheme constituted pay, the Court indicated that 'Article 141 (ex 119) prohibits any discrimination with regard to pay as between men and women, whatever the system which gives rise to such inequality'. Accordingly, even different pensionable ages based upon the difference between the pensionable ages for men and women in national statutory schemes breach Article 141 (ex 119).

In a subsequent case, *Moroni* v *Collo GmbH* (Case C-110/91) [1993] ECR I-6591, the Court of Justice held that benefits under a supplementary pension scheme constitute pay. Consequently, discriminatory pensionable ages in such schemes breach Article 141 (ex 119).

14.5.5 Limitations on the *Barber* judgment

Clearly, the *Barber* ruling had serious implications for the organisation of occupational pension schemes. Aware of the impact of its judgment on contracted-out schemes based upon different retirement ages for men and women, the Court of Justice limited the effect of its ruling to entitlement to pensions from the date of the judgment, save where claims had already been initiated in the national courts. The wording of this limitation gave rise to uncertainties of interpretation. These uncertainties were largely resolved by a Protocol annexed to the Treaty by the Treaty on European Union (*Cases and Materials* (14.3.3)), which provides that, save in the case of claims already instigated, benefits under occupational pension schemes are not to be considered as pay in so far as they are attributable to periods of employment prior to the date of the judgment (17 May 1990).

The Court of Justice has held that this temporal limitation on the effect of *Barber*, whilst it covers benefits under occupational pension schemes, does not apply to discriminatory rules relating to the membership of and access to such schemes. These can be challenged under Article 141 (ex 119) in respect of periods dating back to the decision establishing the direct effect of Article 141 (ex 119) in *Defrenne* (*No. 2*) (Case 43/75) [1976] ECR 455 in *Cases and Materials* (14.1)—(*Vroege* v *NCIV Institut voor Volkshuisvesting BV and Stichting Pensioenfonds NCIV* (Case C-57/93) [1994] ECR I-4541 in *Cases and Materials* (14.3.1)). However, in the case of contributory schemes, successful claimants who wish to exercise their right to back-dated membership will be required to make back payments of contributions (*Fisscher* v *Voorhuis Hengelo BV and Stichting Bedrijfspensioenfonds voor de Detailhandel* (Case C-128/93) [1994] ECR I-4583 in *Cases and Materials* (14.3.3)).

Two pensions cases decided since *Barber* indicate that the Court of Justice has retreated to some degree from its progressive broadening of the definition of 'pay' and of the scope of Article 141 (ex 119).

EXERCISE 14.5 CWS

Look at *Neath* v *Hugh Steeper* (Case C-152/91) [1993] ECR I-6935, [1995] 2 CMLR 357 in *Cases and Materials* (14.3.3). This case concerned (*inter alia*) employer's contributions to a contracted-out occupational pension scheme. What factors gave rise to different payments to men and women? Was the claim that the employer's contributions constituted 'pay' under Article 141 (ex 119) upheld by the Court? Make a brief note of your answer.

Because of the different life expectancies of men and women and the different levels of pension cover required to take account of this, employer contributions into the respective pension funds were greater in respect of female employees. Although the eventual pension payments made to men and women were not discriminatory, the use of sex-based actuarial factors in the calculation of the level of employer contributions to the pension funds resulted, in the event of redundancy, in larger payments to women than to men in the form of transfer benefits or capital sums. The Court of Justice held that, whereas the pension itself constituted pay, neither the employer contributions to the pension funds nor the transfer of capital sums paid on redundancy fell within Article 141 (ex 119).

In a somewhat surprising judgment in *Roberts* v *Birds Eye Walls Ltd* (Case C-132/92) [1993] ECR I-5579, the Court of Justice held that different bridging pension payments made to men and women employees forced to retire early because of ill health did not infringe Article 141 (ex 119). The object of the bridging pension, which was funded by the employer, was to make up the difference between the occupational pension received immediately on early retirement and the overall sum which an employee would receive on reaching state retirement age. Until the age of 60, when neither men nor women had reached state pensionable age, the bridging pension was calculated on the same basis for men and women. However, when a woman reached 60, her bridging pension was reduced because she then became entitled to the state pension. Mrs Roberts claimed that, since the bridging pension constituted pay within Article 141 (ex 119), the payment of a reduced amount to women who had reached the age of 60 infringed the principle of equal pay. The Court disagreed, holding that the mechanisms used for calculating the bridging pension were sexually neutral and not discriminatory.

14.5.6 Significance of the court's broad interpretation of 'pay'

The Court's broad interpretation of 'pay' has significance for the rights of individuals. Since Article 141 (ex 119) is directly effective both vertically and horizontally (*Defrenne* v *SABENA* (*No. 2*) (Case 43/75) [1976] ECR 455, *Cases and Materials* (14.1)), it can be invoked in national courts against both public and private employers. By relying on Article 141 (ex 119), individual claimants are able to avoid the difficulties surrounding reliance on Directives, notably Directive 76/207 on equal treatment for men and women in employment (see 14.8 below).

EXERCISE 14.6

Do you remember the principles developed by the Court of Justice on the direct effect of Community legislation? Look back at Chapter 5 to refresh your memory.

14.6 Article 141 (ex 119) and Directive 75/117: equal work or work of equal value

14.6.1 'Equal work' and 'work of equal value'

Prior to Amsterdam Treaty amendments to the Treaty of Rome, the first paragraph of Article 119 (now 141) provided:

Each Member State shall . . . ensure and subsequently maintain the application of the principle that men and women should receive equal pay for equal work.

The Article did not provide expressly for the application of the equal pay principle to 'work of equal value'.

EXERCISE 14.7   CWS

Write down the definition of 'equal work' contained in Article 1 of Directive 75/117 in *Cases and Materials* (14.4.1).

Article 1 of Directive 75/117 (*Cases and Materials* (14.4.1)) extended the Treaty definition of 'equal work' to the 'same work or . . . work to which equal value is attributed'. In *Jenkins* v *Kingsgate* (*Clothing Productions*) *Ltd* (Case 96/80) [1981] ECR 911 (*Cases and Materials* (14.4.1)), the Court of Justice held that this extended definition of equal work was covered by Article 119 (as it then was) itself. In other words, the Directive merely 'fleshed out' the Treaty provision. Consequently, in respect of claims concerning either the same work or work of equal value, individuals did not need to rely upon Directive 75/117 but could invoke Article 119 (as it then was).

? **QUESTION** 14.2

Why do you think this latter point was important?

Directives are capable only of vertical direct effect, whereas Treaty Articles are capable of both vertical and horizontal direct effect. Since Article 141 (ex 119) is vertically and horizontally directly effective, an individual claimant could avoid any possible difficulties over direct effect by invoking Article 119 (as it then was) rather than Directive 75/117.

 **EXERCISE** 14.8 CWS

Look at paragraph one of Article 141 (ex 119) (*Cases and Materials* (14.1)). In addition to differences of terminology in relation to male and female workers, how have the provisions of the first paragraph been amended and extended?

As a result of Amsterdam Treaty amendments, Article 141 (ex 119) now incorporates the principle of equal pay for work of equal value. Additionally, Article 141 (ex 119) now provides for the adoption by the Council of measures ensuring equal opportunities and equal treatment for men and women in employment, including equal pay for equal work or work of equal value (paragraph 3).

The incorporation into the Treaty of the principle of equal pay for work of equal value does not mean, however, that Directive 75/117 has lost its usefulness. Individuals can continue to rely on the other provisions of the Directive within the context of an Article 141 (ex 119) claim. In particular, Directive 75/117 provides a framework for the identification of 'work of equal value', to which attention now turns.

14.6.2 Directive 75/117: work of equal value

Whilst it may be relatively straightforward to identify 'equal work', it may not be so easy to identify or classify 'work of equal value' so that appropriate pay structures can be set up within an organisation.

 EXERCISE 14.9 CWS

Look at Article 1 of Directive 75/117 in *Cases and Materials* (14.4.1). What term is used for one particular system which may be used within an organisation for determining pay across a range of different jobs?

Article 1 of the Directive refers to job classification systems as a means for determining pay. Typically, under such systems jobs are evaluated according to specific criteria. Those jobs which are not identical but are considered to be of equal value may be classified within the same group or grade and pay is set accordingly. Article 1 requires any such system to be 'based on the same criteria for both men and women and so drawn up as to exclude any discrimination on grounds of sex'. The Directive does not, however, **require** that job classification or job evaluation schemes of this kind be set up within particular organizations.

 EXERCISE 14.10 CWS

In *Commission* v *United Kingdom* (*Equal Pay for Equal Work*) (Case 61/81) [1982] ECR 2601 (*Cases and Materials* (14.4.2)), the Commission claimed that UK legislation implementing Directive 75/117 was deficient. What did the UK legislation provide and how did the UK government defend these provisions? What did the Court of Justice decide? Make a note of your answer.

In this case, enforcement proceedings were brought against the UK by the Commission, which alleged that the UK had failed properly to implement Directive 75/117. The UK legislation required equal pay for work 'rated as equivalent' under a job evaluation scheme but did not permit the introduction of such a scheme without the employer's consent. Moreover, the legislation did not provide any other means by which evaluation could be made. The UK's argument that Directive 75/117 gave an employee no right to job evaluation but only to equal pay once the value of the job had been determined was rejected by the Court of Justice. The Court declared that the UK's interpretation of the Directive amounted to 'a denial of the very existence of a right to equal pay for work of equal value where no classification has been made' and held that the UK had failed in its obligation to implement the Directive. As a result of this judgment, the UK adopted the Equal Pay (Amendment) Regulations 1983 which provide machinery for the assessment of equal value claims.

As has been noted above, Directive 75/117 provides that if a job classification system is used for determining pay, it must be based on non-discriminatory criteria and be drawn up in such a way as to exclude discrimination between men and women. The scheme considered by the Court of Justice in *Rummler* v *Dato-Druck GmbH* (Case 237/85) [1986] ECR 2101 (*Cases and Materials* (14.4.2)), was based on criteria which included the muscular demand or effort involved in performing the job. The Court held that these criteria did not breach Article 1 of Directive 75/117 provided that the work to be performed did require a certain degree of physical strength and the system as a whole did not discriminate on grounds of sex.

14.6.3 **The burden of proof**

The way in which an employer implements criteria for determining levels of pay may not always be entirely clear. If that is the case, how can an employee who suspects discrimination on grounds of sex pursue an equal pay claim? This issue arose in *Handels-og Kontorfunktionaerernes Forbund i Danmark* v *Dansk Arbejdsgiverforening* (*for Danfoss*) (Case 109/88) [1989] ECR 3199 (*Cases and Materials* (14.4.3)). Here, jobs were classified into grades and the basic pay for each grade was the same for men and women. Individual supplements based upon mobility, training and seniority were added to basic pay. Whilst basic pay was equal, it was shown that the average pay for the men in two of the grades was higher than that of the women in the same grades.

The Court of Justice found that because it was unclear which criteria were employed in particular cases and how those criteria were applied, workers were unable to compare the separate components of their pay with those of their colleagues in the same grade. The Court described this system as lacking in 'transparency'. It ruled that in equal pay cases where the pay system lacks transparency and where, in consequence, female workers can establish no more than that the average pay for women is lower than that of males, the burden of proof is reversed.

 EXERCISE 14.11   CWS

Refer to *Danfoss* in *Cases and Materials* (14.4.3). Can you explain how the reversal of the burden of proof in equal pay claims such as that in *Danfoss* can work to the advantage of the employee? Write down your answer in four or five sentences.

You may have written something like this:

Normally, the individual alleging facts in support of a claim must adduce proof of such facts. Thus, in principle, the burden of proof in an equal pay claim lies with the worker who alleges discrimination. However, where it is impossible to determine the precise criteria for the award of pay supplements, or if it is uncertain exactly how those criteria are applied, the claimant employee, even if able to establish that the average pay for women is less than that for men, has very little hope, if any, of establishing discrimination. In *Danfoss*, the Court held that in these circumstances, the burden of proof is reversed and the onus is on the employer to show that its pay policy does not discriminate between men and women.

Directive 97/80 on the burden of proof in sex discrimination cases was adopted under the Agreement on Social Policy (the Social Chapter) in December 1997. It provides that when persons who consider themselves to have been victims of sex discrimination establish facts from which it may be presumed that there has been direct or indirect discrimination, it is for the respondent to show that there has been no breach of the principle of equal treatment (*Cases and Materials* (14.4.3)).

14.6.4 Other provisions of Directive 75/117

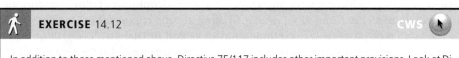

EXERCISE 14.12 CWS

In addition to those mentioned above, Directive 75/117 includes other important provisions. Look at Directive 75/117 in *Cases and Materials* (14.4.1). Which Articles are aimed to ensure that:

(a) employees who wish to pursue equal pay claims can do so through the appropriate national authorities and, if necessary, through the national courts;

(b) Member States take measures to eliminate discriminatory provisions in (*inter alia*) collective agreements and individual contracts of employment;

(c) employers do not take retaliatory action, in the form of dismissal, against employees who pursue equal pay claims against them;

(d) Member States take all the measures necessary to apply the principle of equal pay and to ensure that it is observed?

These important safeguards are contained, respectively, in Articles 2, 4, 5, and 6 of the Directive.

14.7 Indirect discrimination

14.7.1 The distinction between direct and indirect discrimination

Direct discrimination on grounds of sex in relation to pay occurs when an employer sets different levels of pay on the basis of sex alone. Indirect discrimination occurs when pay differentials are purportedly based upon criteria other than sex but in fact result in inequalities of pay between men and women. Similarly, direct and indirect discrimination may occur in relation to the treatment (as well as the pay) of men or women in employment.

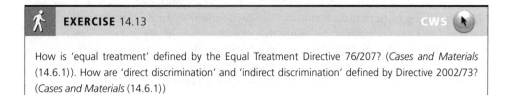

EXERCISE 14.13 CWS

How is 'equal treatment' defined by the Equal Treatment Directive 76/207? (*Cases and Materials* (14.6.1)). How are 'direct discrimination' and 'indirect discrimination' defined by Directive 2002/73? (*Cases and Materials* (14.6.1))

Directive 2002/73, to be implemented by the Member States by 5 October 2005, amends the Equal Treatment Directive 76/207. These Directives are considered in more detail below.

Article 2(1) of Directive 76/207 provides that 'the principle of equal treatment shall mean that there shall be no discrimination whatsoever on grounds of sex either directly or indirectly by reference in particular to marital or family status' (Article 2(1)). This provision remains unamended by Directive 2002/73.

Directive 2002/73 incorporates into Directive 76/207 definitions of 'direct discrimination' and 'indirect discrimination' similar to those already contained in Directive 97/80 on the burden of proof in sex discrimination cases and in Directive 2000/43 on equal treatment between persons irrespective of racial or ethnic origin. Under Article 1 of Directive 2002/73 (Article 2(2) of Directive 76/207, as amended), direct discrimination occurs 'where one person is treated less favourably on grounds of sex than another is, has been or would be treated in a comparable situation'. Indirect discrimination occurs 'where an apparently neutral provision, criterion or practice would put persons of one sex at a particular disadvantage compared with persons of the other sex, unless that provision, criterion or practice is objectively justified by a legitimate aim, and the means of achieving that aim are appropriate and necessary'. Thus, where inequalities between men and women arising from differences in treatment based on criteria other than sex are 'objectively justified' and proportionate, there is no discrimination. By contrast, direct discrimination between men and women can never be justified.

14.7.2 Indirect discrimination and objective justification

In *Jenkins* v *Kingsgate* (*Clothing Productions*) *Ltd* (Case 96/80) [1981] ECR 911 (*Cases and Materials* (14.4.1)), the Court of Justice considered an equal pay claim by a female worker. Here, the Court indicated that Article 141 (ex 119) extends to indirect discrimination.

> **?** **QUESTION** 14.3
>
> In *Jenkins*, which groups of workers received different rates of pay?

The employer in *Jenkins* differentiated between part-time and full-time employees by paying the former group a lower hourly rate than the latter for doing the same job. The Court of Justice was asked to consider whether this pay policy breached Article 141 (ex 119) when the category of part-time workers was predominantly or exclusively comprised of women. The Court responded by ruling that the difference in pay did not breach Article 141 (ex 119) provided that the difference was 'attributable to factors which are objectively justified and are in no way related to any discrimination based on sex'. The judgment suggests that such factors might include the need to encourage more employees to work full-time, justified on economic grounds. Where it is apparent that considerably fewer women than men are able to work full-time because of their domestic responsibilities, the employer must show that its pay policy can be explained by factors other than sex. Otherwise, that policy will breach Article 141 (ex 119).

In *Jenkins*, little guidance was given by the Court of Justice as to what might constitute objective justification. Indeed, the Court expressly stated that it was for the national courts to decide, in the light of the circumstances of each individual case, whether a pay policy was discriminatory. However, in *Bilka-Kaufhaus GmbH* v *Karin Weber von Hartz*

(Case 170/84) [1986] ECR 1607, the Court elucidated the concept of 'objective justification'. Having reiterated that national courts have sole jurisdiction to decide whether the adoption by an employer of a particular pay policy is objectively justified, the Court set out a three-part test which national courts should apply when considering a pay policy adopted apparently without regard to the sex of the workers but which in fact discriminates either against men or against women.

 EXERCISE 14.14   CWS

Look at the *Bilka* case in *Cases and Materials* (14.3.1). Write down the three criteria to be applied in relation to the objective justification of an indirectly discriminatory pay policy.

As in *Jenkins*, the complainant in *Bilka* was a female part-time worker. This case concerned an employer's occupational pension scheme from which part-time workers (except those who had a long period of full-time service with the company) were excluded. Since part-time workers were predominantly female, the adverse effects of this pension policy fell disproportionately upon women employees and the policy was thus indirectly discriminatory. This chapter has already considered the Court of Justice's ruling in *Bilka* that the pension benefits under the employer's scheme constituted pay and therefore fell to be considered under Article 141 (ex 119). However, could the employer's policy be objectively justified? The Court held that apparently indirectly discriminatory measures adopted by an employer will be objectively justified if:

(a) they correspond to a real need of the business;

(b) they are appropriate to achieve the objective pursued; and

(c) they are necessary to achieve that objective.

? **QUESTION** 14.4

Which general principle of Community law do you recognize in the second and third criteria?

This is the principle of proportionality.

You have probably noted that the Court of Justice did not reach any conclusions as to whether the policy in *Bilka* was objectively justified for the reasons advanced by the employer—the encouragement of full-time workers to ensure that certain periods of the week when part-time workers refused to work, namely evenings and Saturdays, were adequately covered. This was left for the national court to decide.

The issue of indirect discrimination in relation to part-time workers arose once again in *Rinner-Kühn* v *FWW Spezial-Gebäudereinigung GmbH* (Case 171/88) [1989] ECR 2743 (*Cases and Materials* (14.3.1)).

> **? QUESTION** 14.5
>
> In *Rinner-Kühn*, the Court of Justice identified one particular aim which it suggested might constitute objective justification for an indirectly discriminatory measure. What was that aim?

The measure in question was German legislation permitting employers to exclude part-time workers from entitlement to sick pay. The Court of Justice suggested that such a measure, which was apparently indirectly discriminatory because its disadvantageous effects fell disproportionately on women, might be justified if it met 'a necessary aim of social policy'. Note that the measure must also be proportionate or, in the words of the judgment, 'suitable and requisite for attaining that aim'. However, the Court did not accept the German government's claim that the legislation was objectively justified because part-time workers were not as integrated into the business as other workers. This argument, it declared, was based upon generalisations about certain categories of workers which could not be identified either as objective or unrelated to any discrimination on grounds of sex.

Generalizations made about certain categories of workers were considered once again by the Court of Justice in *Nimz* v *Freie und Hansestadt Hamburg* (Case 184/89) [1991] ECR 297. The City of Hamburg claimed that its salary classification system, which differentiated between full-time and part-time employees, was objectively justified because full-timers picked up skills more quickly and were able to acquire more experience than part-timers. The Court ruled that these factors were not in themselves sufficient justification. The objectivity of these criteria depended upon the nature of the work performed and the relationship, if any, between the acquisition of experience and the number of hours worked.

The Court of Justice applied the same reasoning in two later decisions *Gerster* v *Freistaat Bayern* (Case C-1/95) [1997] ECR I-5253) and *Kording* v *Senator für Finanzen* (Case C-100/95) [1997] ECR I-5289. German rules made eligibility for promotion (*Gerster*) and exemption from a compulsory professional qualifying examination (*Kording*) dependent upon length of relevant service. Under the rules considered in *Gerster*, periods of employment during which the hours worked were between a half and two-thirds of normal working hours were counted only as two-thirds of normal working hours. In *Kording*, with respect to workers employed no less than half of normal working hours, the rules extended the length of service required proportionately. These rules placed part-timers (predominantly women) at a disadvantage and were thus held to be indirectly discriminatory and in breach of Directive 76/207 unless objectively justified by factors unrelated to any discrimination on grounds of sex.

Recent legislation implementing a framework agreement between employers and unions (the 'social partners') adopted under the Social Chapter aims to eliminate discrimination against part-time workers. Directive 97/81 provides that, in relation to working conditions, part-timers shall not be treated less favourably than full-timers unless the difference in treatment is objectively justified.

So far, cases of indirect discrimination concerning part-time workers have been considered. In *Enderby* v *Frenchay Health Authority and the Secretary of State for Health* (Case C-127/92) [1993] ECR I-5535, [1994] 1 CMLR 8 (*Cases and Materials* (14.5.1)), the Court of Justice held that differences in pay between two different jobs assumed to be of equal value, one of which was performed almost entirely by women and the other predominantly by men, constituted, *prima facie*, sex discrimination.

? **QUESTION** 14.6

In *Enderby*, what were the two justifications offered by the employer in respect of the pay differentials?

In its judgment, the Court of Justice displayed a greater willingness than in some of its previous judgments to give a definitive ruling on a particular justification. The first justification offered by the Frenchay Health Authority, that the levels of pay were set out in separate collective agreements which had been negotiated in a non-discriminatory fashion in collective bargaining, was rejected by the Court of Justice. However, the Court held that the pay differentials might be objectively justified by market forces. This second justification put forward by the employer was based upon the claim that it needed to award higher pay to those performing one of the jobs in question in order to attract suitably qualified candidates, who were in short supply. Whether this did in fact constitute objective justification in this case was a matter for the national court.

In an English case, *Equal Opportunities Commission* v *Secretary of State for Employment* [1994] 1 All ER 910, the House of Lords considered whether certain provisions of the Employment Protection (Consolidation) Act 1978, which discriminated against part-time workers, were objectively justified. It was claimed that these provisions encouraged employers to engage part-time workers and thus achieved a desirable aim, namely an increase in part-time work. It was held that, even if this effect were proved (which it was not), legislation giving rise to such discrimination would not be justified, since it did not constitute a suitable means to achieve the desired objective. The provisions consequently breached Article 141 (ex 119). As a result of this ruling, the legislation was amended by the Employment Protection (Part-time Employment) Regulations 1995.

14.8 Equal treatment for Men and Women in Employment: Directive 76/207 (as amended by Directive 2002/73)

14.8.1 Amendments to the Equal Treatment Directive 76/207

The Equal Treatment Directive 76/207 has been amended by Directive 2002/73, which was adopted in September 2002 and must be implemented by Member States by 5 October 2005.

QUESTION 14.7

Do you remember the meaning of 'implementation'? If not, look back at Chapter 5.

Member States achieve implementation when they bring into force the laws, regulations and administrative provisions necessary to comply with a Directive. Directive 2002/73 incorporates into Directive 76/207 some of the principles already established by the European Court of Justice in the sex discrimination decisions discussed in the following sections. Although the new provisions of the amended Directive will not be capable of direct effect before the implementation deadline has passed, the decisions on which they are based are of course binding.

 QUESTION 14.8

Do you remember the meaning of 'direct effect'? If not, look back at Chapter 5.

14.8.2 Scope of Directive 76/207

As has been noted, Article 141 (ex 119) provides for **equal pay** without discrimination based on sex. Directive 76/207 aims to secure **equal treatment** between men and women in employment.

 EXERCISE 14.15   CWS

Read Article 1 of Directive 76/207 in *Cases and Materials* (14.6.1). Make a note of the three main areas (other than the principle of equal treatment in social security, the scope of which is defined in other secondary legislation) covered by the Directive.

Directive 76/207 is designed to put into effect the principle of equal treatment for men and women as regards:

(a) access to employment (including promotion);

(b) vocational training;

(c) working conditions.

 Directive 2002/73 makes no amendment to the scope of Directive 76/207 but a new Article 1a requires Member States actively to take into account the equality objective when formulating law and policy in these three areas (*Cases and Materials* (14.6.1)).

EXERCISE 14.16

Write down the definition of the principle of equal treatment contained in Article 2(1) of Directive 76/207 (*Cases and Materials* (14.6.1)).

Under Article 2(1) of Directive 76/207, which remains unamended by Directive 2002/73, the principle of equal treatment means that 'there shall be no discrimination whatsoever on grounds of sex either directly or indirectly by reference in particular to marital or family status'. As noted above, Directive 2002/73 provides definitions of direct and indirect discrimination.

14.8.3 The scope of 'discrimination . . . on grounds of sex'

The scope of 'discrimination . . . on grounds of sex' was considered by the Court of Justice in *P* v *S and Cornwall County Council* (Case C-13/94) [1996] ECR I-2143 and *Grant* v *South-West Trains Ltd* (Case C-249/96) [1998] ECR 1-621.

 EXERCISE 14.17

Read the extract from *P* v *S* in *Cases and Materials* (14.6.2). How did the Court of Justice extend the scope of 'sex discrimination' in this case? Make a written note of your answer.

The Court was asked to consider whether the dismissal of a transsexual for reasons of gender reassignment constitutes sex discrimination. The Court's starting point was the principle of equality, a fundamental principle of Community law. It held that, in view of this principle, the scope of Directive 76/207 cannot be limited to protection against discrimination based on gender but extends to discrimination arising from the gender reassignment of the person concerned.

Questions concerning the rights of transsexuals have been raised more recently in *KB* v *The National Health Service Pensions Agency and the Secretary of State for Health* (Case C-117/0), currently pending before the Court of Justice. Here, the appellant considers that she is the victim of sex discrimination under Directive 75/117. Her partner, who was born a woman but has become a man following medical gender reassignment, is not entitled to the survivor's pension under KB's occupational pension scheme to which he would be entitled as a surviving spouse. UK legislation prevents transsexuals from marrying on the basis of their acquired gender.

> **?** **QUESTION** 14.9
>
> In view of the Court's conclusion in *P* v *S*, do you think that differences of treatment based on sexual orientation would violate the principle of equality under Community law? Look at *Grant* (*Cases and Materials* (14.6.2)).

Surprisingly, in *Grant* the Court of Justice declared that South-West Trains' condition requiring a stable relationship with a person of the opposite sex did not constitute discrimination based on sex because it applied regardless of the sex of the worker concerned. Further, since Community law does not at present regard stable homosexual relationships as equivalent to marriage or to stable heterosexual relationships, an employer is not required to treat these situations as equivalent. Finally, whilst discrimination based upon a worker's gender reassignment, like discrimination based upon the fact that a person belongs to a particular sex, is to be prohibited because it is based essentially if not exclusively on the sex of the worker concerned, that reasoning does not apply to differences of treatment based upon sexual orientation.

Since *Grant*, Community legislation has been adopted in this area. Directive 2000/78, which is based on Article 13EC (see 14.3 and *Cases and Materials* (14.2)) establishes a general framework for equal treatment in employment and includes a prohibition on discrimination in relation to sexual orientation.

14.8.4 Other provisions of Directive 76/207

Note also the following provisions of Directive 76/207:

(a) Article 1, paragraph 2 (which remains unamended by Directive 2002/73) requires the adoption of provisions implementing the equal treatment principle in matters of social security. Directive 79/7, concerning statutory social security schemes and Directive 86/378, on occupational schemes, were adopted pursuant to this provision.

(b) Articles 3, 4, and 5 relate to equal treatment in access to employment, vocational

training and working conditions (including dismissal). Directive 2002/73 consolidates all these provisions into a new Article 3 (see *Cases and Materials* (14.6.1)).

(c) Article 6 provides for access to judicial process for complainants. Article 6 is extended by Directive 2002/73, in a new Article 6, to provide wider protection for com-

plainants, including real and effective compensation, without upper limit, in a way that is 'dissuasive and proportionate to the damage suffered' (see *Cases and Materials* (14.6.1)).

(d) Article 7 (which remains substantially unamended by Directive 2002/73) provides protection against dismissal by the employer as a reaction to a complaint of sex discrimination. In *Coote* (*Coote* v *Granada Hospitality Ltd* (Case C-185/97) [1998] ECR 1-5199)), this provision was interpreted broadly by the Court of Justice to include protection against victimisation by the former employer occurring after termination of the employment. Here, Ms Coote claimed that her former employer, against whom she had made a sex discrimination claim, had retaliated by failing to supply a reference to an agency through which she subsequently sought employment.

14.8.5 Equal treatment, social security, and access to employment

Although Article 1(2) of Directive 76/207 excludes social security matters from its scope, leaving the substance, scope and implementation of the equal treatment principle in such matters to be dealt with by separate provisions, the Court of Justice has emphasized that this exclusion is to be interpreted strictly. Accordingly, a social security benefit which is part of a national social security system falls within Directive 76/207 if that benefit is concerned with access to employment. In *Meyers* v *Adjudication Officer* (Case C-116/94) [1995] ECR I-2131, the UK argued that family credit fell outside the scope of the Directive by virtue of Article 1(2). The Court disagreed. It pointed out that the aims of the benefit were to keep poorly paid workers in employment and to encourage unemployed workers to accept work, even if it is low paid, by making financial assistance available to workers whose net income did not exceed a specified amount. Consequently, family credit was concerned with access to employment and fell within Directive 76/207.

14.8.6 Equal treatment and retirement ages

The equal treatment principle has been invoked in a number of UK cases concerning different retirement or pensionable ages for men and women either incorporated into occupational pension schemes or redundancy schemes or forming part of an employer's compulsory retirement policy. Commonly in the UK, pensionable age for these purposes was tied to age of eligibility for state pension (60 for women and 65 for men) and where there was such a link, it was believed that different retirement ages for men and women in occupational pension schemes were permissible under Community law. This was because Directive 79/7, which provides for equal treatment for men and women in matters of social security, allows Member States to exclude from its scope 'the determination of pensionable age for the purposes of granting old-age and retirement pensions and the possible consequences thereof for other benefits' (Article 7(1)(a)). Directive 86/378, which implemented the equal treatment principle in relation to occupational pensions, provided a similar exception (Article 9(a)).

This view was given weight by the decision in *Burton* v *British Railways Board* (Case 19/81) [1982] ECR 555 (*Cases and Materials* (14.6.3)). Here, the applicant challenged as contrary to Directive 76/207 a voluntary redundancy scheme operated by his employer, British Rail, under which women became eligible to take voluntary redundancy at 55 and men at 60. Despite its finding that voluntary redundancy under the scheme constituted 'dismissal' under Article 5 of the Directive, the Court of Justice held that the different ages of access to the scheme did not constitute discriminatory treatment on grounds of sex because, under the terms of the redundancy scheme, those ages had been tied to the state retirement scheme. Consequently, the exception in Article 7(1)(a) of Directive 79/7 applied and Directive 76/207 was not infringed.

Since *Burton*, the Court of Justice has narrowed the scope of the exception in Article 7(1)(a) of Directive 79/7. *Roberts* v *Tate & Lyle Industries* (Case 151/84) [1986] ECR 703

(*Cases and Materials* (14.6.3)) concerned an occupational pension scheme incorporating compulsory retirement for women at 60 and for men at 65 and a compulsory redundancy scheme providing both men and women with an early pension at 55. Mrs Roberts, who, on being made redundant at 53, was refused an early pension, claimed that the scheme was discriminatory since men who were made redundant received an early pension ten years before normal retirement age and women only five years before that age. The Court of Justice chose to characterize the early pension not as a social security benefit falling within the Article 7(1)(a) exception but rather as a condition governing dismissal within the meaning of Article 5 of Directive 76/207. Because the redundancy scheme provided for payment of early pensions at the same age for men and women, it was compatible with the equal treatment principle contained in Directive 76/207.

The Court of Justice adopted the same approach in *Marshall v Southampton and South-West Hampshire Area Health Authority (Teaching)* (Case 152/84) [1986] ECR 723.

 EXERCISE 14.18 CWS

Look at the *Marshall* case in *Cases and Materials* (14.6.3). Write down answers to the following questions:

(a) What policy of her employer did Ms Marshall challenge?

(b) The Court of Justice held that this policy did not fall within the scope of the exception contained in Article 7(1)(a) of Directive 79/7. Why?

Ms Marshall challenged her employer's compulsory retirement policy which required women to retire at 60 but allowed men to stay on until 65. The Court of Justice declared that the exception in Directive 79/7 applies only to 'the determination of pensionable age *for the purposes of granting old-age and retirement pensions* and the possible consequences thereof for other benefits' (emphasis added). This case, the Court held, was not concerned with the consequences of pensionable age for social security benefits but with dismissal within the meaning of Article 5 of Directive 76/207. Consequently, the different treatment of men and women with respect to retirement ages constituted discrimination on grounds of sex in breach of that Directive.

In the later case of *Barber*, the Court of Justice focused upon the discriminatory **effect** of different retirement or pensionable ages for men and women, treating payments made on redundancy and under the contracted-out occupational pension scheme as pay. Here, the Court held that discriminatory retirement ages in occupational pension schemes constituted a breach of the equal pay principle under Article 141 (ex 119) because they resulted in a difference in pay. It should be noted that the Court of Justice reached this decision notwithstanding Article 9 of Directive 86/378 which, as has been mentioned, provided for 'the determination of pensionable age for the purposes of granting old-age or retirement pensions' under occupational pension schemes to be excluded from the equal treatment principle. Article 9 has now been amended by Directive 96/97 to limit the exclusion to schemes for self-employed workers.

EXERCISE 14.19

CWS

Do you recall *Barber* v *Guardian Royal Exchange Assurance Group* (Case C-262/88) [1990] ECR I-1889 in *Cases and Materials* (14.3.1)? If not, look back at 14.5.3 and 14.5.4.

These latest developments in the Court's jurisprudence indicate that the exceptions to the equal treatment principle with respect to pensions and retirement will be given the narrowest scope, to cover only state pension schemes in the strict sense.

14.8.7 Derogation from the equal treatment principle

Directive 76/207 permits a number of exceptions to the equal treatment principle. These exceptions are contained in Article 2. They are amended by Directive 2002/73.

EXERCISE 14.20

CWS

Read Article 2 of Directive 76/207 in *Cases and Materials* (14.6.1). Make a written summary of the exceptions contained in paragraphs 2, 3, and 4 of this Article.

Read Article 1(2) of Directive 2002/73 (*Cases and Materials* (14.6.1)) and note the amended exceptions to be incorporated into Article 2(6)–(8) of Directive 76/207, as amended.

Your summary might look something like this:

Article 2 of Directive 76/207, before amendment, provides for the following exceptions to the equal treatment principle:

(a) Those occupational activities (and appropriate training) for which, because of their nature or the context in which they are carried out, the sex of the worker constitutes a determining factor (Article 2(2)).

After amendment by Directive 2002/73, Article 2(2) becomes Article 2(6) and provides that, to fall within the derogation, a difference of treatment based on characteristics related to sex must be a 'genuine and determining occupational requirement' and that the objective must be legitimate and the requirement proportionate (see *Cases and Materials* (14.6.1)). This amendment reiterates the proportionality principle already laid down by the Court of Justice in this context (see the discussion of *Kreil* v *Germany* (Case C-285/98) at 14.8.7.1).

(b) Provisions concerning the protection of women, particularly as regards pregnancy and maternity (Article 2(3)).

This derogation is retained in Article 2(7) of the amended Directive 76/207. Article 2(7) also elaborates on the original provision. It provides that after a period of maternity leave, a woman shall be entitled to return to her job on no less favourable terms and to benefit from any improvement in working conditions to which she would have been entitled during her absence. Any less favourable treatment of women related to pregnancy or maternity constitutes discrimination. Further, the equal treatment principle does not affect the right to parental leave under Directive 92/85, nor the provisions of Directive 92/85 on the health and safety of pregnant workers and workers who have recently given birth or are breastfeeding.

(c) Measures to promote equal opportunity for men and women (Article 2(4)).

This provision, renumbered Article 2(8) after amendment, is amended by Directive 2002/73 to refer directly to Article 141(4) EC, which allows Members States to 'maintain or adopt measures providing for special advantages . . . to make it easier for the under-represented sex to pursue a vocational activity or to prevent or compensate for disadvantages in professional careers' with a view to ensuring equality in practice between men and women (see *Cases and Materials* (14.1)).

14.8.7.1 **Article 2(2) (Article 2(6), as amended)**

In *Commission* v *United Kingdom* (*Equal Treatment for Men and Women*) (Case 165/82) [1983] ECR 3431, the Court of Justice considered three exemptions to the equal treatment principle contained in the Sex Discrimination Act 1975, which the UK argued fell within the scope of Article 2(2).

 EXERCISE 14.21 CWS

Look at *Commission* v *United Kingdom* in *Cases and Materials* (14.6.4.1). What were the three exemptions? Did the Court of Justice decide that these exemptions came within Article 2(2)?

The Court of Justice held that the exemptions concerning employment in private households and in undertakings employing no more than five persons did not fall within the Article 2(2) exception. The Court ruled that, although such exemptions might be appropriate in individual cases, for instance where the aim was to maintain respect for private life in a particular private household, blanket exemptions of this kind went beyond the objective contained in Article 2(2). By contrast, the limitations concerning access to the profession of midwifery were held to conform with Article 2(2), in view of the 'personal sensitivities' involved in relations between midwife and patient. In fact, the restrictions on male access to the profession of midwifery in the UK have now been removed by an amendment to the 1975 Act.

The scope of Article 2(2) was considered again in *Johnston* v *Chief Constable of the Royal Ulster Constabulary* (Case 222/84) [1986] ECR 1651 (*Cases and Materials* (14.6.4.1)). The complainant, a female member of the Royal Ulster Constabulary (RUC) Reserve challenged the RUC's decision not to renew her contract, taken pursuant to the RUC's newly adopted policy on the carrying of firearms by its officers.

EXERCISE 14.22

Summarize in a short paragraph the decision of the Court of Justice in *Johnston* in relation to Article 2(2) of Directive 76/207.

The Court of Justice accepted the UK's argument that, if women were armed, they would be more likely to become targets for assassination and ruled that 'the context of certain policing activities may be such that the sex of police officers constitutes a determining factor for carrying them out'. However, it was for the national court, applying the principle of proportionality, to decide whether the RUC was justified in refusing to renew Mrs Johnston's contract. Moreover, if found to be justified under Article 2(2), that policy must be reviewed from time to time in the light of changing circumstances to ensure that it continued to be justified.

In a more recent case, a British Army chef, Mrs Sirdar, claimed that she had been the victim of sex discrimination when she was refused a transfer into the Royal Marines. Women were excluded from the regiment because of the 'interoperability' rule, which required all members of the corps, whatever their specialization, to be engaged and trained to serve as front-line commandos. The Court of Justice recognized the special character of the Royal Marines, as a small force intended to be the first line of attack. This, together with the interoperability rule, justified the exclusively male composition of the force. The Court decided that the exclusion of women from service in special combat units, such as the British Royal Marines, may be justified under Article 2(2) by reason of the nature of the activities in question and the context in which they are carried out. (*Sirdar* v *The Army Board and Secretary of State for Defence* (Case C-273/97), [1999] ECR I-7403).

However, any derogation from the right of equal treatment must be appropriate and necessary to the aim in view. Thus, German legislation excluding women from all military posts involving the use of arms, allowing them access only to medical and military-music services, went further than was necessary to guarantee public security and could not be justified under Article 2(2). Here, women were denied access not simply to specific duties but to all armed units. Nor could the national legislation be justified under Article 2(3) concerning the protection of women as regards pregnancy and maternity (see 14.8.7.2) (*Kreil* v *Germany* (Case C-285/98), [2000] ECR I-69).

In *Sirdar* and *Kreil* the Court of Justice declared that decisions of the Member States concerning the organization of their armed forces cannot be completely excluded from the application of Community law. However, the Court stressed that matters of military organization remain within the competence of Member States where the defence of their territory or of their essential interests are at issue. Reiterating these principles in *Dory* v *Germany* (Case C-186/01) judgment of 11 March 2003, the Court held that national rules requiring men only to complete a period of compulsory military service was outside the scope of Community law, even if that rule tended to delay the careers of those called up for such service.

14.8.7.2 **Article 2(3) (Article 2(7), as amended)**

The Court of Justice has limited the scope of Article 2(3) of the Directive to two specific areas: the protection of a woman's biological condition during and after pregnancy and the protection of the special relationship which exists between mother and child in the period following the birth.

Hence, a German law granting leave to the mother but not to the father after the birth of a child was compatible with Directive 76/207 (*Hofmann* v *Barmer Ersatzkasse* (Case 184/83) [1984] ECR 3047). It should be noted that the Pregnancy and Maternity Directive 92/85 requires Member States to provide a period of maternity leave for women and the Parental Leave Directive 96/34, adopted under the Social Chapter in June 1996, provides for a right to parental leave of at least three months for men and women workers on the grounds of the birth or adoption of a child.

In *Hofmann*, the Court of Justice declared that Directive 76/207 'is not designed to settle questions concerned with the organisation of the family, or to alter the division of responsibility between parents'. The Court took the same view in *Commission* v *France* (Case 312/86) [1988] ECR 6315 and ruled that French legislation allowing special privileges for married women, such as days off at the start of the school year and leave when their children were ill, did not come within the Article 2(3) exception because such privileges were unconnected with pregnancy and maternity.

Adopting the same interpretation of 'provisions concerning the protection of women, particularly as regards pregnancy and maternity' in *Johnston*, the Court of Justice dismissed the RUC's attempts to justify its employment policy under Article 2(3). Even though public opinion might demand that women be given greater protection than men against the risks inherent in the exercise of police duties in Northern Ireland, those risks were not covered by the Article 2(3) exception.

The limited scope of Article 2(3) was again emphasized by the Court of Justice in two cases concerning, respectively, the prohibition and limitation under national legislation of night-working for women. The Court held that such provisions would only be acceptable under Community law in the context of pregnancy and maternity (*Criminal proceedings against Stoeckel* (Case C-345/89) [1991] ECR I-4047 (*Cases and Materials* (14.6.4.2)); *Office Nationale de l'Emploi* v *Minne* (Case C-13/93) [1994] ECR I-371).

14.8.7.3 **Article 2(4) (Article 2(8), as amended)**

This third exception to the principle of equal treatment allows measures which, although discriminatory on their face, are designed to eliminate or reduce actual instances of inequality between men and women arising from the realities of social life. Such measures are often described as measures of 'positive action', or 'positive discrimination'. In *Commission* v *France* (Case 312/86) [1988] ECR 6315 the Court of Justice, apparently taking the view that there was no existing inequality between men and women with respect to the matters covered by the French legislation under challenge, dismissed the French government's argument that the granting of special rights to women fell within the Article 2(4) exception.

The Court of Justice again adopted a strict interpretation of this article in relation to a German law giving automatic priority to women applicants for promotion to posts for which they hold qualifications equal to those of male applicants, in sectors where women were under-represented. The Court declared that 'national rules which guarantee women absolute and unconditional priority for appointment or promotion go beyond promoting equal opportunities and overstep the limits of the exception in Article 2(4) of the Directive'. Such rules provide not for the desired aim of equality of opportunity but for a result which is only to be arrived at by means of equality of opportunity (*Kalanke* v *Freie Hansestadt Bremen* (Case C-450/93) [1995] ECR I-3051). However, where national legislation giving priority to women candidates provides that such priority is not automatic but is overridden by criteria which tilt the balance in favour of a male candidate, the Article 2(4) exception applies (*Marschall* v *Land Nordrhein-Westfalen* (Case C-409/95) [1997] ECR I-6363; *Badeck and Others* (Case C-158/97) [2000] ECR I-1875).

Similarly, a subsidized crèche scheme, set up by the Netherlands Ministry of Agriculture to tackle the under-representation of women within the Ministry and which in principle reserved places for the children of women employees only, fell within the Article 2(4) exception because it allowed access to the scheme by male employees 'in the case of an emergency'. There would be no unlawful discrimination provided that this exception in favour of male employees allowed those of them taking care of children on their own to have access to the nursery places on the same conditions as female employee (*Lommers* v *Minister van Landbouw, Natuurbeheer en Visserij* (Case C-476/99) [2002] ECR I-2691).

Lommers, and other cases concerning positive discrimination in favour of women, raise the question as to how far measures purportedly benefiting women do in fact operate to their benefit. The subsidized scheme in *Lommers* could be seen as reinforcing the existing stereotyping of the woman's role as principal child-carer within the family, arguably creating a significant obstacle to the achievement of equality between men and women, not only in relation to their roles and responsibilities within the family, but also in relation to access to and progression in the employment market.

? QUESTION 14.10 CWS

Which paragraph of Article 141 (ex 119) EC allows Member States to maintain or adopt provisions of 'positive action' without infringing the equal treatment principle? (See *Cases and Materials* (14.1)).

Following Amsterdam Treaty amendments, paragraph 4 of Article 141 (ex 119) allows Member States, without infringing the equal treatment principle, to maintain or adopt measures granting 'specific advantages' to 'make it easier for the under-represented sex to pursue vocational activity or to prevent or compensate for disadvantages in professional careers'.

In *Badeck*, a dispute concerning positive action in favour of women in relation to posts in the public service, the question framed by the national court sought interpretation of Article 2(4) of Directive 76/207. The Court of Justice referred to Article 141(4) in setting out the legal background but went on to declare that since the question referred concerned the Directive, Article 141(4) would only be material to the outcome of the case if the national legislation was found to be incompatible with the Directive. The Court thus drew a distinction between these two provisions, suggesting that the Article 141(4) exception is wider in scope than Article 2(4) of the Directive. This distinction was reiterated in the later case of *Abrahamsson* v *Fogelqvist* (Case C-407/98) [2000] ECR I-5539, where the Court of Justice, after first concluding that parts of the legislation at issue were incompatible with the Directive, went on to consider their compatibility with Article 141EC. Following amendments by Directive 2002/73 to Article 2(4), the 'positive action' exception, contained in Article 2(8) after amendment, incorporates the wording of Article 141(4)EC. Any existing distinction between the respective provisions is thereby removed.

Kalanke, *Marshall*, and *Badeck* concerned rules which allowed for preference to be given to members of the under-represented sex where male and female candidates were equally qualified for a job. By contrast, *Abrahamsson* concerned national legislation which enabled automatic preference to be given to candidates of the under-represented sex who, although they held sufficient qualifications for the job, did not have qualifications equal to those of other candidates. Here, the Court held the scheme in question to be outside the scope of Article 141(4)EC and Article 2(4) of the Directive, since the selection process was not based upon an objective assessment of the merits of candidates and the criteria to be applied were unclear. It seems, however, that a scheme of this kind that did satisfy the requirements of clarity and objectivity would be compatible with Community law, provided also that the criteria applied in assessing candidates had the genuine aim of reducing inequality and were proportionate to that aim.

The cases so far considered concern measures of positive discrimination in favour of women. It is clear from *Schnorbus* v *Land Hessen* (Case C-79/99) [2000] ECR 1-1099 that measures of positive discrimination which benefit men may equally be compatible with Directive 76/207. Here, the Court of Justice was asked to consider German rules governing access to practical legal training which gave preference to applicants who had completed compulsory military or civilian service. The applicant, Julia Schnorbus, complained that the selection procedure discriminated against women because such service could only be done by men. The Court held that, whilst these procedures constituted indirect discrimination against women, they were justified because they compensated for the delay suffered by men in the completion of their education as a result of their military service requirement. It is worth noting that, despite the fact that the national court had asked specifically whether the procedure in question fell within the Article 2(4) derogation, the Court chose to base its finding on the objective justification of these indirectly discriminatory rules.

14.8.8 Dismissal or refusal to appoint by reason of pregnancy

From the employer's point of view, the pregnancy of an employee creates financial and organisational difficulties. Either a temporary replacement has to be found or other staff must take up extra workload during the woman's absence immediately before and after the confinement. Employers have therefore sought to justify the dismissal of or the refusal to engage a pregnant woman on economic grounds. Does this behaviour amount to discrimination on grounds of sex contrary to Directive 76/207?

EXERCISE 14.23

Look at the extracts from the judgments in the following cases:

(a) *Dekker* v *Stichting Vormingscentrum voor Jong Volwassenen Plus* (Case C-177/88) [1990] ECR I-3941 (*Cases and Materials* (14.6.5)).

(b) *Handels-og Kontorfunktionaerernes Forbund i Danmark* v *Dansk Arbejdsgiverforening* (*Hertz*) (Case 179/88) [1990] ECR I-3979 (*Cases and Materials* (14.6.5)).

(c) *Habermann-Beltermann* v *Arbeiterwohlfahrt Bezirksverband* (Case C-421/92) [1994] ECR I-1657 (*Cases and Materials* (14.6.5)).

(d) *Webb* v *EMO Air Cargo* (*UK*) *Ltd* (Case C-32/93) [1994] ECR I-3567 (*Cases and Materials* (14.6.5)).

Summarize the Court's rulings in four paragraphs.

You might have written something like this:

(a) The refusal to engage a woman for reasons connected with pregnancy constitutes direct discrimination on grounds of sex in breach of Directive 76/207. Such an action cannot be justified by the employer on the basis of financial detriment (*Dekker*).

(b) However, whereas the dismissal of (as well as the refusal to appoint) a pregnant worker constitutes direct discrimination on grounds of sex, an employer did not act in breach of the principle of equal treatment by dismissing a woman whose pregnancy-related illness, which gave rise to extended periods of absence from work following the birth of her child, occurred after the end of her maternity leave. Here, the Court declared, there is no reason to treat an illness attributable to pregnancy or confinement differently from any other illness or to apply to it different rules relating to absence and dismissal (*Hertz*).

The same reasoning was applied by the Court of Justice in relation to the dismissal of a woman whose pregnancy-related illness arose during pregnancy and continued during and after the end of her maternity leave (*Handels- og Kontorfunktionaererernes Forbund i Danmark*, acting on behalf of *Helle Elisabeth Larsson* v *Dansk Handel & Service* acting on behalf of *Føtex Supermarked A/S* (Case C-400/95) [1997] ECR I-2757).

The Court of Justice's ruling in *Hertz* was in line with the Pregnancy and Maternity Directive 92/85, which at the time of the judgment had not passed its implementation date (19 October 1994). Article 10 of the Directive requires Member States to prohibit the dismissal of pregnant workers from the beginning of their pregnancy to the end of the period of maternity leave (as defined by the Directive) but does not grant protection from dismissal after the end of maternity leave. Further, Directive 92/85 does not cover the refusal to employ a woman because she is pregnant, though Directive 76/207 (and *Dekker*) would still apply in this situation.

(c) A statutory prohibition on night-working by pregnant women which temporarily prevented a woman from performing night work did not justify the termination of her employment contract without a fixed term on account of her pregnancy (*Habermann-Beltermann*).

In *Mahlburg* v *Land Mecklenburg-Vorpommern* (Case C-207/98), [2000] ECR 1-549, the Court of Justice was asked to consider the refusal by an employer to appoint a pregnant woman to a permanent post on the ground that a statutory provision prevented her, for reasons of health, from being employed in that particular post throughout her pregnancy. The Court held that such a refusal was incompatible with Article 2(1) and (3) of Directive 76/207.

Similarly, the refusal of an employer to allow a woman, on account of her pregnancy, to return to work before the end of a period of parental leave was incompatible with the Equal Treatment Directive 76/207 and the Pregnancy Directive 92/85. Here, the principles set out by the Court in *Habermann-Beltermann*, *Dekker*, and *Mahlburg* applied. Neither legislative prohibitions on the performance of certain duties by pregnant women for their protection during pregnancy nor the financial loss suffered by the employer justify refusing employment on grounds of pregnancy. (*Busch* v *Klinikum Neustadt GmbH & Co. Betriebs-KG* (Case C-320/01), judgment of 27 February 2003).

(d) The dismissal of a woman engaged under a permanent contract partly to cover for another worker on maternity leave and who on taking up that employment discovered that she too was pregnant could not be justified under Community law (*Webb*).

Following *Webb* and *Habermann-Beltermann*, there was some doubt as to whether the right not to be dismissed on account of pregnancy applied to pregnant workers on fixed-term contracts as well as to those on permanent contracts. This doubt was dispelled by Directive 92/85, which makes no distinction between these two categories of workers.

As has been noted, the dismissal of a woman from her employment for reasons of pregnancy constitutes direct sex discrimination. In *Thibault*, the Court of Justice considered the situation of a woman who was accorded unfavourable treatment regarding her working conditions as a result of her absence from work on maternity leave. Because of this absence, Mrs Thibault was deprived by her employer of the right to an annual assessment of her performance and consequently of her opportunity to qualify for promotion. The Court held that such conduct on the part of the employer constituted discrimination based directly on grounds of sex within the meaning of Directive 76/207 (Case C-136/95 *Caisse nationale d'assurance vieillesse des travailleurs salariés* (CNAVTS) v *Thibault* [1998] ECR I-2011).

14.8.9 Harassment and sexual harassment

In addition to the amendments to Directive 76/207 already referred to above, Directive 2002/73 also sets out new provisions for incorporation into Directive 76/207 concerning harassment and sexual harassment. Both harassment ('unwanted conduct related to the sex of a person . . .' (Article 2(2) of Directive 76/207, as amended)) and sexual harassment ('any form of unwanted verbal, non-verbal or physical conduct of a sexual nature. . . .' (also Article 2(2) of Directive 76/207, as amended)) are deemed to be discrimination on grounds of sex and therefore prohibited.

14.9 Directive 79/7: equal treatment in matters of social security

Directive 79/7 has as its aim 'the progressive implementation, in the field of social security . . . of the principle of equal treatment for men and women'. It applies to the 'working population' and covers statutory schemes providing protection against sickness, invalidity, old age, accidents at work, occupational diseases and unemployment.

14.10 Directive 86/378 (amended by Directive 96/97): equal treatment in occupational social security schemes

Directive 86/378 has as its objective the implementation of the equal treatment principle in occupational social security schemes. Amendments adopted in Directive 96/97 take account of the jurisprudence of the Court of Justice on occupational pension schemes (see 14.5.4 and 14.5.5).

14.11 Directive 86/613: equal treatment in self-employment

Directive 86/613 contains provisions relating to the self-employed which complement those in Directive 76/207 on equal treatment for men and women in employment. In particular, Member States are required to take all necessary measures for the elimination of discrimination 'especially in respect of the establishment, equipment or extension of a business or the launching or extension of any other form of self-employed activity including financial facilities' (Article 4). They must ensure that it is no more difficult for spouses than for unmarried persons to form a company between them (Article 5) and that spouses of self-employed persons who participate in the business and are not protected by the self-employed worker's social security scheme have access to a contributory social security scheme (Article 6).

14.12 Remedies

The subject of remedies has been dealt with in detail in **Chapter 5**.

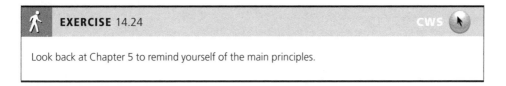

EXERCISE 14.24   CWS

Look back at Chapter 5 to remind yourself of the main principles.

Once discrimination on grounds of sex has been established, Member States are required to do all that is necessary to give effect to Community law. Article 6 of Directive 76/207, which requires Member States to 'introduce into their national legal systems such measures as are necessary to enable persons who consider themselves wronged by failure to apply to them the principle of equal treatment . . . to pursue their claims by judicial process after possible recourse to other competent authorities', has been interpreted to mean that national remedies must provide sufficient, real and effective protection of individual rights under Community law. These provisions on remedies are strengthened by Directive 2002/73. The Directive provides, for instance, that compensation for damage suffered as a result of discrimination must be proportionate and not, except in certain cases, subject to an upper limit.

 CONCLUSIONS

From relatively modest beginnings, founded initially upon the equal pay principle, Community sex discrimination law has developed into a substantial body of legislation according extensive rights to individuals with respect to equal treatment in employment and in matters of social security. The Court of Justice has contributed in large measure to the promotion of these individual rights, particularly through its broad interpretation of 'pay' and through its development of the concept of indirect discrimination. However, although it is clear that Community sex discrimination law has been interpreted as a vehicle for the achievement of social as well as economic objectives, it still remains firmly confined within the context of employment.

 CHAPTER 14: ASSESSMENT EXERCISE   CWS

(a) Outline the role played by the Court of Justice in the extension of individual rights under Community sex discrimination law through its broad interpretation of the concept of 'pay' contained in Article 141 (ex 119) EC.

(b) Assess the importance of *Jenkins* v *Kingsgate* (*Clothing Productions*) *Ltd* (Case 96/80) and *Bilka-Kaufhaus GmbH* v *Karin Weber von Hartz* (Case 170/84) in the development of the concepts of indirect discrimination and objective justification in Community sex discrimination law.

(c) 'From relatively modest beginnings, Community sex discrimination law has developed into a substantial body of law according extensive rights to individuals in employment. Discuss.

See *Cases and Materials* (14.8) for specimen answers.

■ INDEX